Niki Gorick Dock Life Renewed

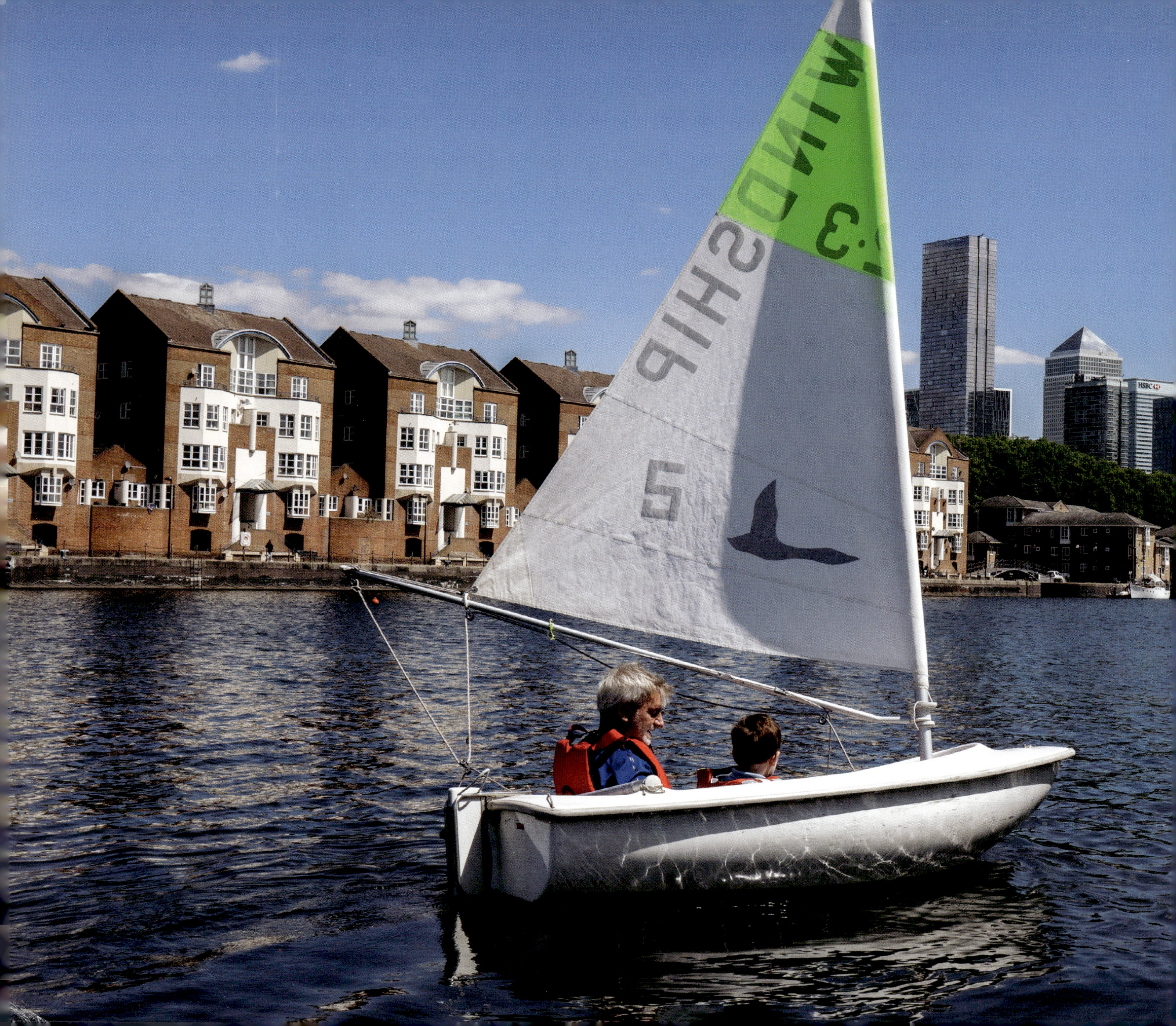
WINDSHIP
HSBC

Niki Gorick Dock Life Renewed

HOW LONDON'S DOCKS ARE THRIVING AGAIN

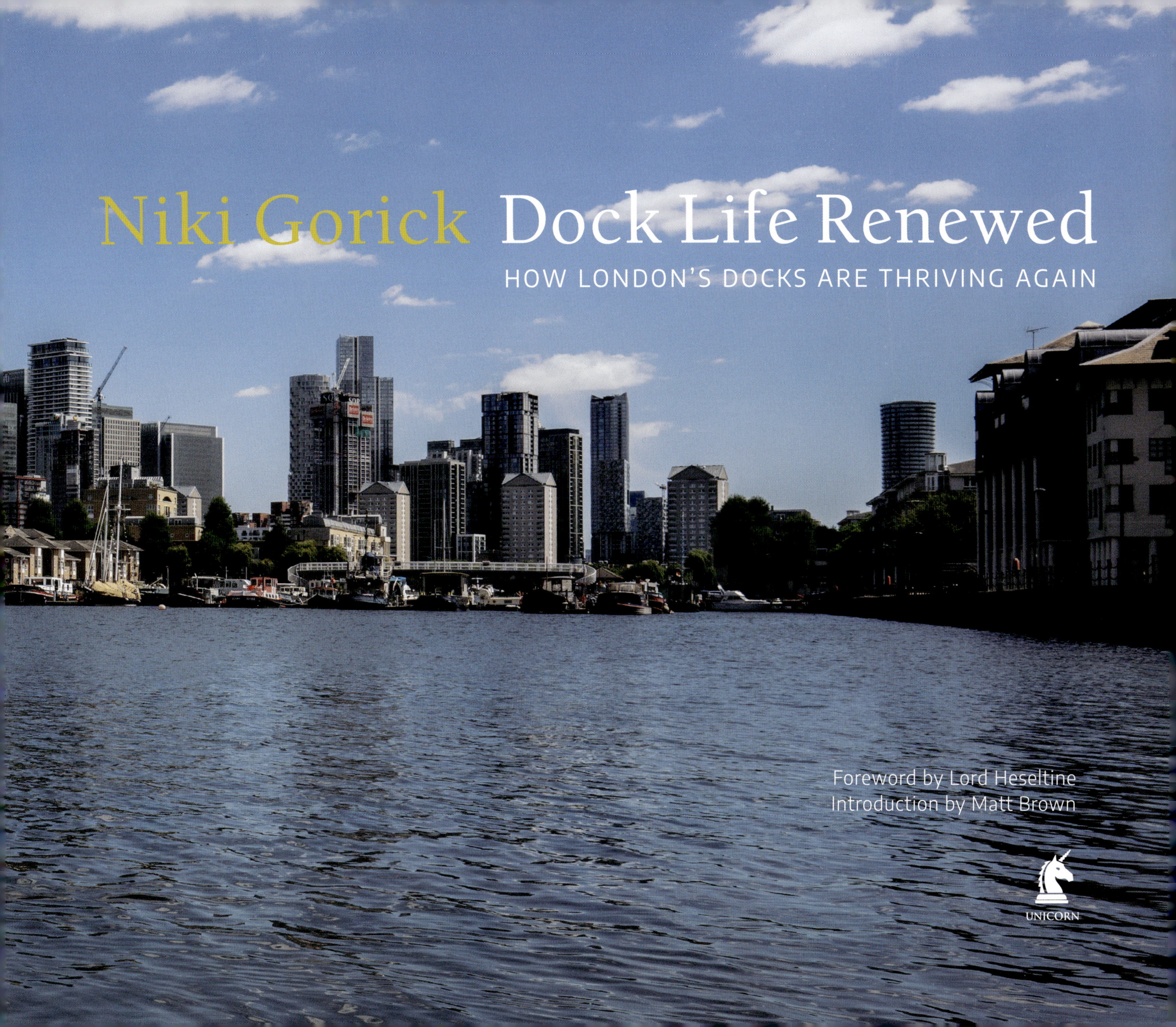

Foreword by Lord Heseltine
Introduction by Matt Brown

UNICORN

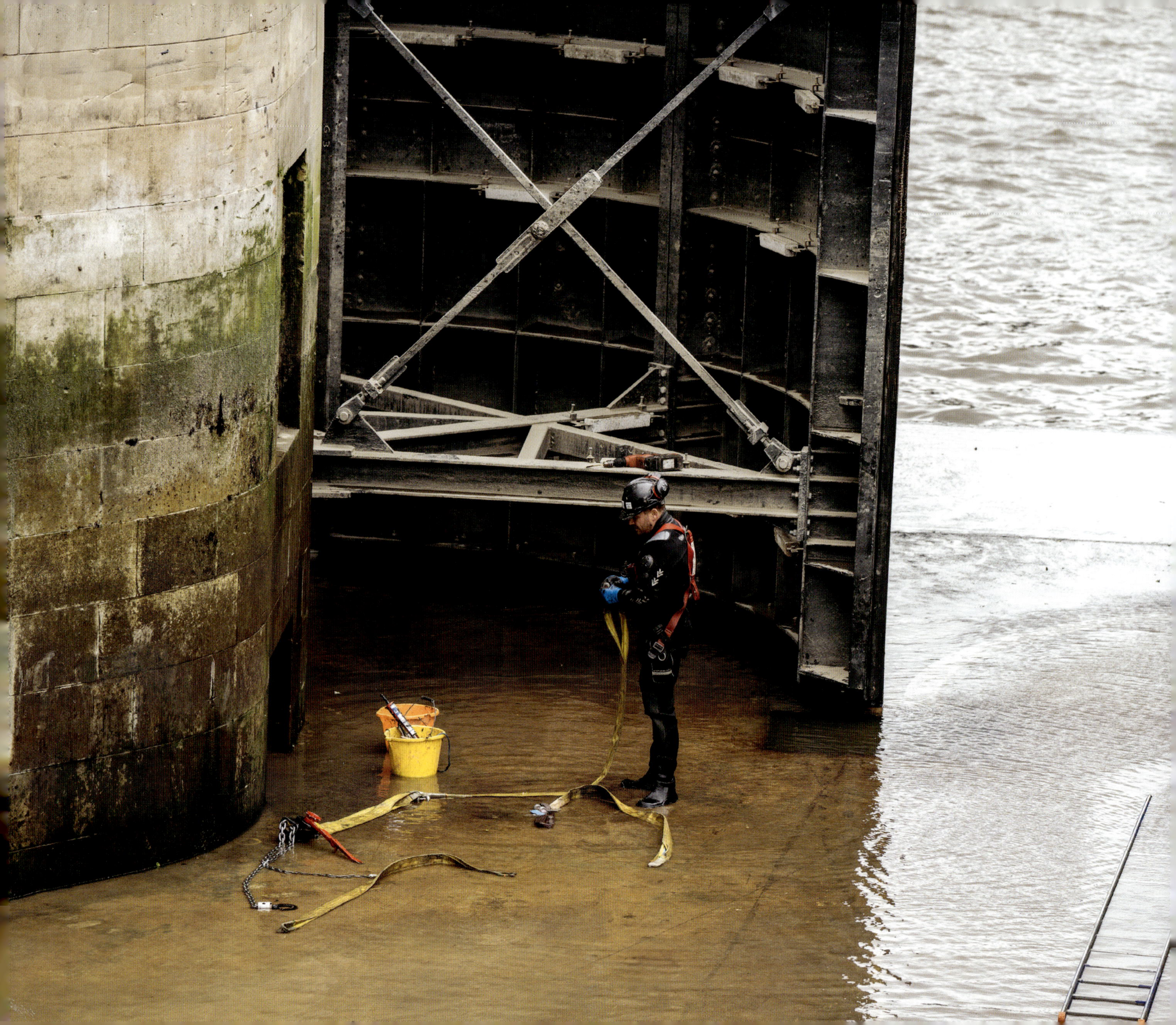

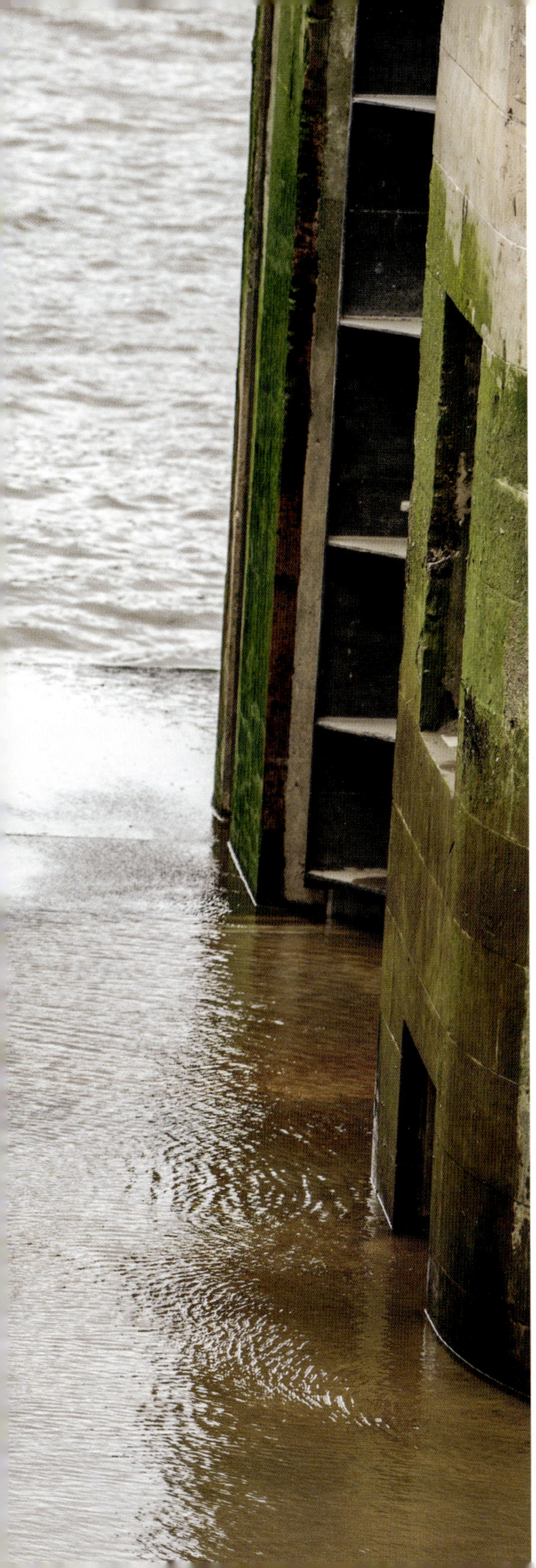

Contents

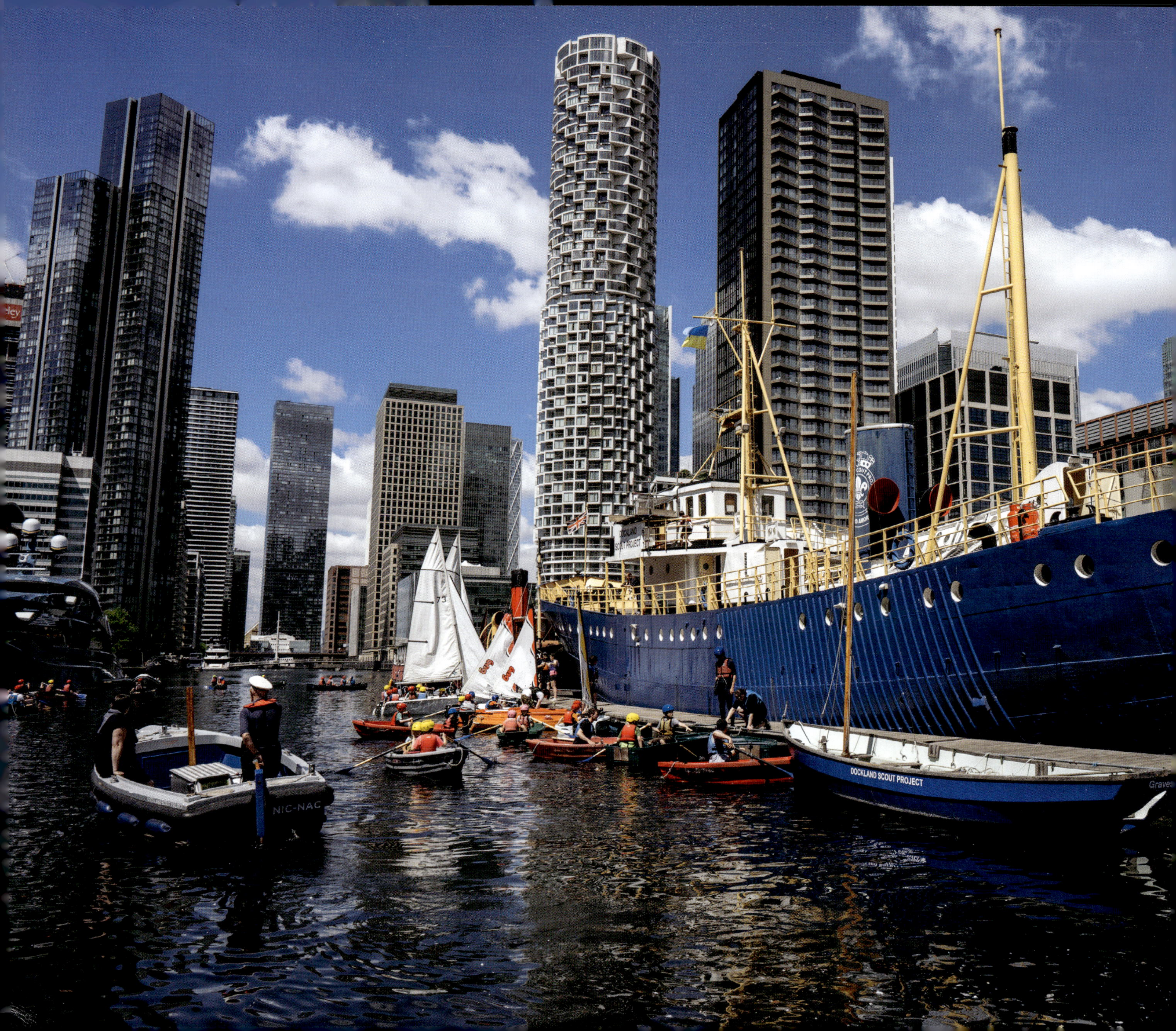
NIC-NAC
DOCKLAND SCOUT PROJECT

Foreword

LORD HESELTINE

Six thousand acres of forgotten wasteland – this was my horrified appraisal of London's old docks whilst flying over them in a plane forty-two years ago. By setting up the London Docklands Development Corporation, we aimed to regenerate these derelict areas and I am still very proud of the corporation's success in creating new financial, commercial and residential communities.

I am delighted that this book specifically celebrates the regeneration of life on the waters of the old docks, reminding us of their working heritage as the great Port of London. Although cargo ships are no longer arriving to unload, an extraordinary diversity of vessels are thriving in the docks for business, living and recreation. Back in the 1980s, I certainly wouldn't have predicted that there would still be a working Surrey Docks boatyard, or that hot tubs now navigate the waterways of the Isle of Dogs and superyachts visit St Katharine Docks. Come to think of it, I would not have predicted virtually any of the big changes that the development corporation created! That is what happens when you create a powerful organisation with effective leadership, appropriate powers and resources and the right incentives. It's a remarkable transformation.

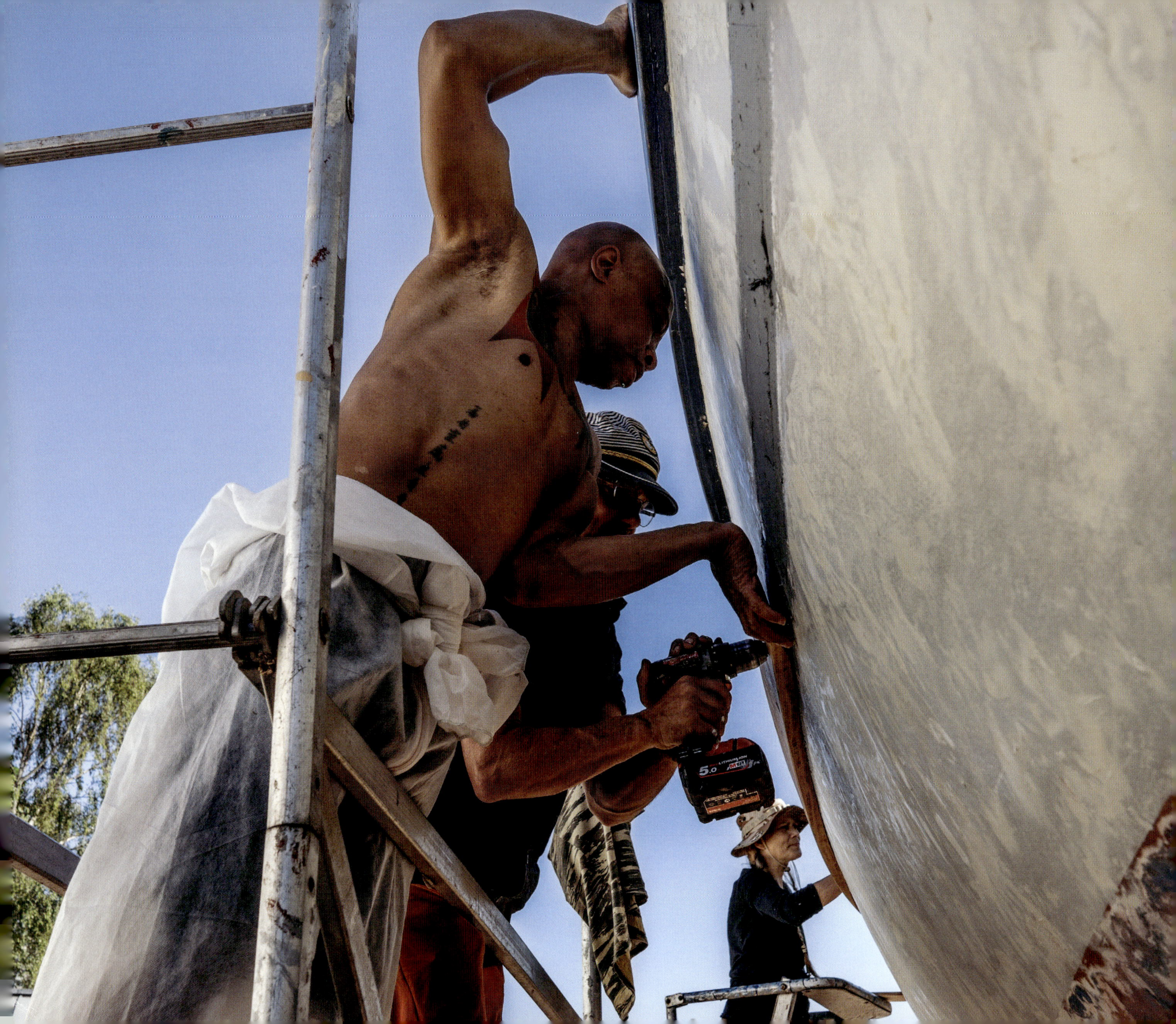
5.0

Preface

NIKI GORICK

When I first moved to Surrey Quays, a visiting friend described the beautiful surroundings of open spaces, trees, water and boats as the land of Narnia. Comparing this part of London's old docklands to a fantasy world of magic is, of course, a bit of a stretch but there is no doubt that these converted commercial docks are hugely attractive places to live. And not just for flat-dwellers like me. In the early days of Covid in 2020 and strictly local walks, I became fascinated by the variety of boats surrounding me and those living on them. It was intriguing to see that these enclosed waters, once used by commercial traffic for over two centuries and then left unused for a whole decade, were now supporting a thriving floating community. As a photographer, I felt drawn to try and capture this hidden world of homes attached to pontoons in the centre of London.

I started chatting to my water-based neighbours, gaining their trust and permission to photograph. I soon discovered many different personalities and a tightknit, welcoming community of all types, from pensioners to families, business executives to artists. Many have lived on boats for years, others are newcomers, but the waiting list for residential moorings is long. One of the main attractions of South Dock Marina is being able to live in central London relatively cheaply. Southwark Council's mooring fees are reasonable and boats are much more affordable than onshore options. As an urban marina, it is also safely cordoned off inside a gated network of pontoons, creating a world apart – a comfortable harbour for some, for others a real sanctuary.

I knew very little about the practicalities of renovating and living on boats but became increasingly curious about the many activities going on, particularly in the busy boatyard. I was fascinated to see how ancient marine trades were being maintained and updated, and made repeated visits to photograph progress on different boats with the help of my own entry fob kindly supplied by the harbour master.

It was the perfect project to embark on during the pandemic, as most activities were outside and no masks had to be worn, so, thankfully, faces and expressions could be properly captured. I expanded my focus to include two other dock areas, St Katharine Docks and the Isle of Dogs, as both of these are run by different organisations and have contrasting characters to each other and to South Dock Marina in Surrey Quays. Working with tip-offs from the harbour masters allowed me to capture their 'liveaboard' communities and also a new world (to me) of visiting superyachts and warships, floating arts spaces, yoga paddleboarding and classic boat festivals, right through to serious dock maintenance, heritage enthusiasts and energetic sea scouts.

Two years of photographing have resulted in a collection of images that I hope conveys the extraordinary diversity of what is happening on the waters of London's old docks. It's certainly been a revelation to me. The great commercial Port of London may have disappeared into history but a twenty-first-century reincarnation means that life in many forms has returned.

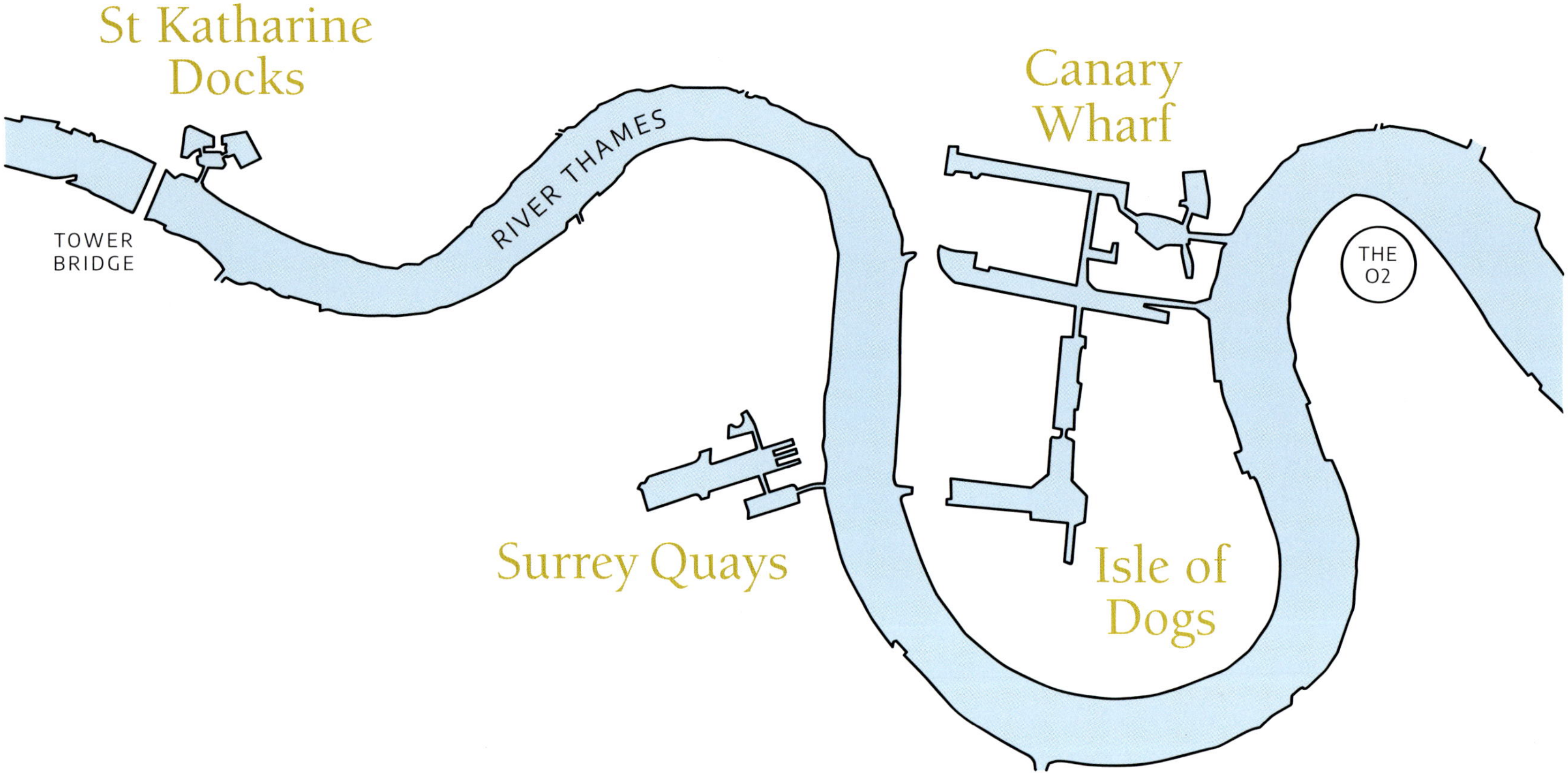
St Katharine
Docks
TOWER
BRIDGE
RIVER THAMES
Canary
Wharf
THE
O2
Surrey Quays
Isle of
Dogs

Introduction

MATT BROWN, EDITOR-AT-LARGE, *LONDONIST*

The oldest structure ever found in London is a jetty. Its Mesolithic timbers, still visible at Vauxhall during low tides, may be 6,500 years old. Raising cargo out of the river and on to dry land is, by extension, London's oldest documented profession. The Romans, millennia later, serviced their newly minted city of Londinium from a mile-long quayside. Their Anglo-Saxon successors built up a port near Covent Garden, described by the Venerable Bede as 'a trading centre for many nations who visit it by land and sea'. Generations later, the Port of London was the commercial hub of the largest empire in history. London has always been a city of docks.

I'm writing these words from a café in St Katharine Docks, immediately east of the Tower of London. Despite heavy war damage and redevelopment, this is one of London's best-preserved docks, with original warehousing and heritage features. It's also among the more attractive, as numerous photographs in this volume attest. A popular marina and dining spot, St Katharine Docks is a place of leisure, relaxation and entertainment. Children swing around poles and jeté off mooring posts. Houseboats and pleasure craft crowd the edges. Their number has included Édith Piaf's 'love boat' and the late Queen's gilt rowbarge, *Gloriana*.

This would have been inconceivable just a couple of generations ago. St Katharine Docks was a place of graft and grit. You would not bring your family here. Nobody sat down for a quayside cappuccino. Nobody sat down at all, unless it was to file paperwork. In just a few short decades, St Katharine and the other docks in this book have transformed beyond imagination. A dock worker transported from the nineteenth century would find himself in a different world.*

Of course, the docks have always seen radical change. Their very creation was an act of upheaval, displacement and engineering on a grand scale. Stand at one end of Rotherhithe's Greenland Dock today, and just imagine the human effort required to scoop out such volumes at a time before efficient engines and heavy machinery. In some cases, thousands of people lost their homes to development and historic buildings were torn down. The tumult was not restricted to the dock sites themselves. Their creation necessitated new roads and rail links that would carve canyons into the neighbouring boroughs and beyond. Landscapes were redefined across the capital. The marshes west of Nine Elms, for example, were transformed into Battersea Park thanks to a soil transplant from the digs of the East End. Wealthy Belgravia rests upon the loams of St Katharine.

Later on, the docks themselves would face upheaval. Lengthy labour disputes disrupted operations in the late nineteenth century and led to the unionisation of the workforce. The First World War brought an urgent change in priorities to the Port of London, along with the new threat of aerial bombardment. The Second World War realised that threat in full. An estimated 25,000 explosives and firebombs rained down on the area, with devastating results. But the docks never closed. Their resilient industries bounced back stronger from each challenge. When the end came – within living memory – it was through obsolescence. The world embraced container shipping. The inner London docks lacked both the infrastructure and the deep water needed to handle such vessels. By the 1980s, the quaysides lay in silence.

In every ending is a new beginning. Nowhere better demonstrates this aphorism than London's docks. Half a lifetime ago, the spent quaysides were fenced off, weeded over, fit only as a backdrop for gritty police dramas. A few short decades later and the docks are once again among London's most energetic and affluent areas. This book is a celebration of that transformation. It examines, through photography, how these former pools of industry have been co-opted for new purposes and

* In one sense, the cliché is literal. St Katharine Docks contains an outcast prop from the movie *2001: A Space Odyssey*. A huge acrylic block pinned to a building at the south of the marina was originally intended as the film's iconic alien Monolith, before Kubrick changed his mind and went obsidian. What would a Victorian stevedore have made of that?

pastimes. Some changes, as Lord Heseltine notes in his Foreword, would surprise even the London Docklands Development Corporation (LDDC), whose job it was to recall the docks to life.

As a resident of Surrey Quays, photographer Niki Gorick has a local's eye for detail. But one only has to spend a few moments with her work to spot her real passion: not the docks themselves but the people who inhabit the boats, quays and jetties. In these pages, we're gifted a unique glimpse into the diverse characters who enliven the modern docks, and the boundless variety of their activities. Such a project is potentially infinite. A million people live or work here. The Docklands stretch way beyond the Isle of Dogs to encompass the vast Royal Docks. To bring focus to the project, Niki has concentrated on just three areas.

St Katharine Docks is the smallest of the three, immediately east of the Tower of London. Its now tranquil basins were once a dense warren of slum housing, clustered around the medieval hospital of St Katharine's. But by the 1820s, London needed more dock space, and this land, so close to the City, was a prime site. The homes of more than 10,000 people were swept away by the 'unfeeling and encroaching hand of commerce'. The development came with the full heft of the Industrial Revolution: Thomas Telford masterminded the new docks, while Messers Boulton and Watt provided the steam power. Even so, the docks were only moderately successful in the long term. Heavily bombed and of limited capacity, they were among the first to close after the Second World War but also among the earliest to be redeveloped. First came the gargantuan concrete wall of the Tower Hotel, followed by new commercial blocks and the sensitive redevelopment of the surviving warehouses. Over the past three decades, this slum-turned-docks-turned-marina has thrived. It is an astonishing, multipartite transformation.

Heading southeast, we reach the old Surrey Commercial Docks – or what remains of them. Until the 1970s almost everything east of the Overground railway was either water or quay. This sprawling complex occupied an area similar to that of Monaco. Imagine how many lives this mega-dock, known especially for its timber trade, must have touched over almost 300 years of operation. In a now-familiar story, heavy bombing in the Second World War, followed by changes in transportation, led to the gradual stagnation of the Surrey Commercial Docks. By the 1980s, some 90 per cent had been filled in. Much of this newly released land was converted to residential use, with the Surrey Quays shopping centre providing a commercial hub. The huge Greenland Dock and adjacent South Dock were retained, along with a few smaller pools.

Impressive though this transformation was, still loftier ambitions would be fulfilled across the water at West India Docks, to the north of the Isle of Dogs. These docks opened at the dawn of the nineteenth century, tasked with facilitating trade with the West Indies. They remained successful until, once again, the twin ravages of war and commercial enfeeblement signalled the end. The utter transformation that followed is best seen from Greenwich Hill. The view to the north is a crenelated wall of towers, nine of which would have been London's tallest building had they been erected before the 1980s. Yet among these giants, many dock spaces and other remnants survive, including a Grade I-listed sugar warehouse that is now home to the Museum of London Docklands.

In all three cases, we can thank the London Docklands Development Corporation for making change happen. The organisation was set up by the UK government in 1981 to bring new purpose to the riverside, with a purview that stretched over 22 square kilometres of former dock land. Redevelopment was not always smooth sailing. Wholesale change on this scale never is. Entire books can, and have, been written about the opposition the LDDC faced. Despite protests, accusations, recessions and bankruptcies, the project soldiered on to fruition. This book is all about what came next.

Until very recently, the only verbs associated with these docks would have been work, graft, labour and toil. But we now find other activities: fishing, jogging, mudlarking, windsurfing, open swimming, fine dining, yoga, paddleboarding … even yoga-paddleboarding. Families live here. Cormorants live here. Luxury yachts bob beside thrifty houseboats; dragon boats share waters with armour-plated battleships. Sails, paddles, outboard motors. Diversity without end. It is the wider metropolis in marine microcosm.

On my own docklands wanderings I've tried my hand at bowls, kayaked to a brewery, got lost in an endless shopping centre, sipped martinis in a geodesic dome, encountered a bus-sized rubber duck, walked across the largest roof in London and admired a plantation of dawn redwoods – a tree unknown to western science until the 1940s. Any and all of this would have been inconceivable to the dockers who worked these quays just two generations ago. And yet it seems I've barely had my eyes open. Niki's photographs reveal dozens of unexpected activities in these once industrial waters – from floating hot tubs to cactus farming to an amphibious church and an aquatic theatre.

The character and appearance of the docks may have changed beyond recognition but – and here lies the most striking aspect of this book – the old trades have not vanished completely. Niki's lens is at its keenest when exploring the boatyards and service areas that still form a crucial part of the motley dockland admixture. The docks may no longer be industrial but they remain industrious. The heart of this book lies with the metal fabricators, engineers, fibreglass fitters, rot detectives, woodwork apprentices, painters, fitters and mechanics whose work goes largely unseen – until now. And these waters, Niki reminds us, still reach outwards like the docks of old. Vessels journey from all over the world to be here. You might stumble across a fully-rigged ship from the Royal Navy of Oman, a Swedish East Indiaman, a Goan barque and even, just occasionally, a sail vessel of trade, bringing goods from overseas on the reappraised and virtuous puff of wind power.

It is impossible to know what our descendants, 6,500 years from now, might uncover from the mud of the Thames to cast light upon our long-vanished age. The line of a stone quayside, perhaps, or the rusted hulk of a toppled crane. We can only hope that their archives retain a copy of this magnificent book, whose images offer a rich insight into the post-industrial docks of the early twenty-first century. I hope you enjoy these photographs as much as I have, and that they inspire you to explore and appreciate London's docklands further. If history tells us anything, they will not stay this way for ever.

Havens of diversity

These stretches of urban water attract an extraordinary mix of residents and visitors.

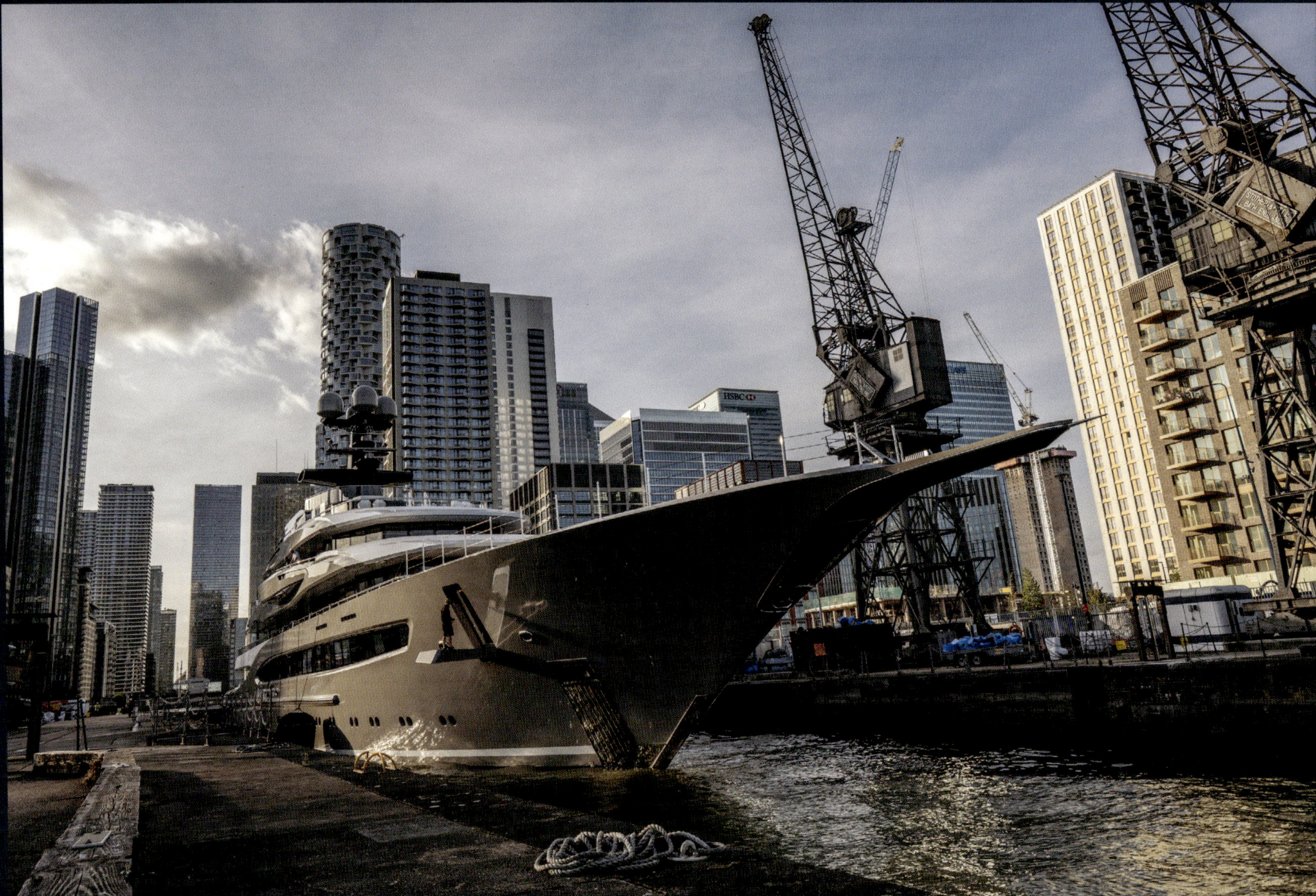

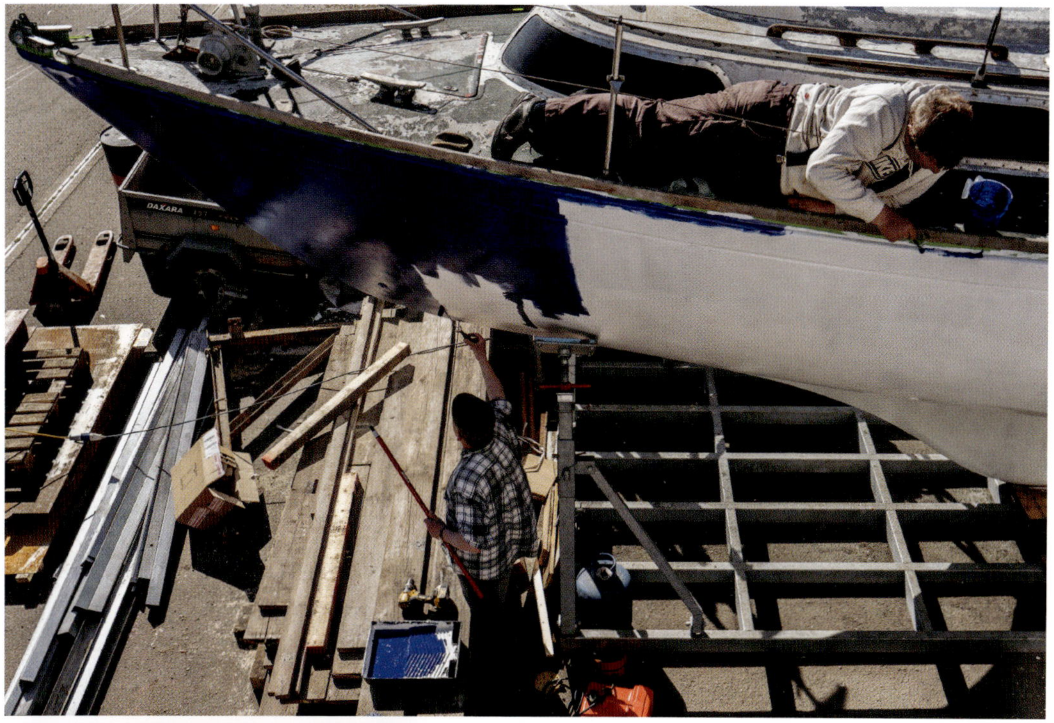

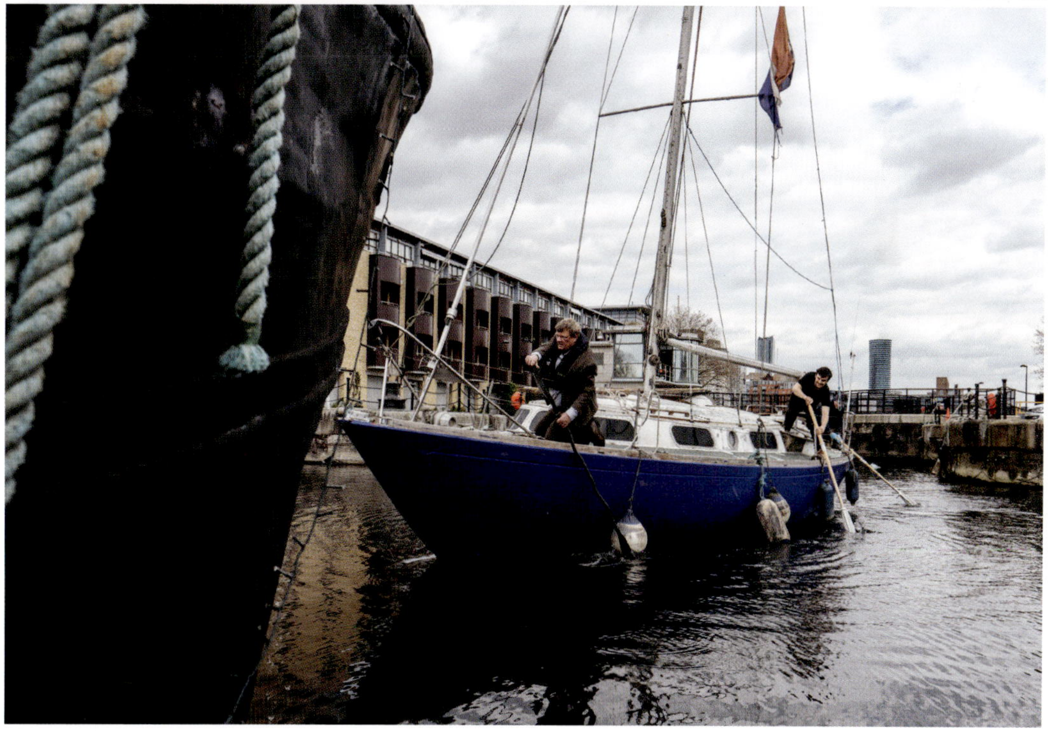

Two ends of the spectrum

Superyachts with big powerful engines frequently add a touch of glamour to West India Docks at Canary Wharf. By contrast, the charity Good4you is renovating a derelict, old sailing boat, *Boudicca*, which has no engine. She will stay in South Dock Marina in Surrey Quays to create a permanent home for a disabled man who was homeless in London for seven years.
www.good4you.org.uk

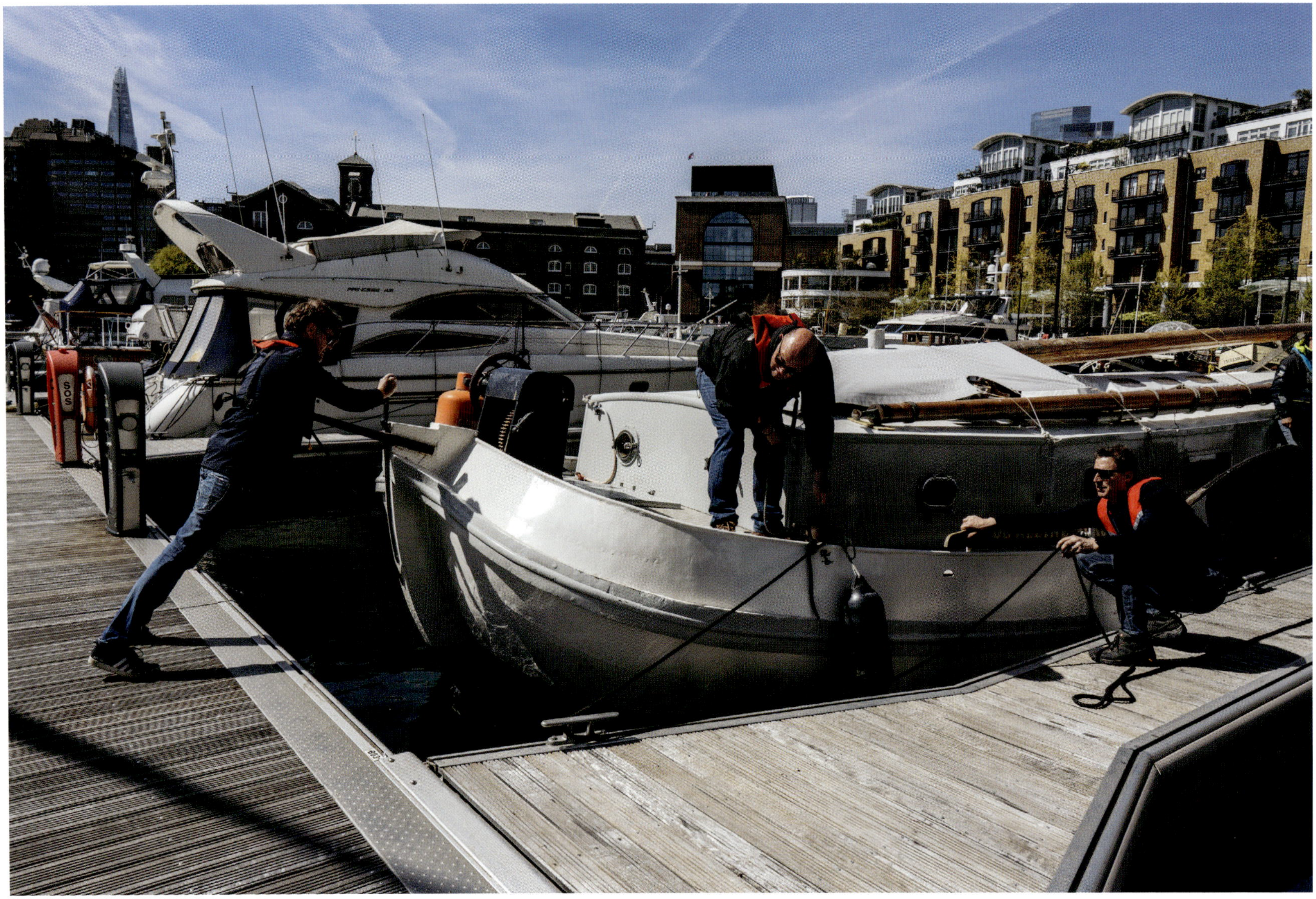

Mooring up

The freshly restored *De Kleine Aukje* arrives at her new berth in St Katharine Docks. This beautiful example of an early 20th-century Dutch barge will become a liveaboard for someone wanting a more affordable version of a central London pied-à-terre. No full-time living is allowed in St Kats, with proof of another main residence required.

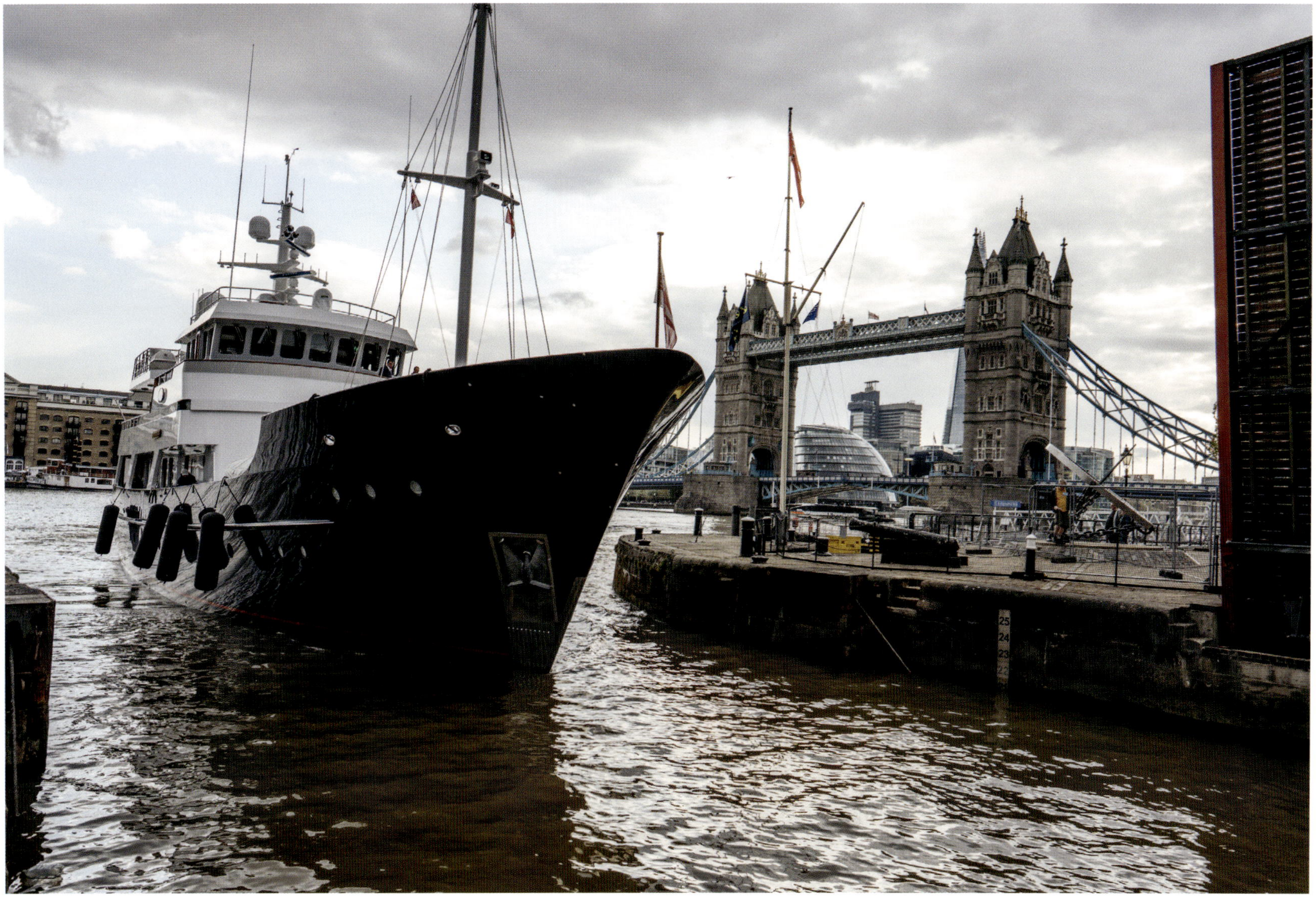

Visiting elites

St Katharine Docks' central location by the City of London makes it a popular destination for the luxury end of the boat-owning market. Run by private company Island Global Yachting (IGY) Marinas, it is a prestigious destination within its global network of moorings.

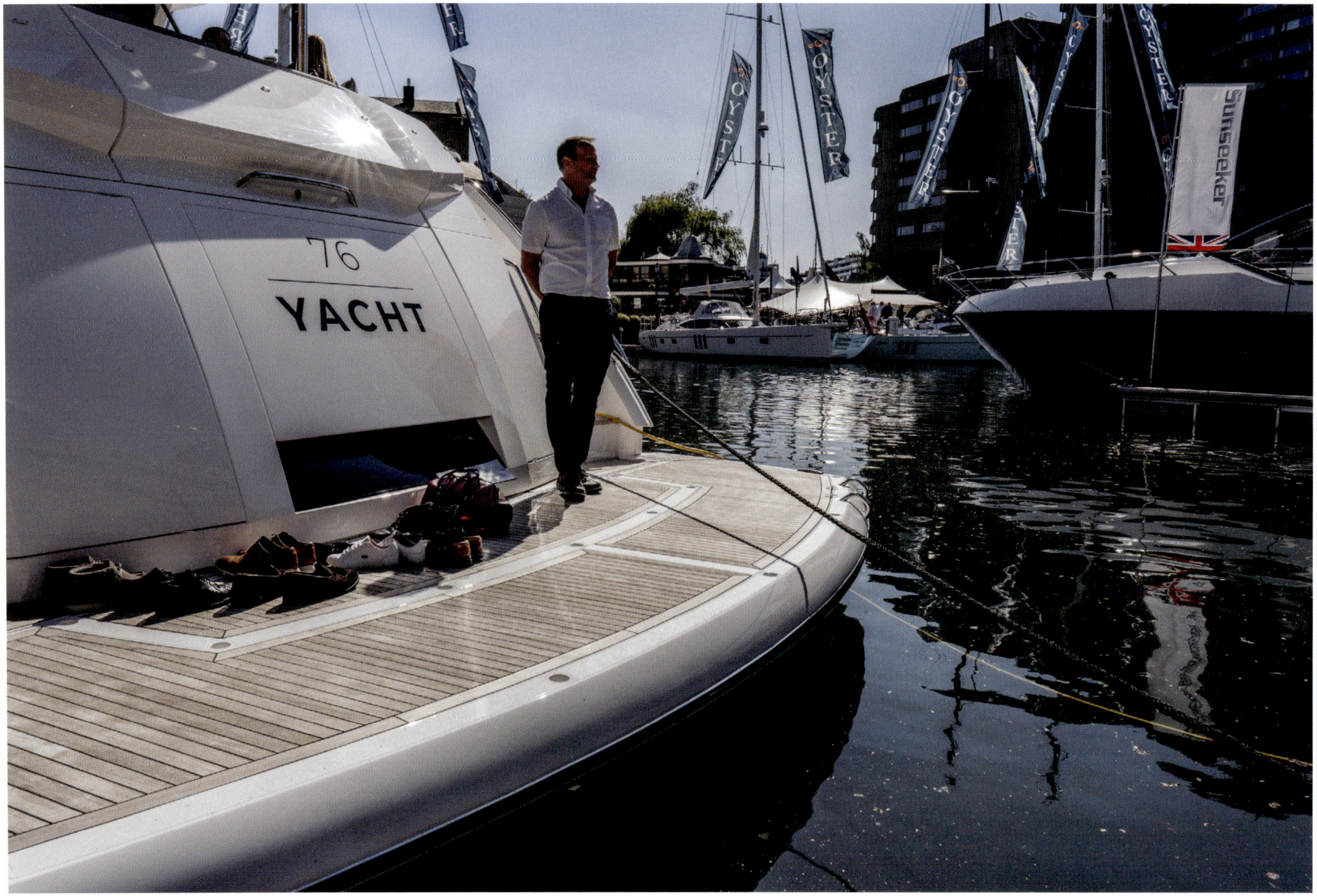

Marine showcase

Springtime sees St Katharine Docks transformed into a high-end yacht market with a floating display of luxury boat brands competing for customers. Organised by British Marine, the UK's marine industry trade association, this pristine line-up of the very latest models entices prospective buyers on board, while all footwear is guarded outside.

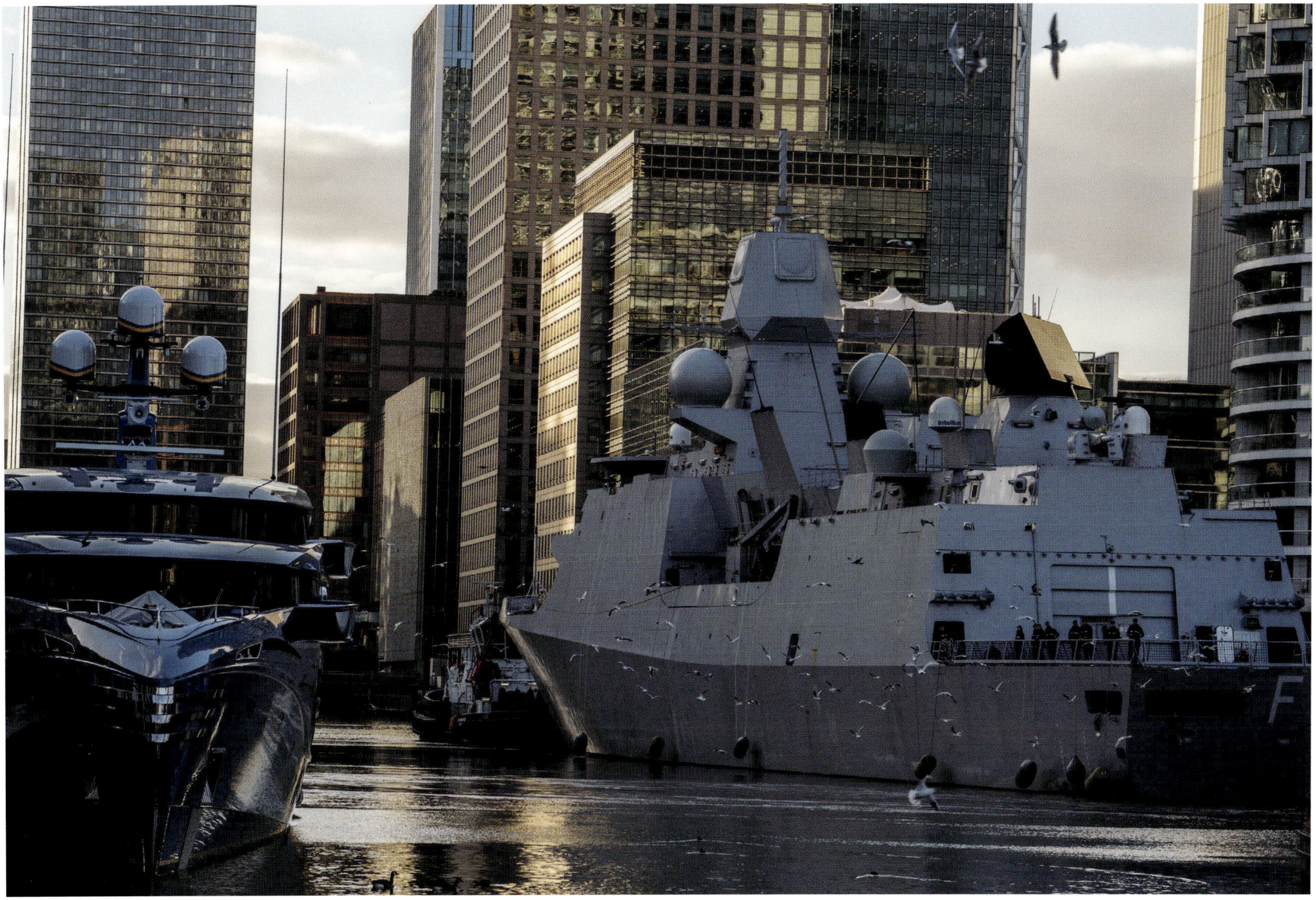

War and peace

Among the skyscrapers of Canary Wharf, West India Docks hosts a contrasting range of the larger vessels visiting London. At 10-metres deep, it can safely handle such warships as the Dutch 6,000-ton frigate HNLMS *Tromp*, as it manoeuvres past the smaller but still substantial superyacht.

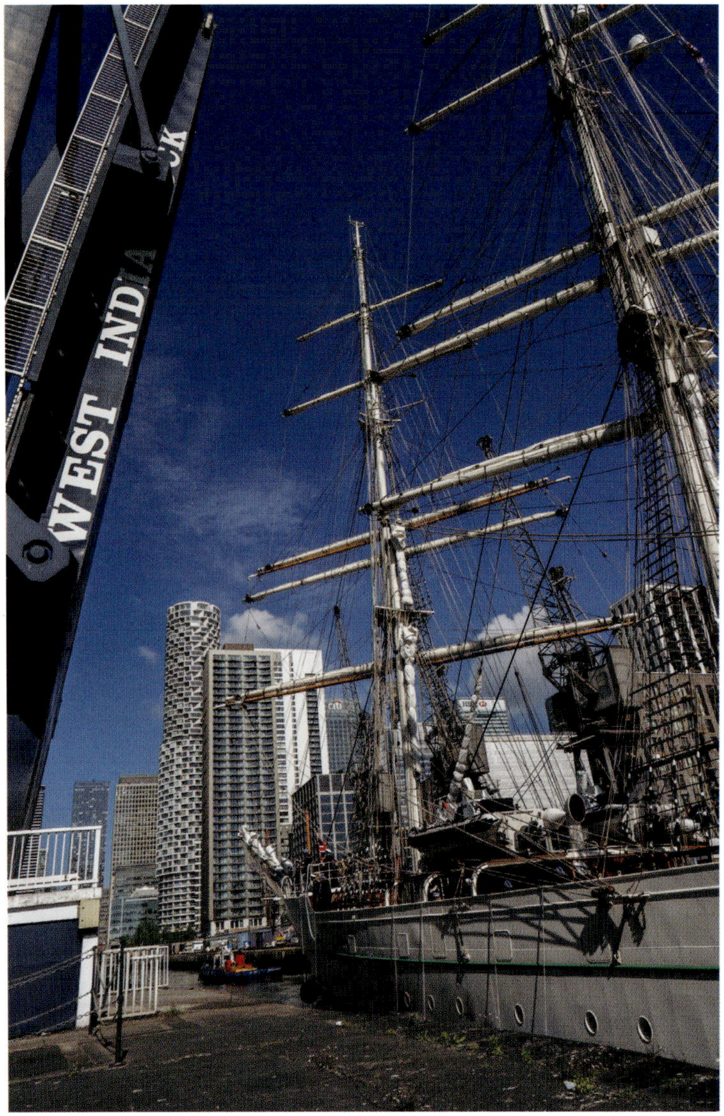

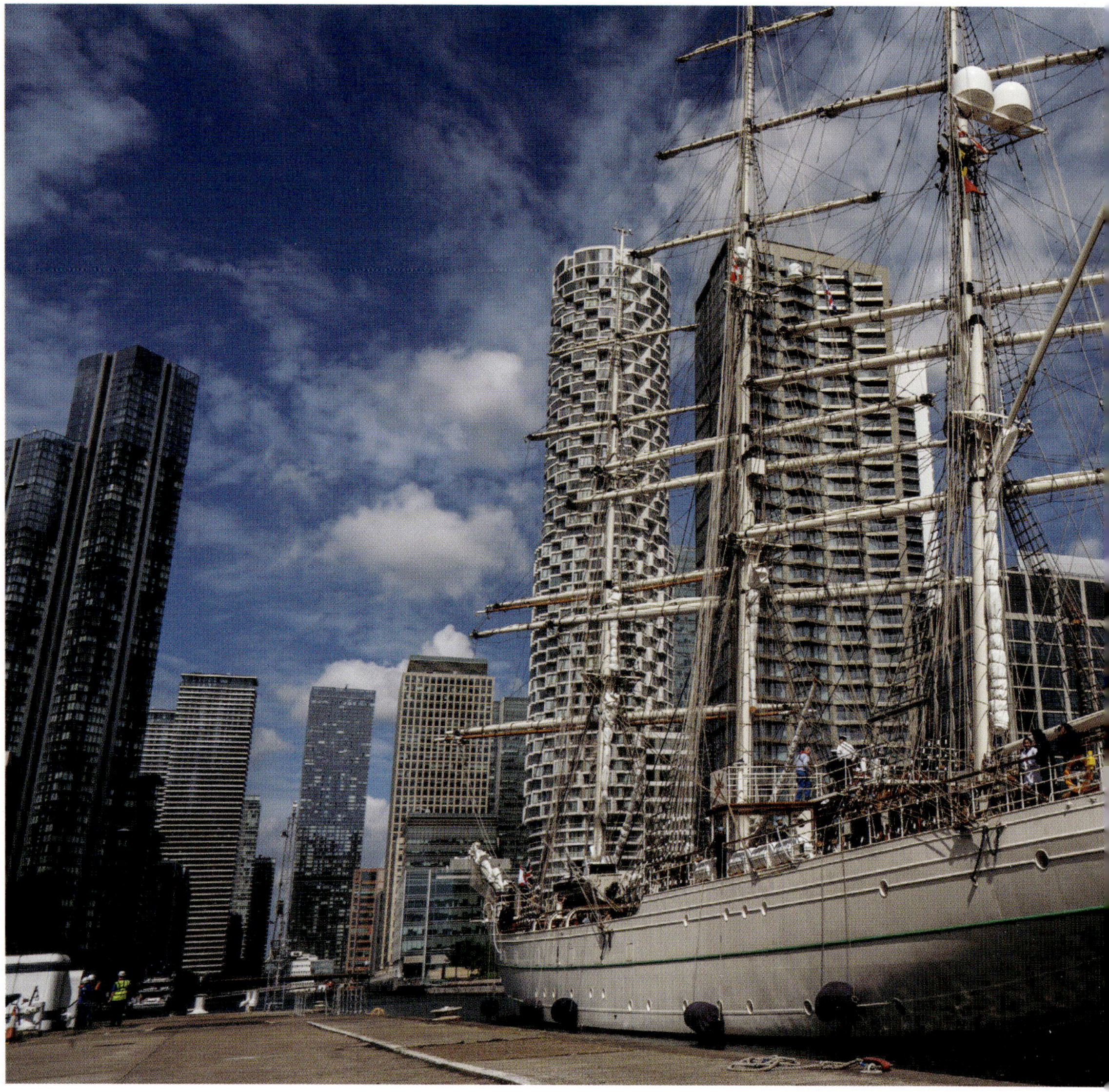

Training in style

Cadets training with the Royal Navy of Oman arrive in the Isle of Dogs on *Shabab Oman II*, a spectacular three-masted square-rigged clipper built in 2014. This blend of traditional sails and rigging with modern computerised navigation, gives a crew of 94 all-round experience in seafaring skills. With a total of 34 sails, it is built for speed like its forebears and is a regular in Tall Ships races.

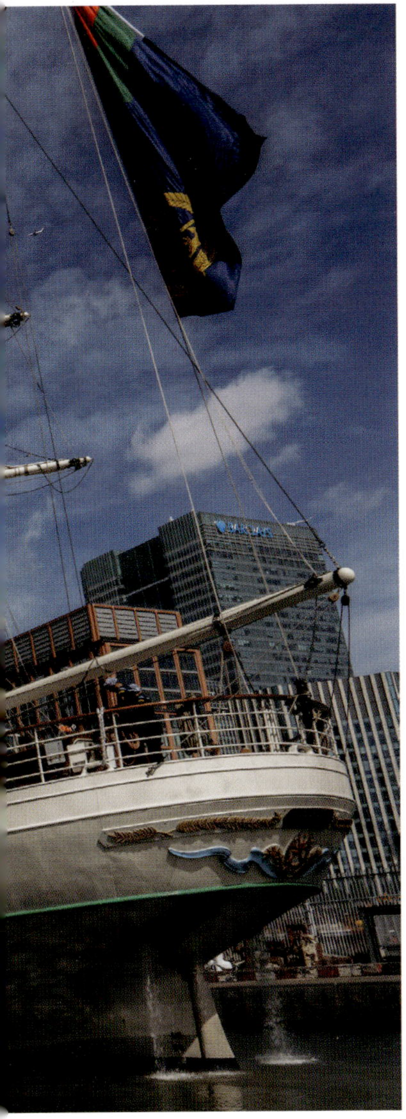

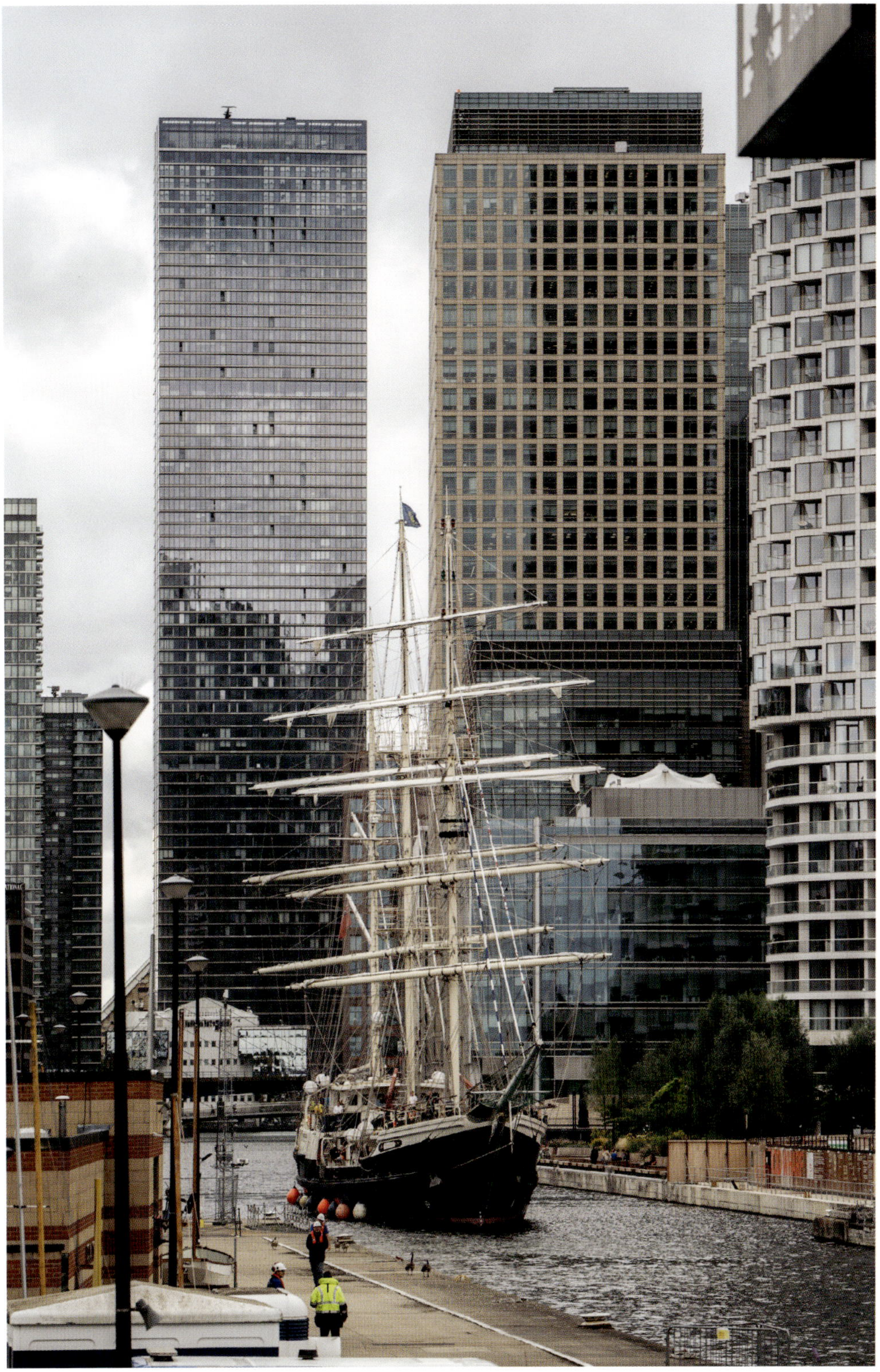

Tall story

Owned by the Jubilee Sailing Trust, SV *Tenacious* is not only the UK's largest working tall ship but is unique in being cleverly designed to be sailed by mixed-ability crews, including wheelchair users. Since its launch in 2000, the ship has sailed over 270,000 kilometres, including six voyages across the Atlantic. Having picked up some crew in London, it is heading for the sea again out of West India Docks.
www.jst.org.uk

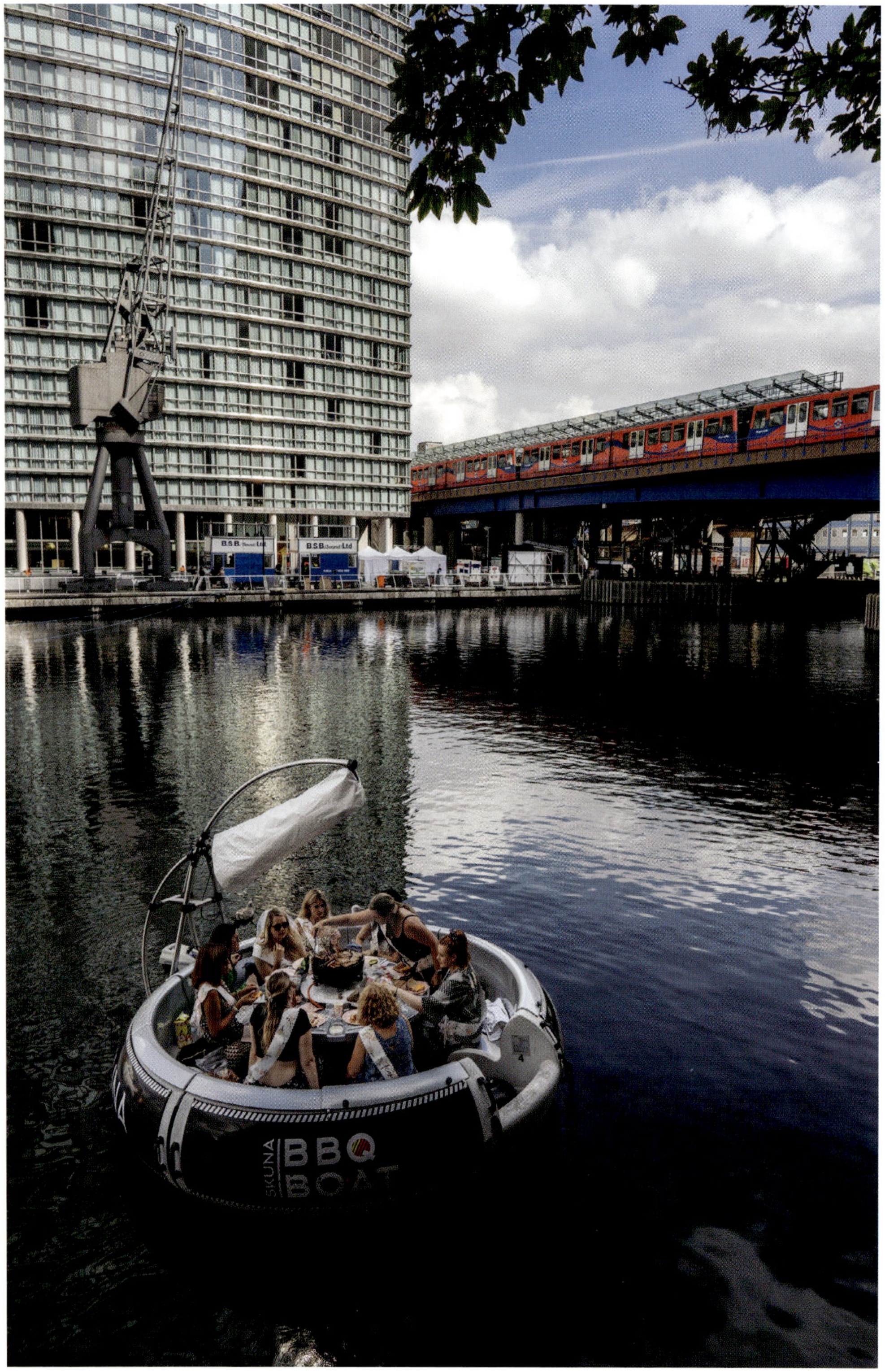

Fire and water

Popular al fresco dining is on the move below Canary Wharf's DLR line and the suspended shipping cranes preserved on the quayside. A hen party meanders peacefully around the waters of West India Quay, with the bride-to-be and friends sipping wine and enjoying a BBQ lunch.
www.skunaboats.com

Funnelling the past

Gentle puffs from the hot tub's wood-burning stove evoke faint reminders of how commercial ships used to belch smoke and unload cargo on the Isle of Dogs' industrial waterways.

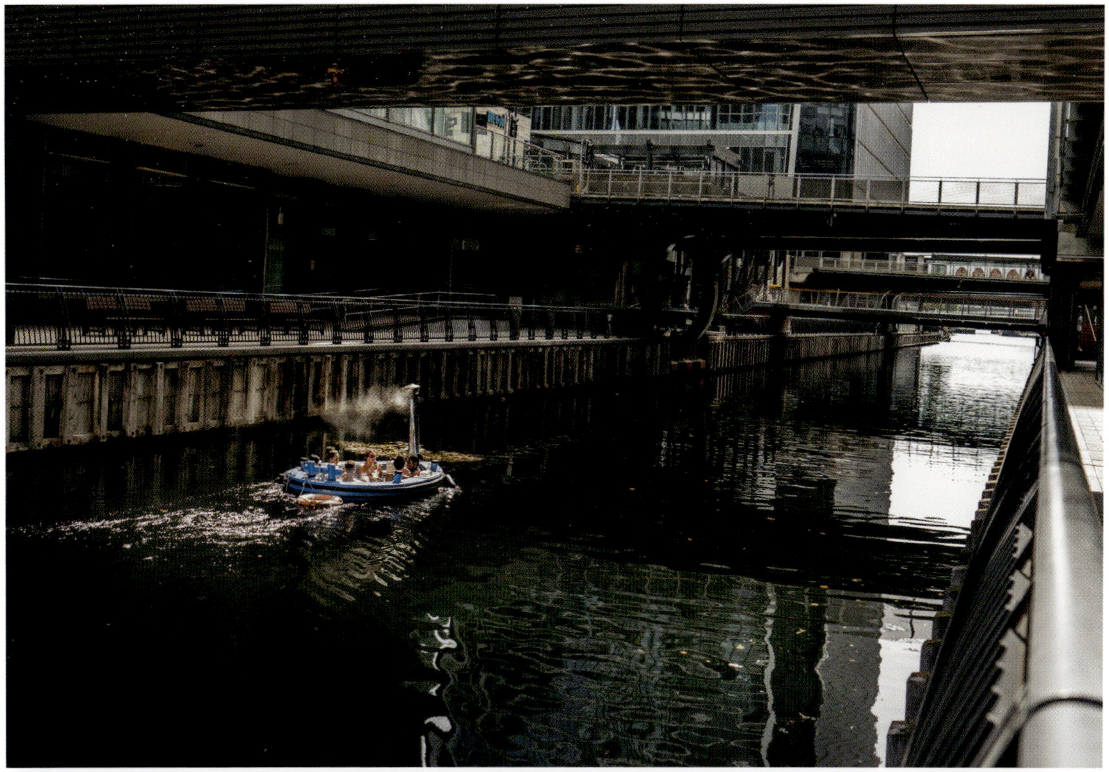

Temperature controlled

With the hot tub water kept at a toasty 38°C, semi-clad journeying through the deep waters of the Isle of Dogs' 19th-century docks is a year round attraction.
www.skunaboats.com

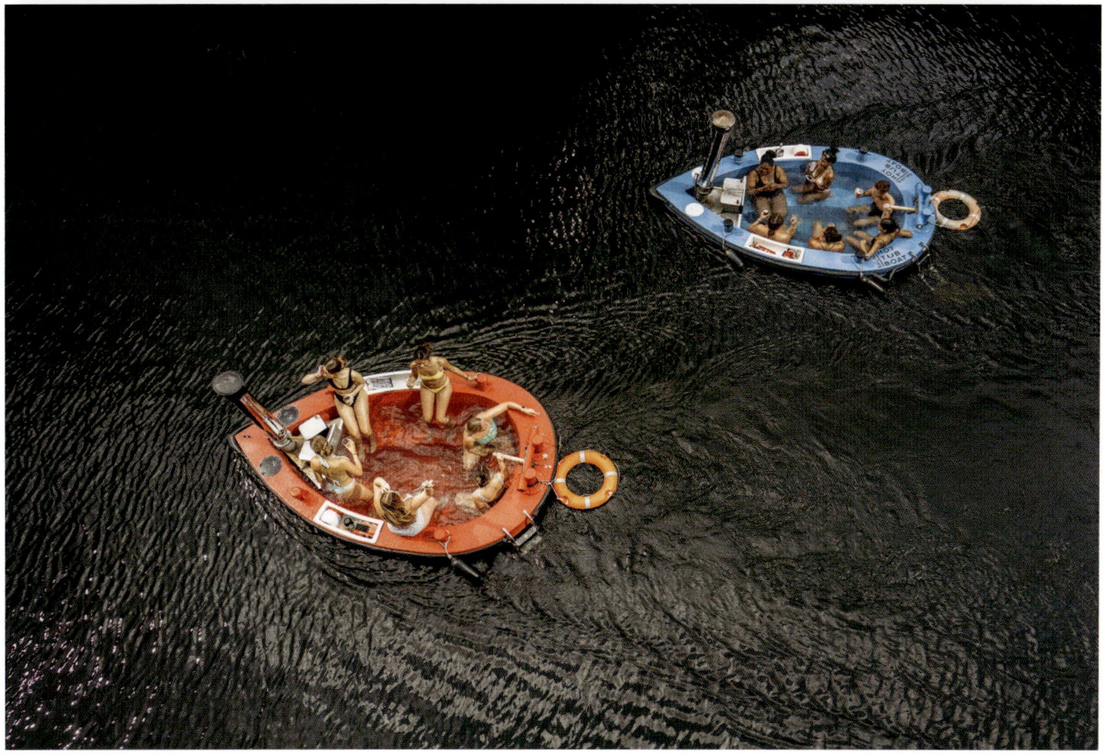

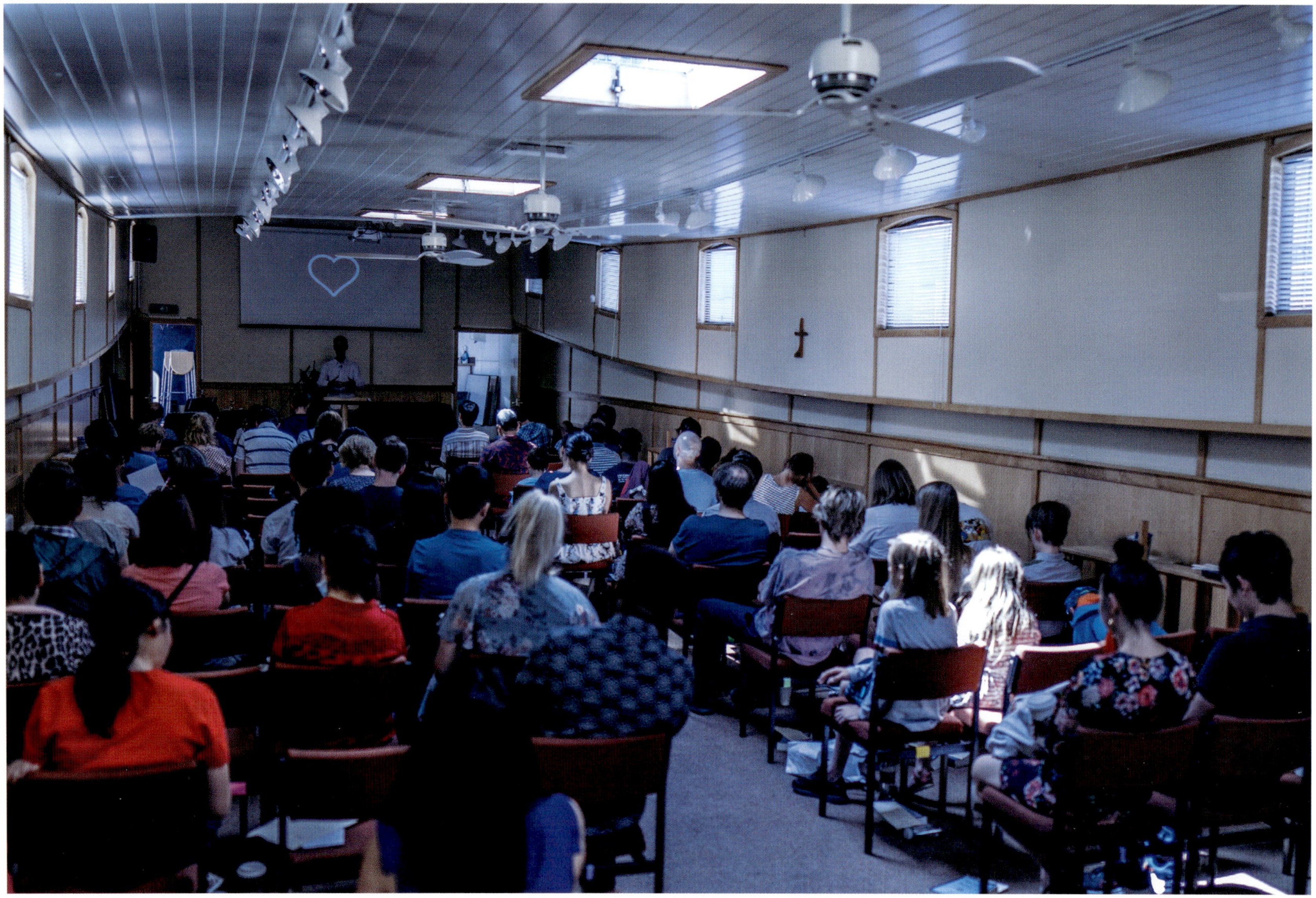

Buoyant worship

As London's floating church, St Peter's Barge has been permanently moored on West India Quay since 2003 and has built up a popular following from those living and working in the Canary Wharf area. The Senior Pastor, Rev. Marcus Nodder, preaches at a busy Sunday service on this beautifully converted Dutch freight barge.
www.stpetersbarge.org

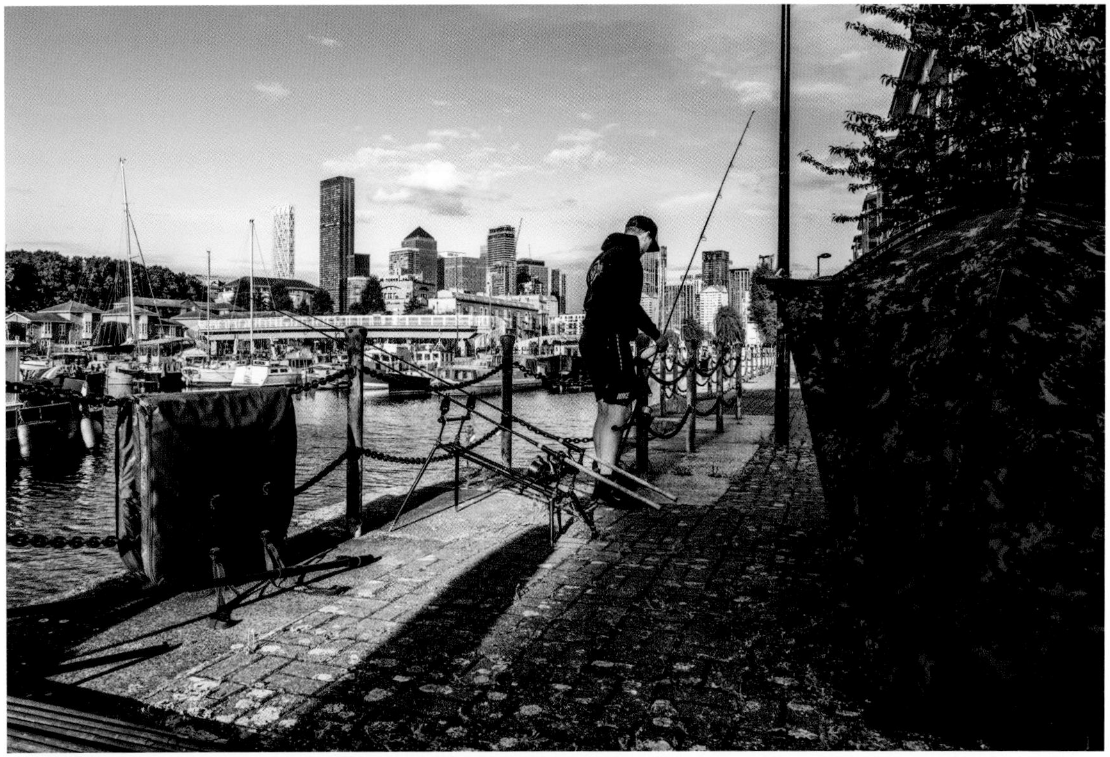

Hooked on fishing

Members of the Surrey Docks Angling club often camp overnight to take full advantage of their designated 48-hour slot beside Greenland Dock, hoping to catch Thames fish such as carp, bream, perch, tench, rudd and even the odd eel. Purely for sport, strict rules require all catches to be returned and the emphasis is on conserving the quality of both the water and the fish.
www.sdangling.club

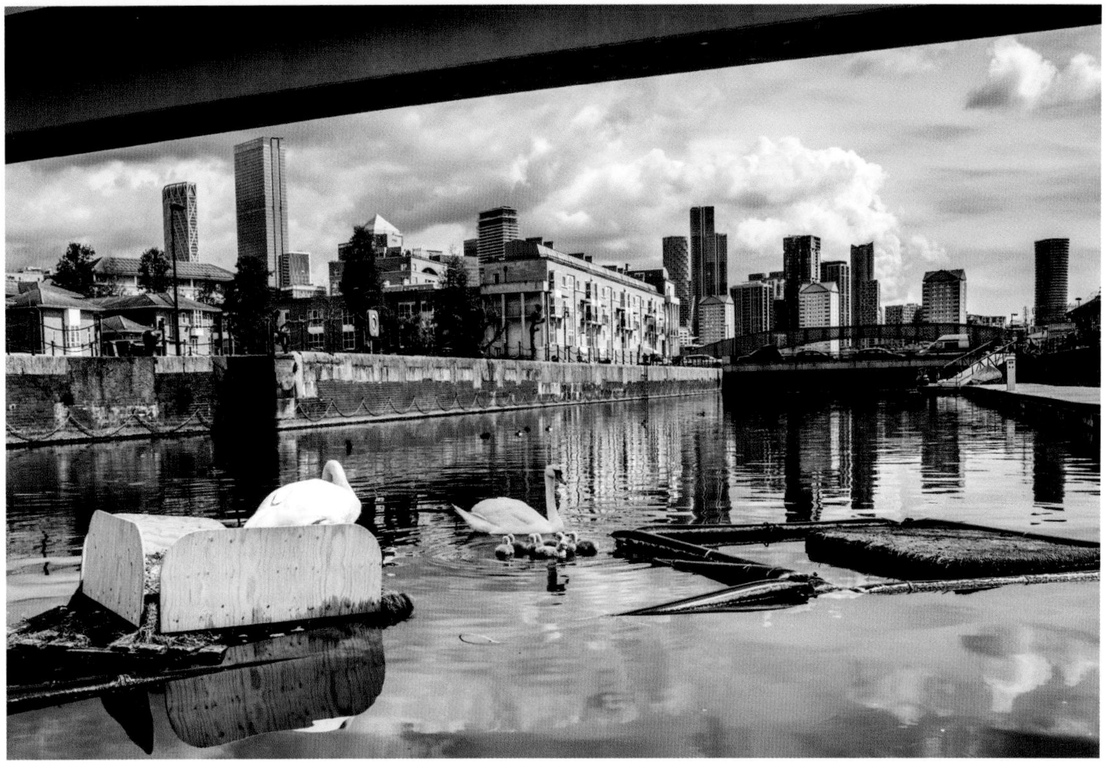

Rewilded

With the noise and commotion of the working docks in the past, wildlife of many types soon returned, particularly birds. Now, specially built floating platforms, such these in Greenland Dock's old lock, encourage large families of breeding swans every year, as well as residential geese, grebes and coots. Winter visitors, such as cormorants, terns and gulls add to this thriving avian community.

Life on board

Boat-dwellers are as varied as their vessels but the unique conditions of living on the water create a strong sense of community.

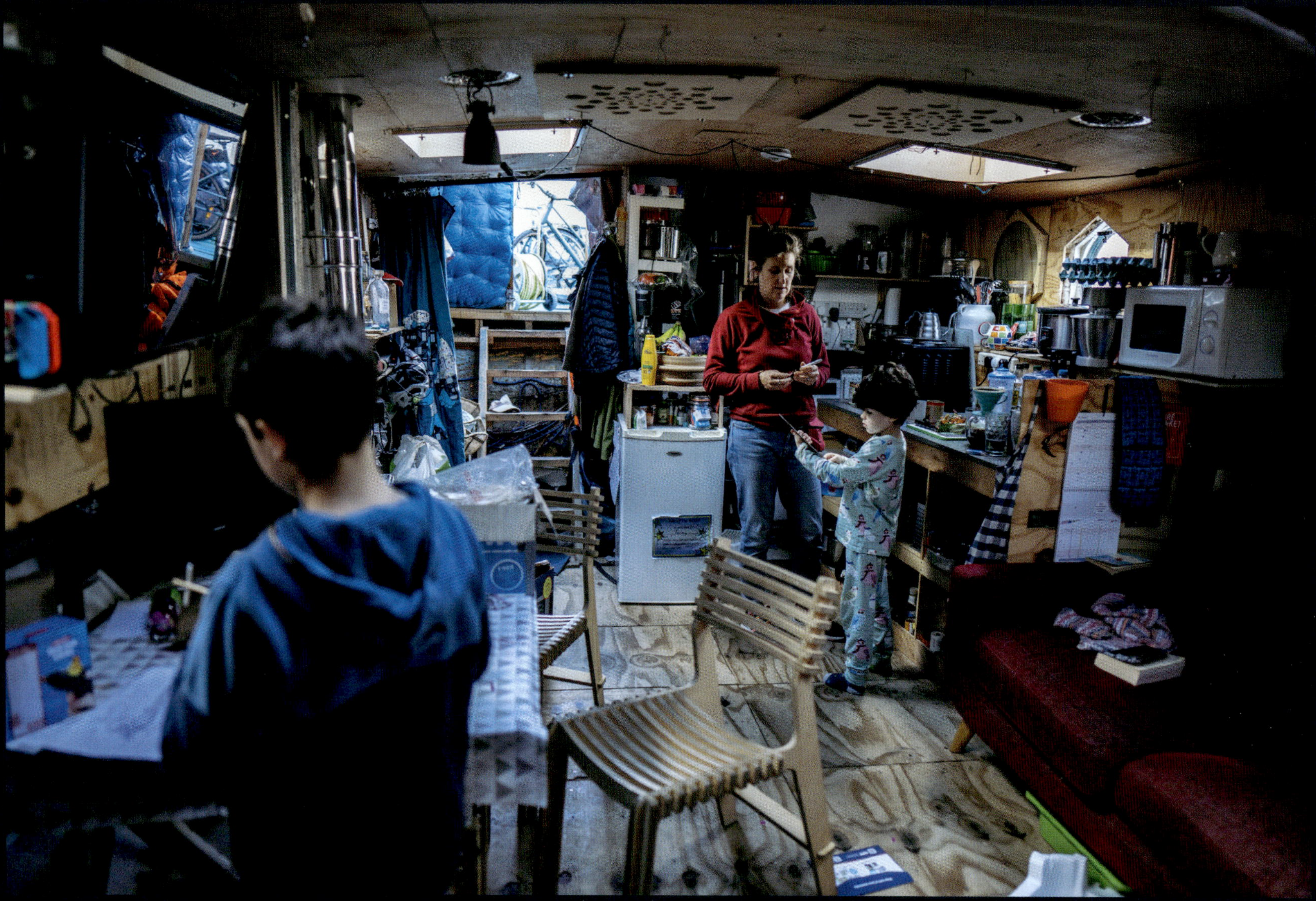

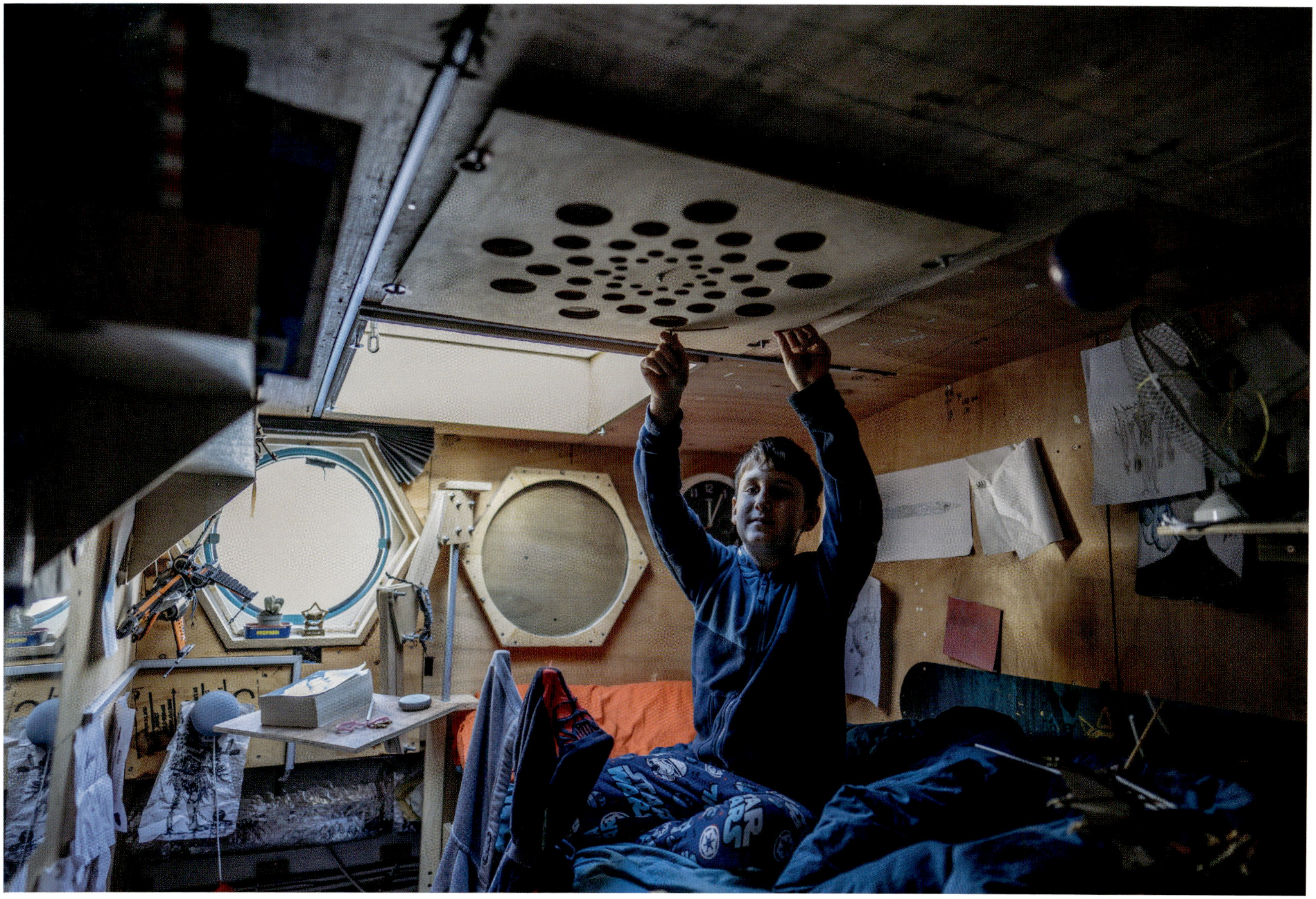

Build your own boat

‹ Knowing that they had the right design and computer woodworking skills, Simon and Rebecca bought a new wide-beam houseboat shell and then set about creating a family home to their own specifications. Using their CNC machine and boatyard workshop, they have produced and fitted everything in bespoke engineered timber, from the insulation panels and ceiling shutters to the cupboards, tables and chairs. Not quite finished, the next stage will be to move the temporary kitchen into a new extension space on the rear deck. www.studioshillito.com

Detailed design

Eli proudly demonstrates how shutters can block the light from the window above his bed but the fretwork can also be half-opened to create a breeze when needed.

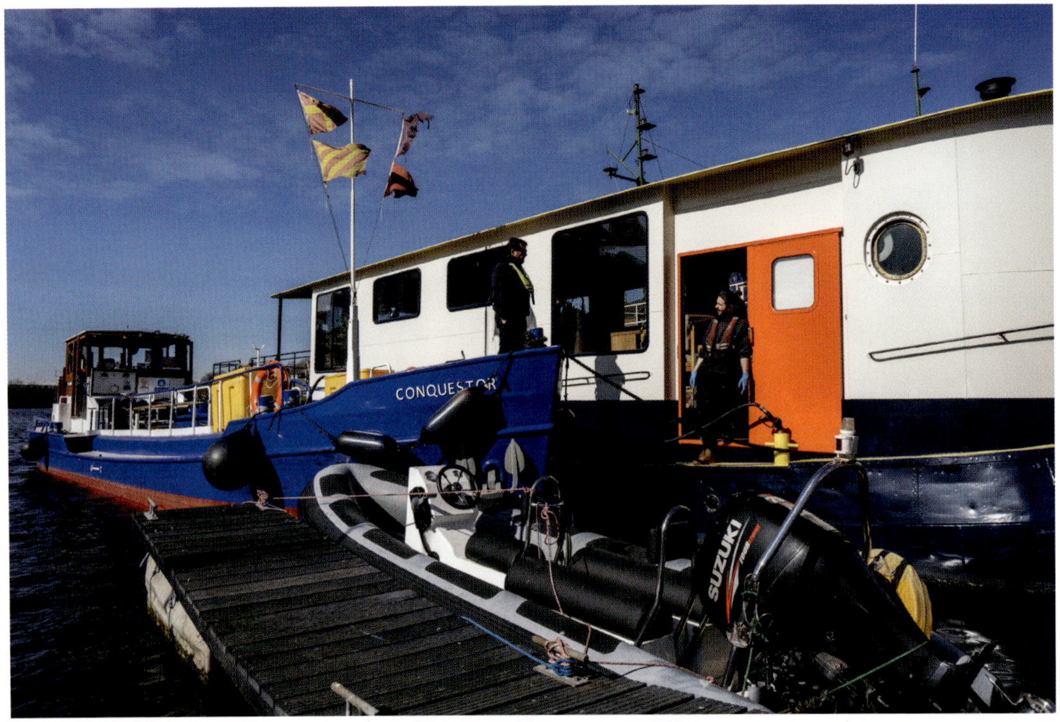

Fuelling up

Most liveaboards need regular top-ups of diesel to generate electricity, even when only stationary, with some of the larger Dutch barges on Greenland Dock holding 1,000 litres. Thames Marine Services' fleet of different-sized tankers supply boats up and down the river. www.thamesmarineservices.co.uk

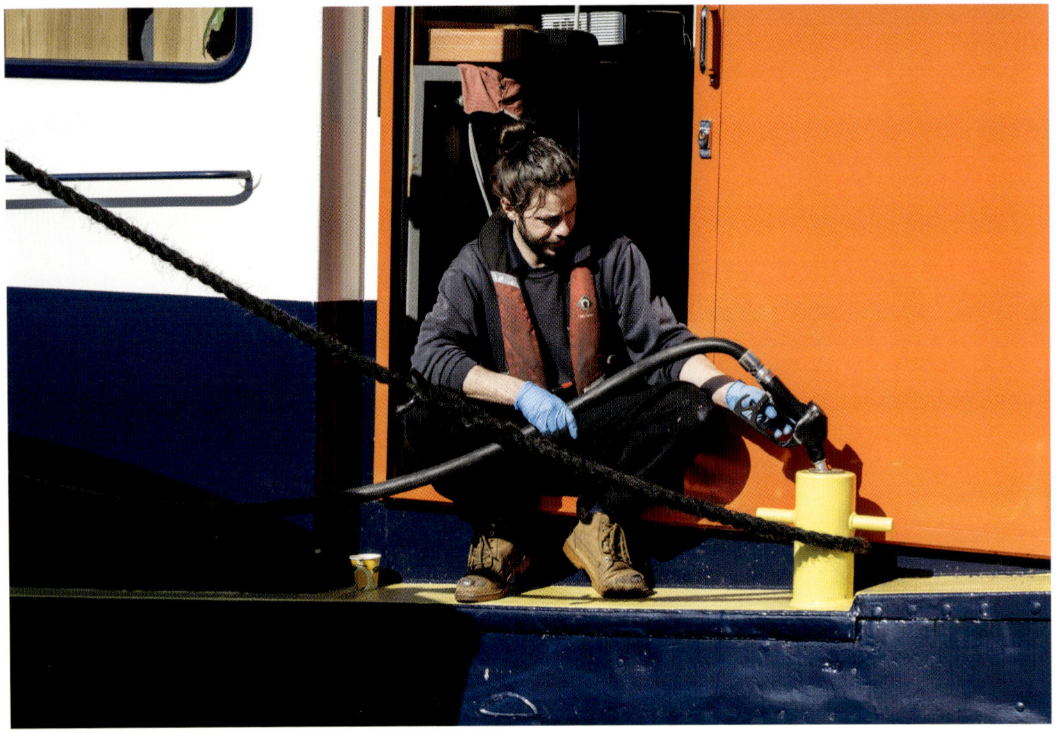

Traditions run deep

Max, of Thames Marine Services, comes from a family with a long line of generations with a rich history of working on the river.

Urban backdrop

A peaceful summer's morning and Mark and Sarah relax on the deck of their beautifully converted Belgian barge home in Blackwall Basin by the towers of Canary Wharf.

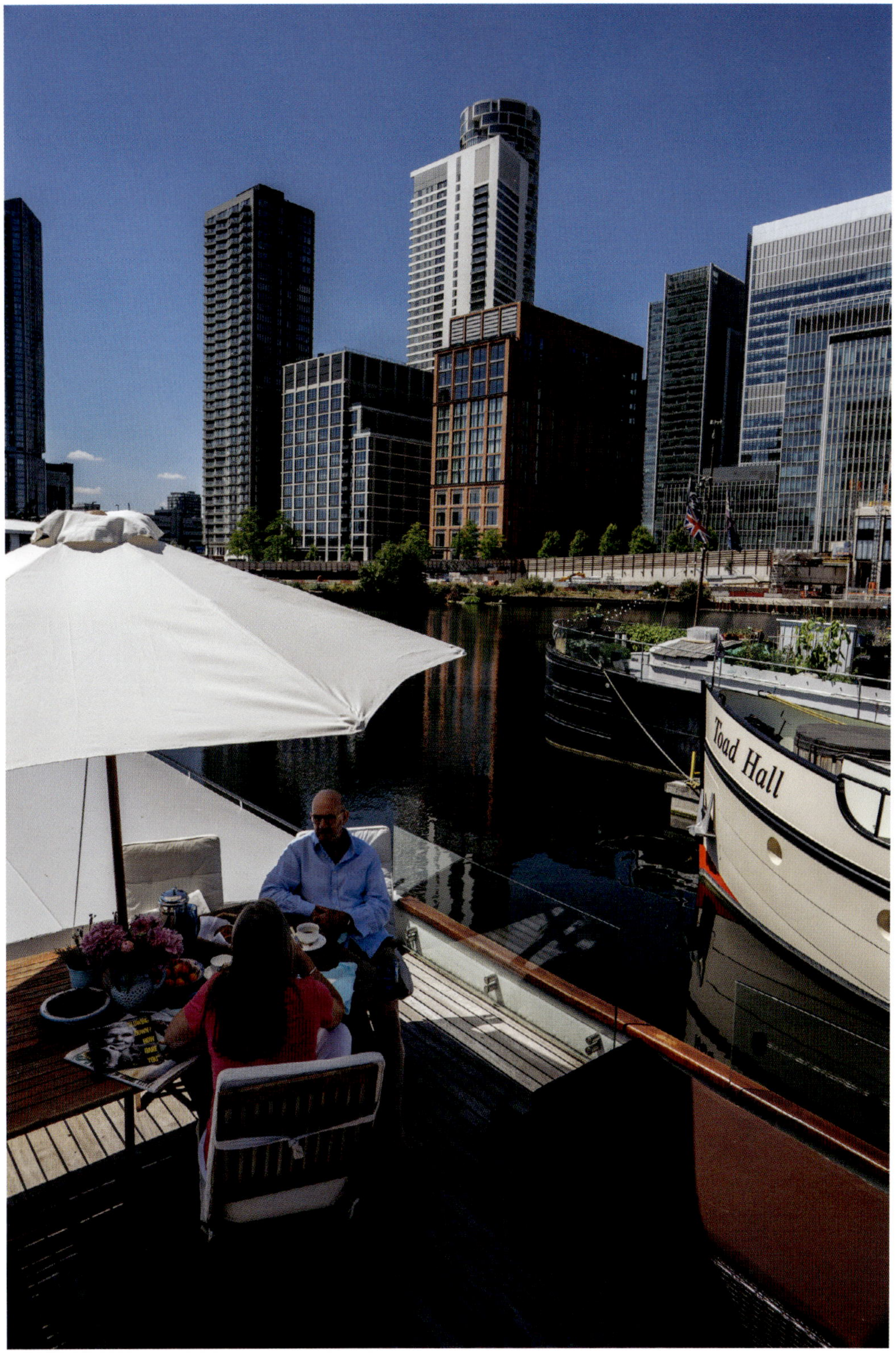

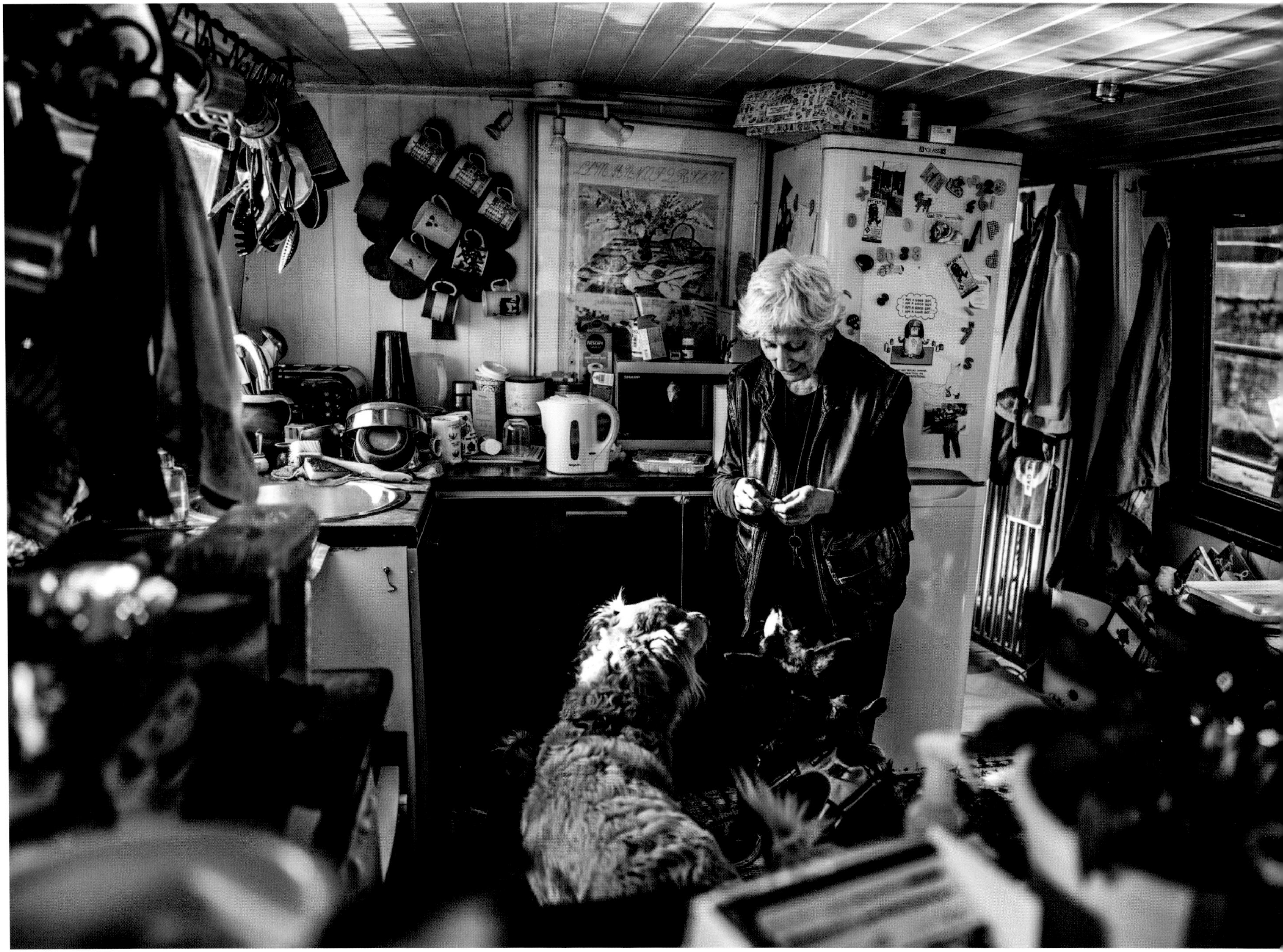

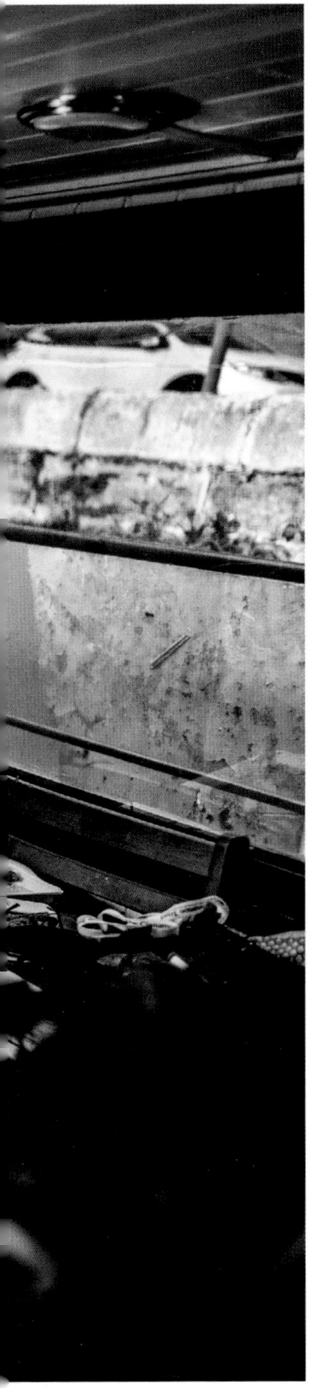

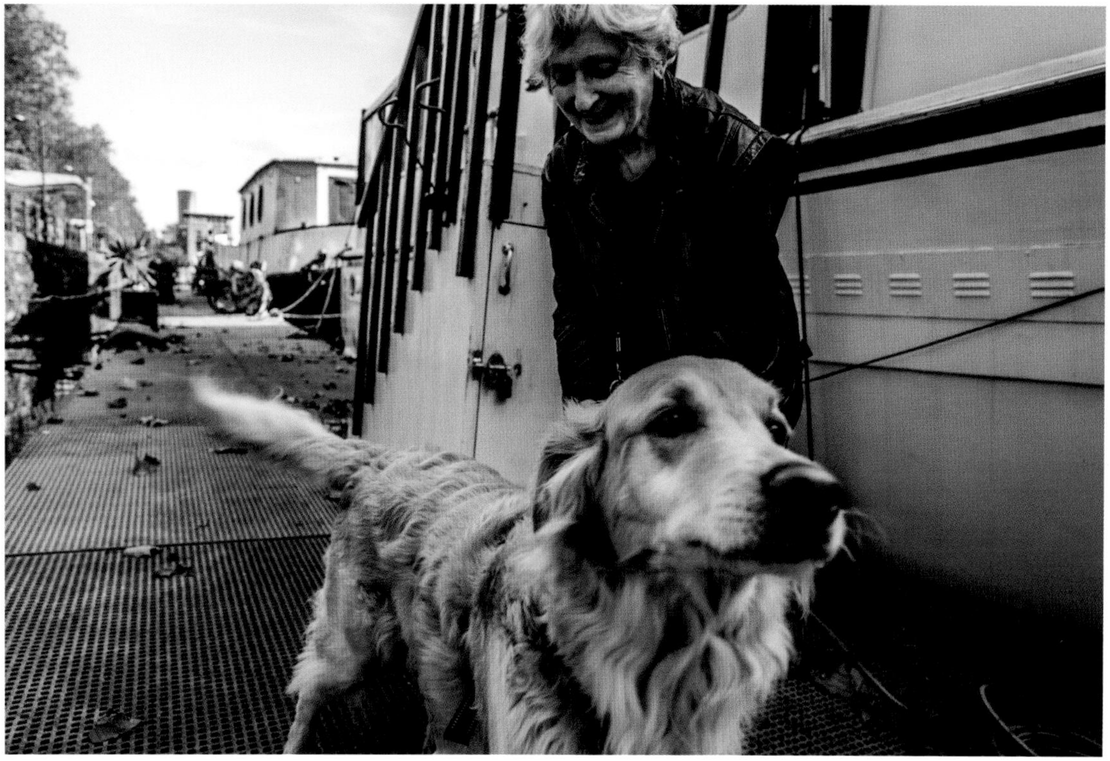

Canine care

For many years, Eva has welcomed dogs from the Cinnamon Trust on to her cosy boat, looking after up to five animals while their owners are in hospital or unable to care for them. A spry 83-year-old, she is frequently out and about walking her charges along Surrey Dock Marina's pontoons and quaysides.
www.cinnamon.org.uk

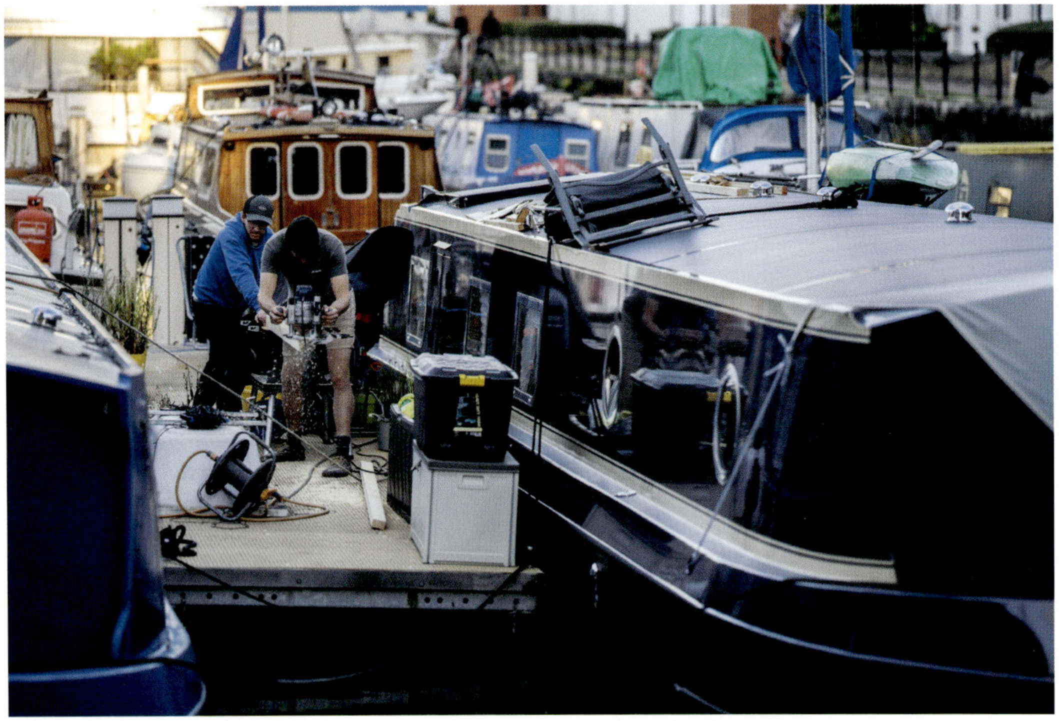

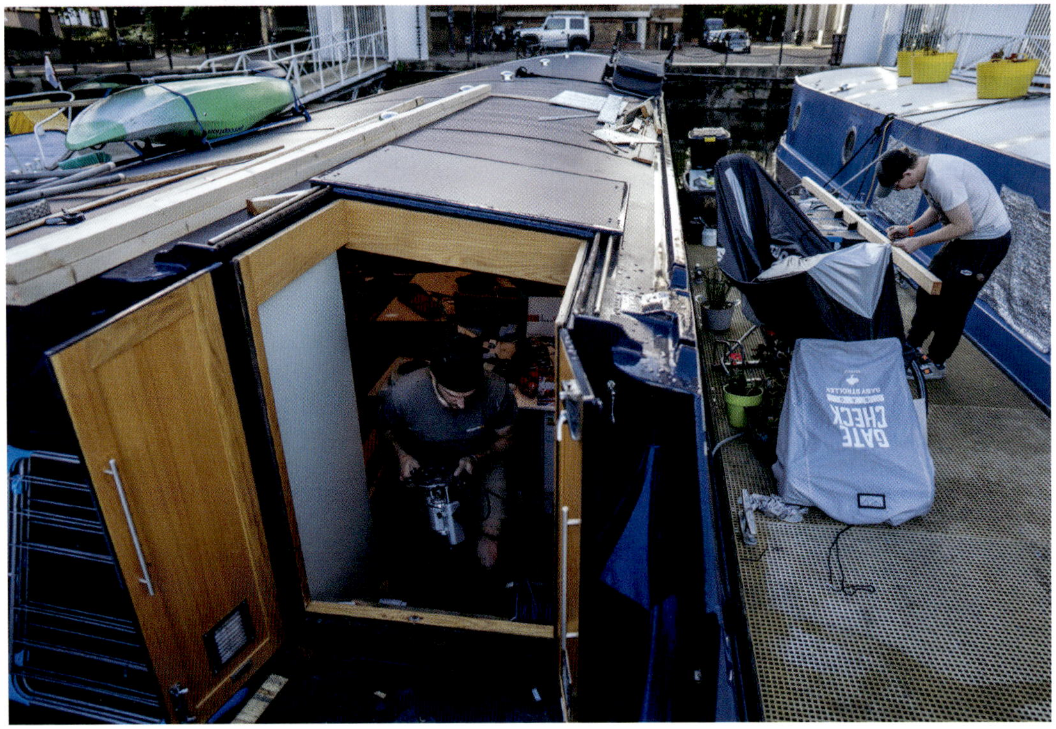

Baby on board

For John it was a race against time to create a kitchen and a nursery within the basic shell of his new boat. Using the pontoon as a makeshift workshop and with the help of expert carpenter Chris Lees, all was more or less in place by the time his wife, baby son Artu and in-laws from Argentina arrived. Some finishing touches are still needed but the boat has now been transformed into a wonderfully comfortable family home.

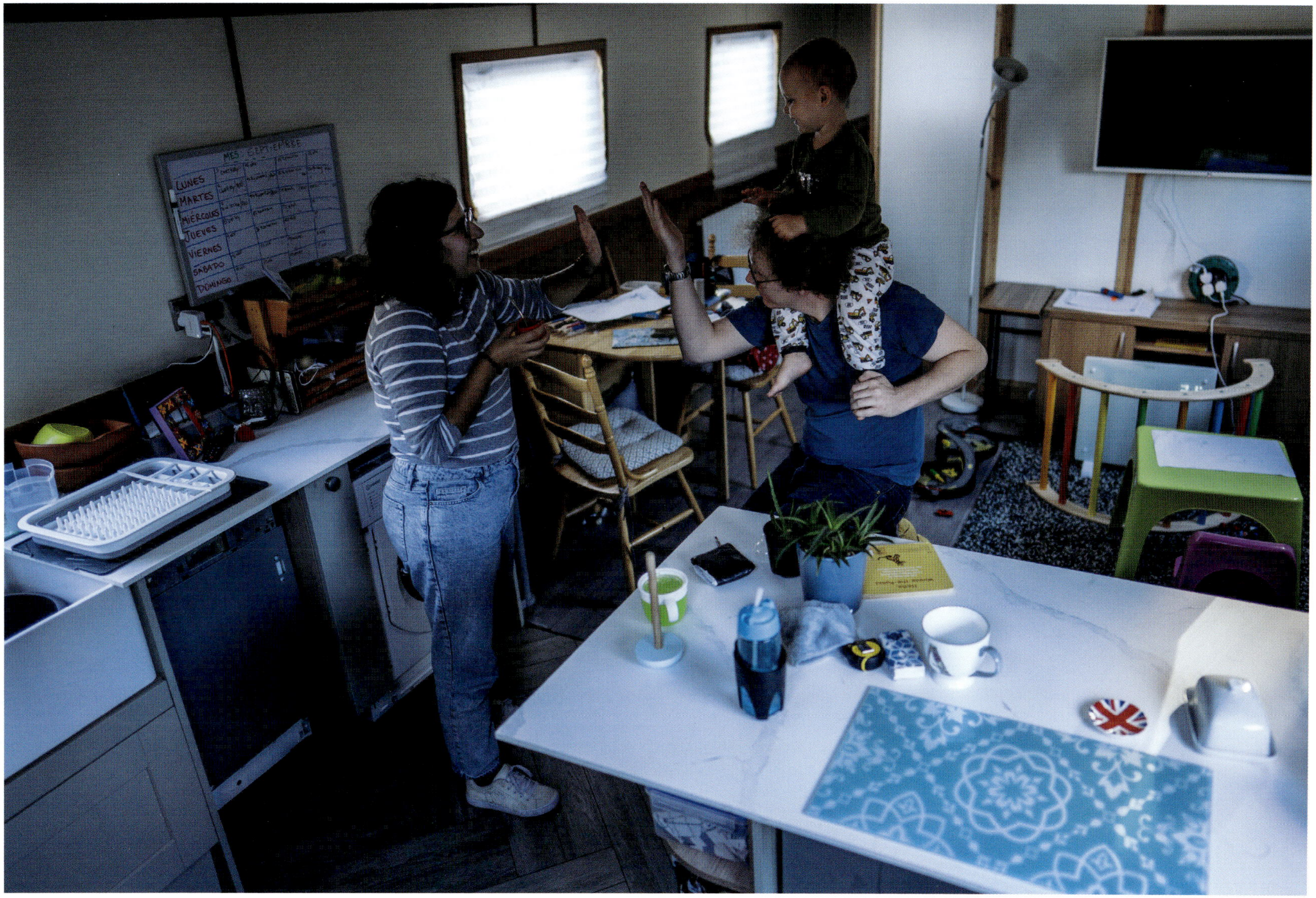
LUNES
MARTES
MIÉRCOLES
JUEVES
VIERNES
SABADO
DOMINGO

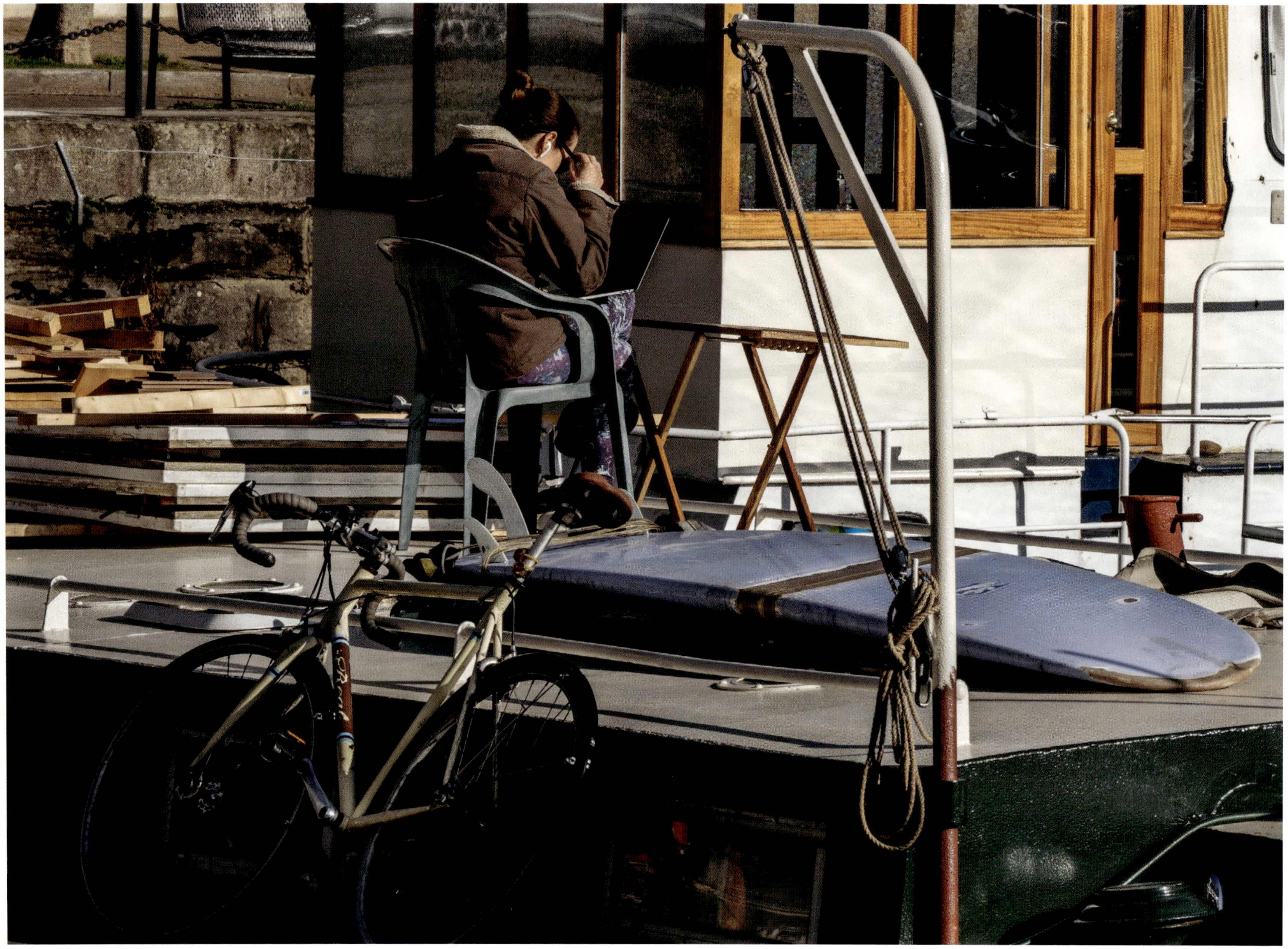

Working from home

South Dock Marina's quiet, central location in Surrey Quays has always encouraged some residents to use their boats as offices. Since the Covid pandemic, the delights of being able to create an impromptu workstation on your sunny deck have found even more takers.

Outside space

Decks and pontoons are precious extensions for boat dwellers. Like the gardens and balconies of their land-based neighbours, good weather brings out everything from full-blown washdays to pot-planting and barbecues.

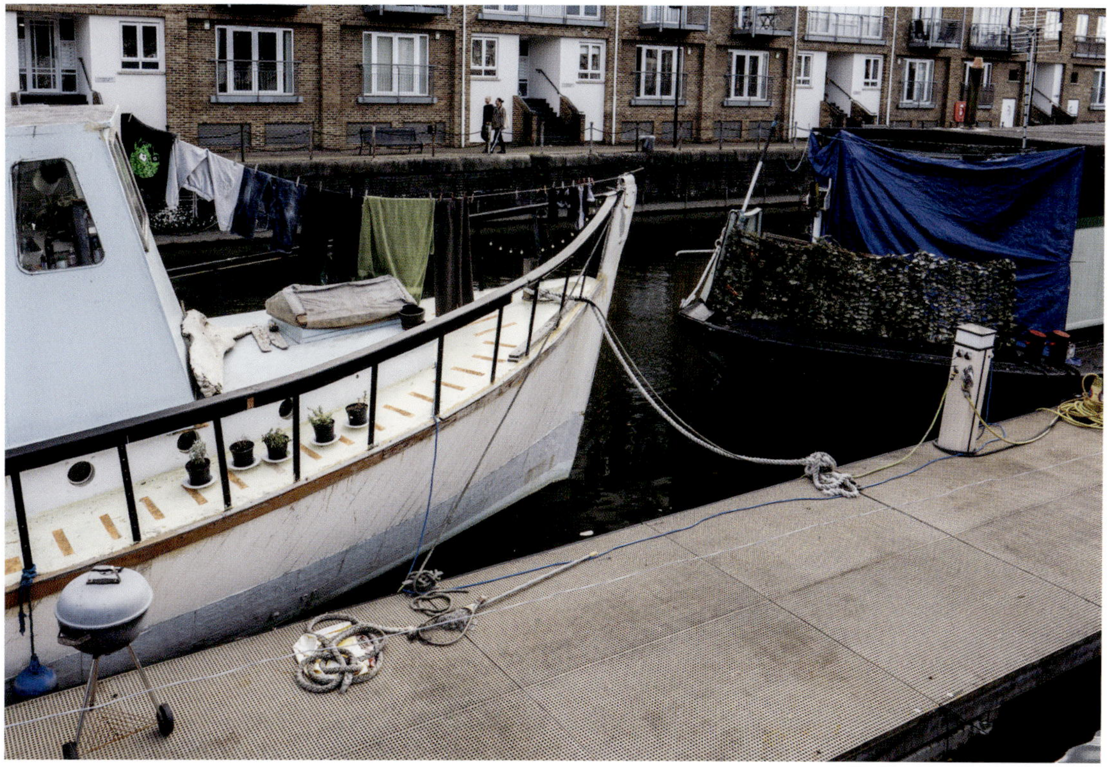

Deck garden

Twenty-seven residential vessels moor up in Blackwall Basin beside Canary Wharf, including one belonging to cacti propagator, Duncan. First started five years ago to supplement his wife's flower shop, he still finds tending to this collection of over 1,000 specimens a therapeutic end to his day.

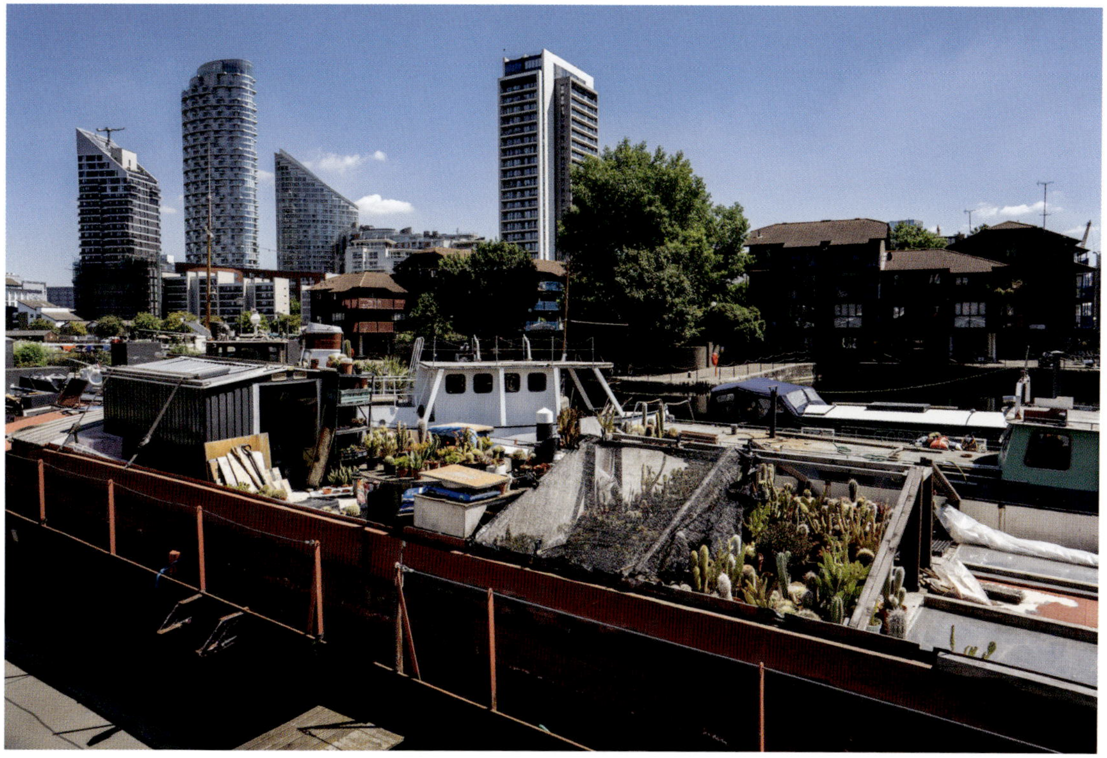

Inner workings

Locks and docks with moving boats are complicated environments needing constant maintenance and coordinated teamwork.

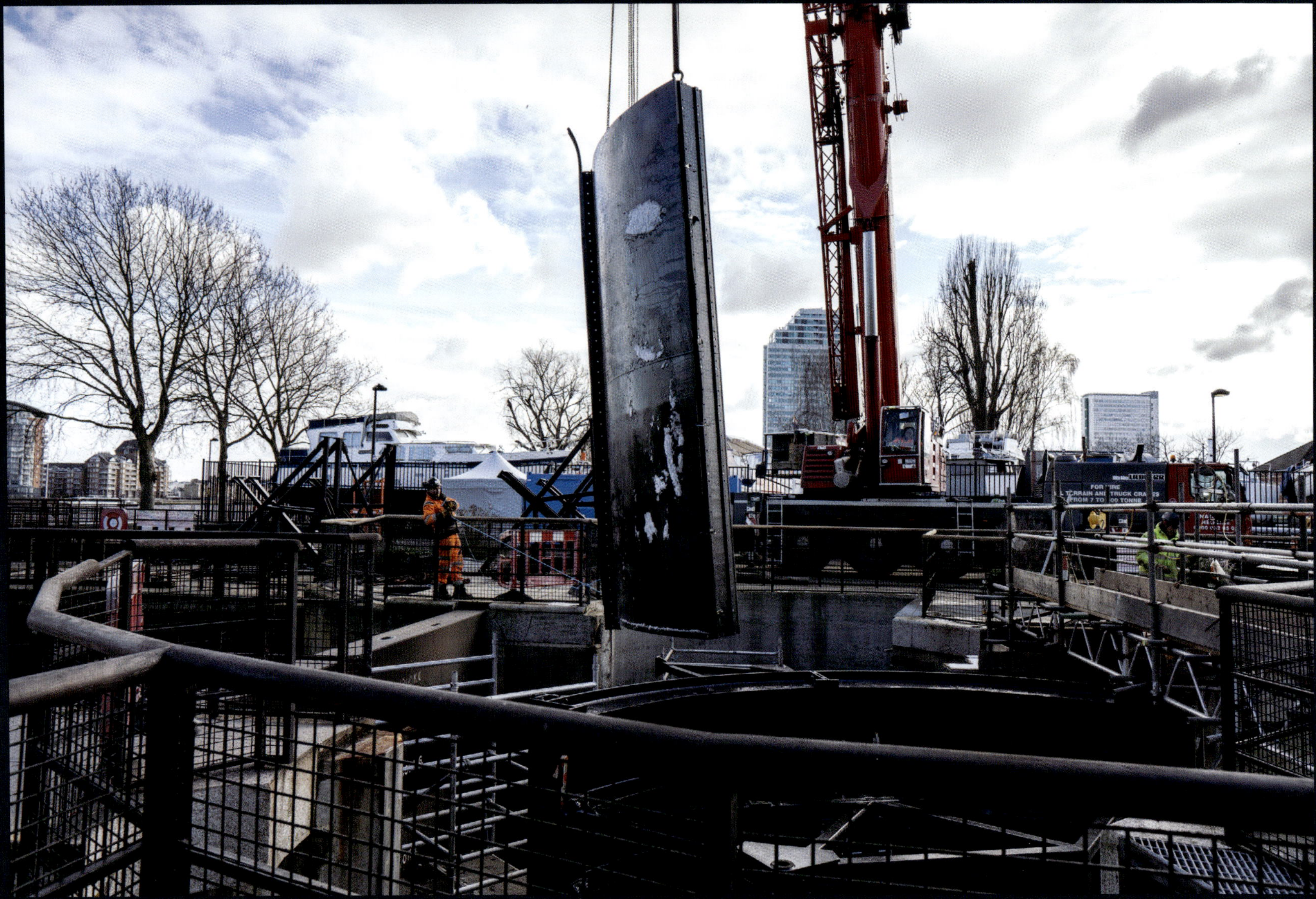

Locked in

For four winter months into 2021, the South Dock Marina lock was drained for a much-needed total refurbishment. No boats could get in or out during this time. Huge steel beams were installed to create a 'stoplog dam' to block off the river, while major engineering feats, such as lifting out and later reinstalling the massive reconditioned gate 'skins', took place.
www.diveco.co.uk

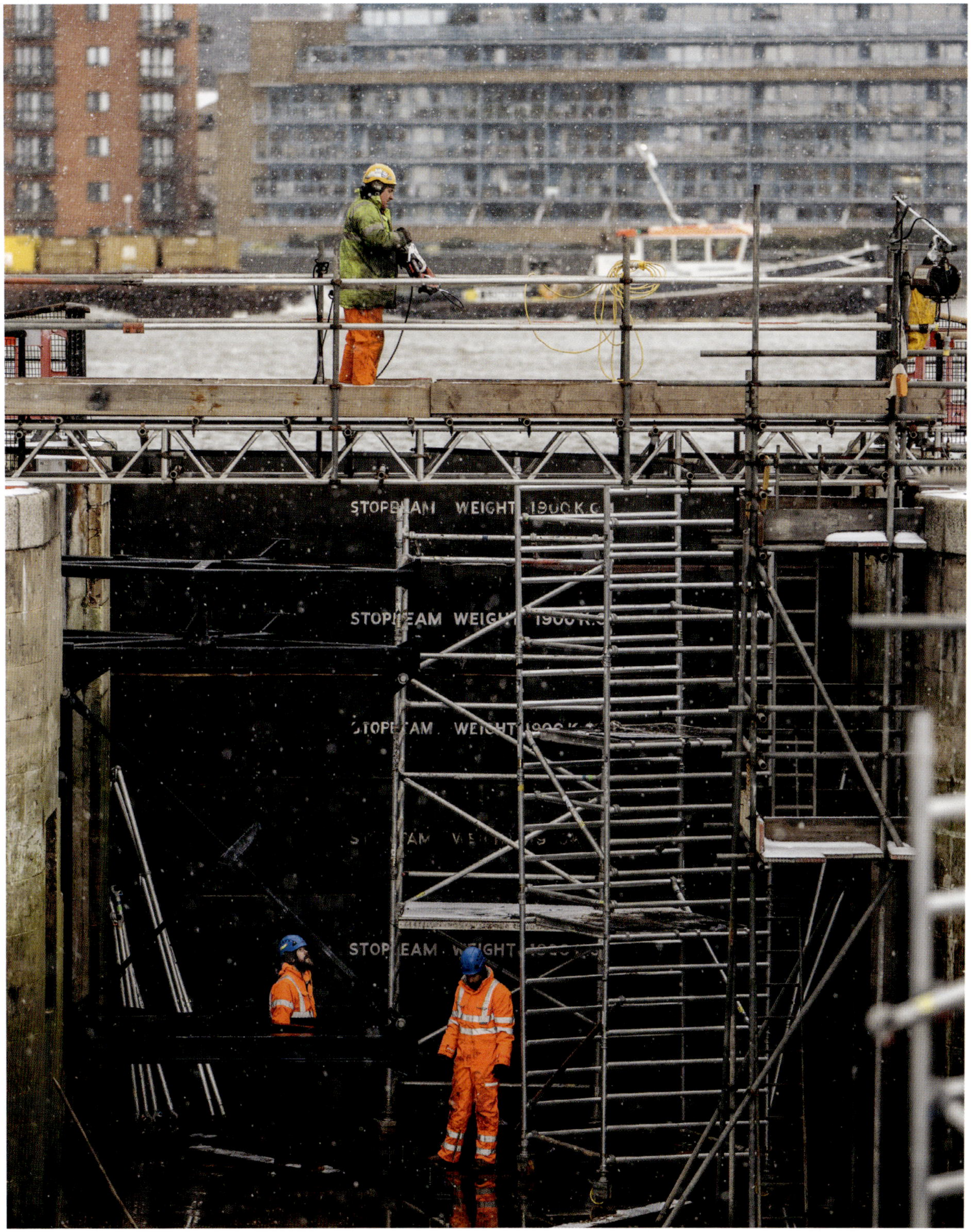

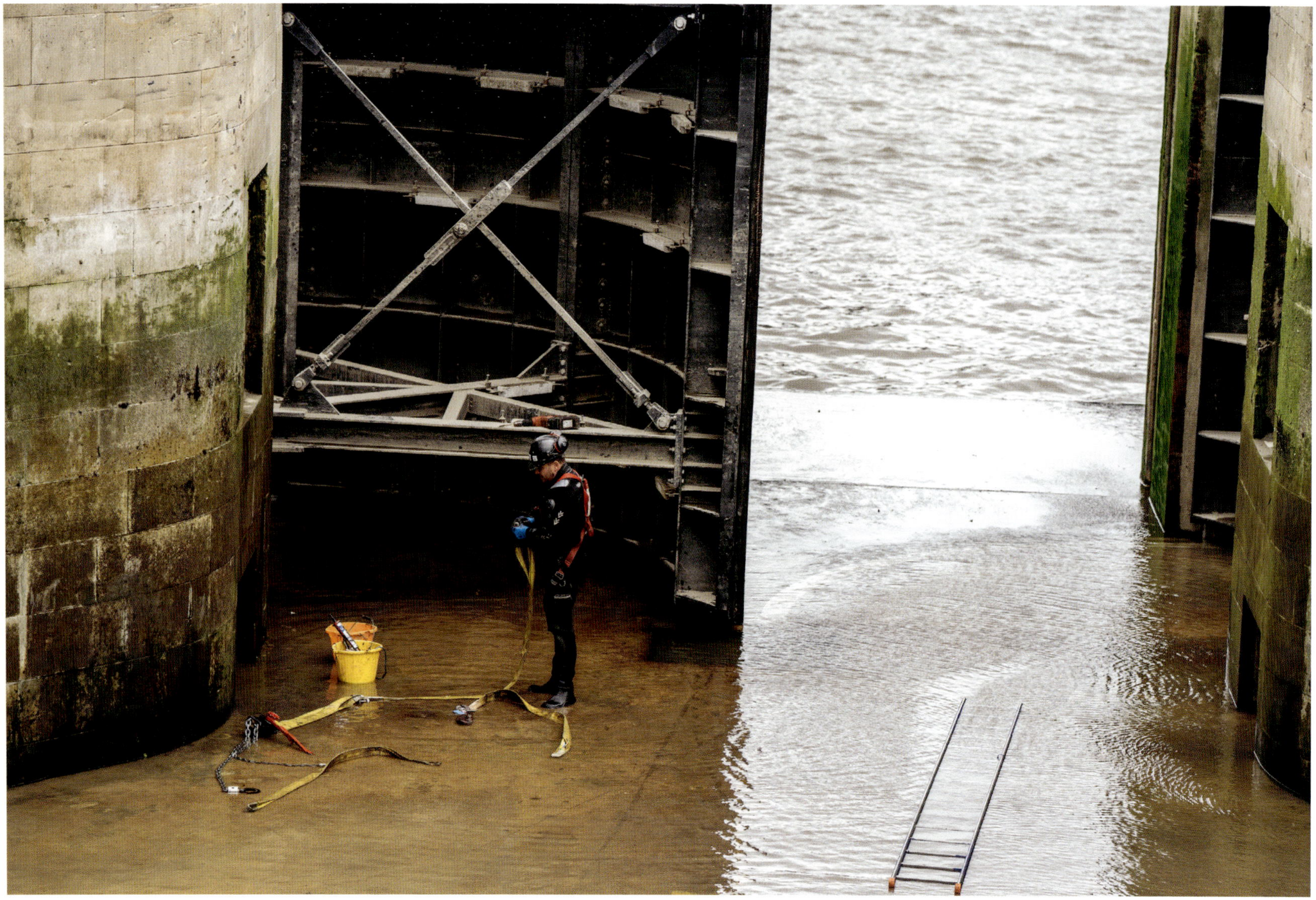

Tidal timing

Now back to full working order, regular maintenance of the South Dock Marina lock is governed by the tides. With the river rising, a diver from DiveCo Marine begins to pack up.

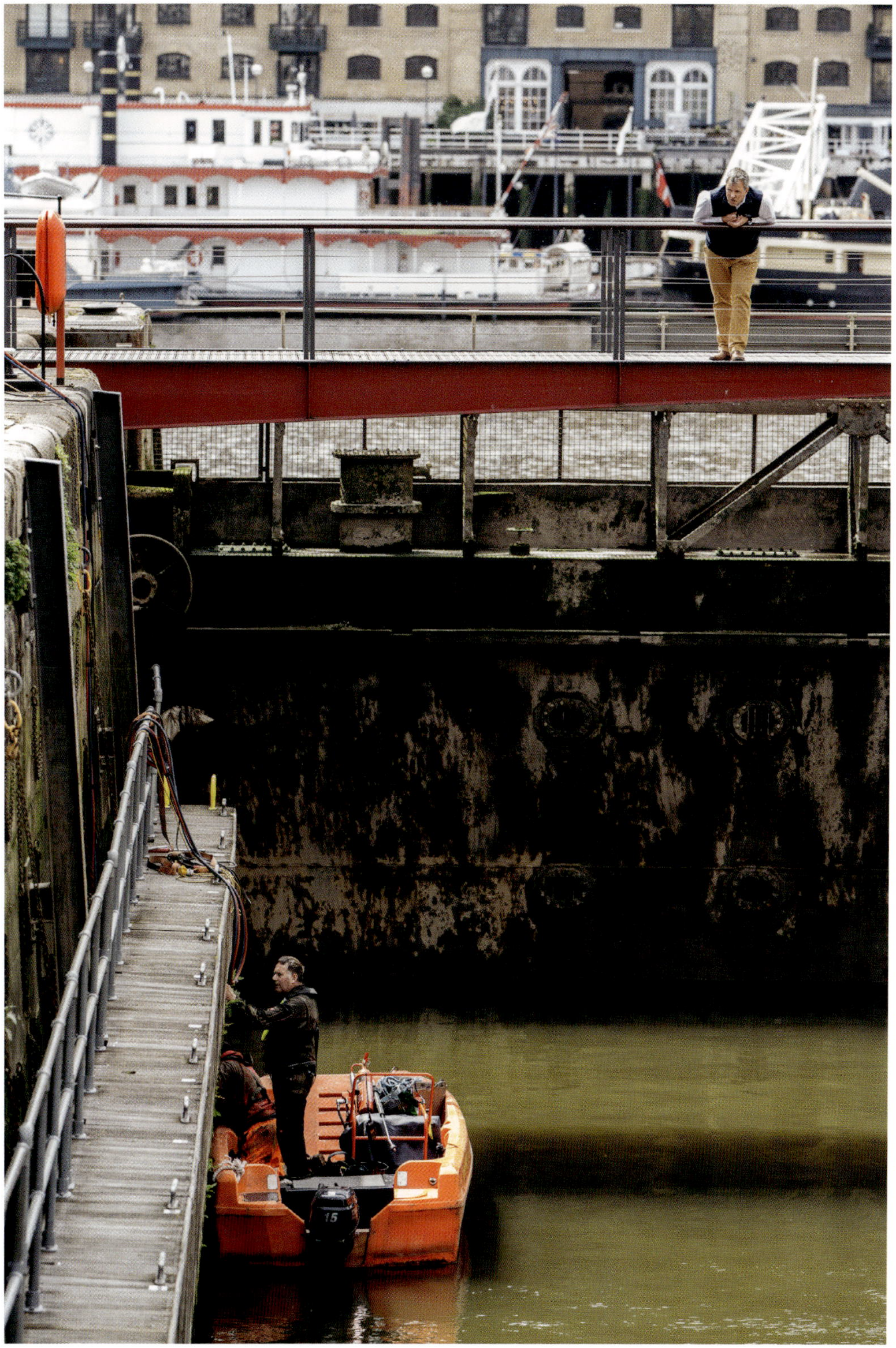

Moving parts

Thomas Telford's early 19th-century engineering for St Katharine Docks has stood the test of time but all lock mechanisms need systematic checking, here overseen by the then General Manager, Paul Tetlow.

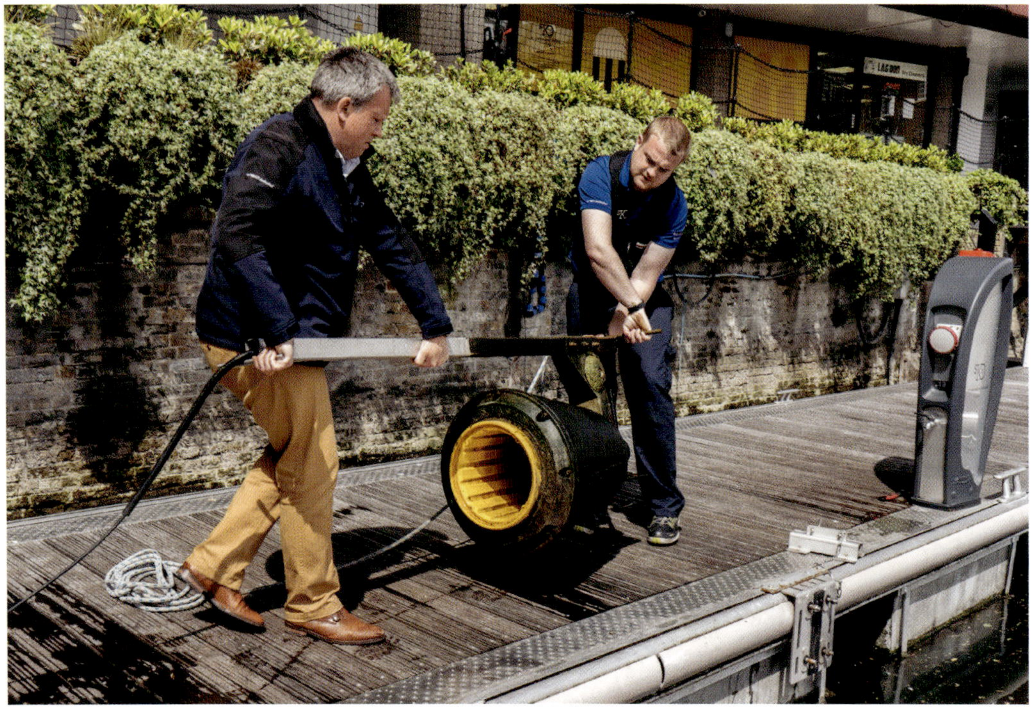

Marina nuts and bolts

Maintaining the upmarket sophistication of St Katharine Docks requires a great deal of behind-the-scenes work by the marina team, including cleaning out the Seabins of debris coming in from the river.

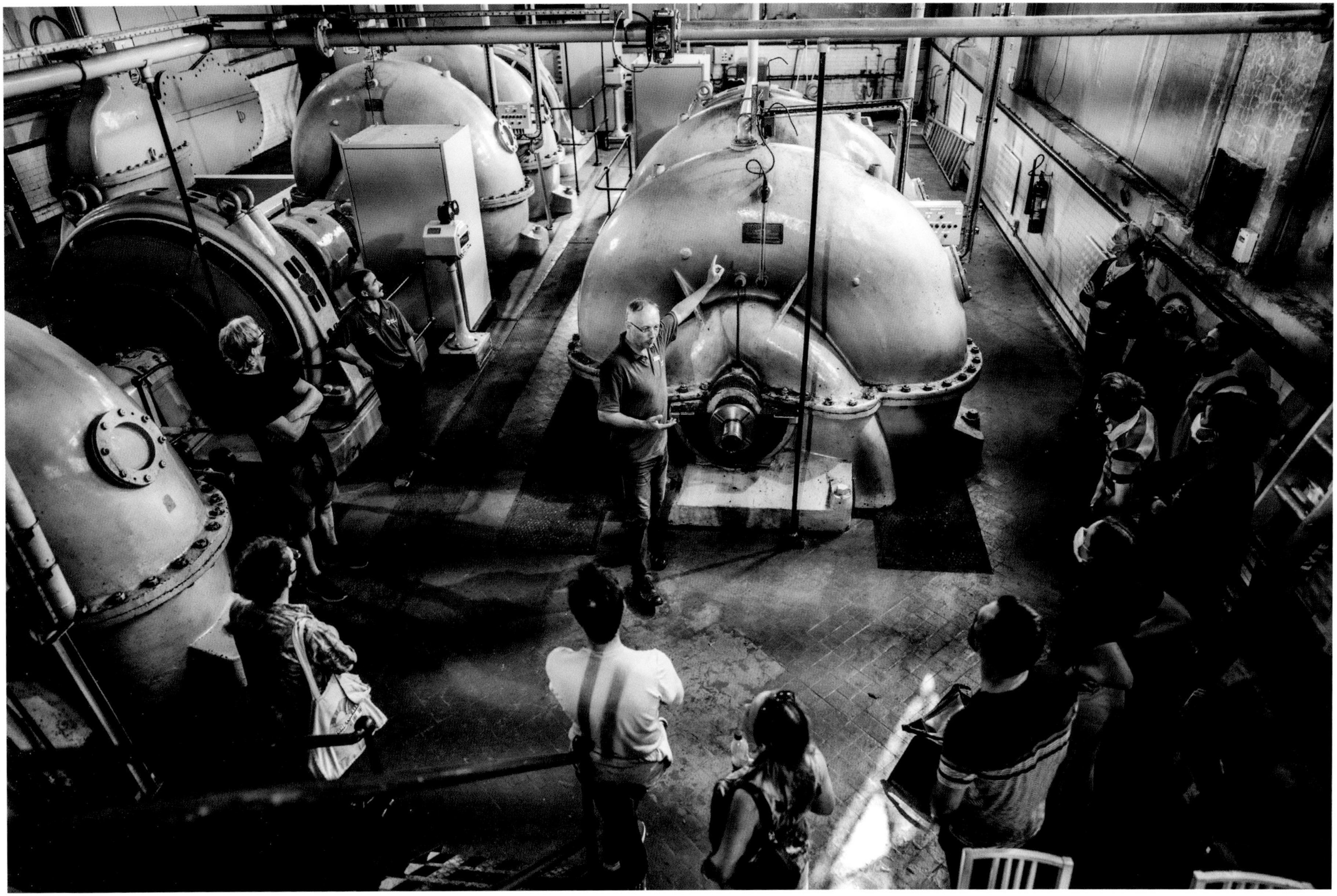

Levelling up

During a popular Open House visiting day, Phil Emery from the Canal & River Trust explains how pumps at the Isle of Dogs Impounding Station have been performing the vital role of maintaining water levels in the West India and Millwall Docks since 1929. Transferring water directly from the Thames, these three massive pumps deal with four million tons a year and could fill an Olympic-size swimming pool in nine minutes. With water continually lost through evaporation and lock movements, they are a key part of the dock infrastructure.
www.canalrivertrust.org.uk

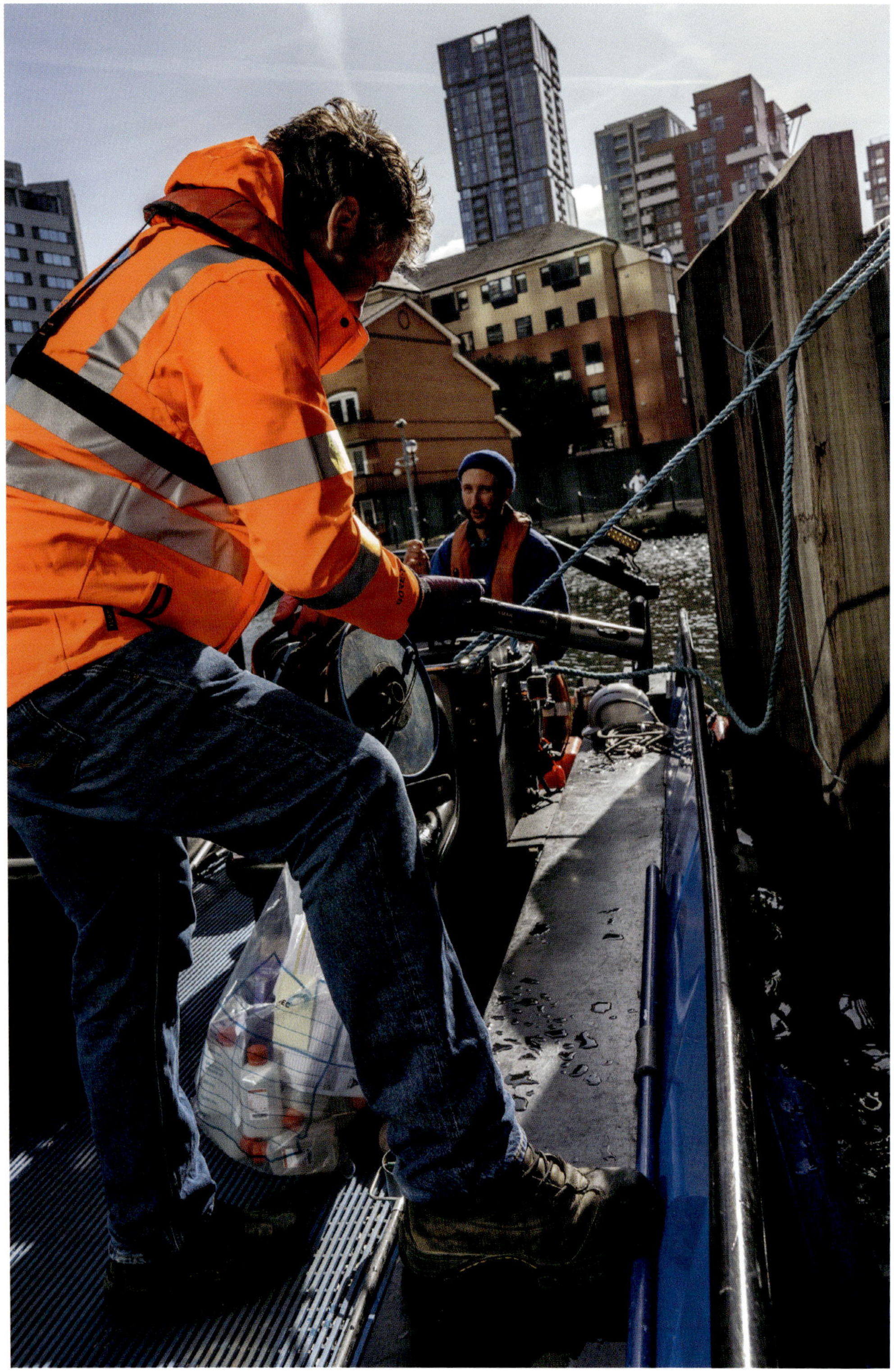

Quality control

Every month an environmental scientist is ferried around West India Docks to methodically take water samples at six carefully chosen locations. For all those living on, working near or generally enjoying the Isle of Dogs' waters, the Canal & River Trust hires specialists SOCOTEC to test for potential common contaminants such as metals and nitrates, as well as to check the oxygen levels and pH balance.
www.socotec.co.uk

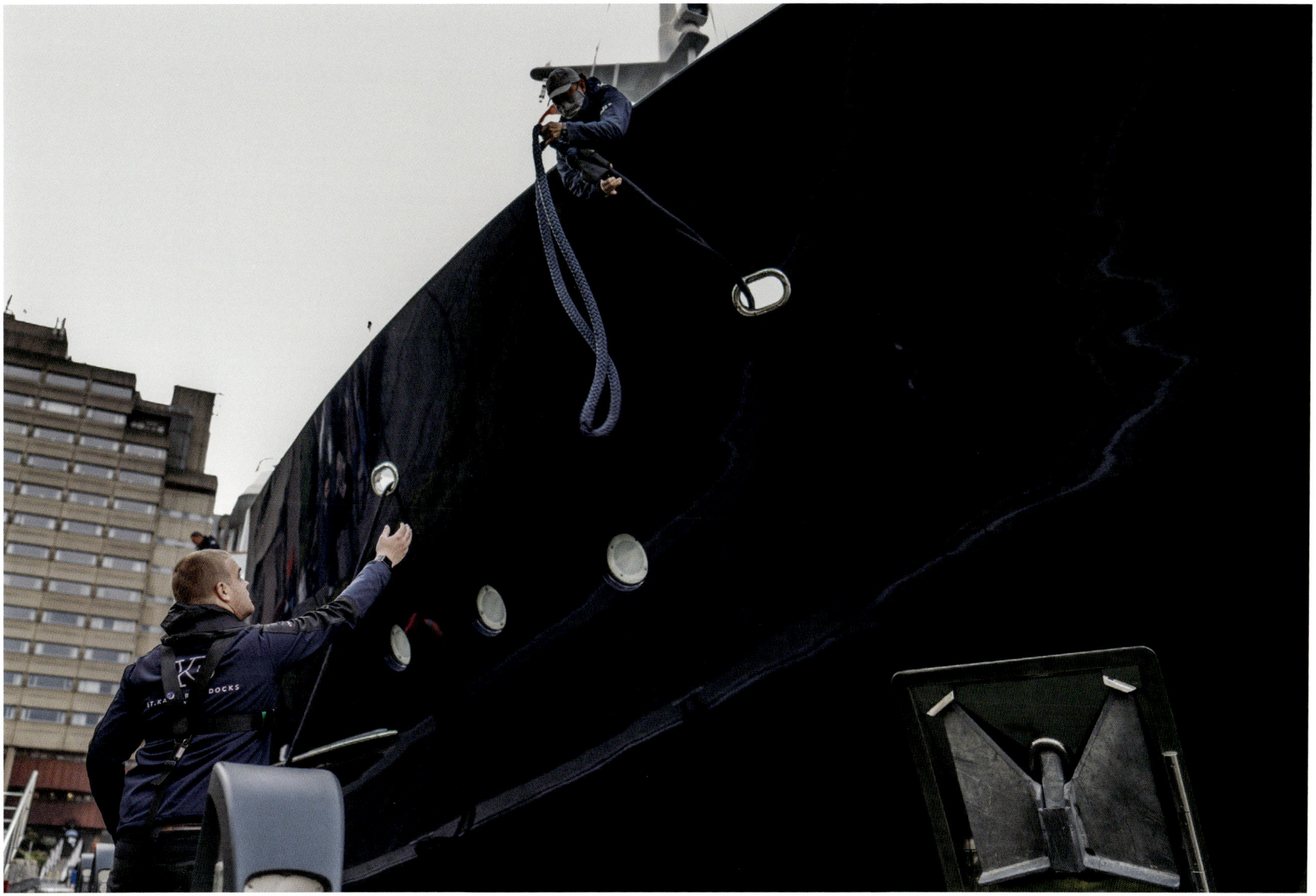

Good catch

Even a superyacht needs two people at either end of a rope to moor up safely. At St Katharine Docks, the marina team has it down to a fine art.

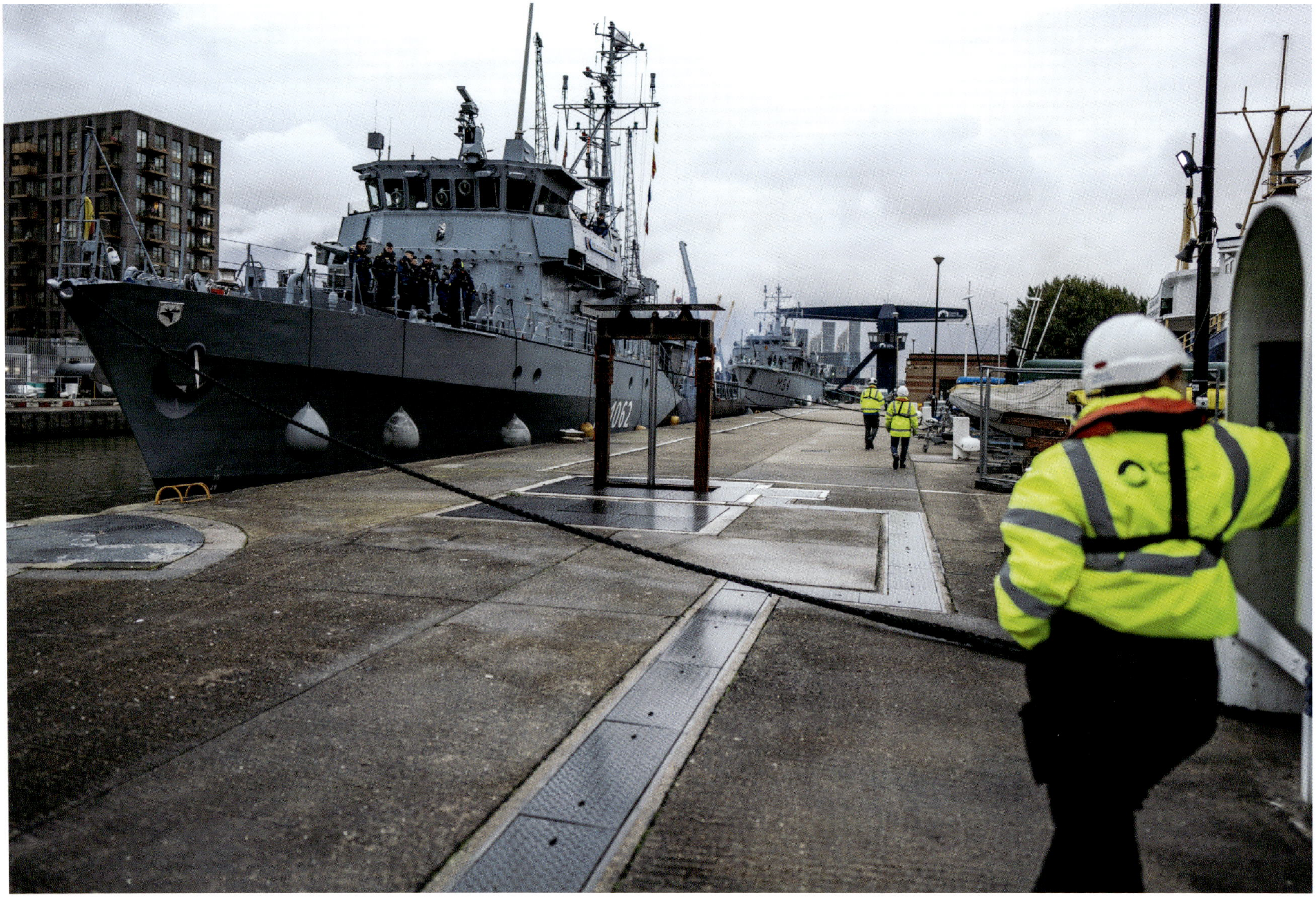

Full house

The arrival of six NATO warships into the Isle of Dogs keeps the West India Docks lock busy for over two hours. Coming in three-by-three, this fleet requires two lifts of the road bridge and shows off the coordinated expertise of the Canal & River Trust's team. With the first three ships safely into the lock, the inner sluice gate's mechanism is now rising up out of the quay to allow water to enter.

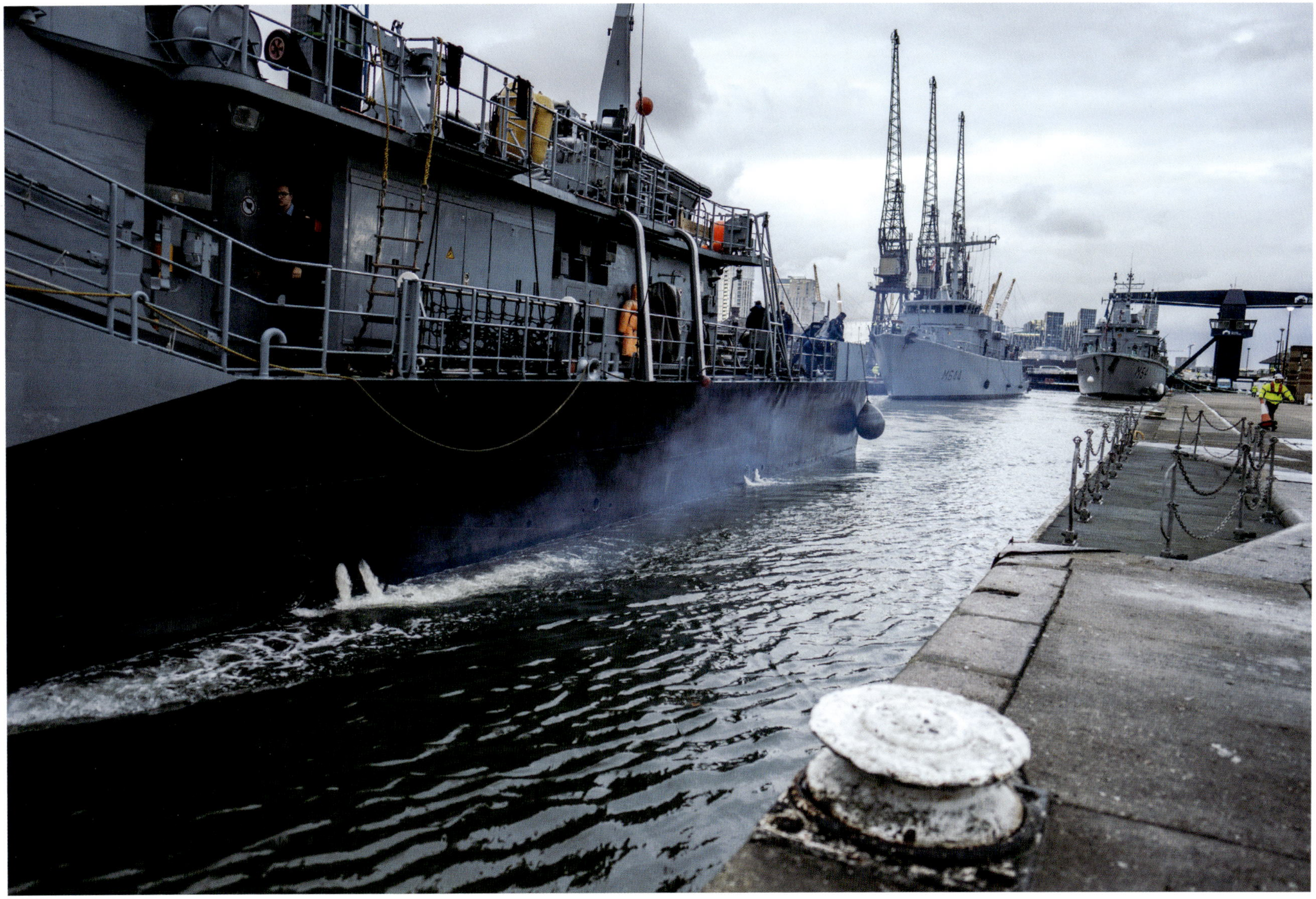

Moving on in

With the water level in the lock now correct and the inner gates open, these three warships head off into West India Docks to moor up. The old dockside cranes in the background are a reminder of how the arrival of large ships used to be a daily occurrence when these were busy commercial docks unloading cargo.

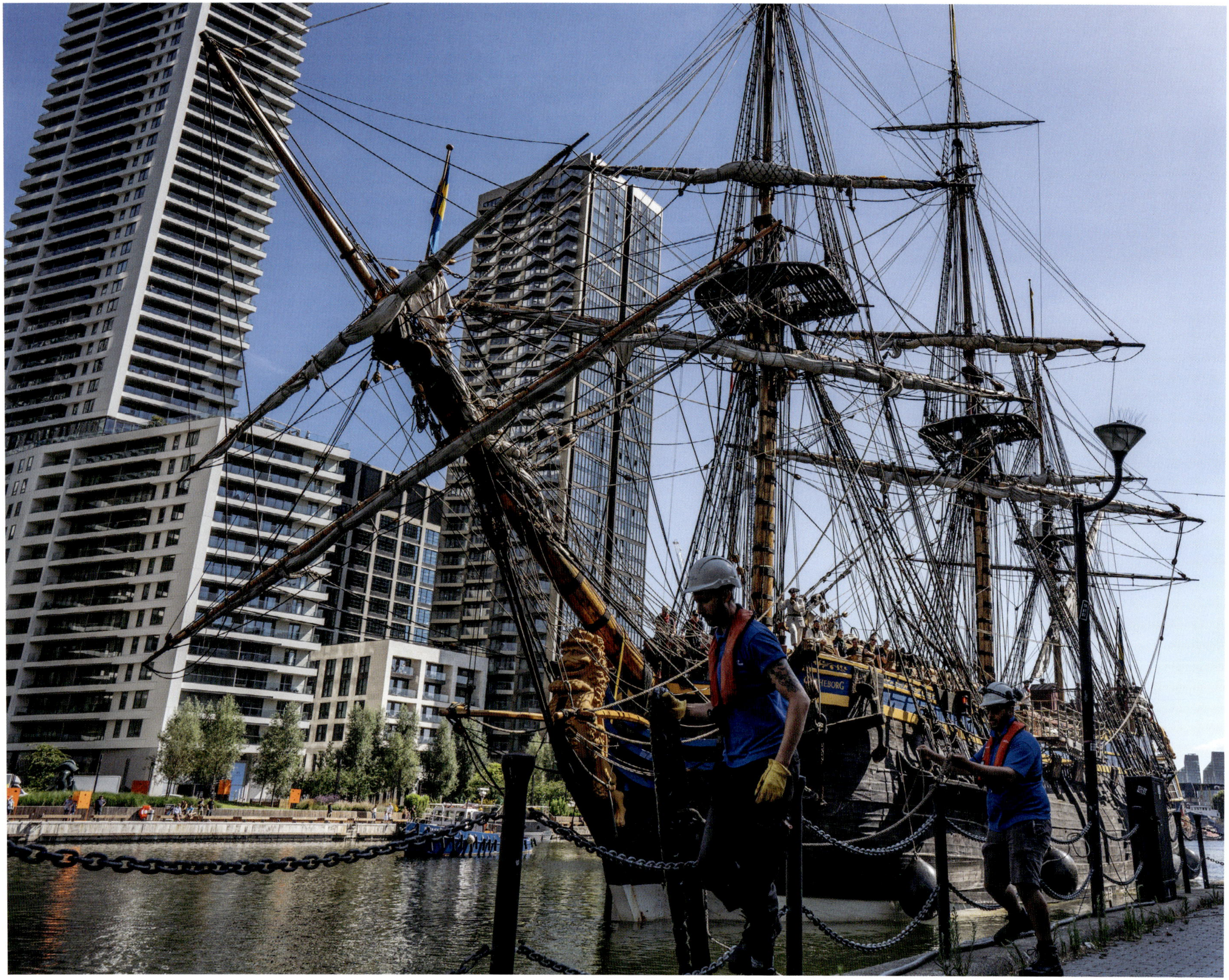

Push and pull

Manoeuvring in locks and docks can be tricky for large ships, so tugboats are often needed. Despite their small size, a tug's huge propellors and powerful engines allow it to act as a rudder and pull or push a larger ship safely into position. For the Indian Navy's three-masted barque training ship, INS *Tarangini*, two tugs are on hand to help her negotiate the Thames' currents and safely enter the lock at the West India Docks.

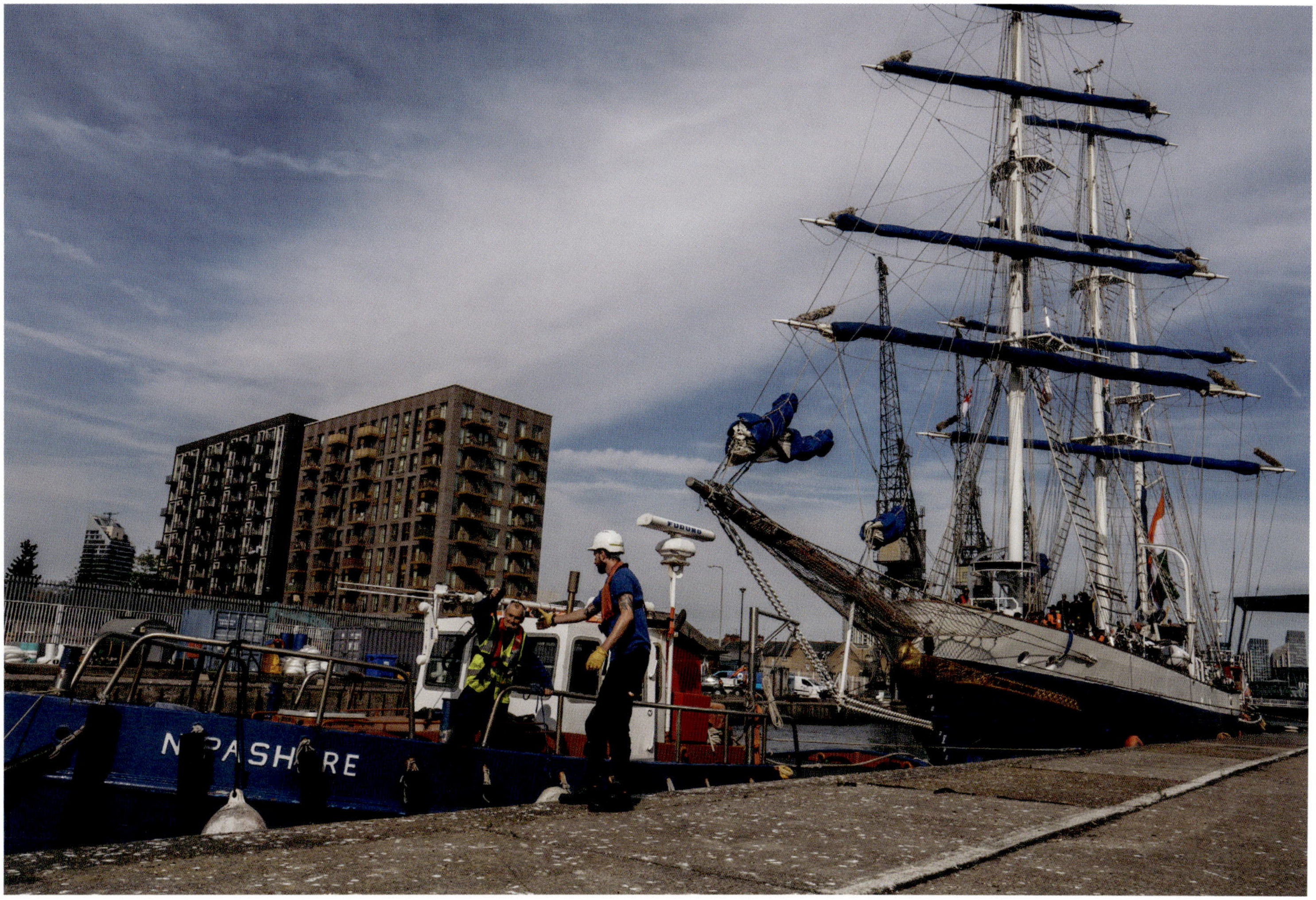

Ready for anything

‹ Visitors to the Isle of Dogs come in all shapes and sizes. Here, the Canal & River Trust team is called upon to guide the impressive replica of the Swedish East Indiaman *Götheborg* to a safe mooring.

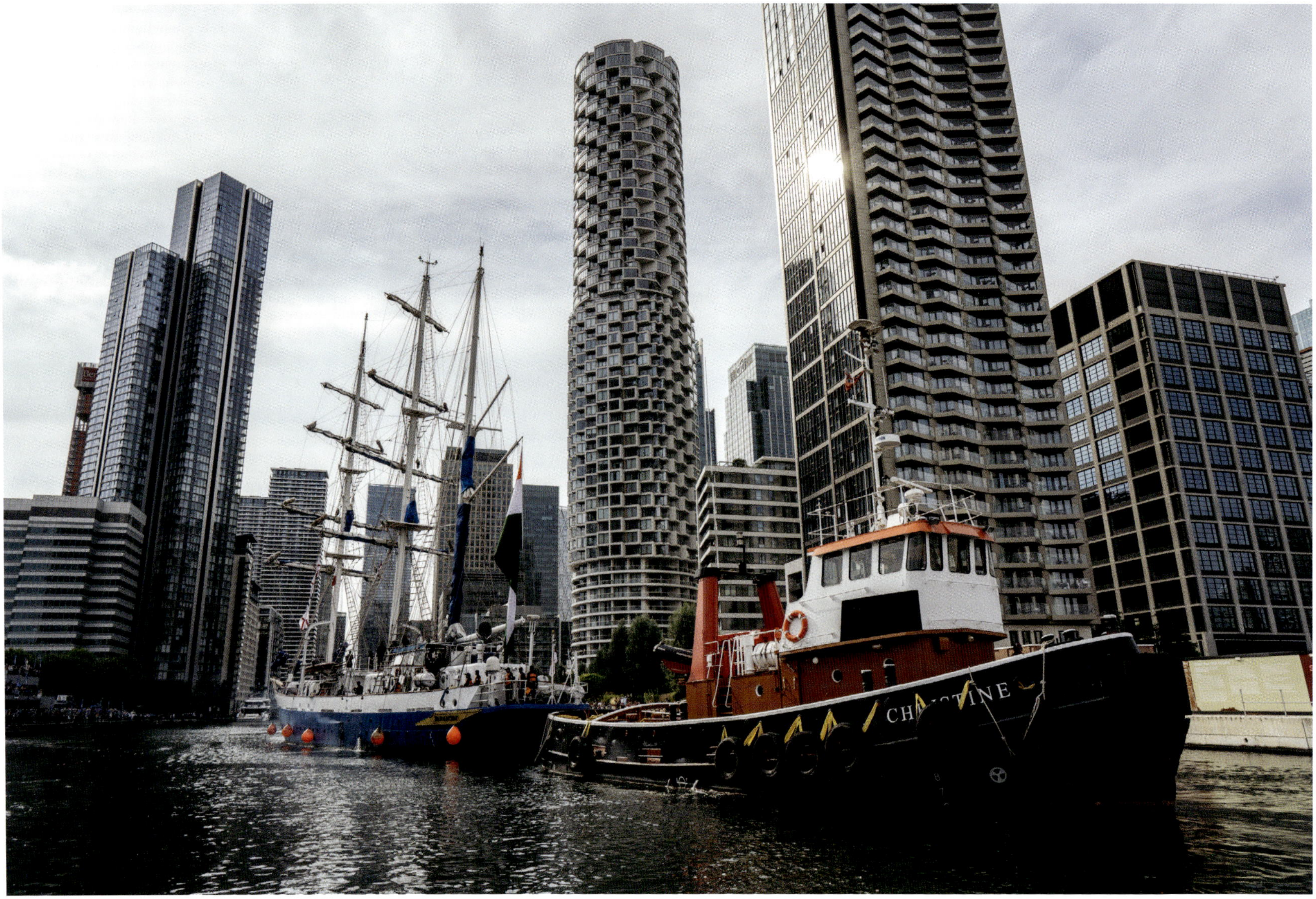

Well-timed arrival

Escorted by her trusty tugs, INS *Tarangini* powers across Canary Wharf's West India Docks towards the crowds on the quayside waiting to celebrate India's 76th Independence Day.

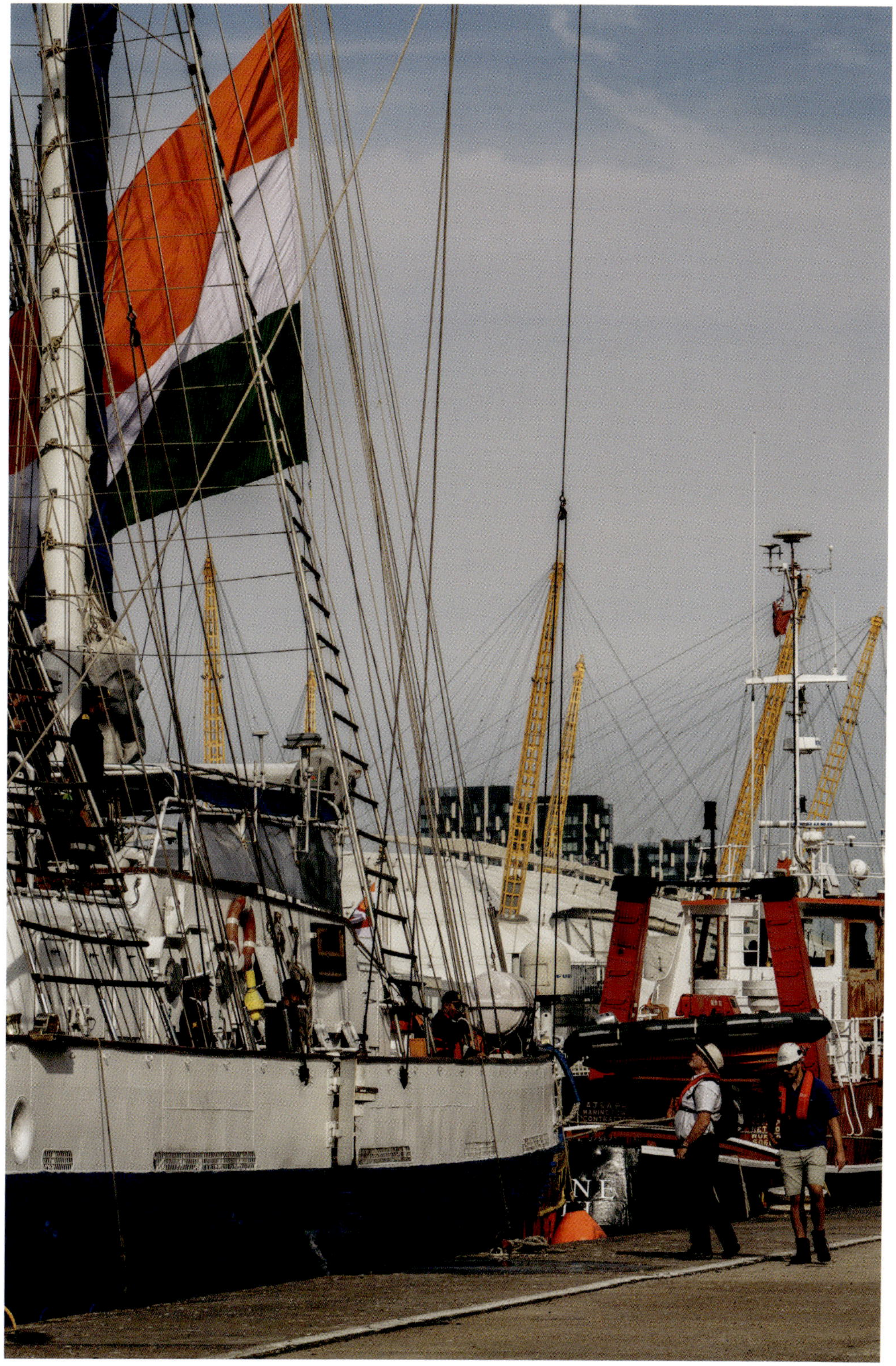

Master mariner

Heading up the Canal & River Trust's team on the Isle of Dogs, the harbour master's role is pivotal to the smooth running of dock activities. Here he is on the dockside in his trademark Panama hat to check mooring details with the captain of the tall ship INS *Tarangini*.

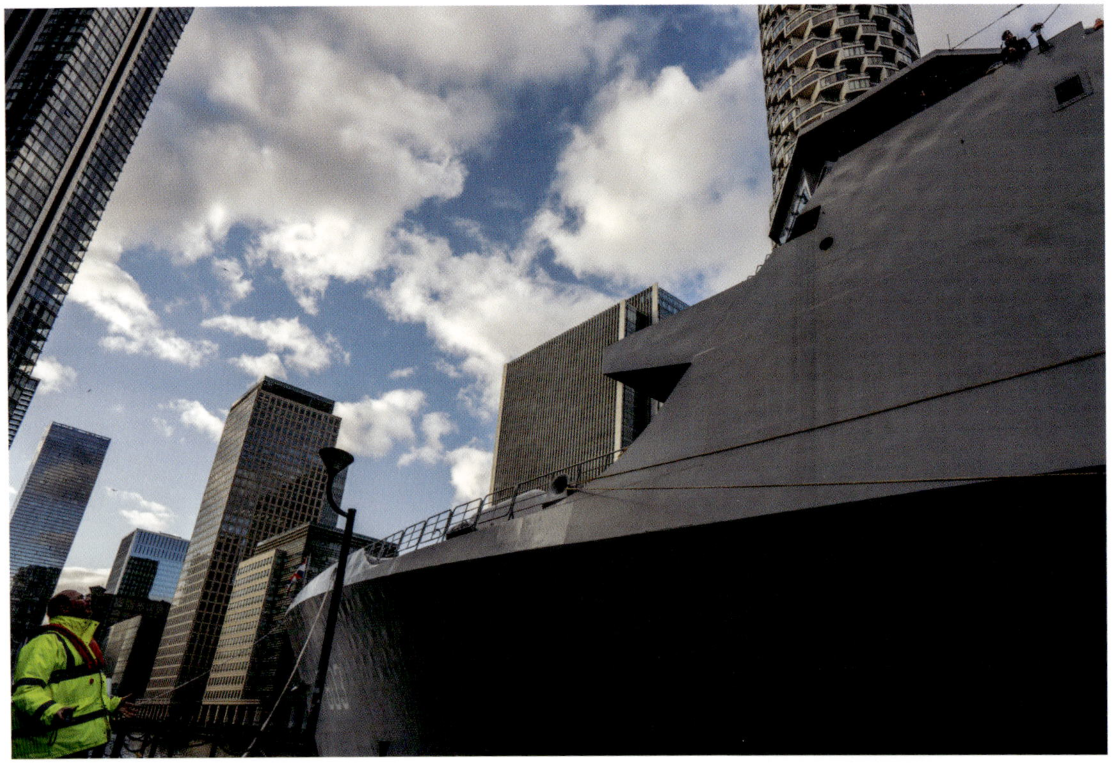

Testing times

The harbour master personally gives the go-ahead to the captain of the Dutch warship HNLMS *Tromp* that it is finally time to leave. A combination of factors has tested his experienced judgment to the full, with an unusually powerful storm suggesting that high tide may not reach the height needed for this massive ship to exit into the Thames with the help of two incoming tugs. Calmly studying the tide technical data, he makes the call that all will be well.

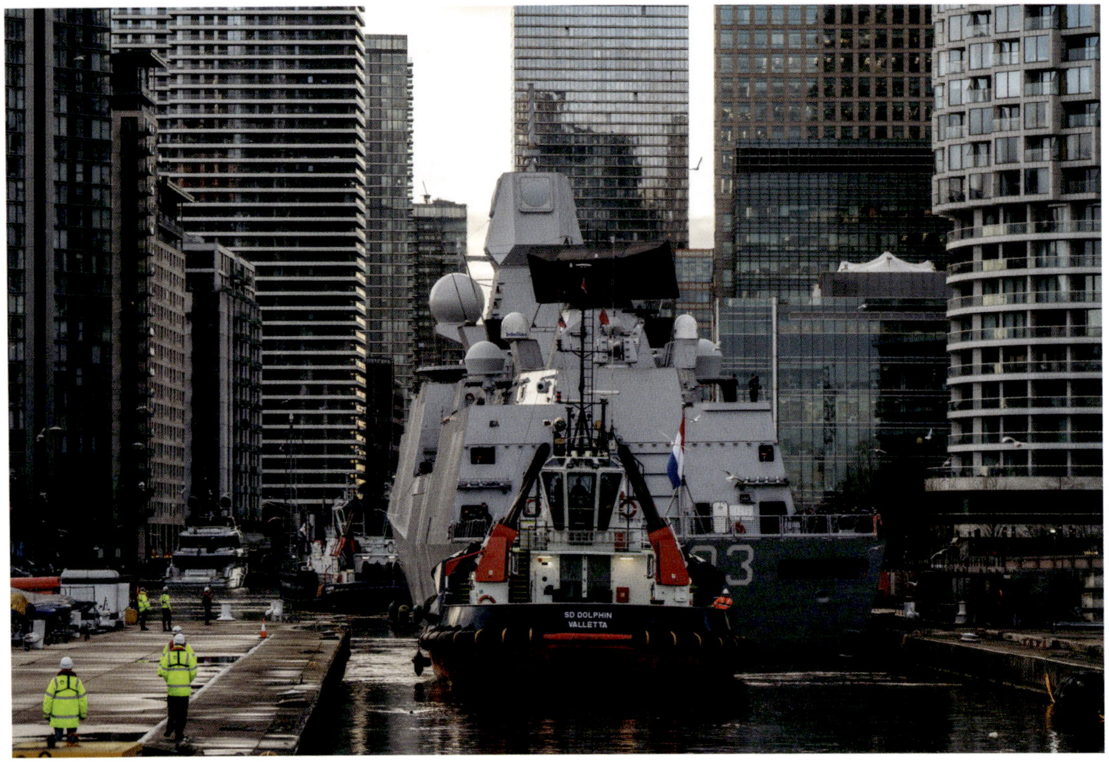

Successful exit

The two large tugs finally make it into West India Docks to help HNLMS *Tromp* manoeuvre carefully into the lock. There is no room for this 144-metre warship to turn around, so the tugs skilfully pull and push her in backwards and then out into the Thames and safely away to sea again.

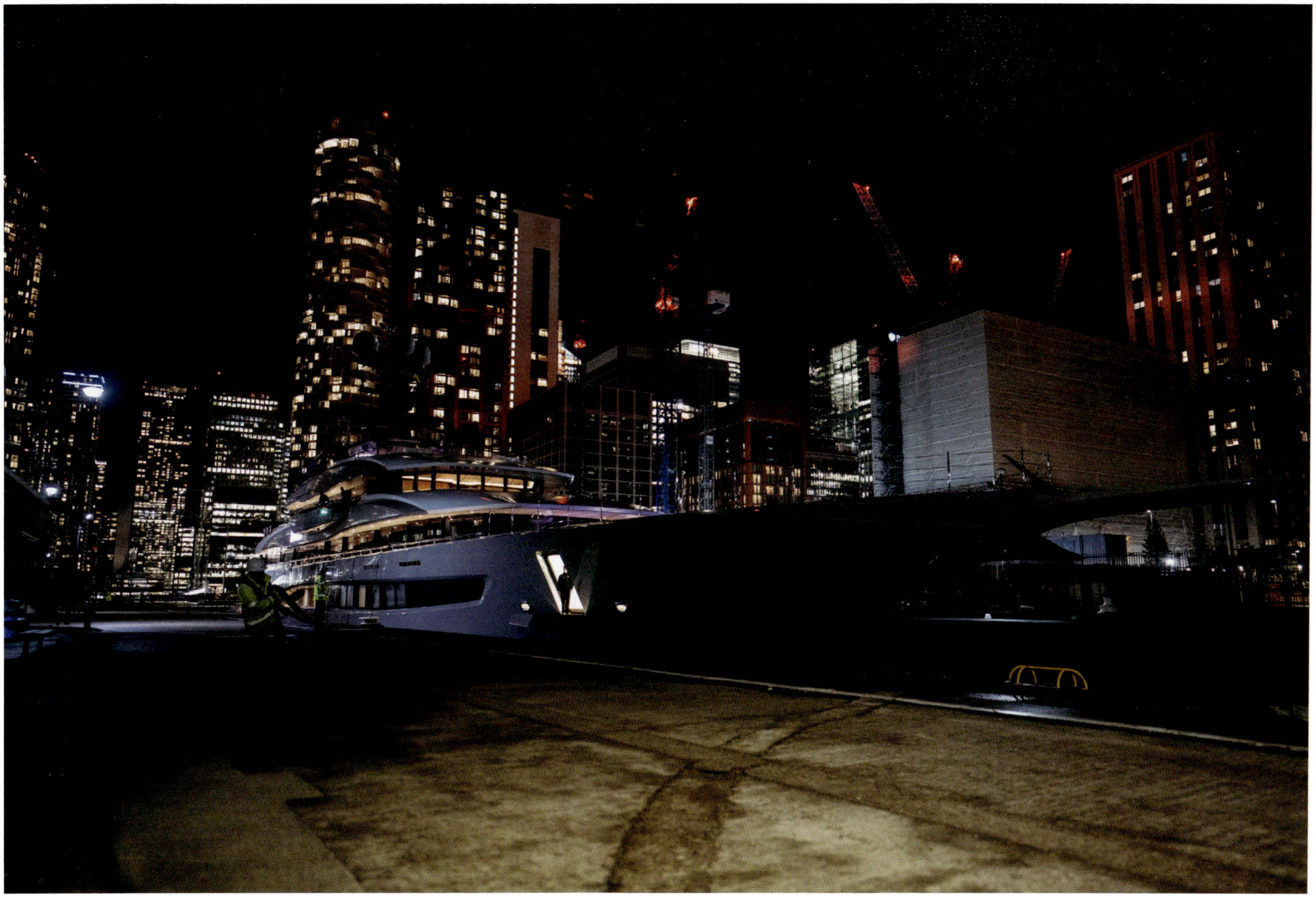

High tides rule

Due to the River Thames' large tidal range, entry and exits for London's docks are only possible twice a day at high tide. Marina teams often have to work in the early mornings and late at night to help boat owners time it right, as here, for example, when a superyacht arrives under the bright lights of Canary Wharf.

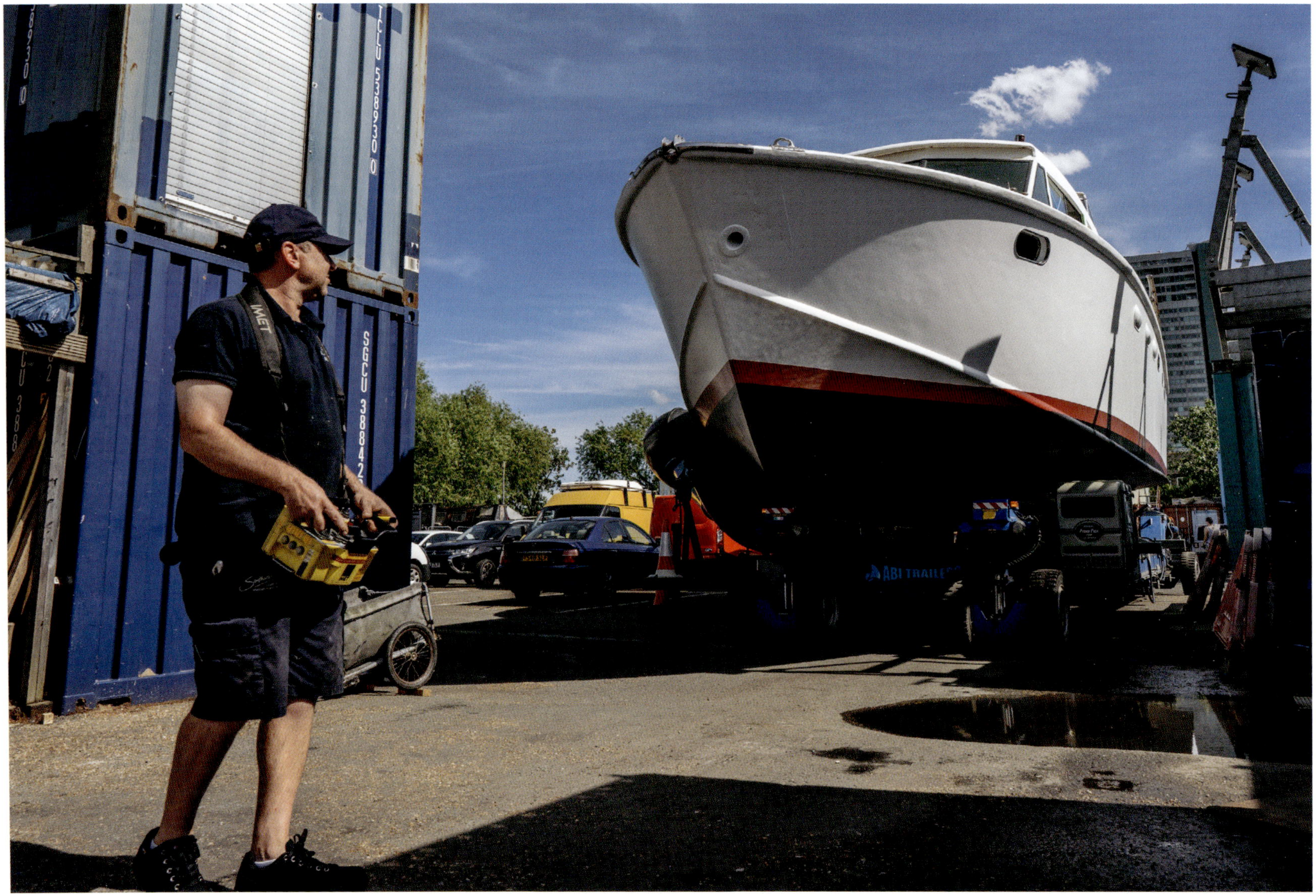

Onshore movements

Matt, from the South Dock Marina team, skilfully guides a newly refurbished boat on a motorised cradle out of the boatyard using a remote control.

There is a high turnover of different boats being brought in to be worked on and then needing to be helped back into the water.

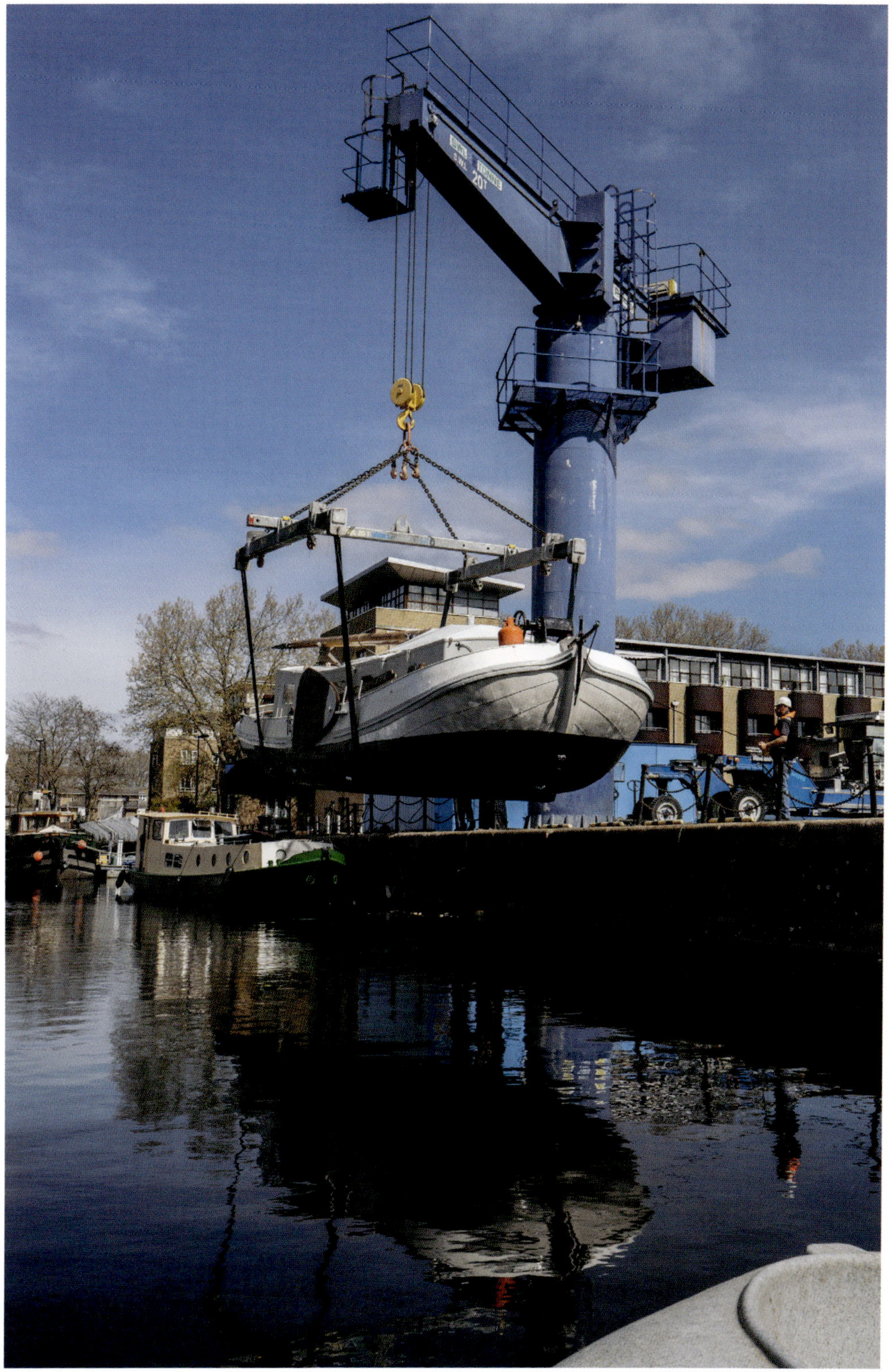

Precision hoisting

South Dock Marina's pedestal crane can lift boats of up to 20 tons. The marina team makes it look easy but great care is needed: if the lifting straps are put too near the aft end, the propellor shafts can be damaged; too far forward and the boat won't be level and may fall into the dock, causing a tsunami.

Keeping afloat

Strict safety rules require all boats to be regularly lifted out of the water for surveys and repairs.

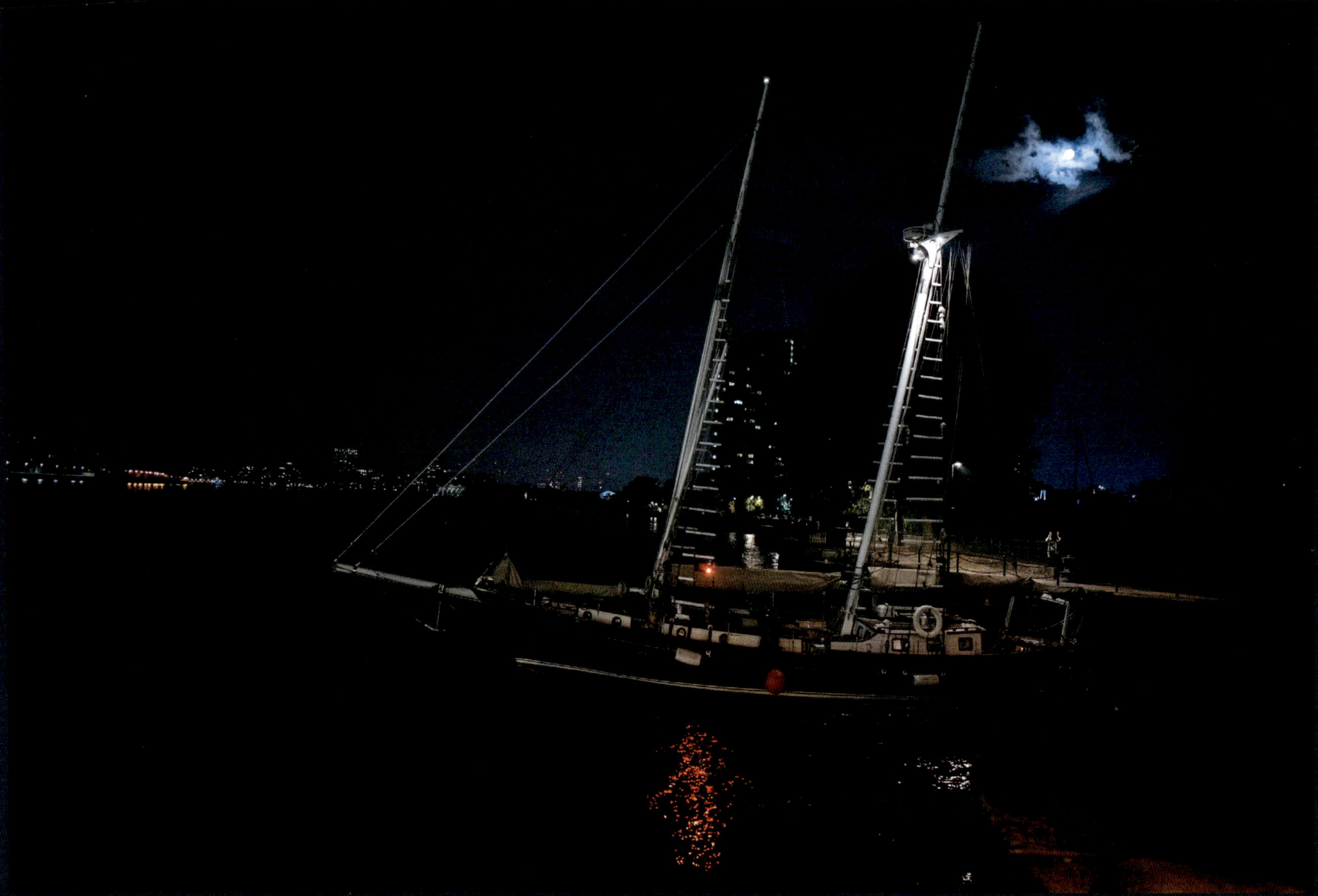

The big lift

Occasionally a few boat owners with vessels too heavy for the South Dock Marina crane to lift will club together to hire in a mega-mobile one. Here *Zeewolf* is hoisted out and her hull cleaned of marine growth ready for surveying, before being swung on to a motorised cradle for transfer into the boatyard. It's a quicker and more convenient option than making the 12-hour journey down-river to find a larger crane, as it not only allows for on-the-spot surveys and repairs but owners can continue to live aboard locally while this happens.

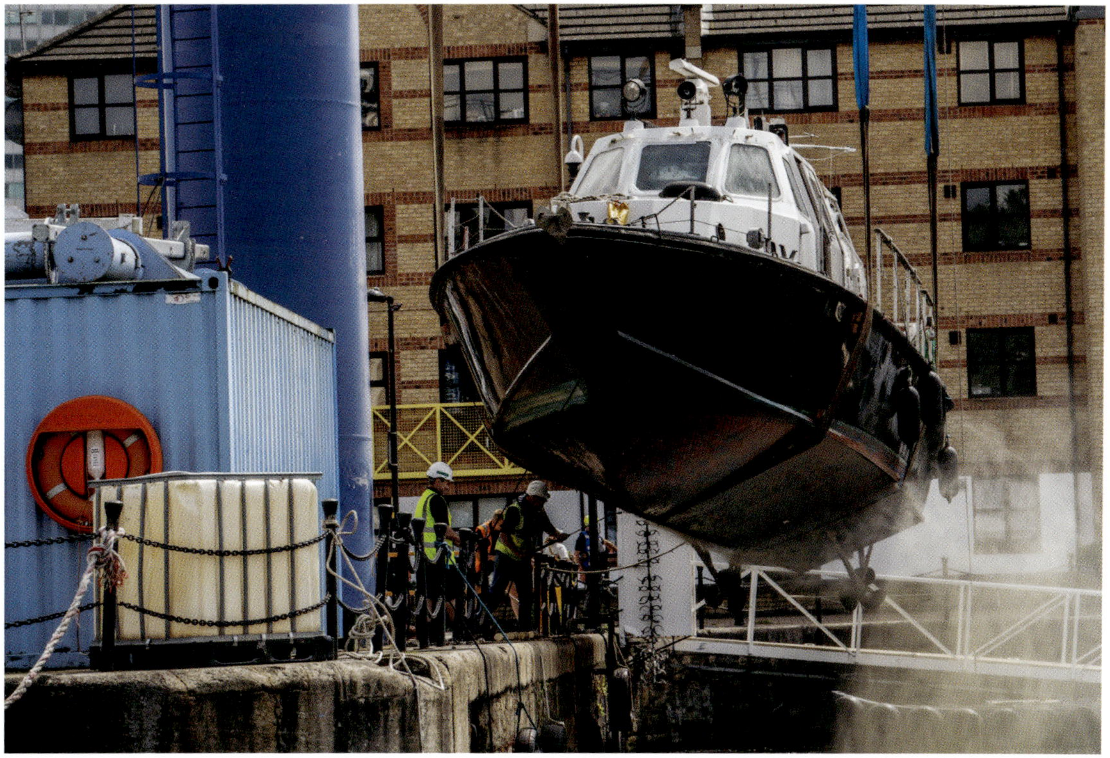

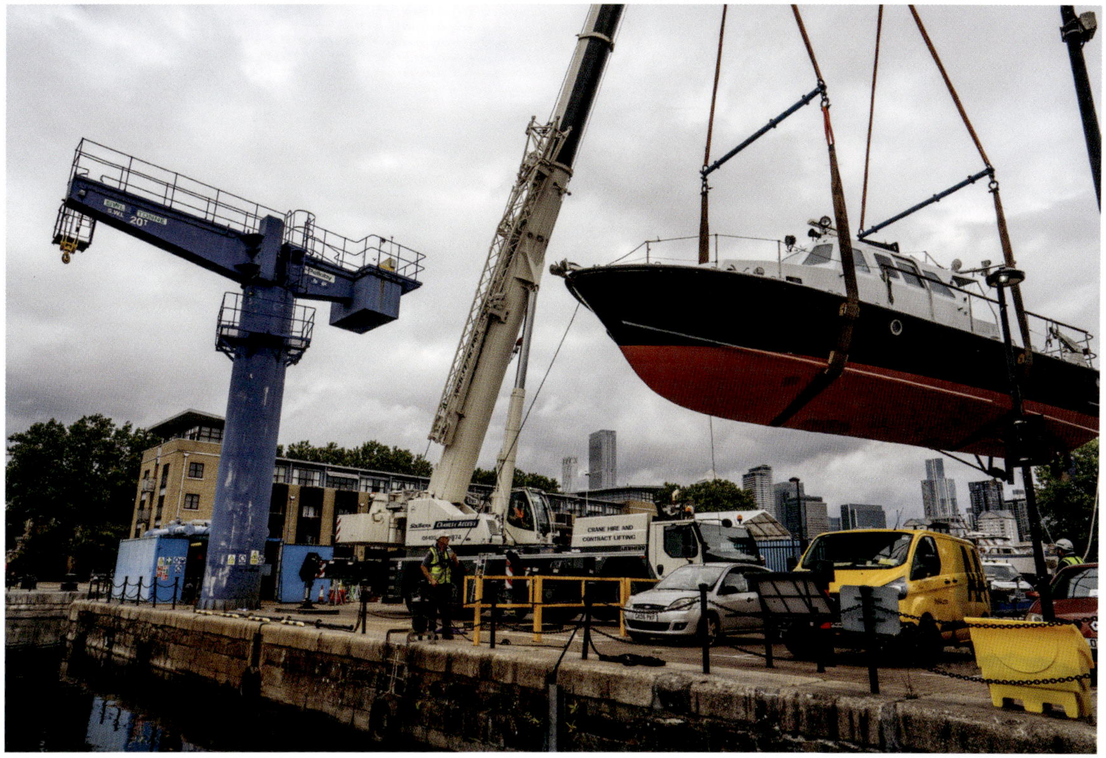

Midnight moonlight

‹ *Nathanael* exits Surrey Quays' South Dock Marina, catching the high tide on to the Thames. She's heading down-river for Gillingham, which has a crane large enough to lift her out for her five-yearly insurance survey. This beautiful schooner with a steel hull and wooden decks was built in a French tank factory and is one of only three constructed to this design. A true seagoing vessel, her owner sailed her all the way back from Hong Kong to her current berth in Greenland Dock.

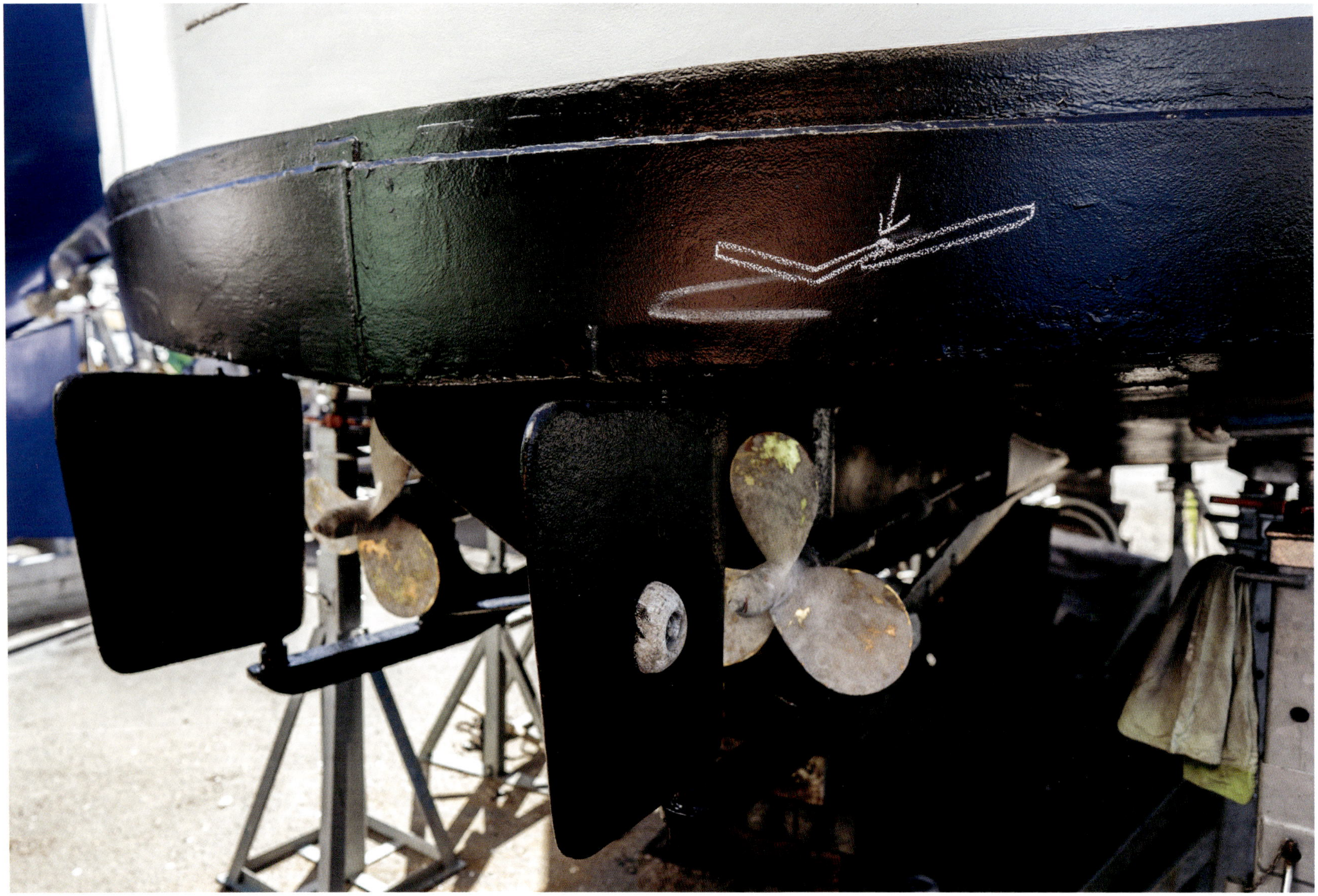

Making their mark

Marine surveyors are the detectives of the boat world, their regular examinations of hulls, particularly for liveaboards, are vital to identify any degradation that might result in leaks. With boats sitting in the water for long periods, corrosion of some sort is inevitable. Here, on newly-surveyed *Ramesses II*, tell-tale chalk marks clearly show where repair work needs to be done on its steel hull.

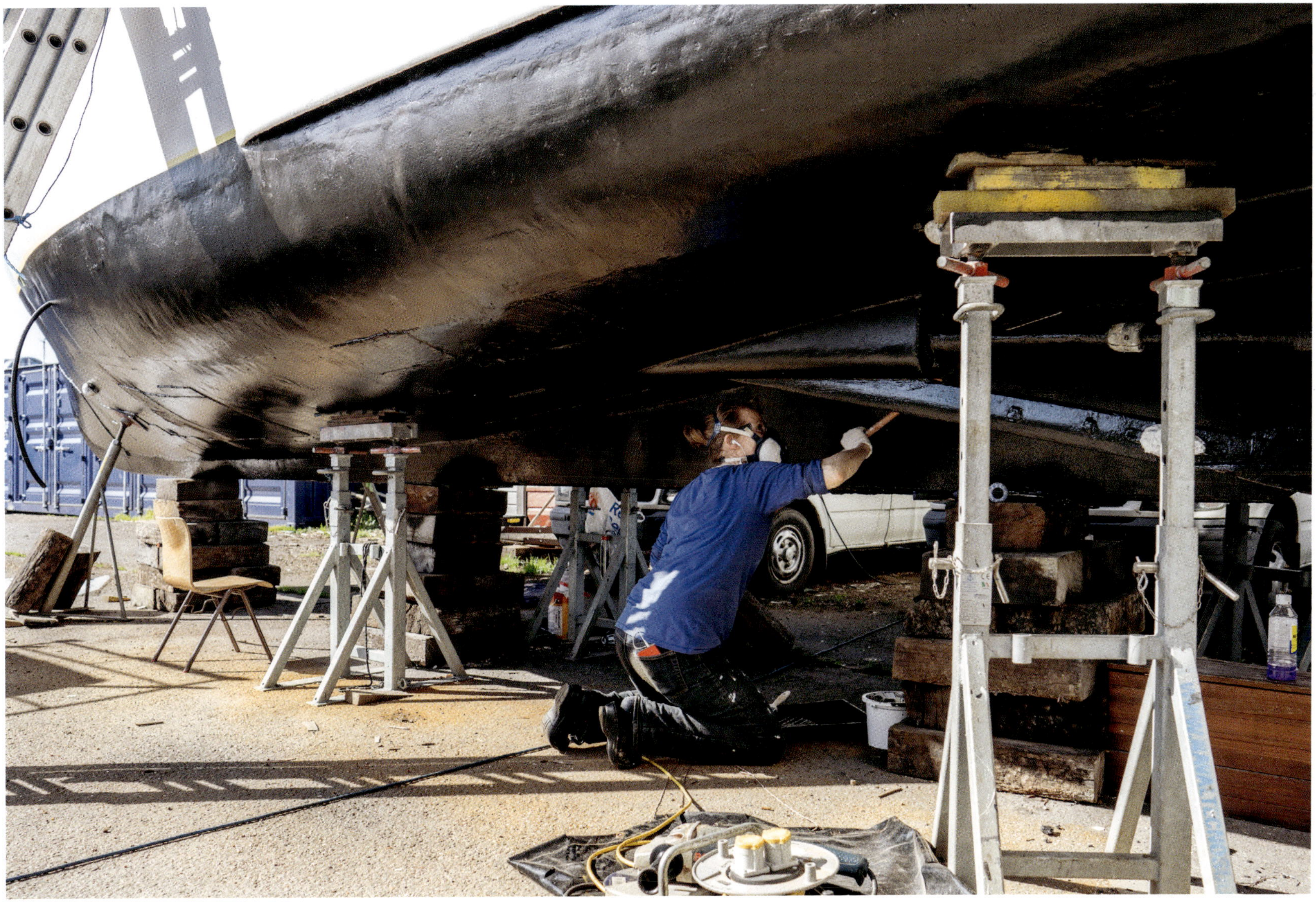

Boatyard DIY

With a clean bill of health from the surveyor and repairs completed, Charlie can now go ahead and repaint *Ramesses II*, the 1960s Dutch 'gentleman's cruiser' that she's been comfortably living on for over eight years in Surrey Quays' South Dock Marina. Many boat owners carry out their own non-specialist work to save both money and time. However, they need to have technical and safety know-how. The waterproof anti-fouling paint gives off toxic fumes; hence Charlie's care to wear protective clothing.

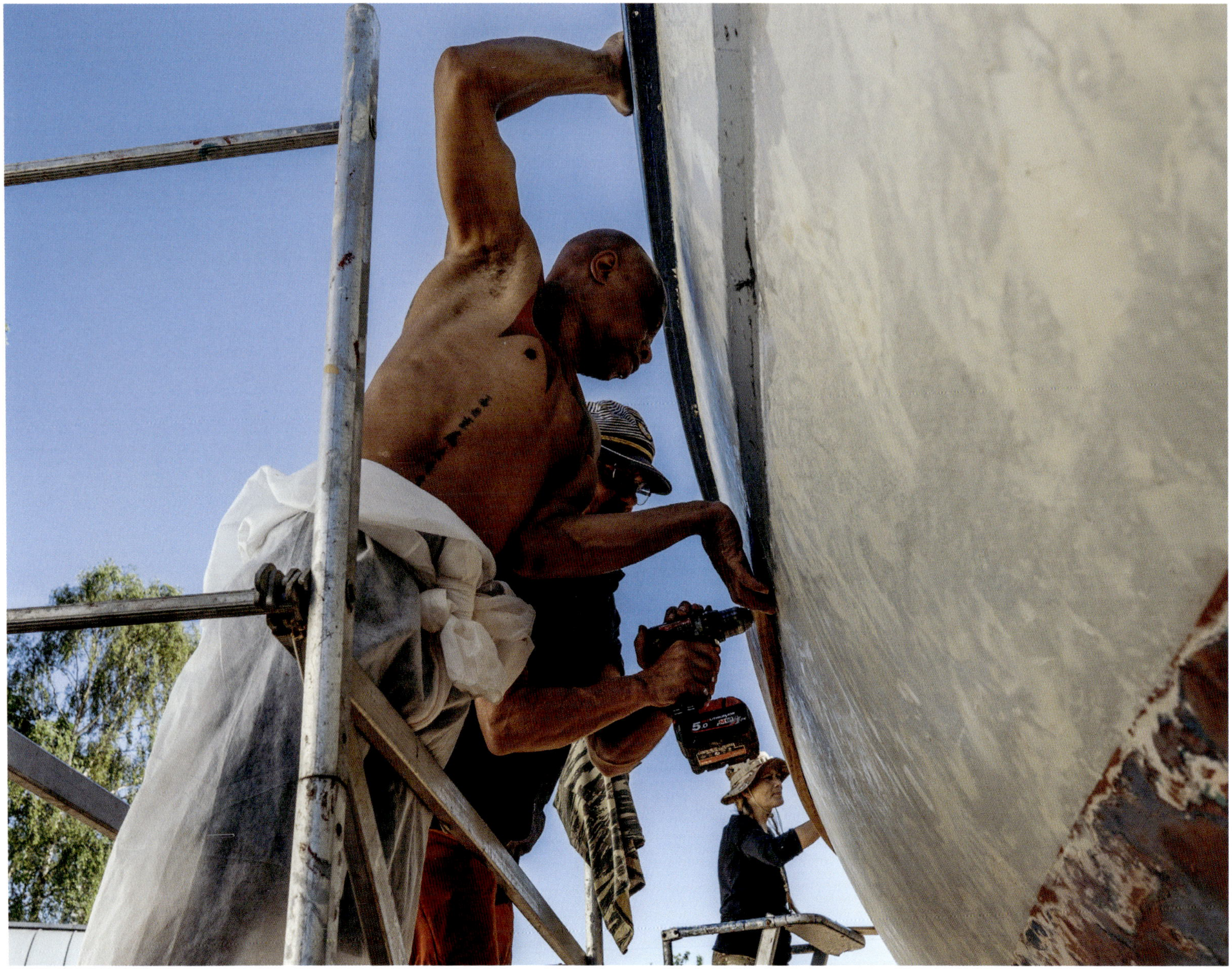

Curved carpentry

For major boat refurbishments, South Dock Marina boatyard provides expertise from specialists such as marine carpenter Nick Kenny. A whole new 'rubbing strake' is needed for one side of a completely stripped-down wooden boat. To create the right curve in the timber, Nick has first steamed the long plank in a custom-made box using a simple wallpaper steamer. While the wood is still moist and malleable, he quickly fixes it on to the length of the hull with the help of assistants, Wayne and Nina, cleverly achieving exactly the right fit. This replacement perfectly matches an original one on the other side of the hull and will help protect the boat from wear.

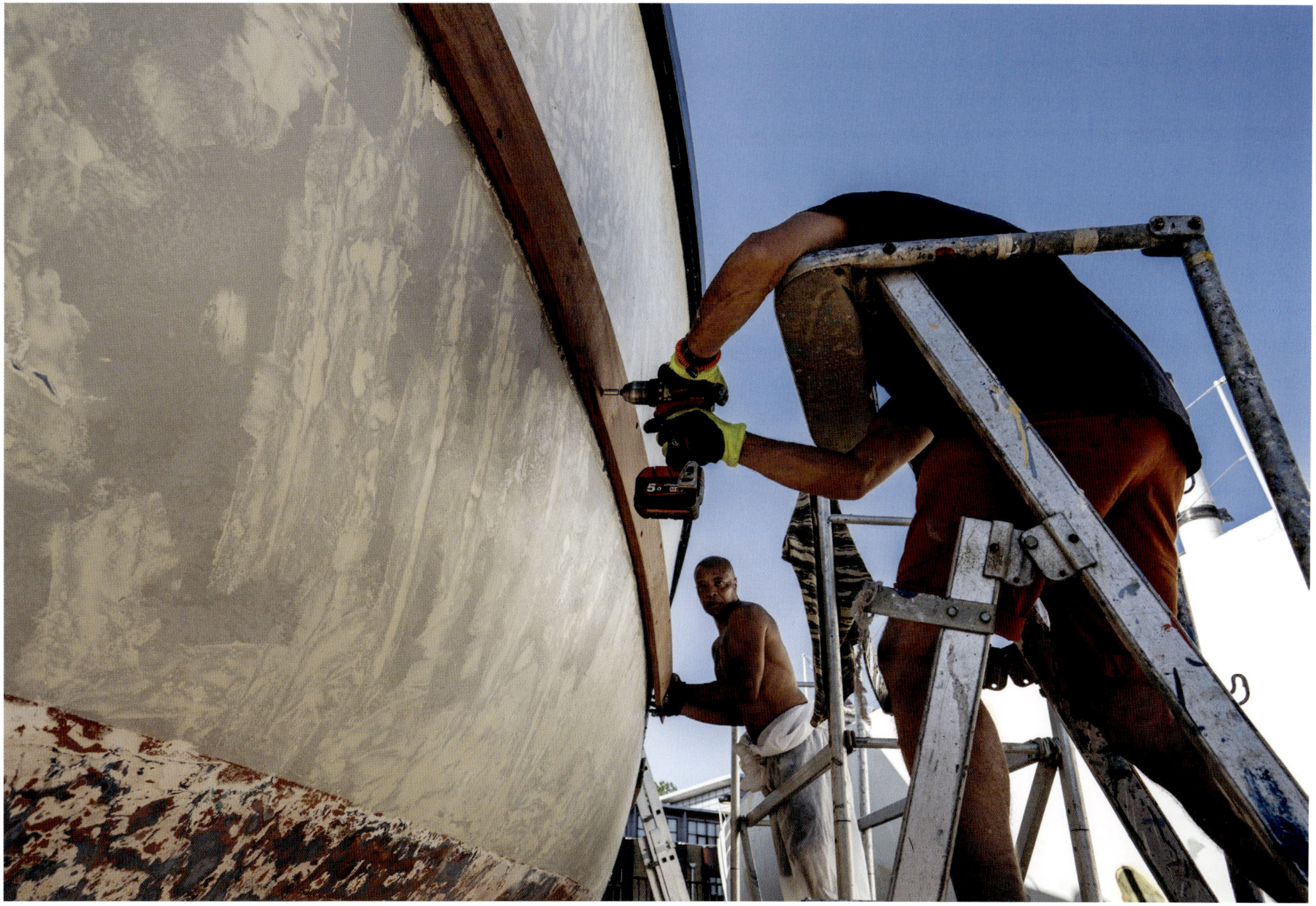

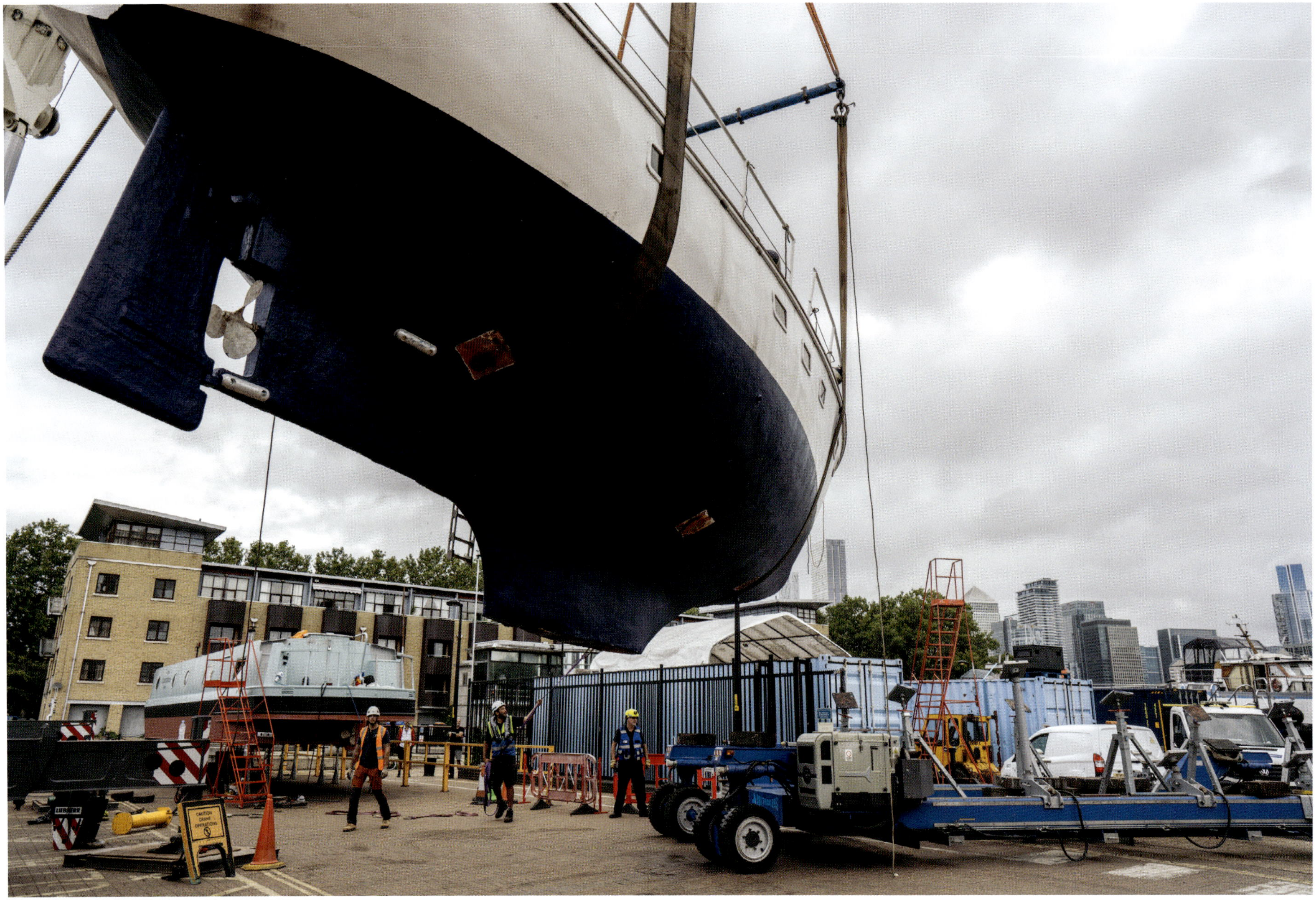

Heavy lifting

Unusually made from concrete (a steel frame and ferro-cement to be precise), *Con Artist* is one of the heaviest boats in South Dock Marina, needing the extra-strong hired crane to lift it in and out for survey and repair in the boatyard.

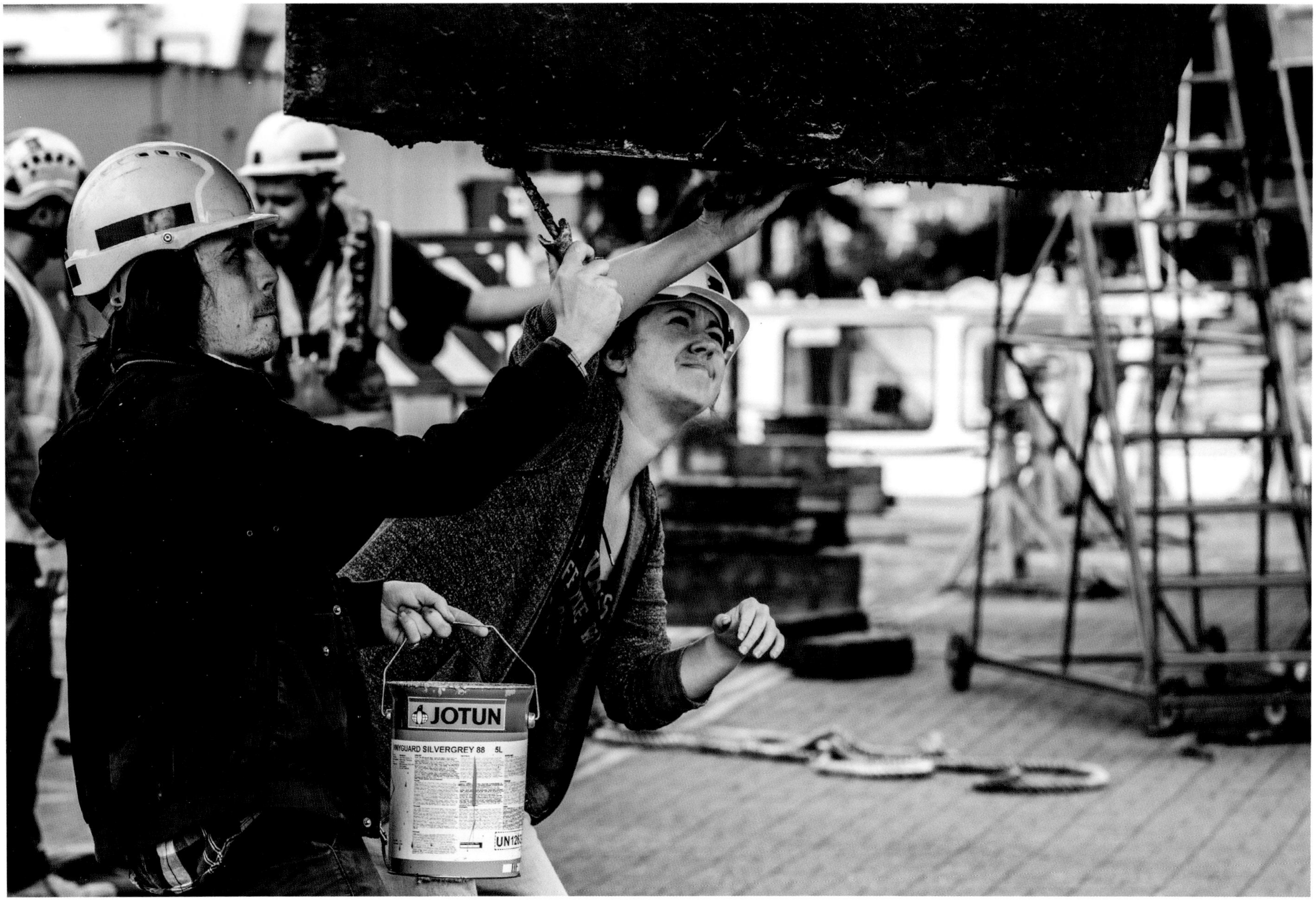

Final touches

Actor Felix and screenwriter Meghan take advantage of the huge crane lifting their liveaboard's keel completely off the ground to finish its month-long refurbishment with some scraping and a quick bit of fast-drying protective paint. A few minutes later, *Con Artist* is back on its South Dock Marina mooring as the couple's floating home.

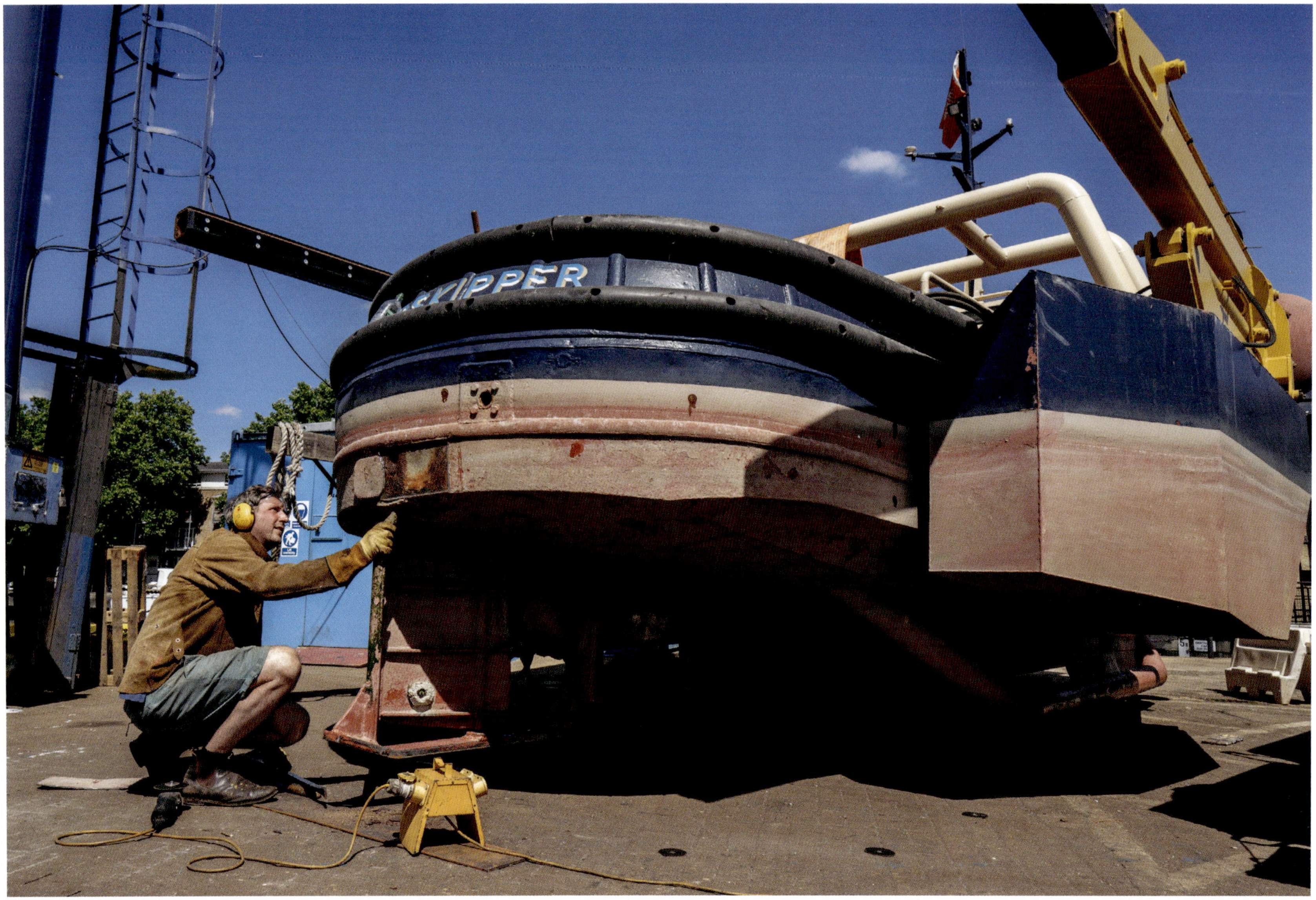

A walking ship

Artist James Capper has brought his fully mobile sculpture, *Mudskipper*, back to South Dock Marina boatyard, where he created it in 2019. It's out of the water for the five-year check required by the Port of London Authority – but there's a problem. James' magnificent artwork conversion of a 1980s Thames workboat may be able to move across both water and land using a set of hydraulic propulsion legs but the survey has shown that it has a hole that needs fixing.

The art of welding

James is an unusual artist. As well as being an expert in hydraulics, he is a trained welder and fully able to do his own repairs. Improvising with a circular sanding pad, he has soon marked out what he needs to remove and sets to with welding equipment brought from his workshop just down the road.

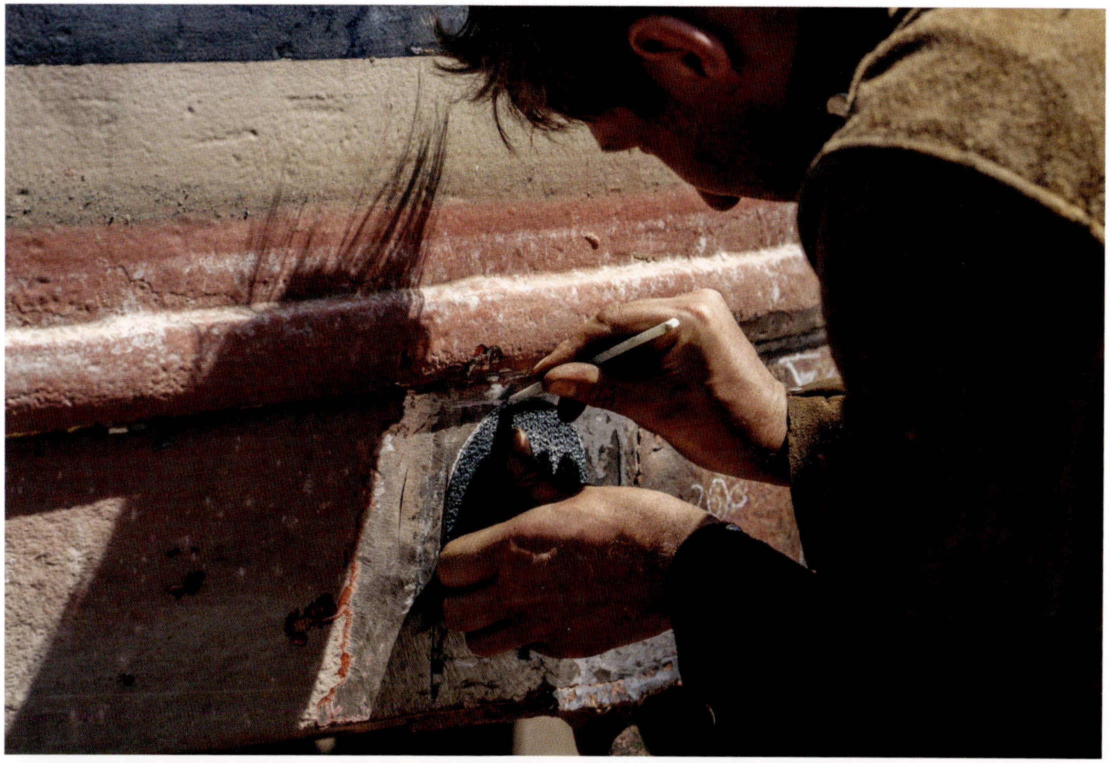

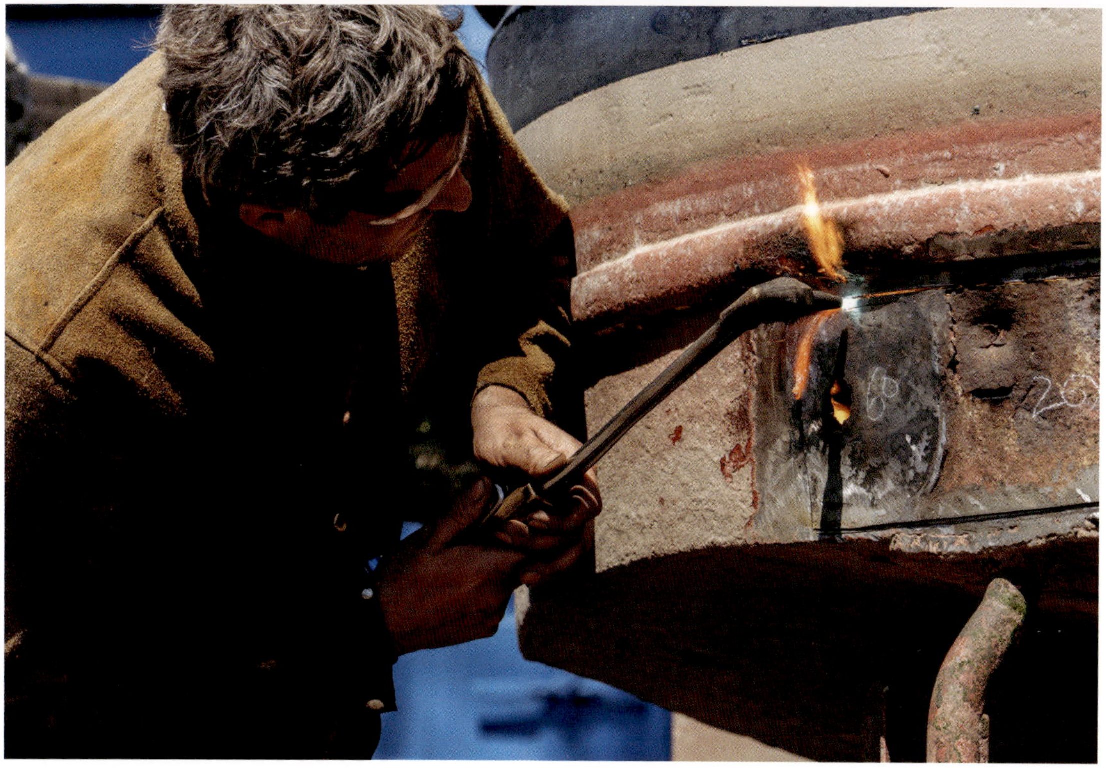

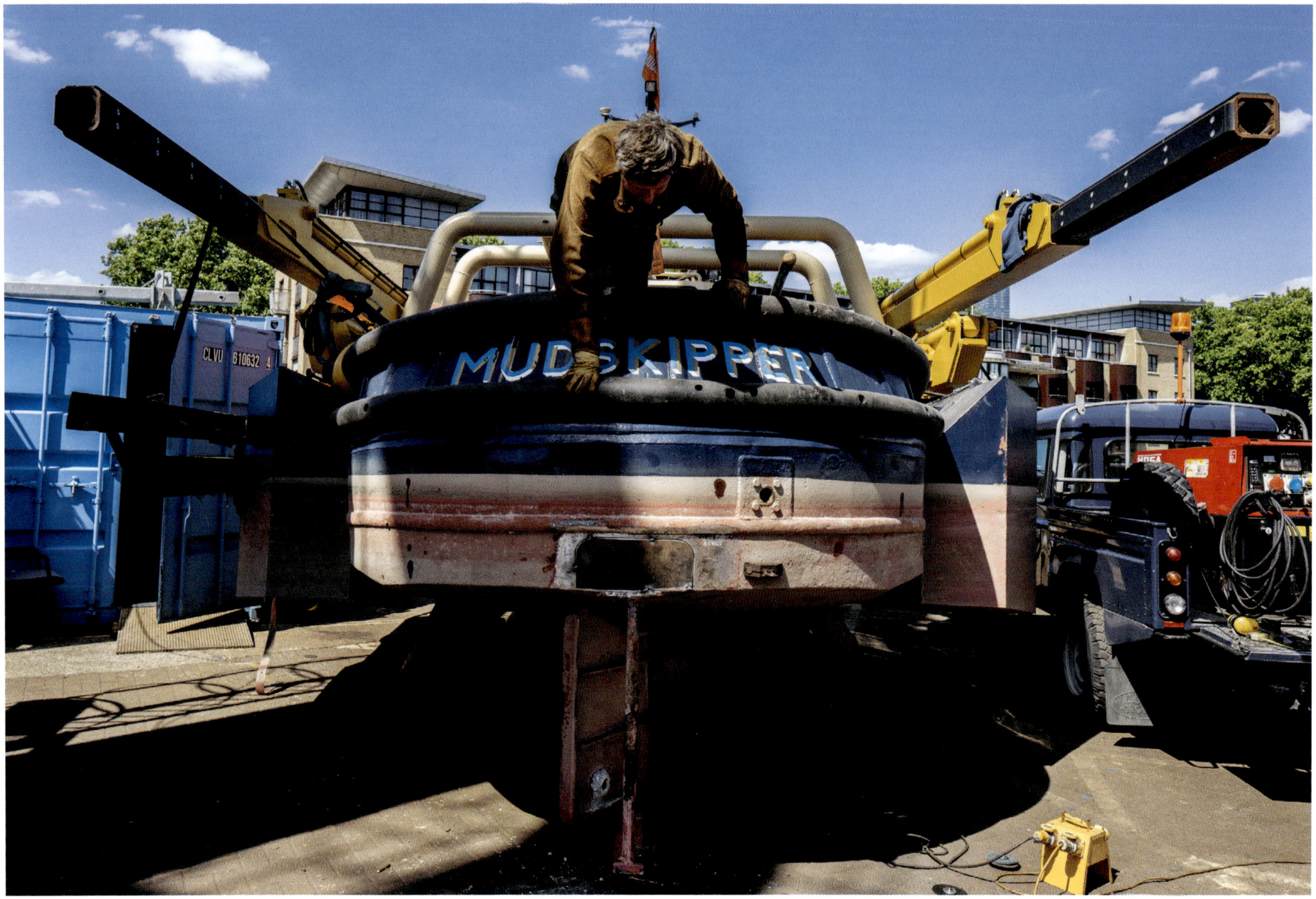

Getting shipshape

With the corroded parts cut out and a new steel plate fitted, James checks that it all looks good from above. As an experimental sculpture weighing 14.5 tons, it needs to be absolutely watertight again.

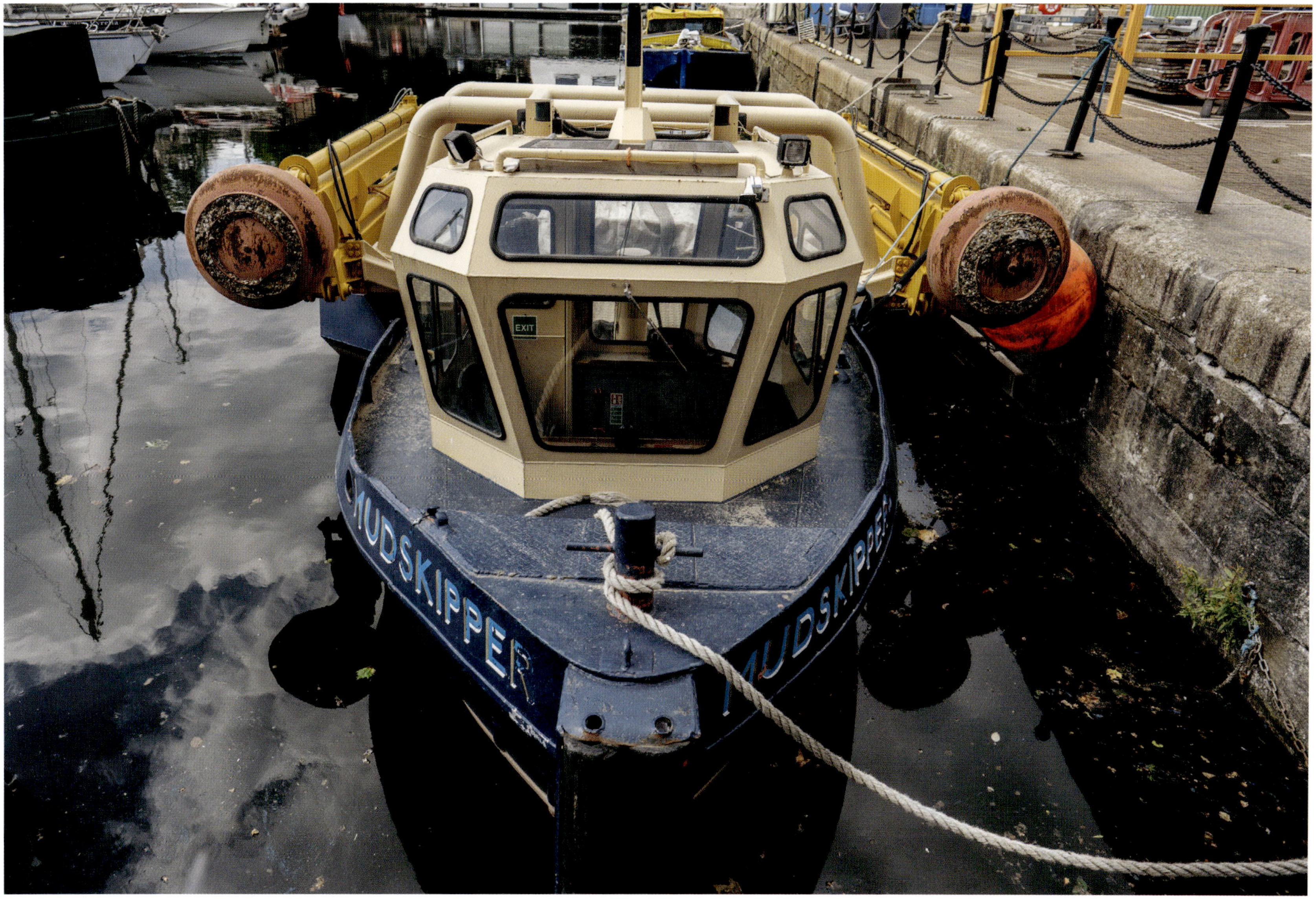

Amphibious again

Mudskipper is now back in South Dock Marina and ready to head out on to the Thames to resume live demonstrations of James' unique melding of artistic and engineering talent.
www.illuminateproductions.co.uk/mudskipper

Boatyard tales

South Dock Marina in Surrey Quays runs the last working boatyard in central London – it's a hive of activity.

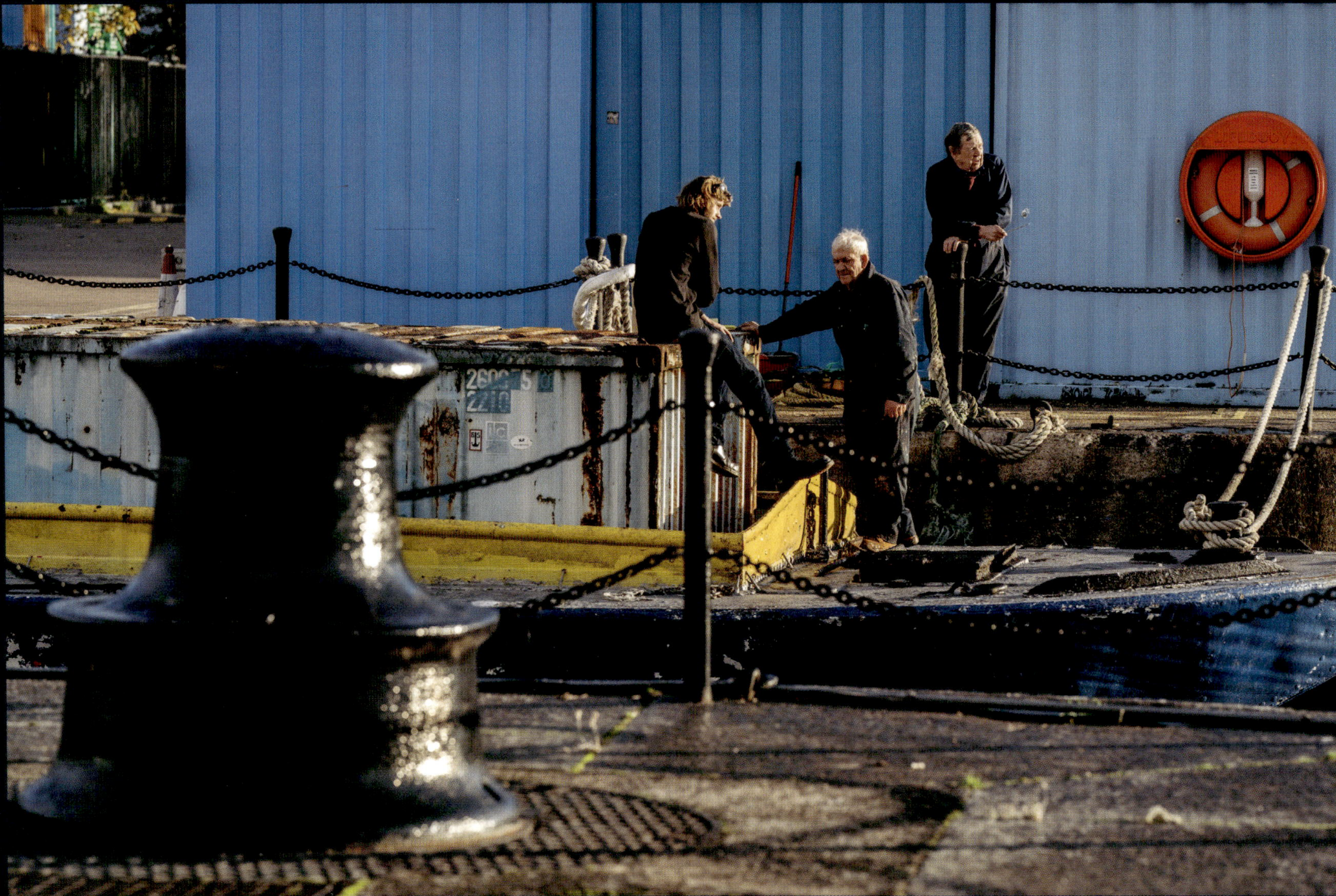

Learning from experience

Brenden runs a busy workshop in South Dock Marina boatyard, repairing other people's boats but also working on his own fleet. He has bought an old 'beaver boat', built as a tug to move wood on Canadian logging rivers. As it's small but has a very powerful engine, Brenden knows that it will be in demand for working in the tighter spaces of the Upper Thames. For such major refurbishments, Brenden always turns to Phil and Bill, full of admiration for their experience and skills learnt during the Port of London's heyday. First of all, he takes advice from Phil on how best to create a whole new pushing fender for the tug's bow.
www.osheasmarineservices.com

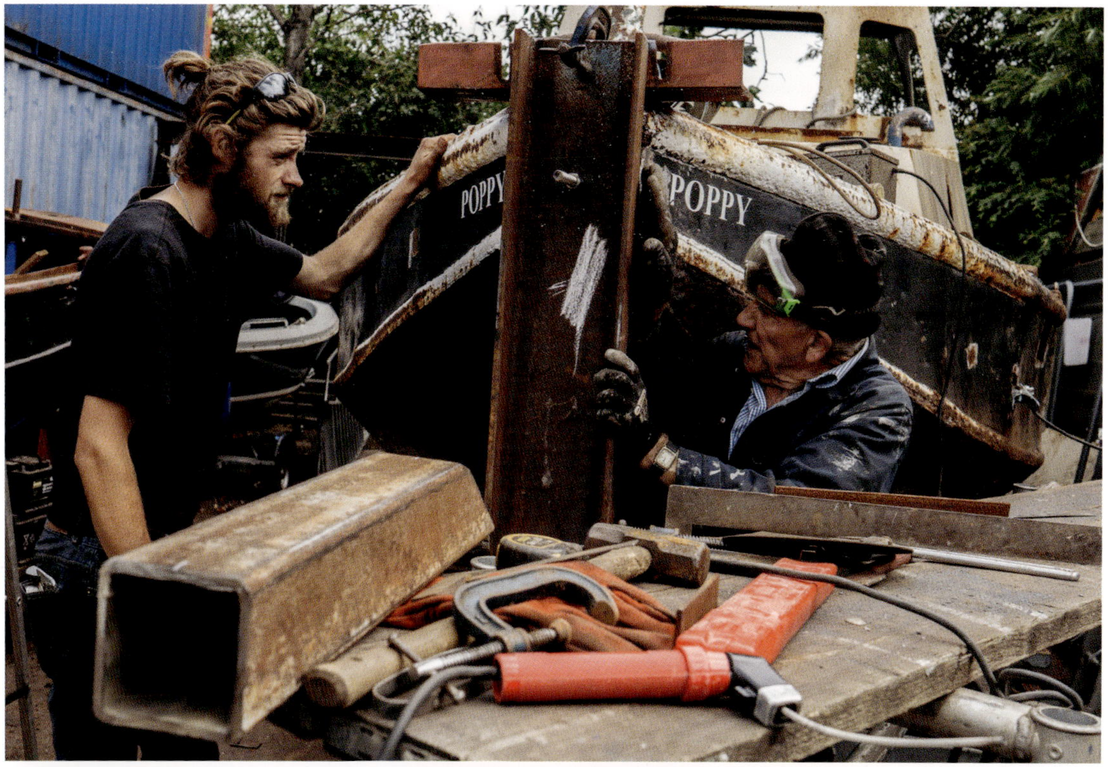

Practised partnership

The new bow structure is soon taking shape. Phil and Bill first met in the 1970s when they were building the Thames Barrier. Decades later, they are still the best of friends and despite their age, maintain a formidable work rate.

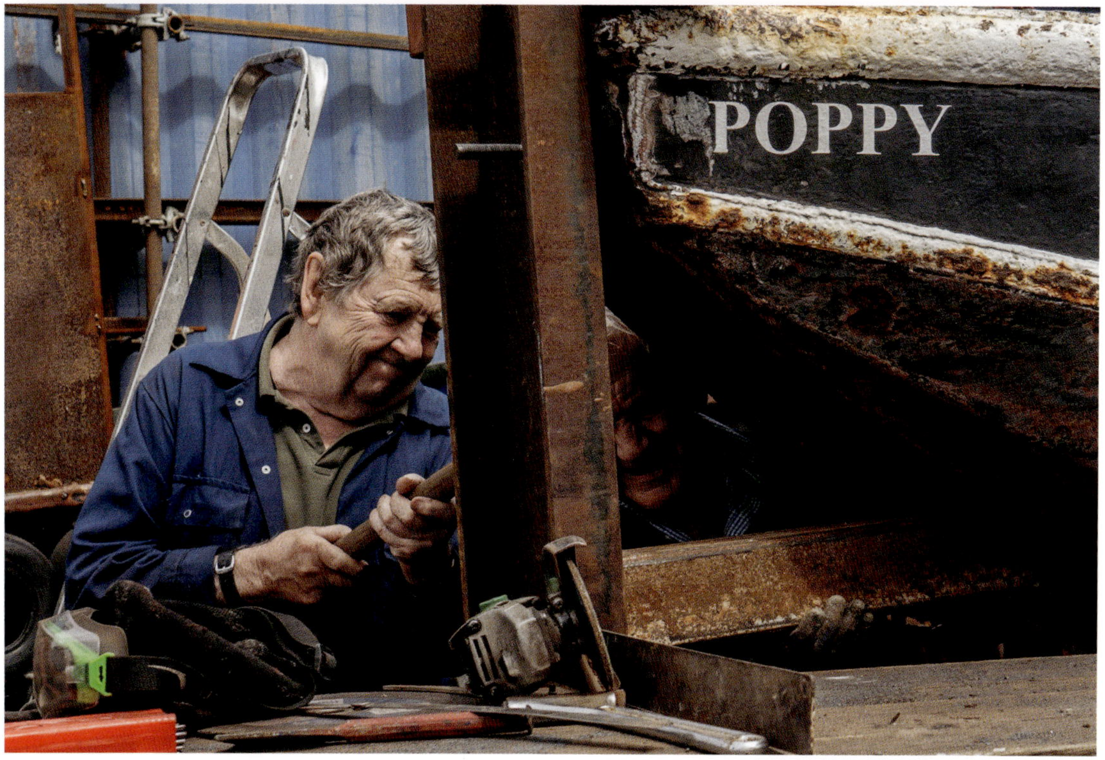

Age range

‹ Still in his early 20s, entrepreneur Brenden has teamed up with Bill and Phil, both well into their 70s, to start River Skips Ltd, a refuse management business collecting general rubbish from piers on the Thames to take down-river for disposal. Combining septuagenarian know-how with the energy of youth to convert two old 'lighter' barges to do the towing, it's a highly successful blend of talents.
www.riverskipslimited.com

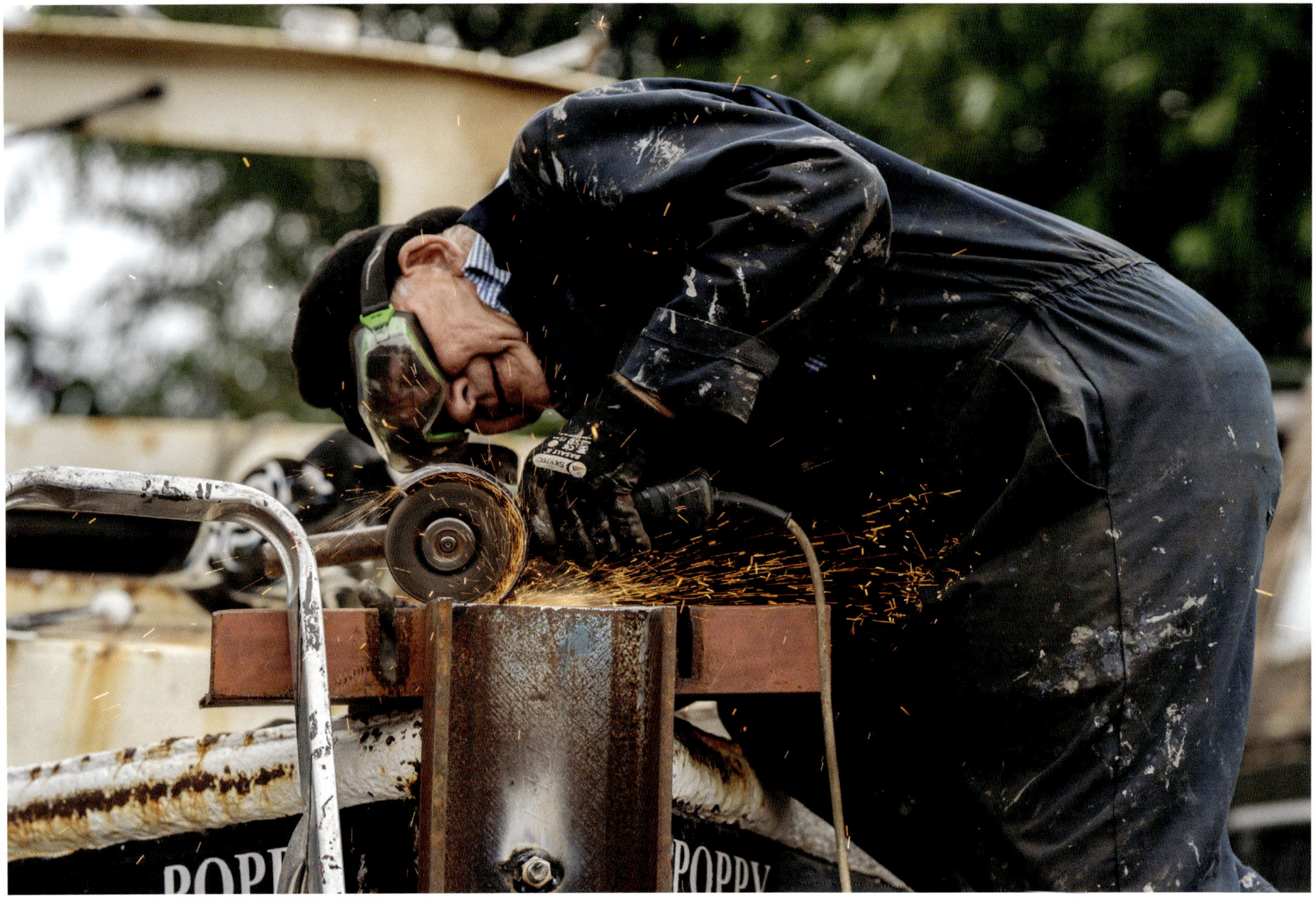

Division of labour

This old tugboat certainly has a lot of corrosion to cut out and new plating to fit. Phil is the expert with angle-grinding, skillfully cutting metal as well as smoothing welds after Bill has done his work.

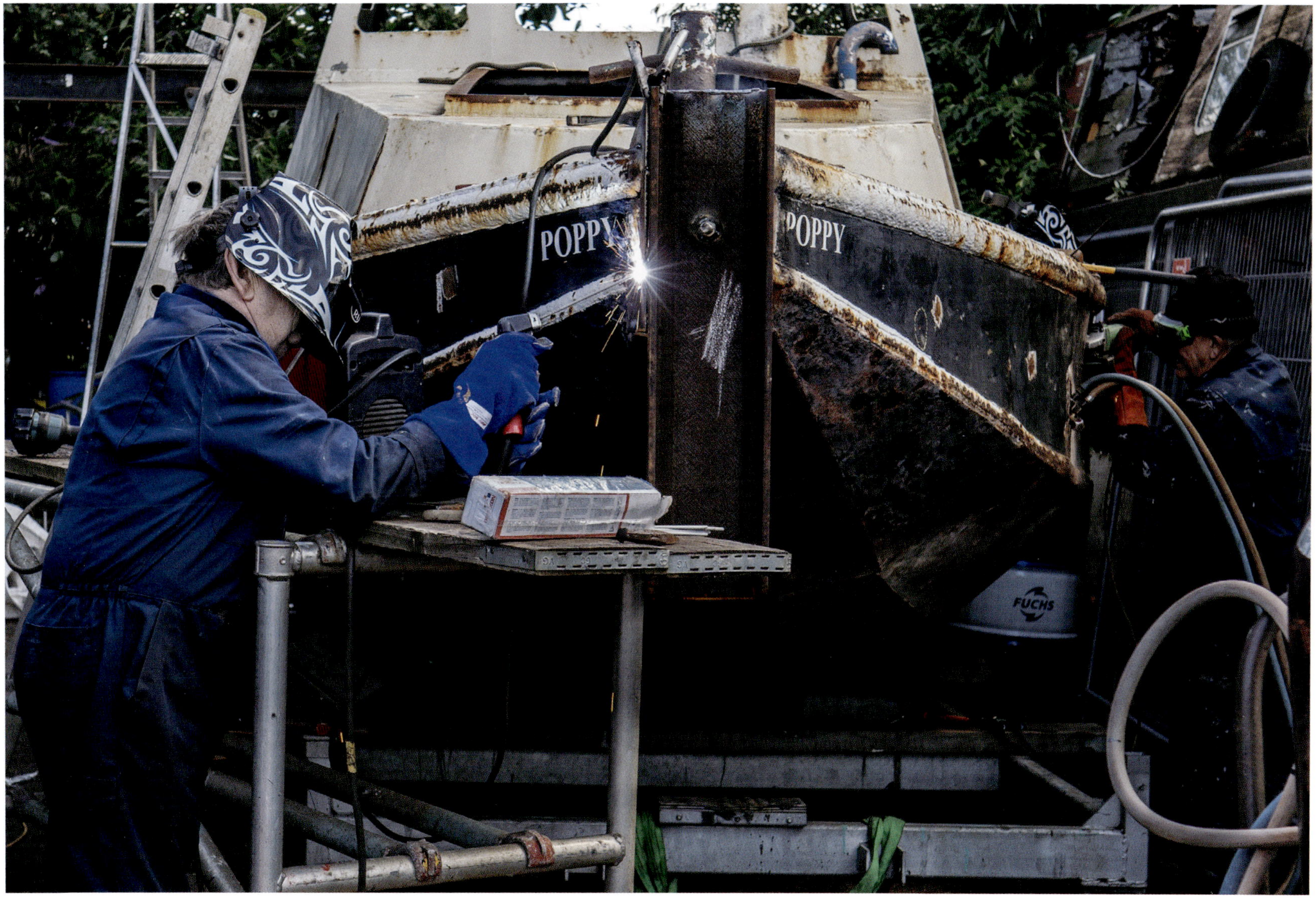

Disappearing skills

Bill is a master of 'stick-welding', proud that he originally trained as one of an elite band of Lloyds A1 welders. Both he and Phil have stories of London's commercial docks when there were hundreds of skilled workmen like themselves. Now they are a dying breed. Brenden is worried that when they go, their particular marine skill set will disappear with them.

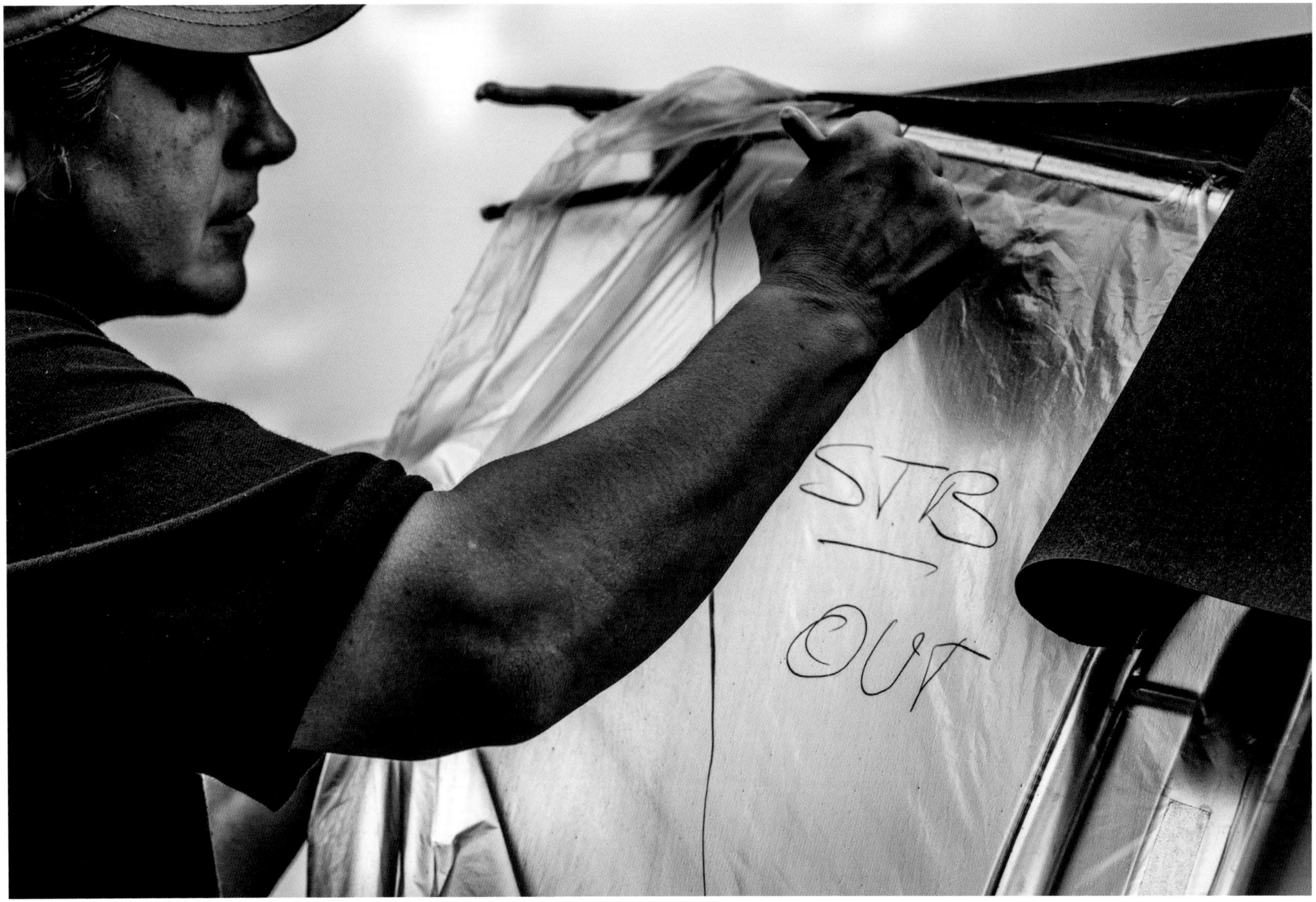

A cut above

For over 10 years, two sisters from the mountains of Patagonia have been creating boat covers and upholstery from their office and workshop in South Dock Marina boatyard. With an intrepid history of constructing their own boat in Argentina and then sailing it around the world, Patricia and Miryam have built Marine Canvas Hut into a thriving business catering for boats of all shapes and sizes. Very much a bespoke service, the initial measuring up is very carefully marked out on special sheeting. www.marinecanvashut.co.uk

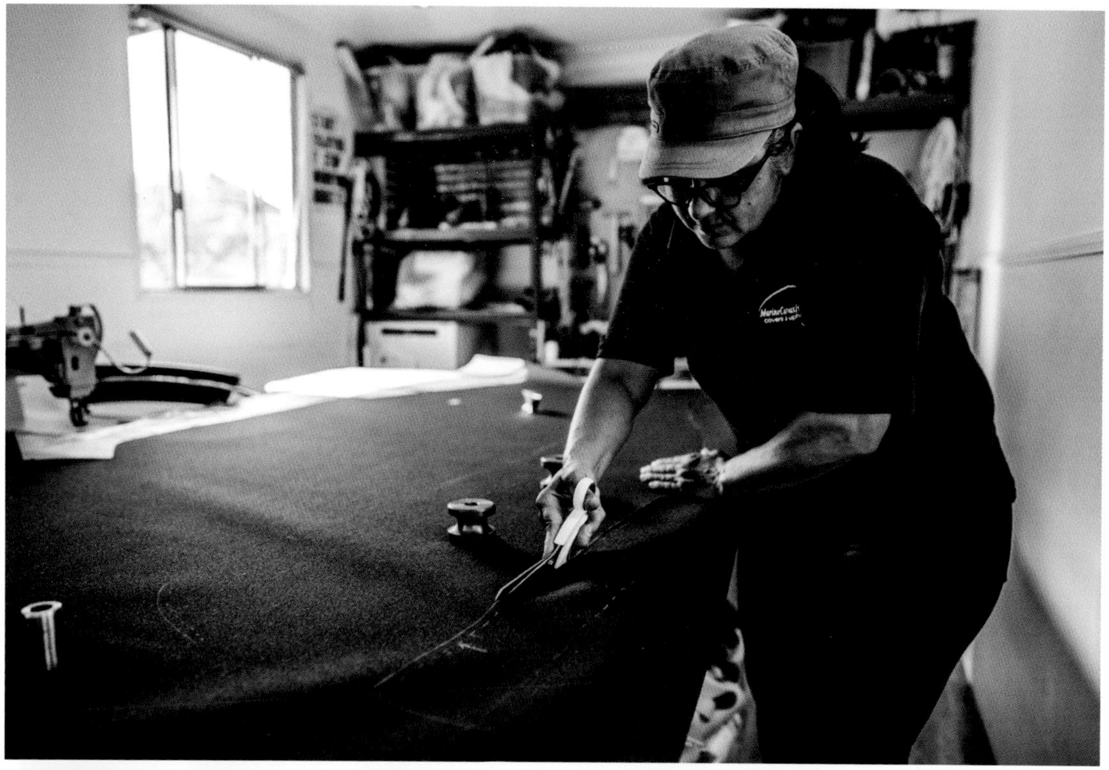

Following the curve

Every boat is different and there are very few straight lines. Careful cutting is needed to tailor each cover to the particular contours of the boat.

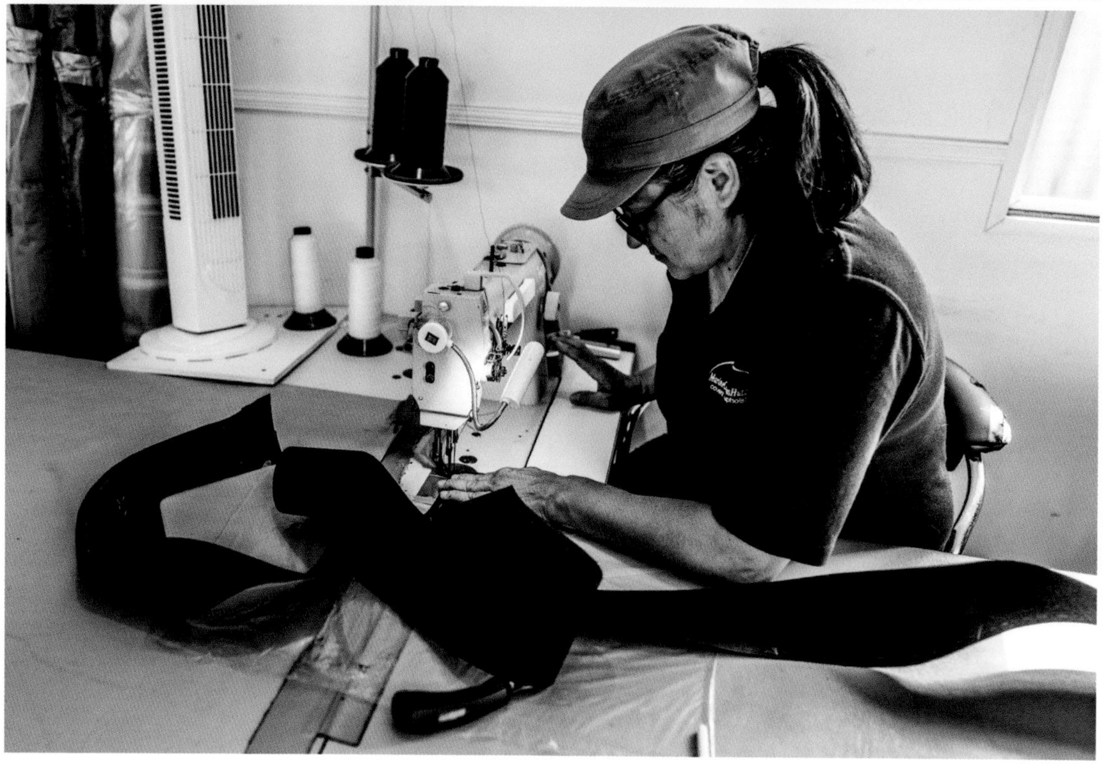

All sewn up

Using a specially calibrated machine, Patricia stitches together the cloth segments to create a three-dimensional cover ready for fitting.

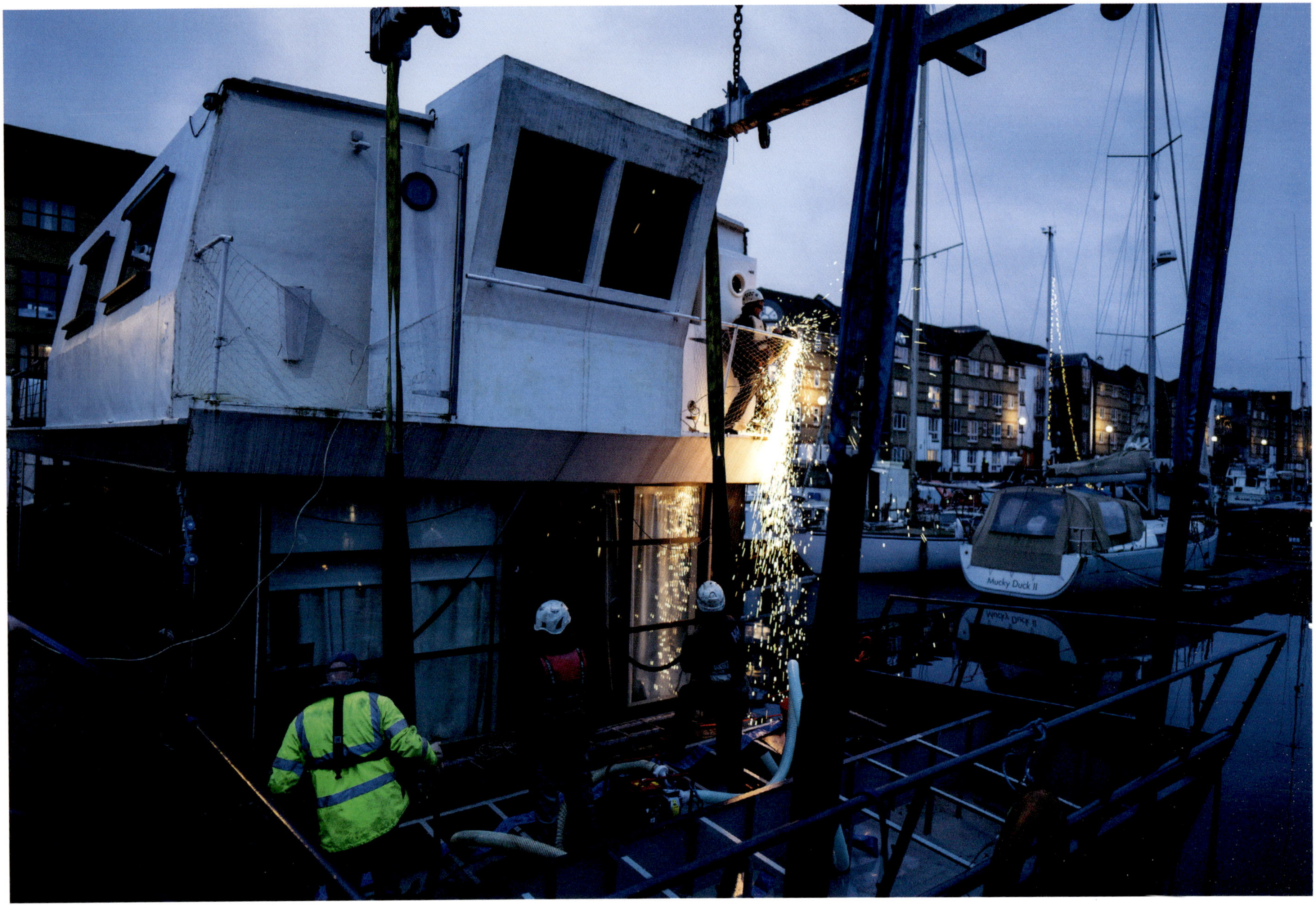

Home improvements

Metal fabricator Mike Pearce dramatically prepares to attach a new extension to *Arcadia*, with the help of the South Dock Marina crane team. Mike has been given the task of rebalancing this now rather wobbly vessel, originally built as a prototype for a never-realised floating village. It's a challenge requiring all his design and practical ingenuity.

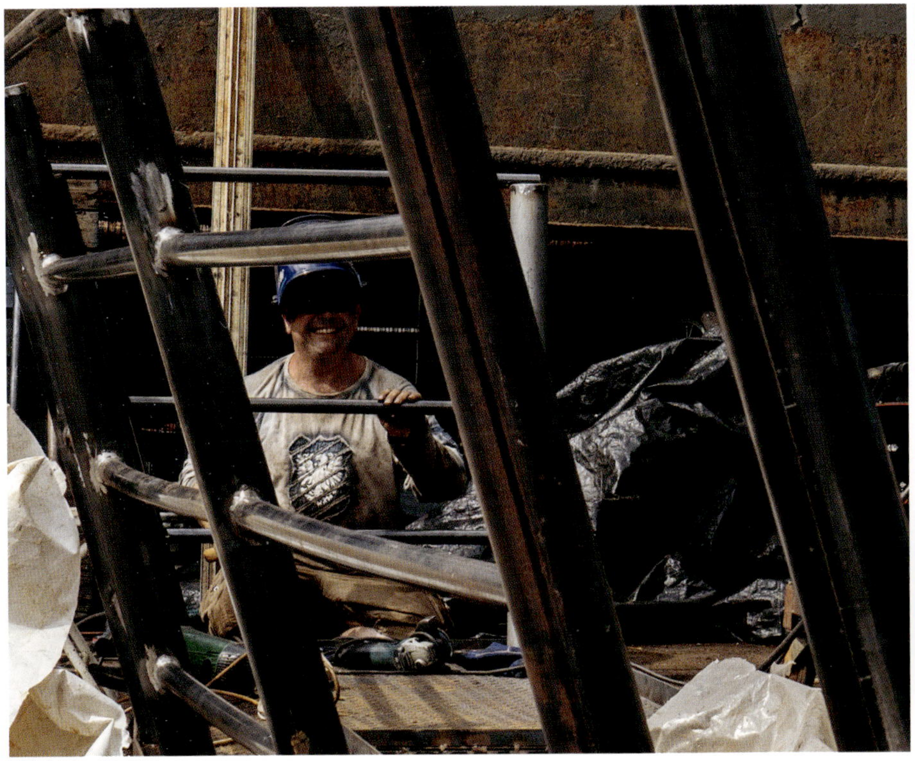

Artistic license

In his well-established workshop in South Dock Marina boatyard, Mike creates bespoke structures from scratch and relishes the artistry involved in metal fabrication, as well as being in total control of how a project evolves. Combining an art school background with welding training, he offers a unique set of skills. The new balcony he's now creating for *Arcadia* will not only meet practical requirements but will also look good.

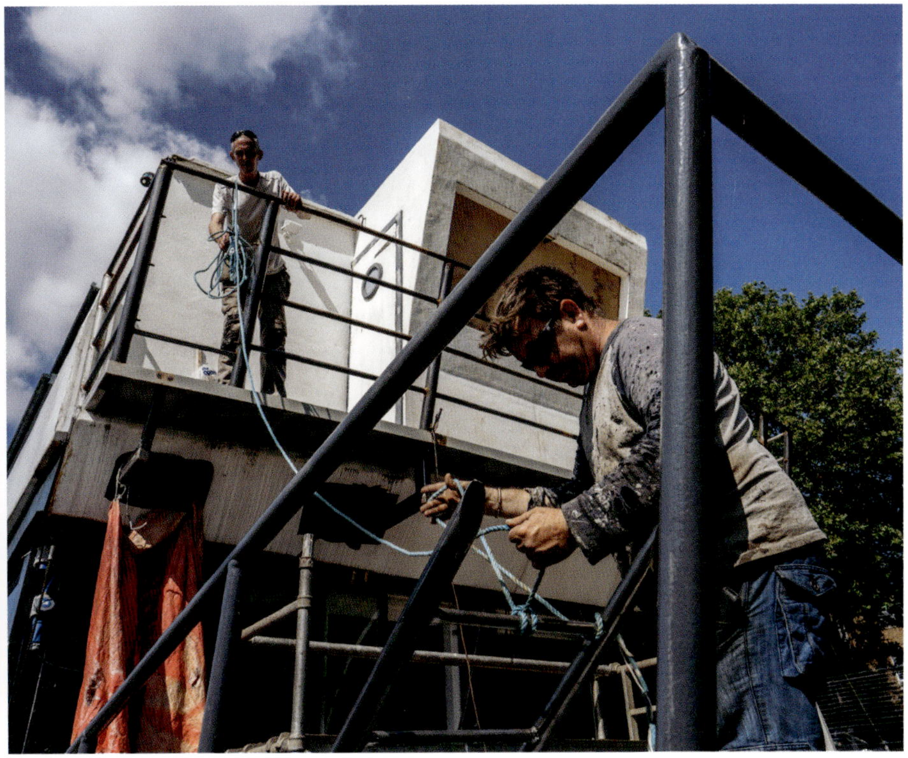

Function with style

With the new balcony fitted, Mike lines up one of the accompanying ladders he has designed to specifically complement *Arcadia*'s large dimensions. Once welded into place, these ladders will allow deck access to the top level and help balance the overall look of this unusual vessel.

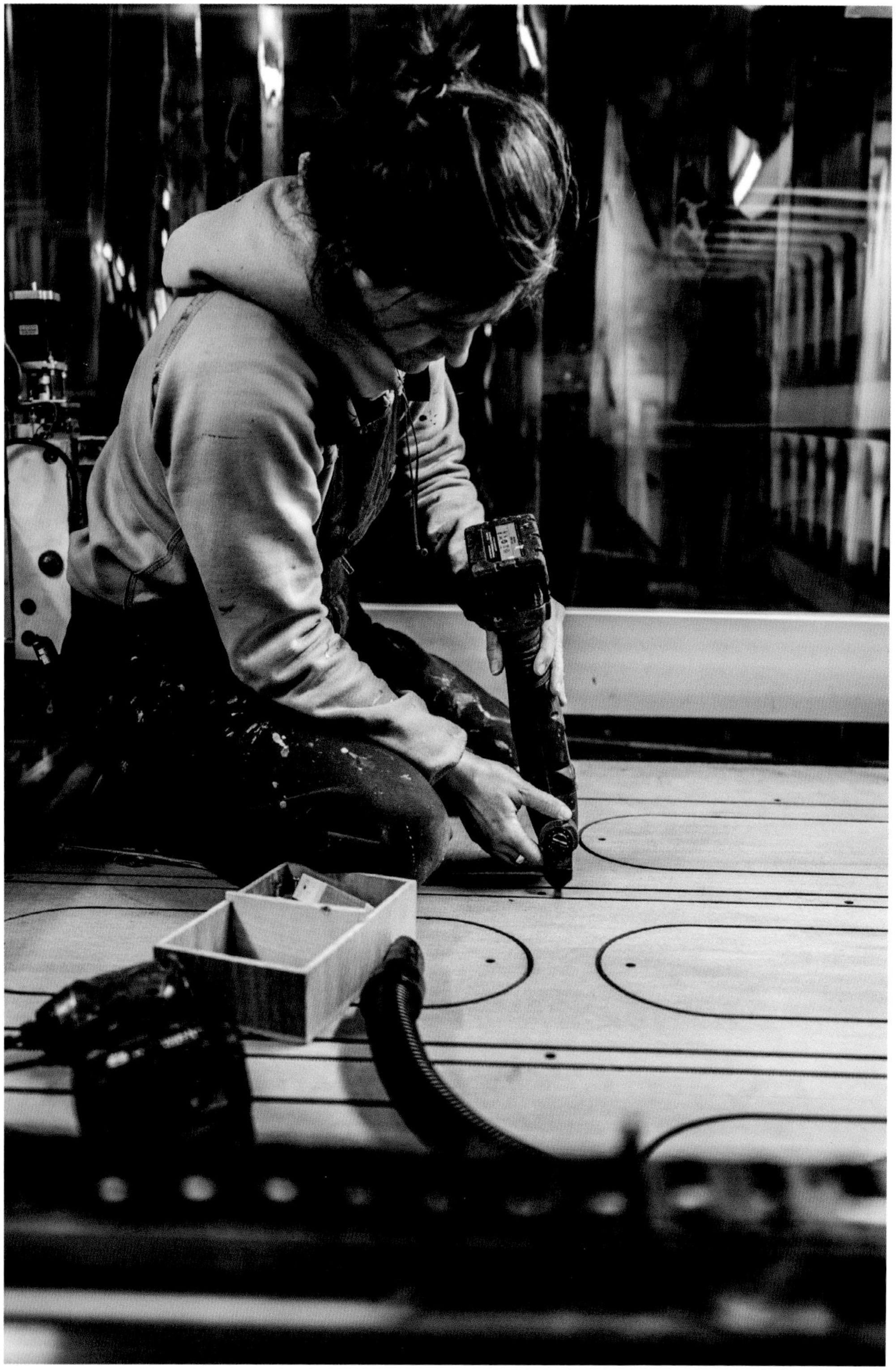

Creating by numbers

One of the converted shipping containers in South Dock Marina boatyard houses the bespoke woodworking and furniture design company Studio Shillito. Central to this husband-and-wife business is the CNC machine that enables the couple to digitally create any three-dimensional shape in wood imaginable, with both speed and incredible accuracy. Here, Rebecca is fulfilling an order for curved window frames to replace rotting ones on the 1960s superyacht *Maserati*. To have created all these by hand would have taken days of work but under Rebecca's guidance, digitised coordinates produce results in just a few hours.

Making the cut

To create the window frames for *Maserati*, Rebecca calibrates the CNC machine to the wood's exact thickness and then programmes it to make three cutting passes across each sheet. She enjoys working out how to get as many items as possible from one piece of wood, a particularly important skill when, as in this case, using specially treated and expensive marine plywood. Wastage is minimal.

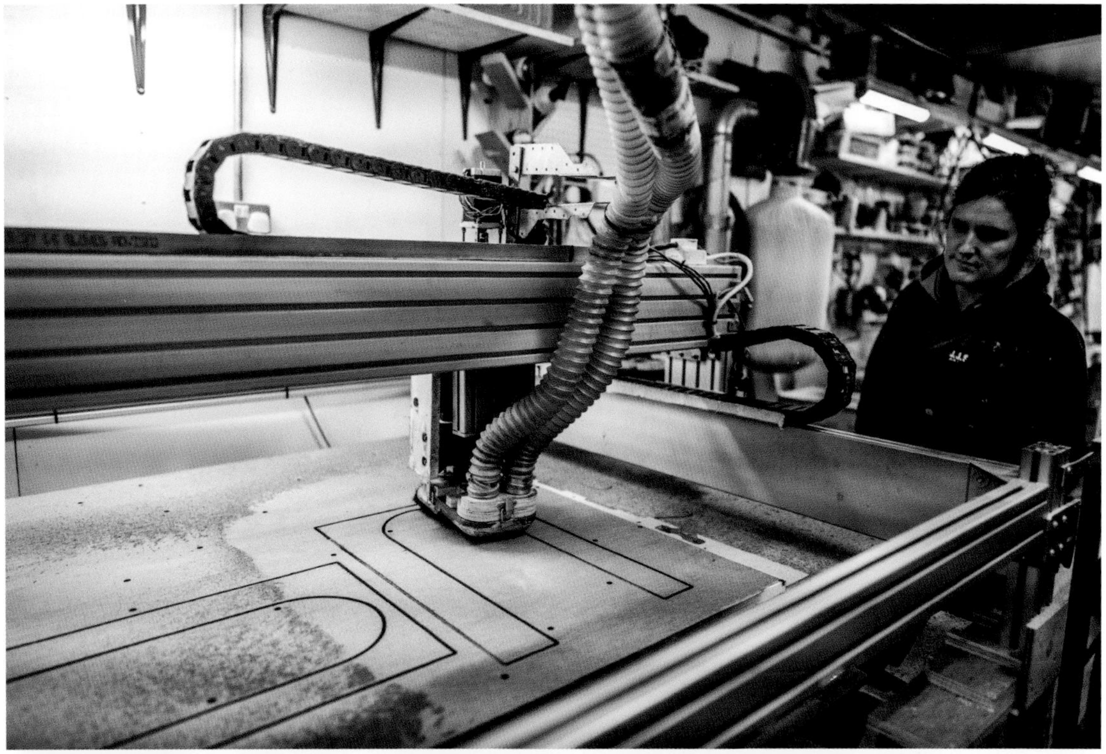

Getting physical

Once the computerised machine has done its work, it is then up to Rebecca to climb up and carefully cut all the holding tabs of wood that were needed to keep everything in place (see opposite). She can then finally lift the frames free, ready for delivery to the team working on *Maserati*.
www.studioshillito.com

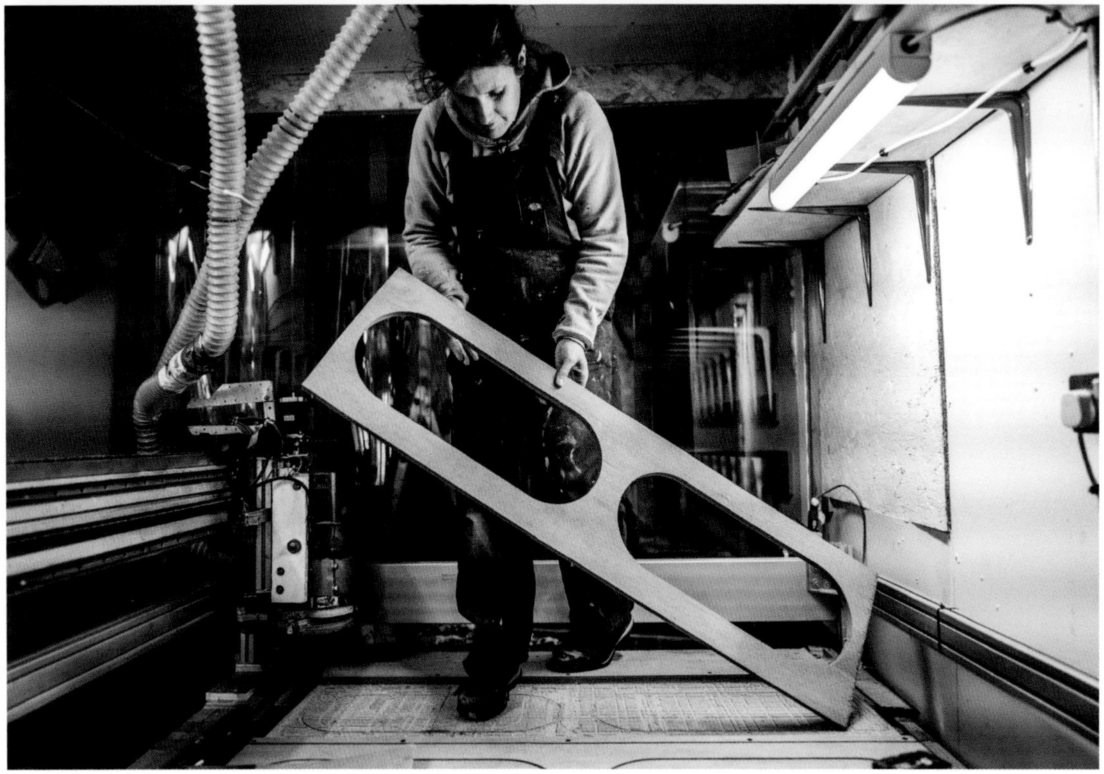

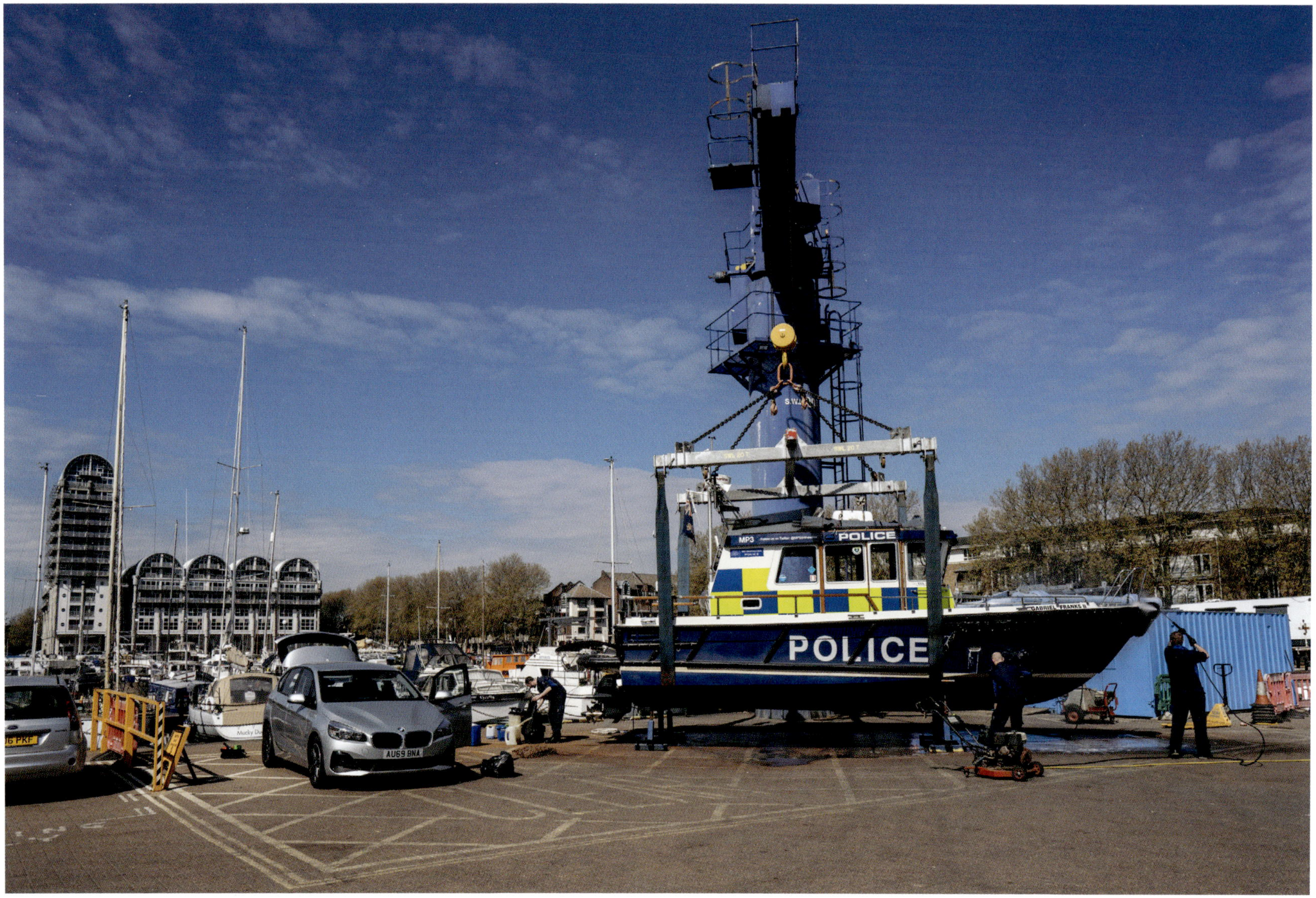

Police presence

A fast-response boat from the Marine Policing Unit (MPU) gets a quick clean at South Dock Marina before returning to the river. This needs to be done regularly, as any dirt or algae build-up on the hull can slow speeds considerably.

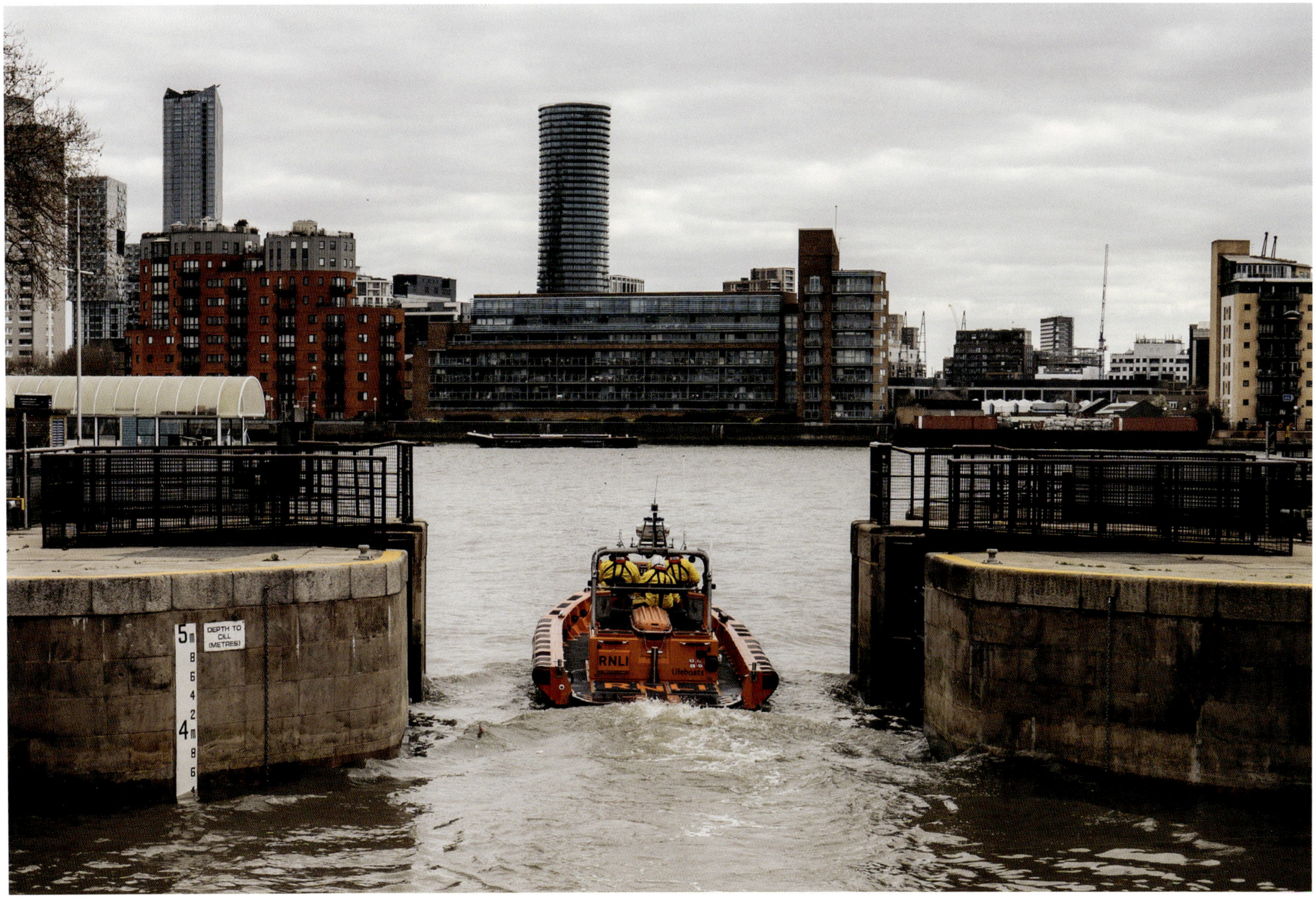

Keeping it clean

An E class lifeboat manned by the Royal National Lifeboat Institution (RNLI) exits on to the Thames through South Dock Marina lock, heading back to its base at Westminster's Tower Lifeboat Station, where a crew is on duty around the clock. It has also just had one of its regular pressure washes to maintain a clean hull. Fast, tough and manoeuvrable, this inshore lifeboat is specially designed to cope with the Thames' tidal currents, submerged debris and heavy traffic.

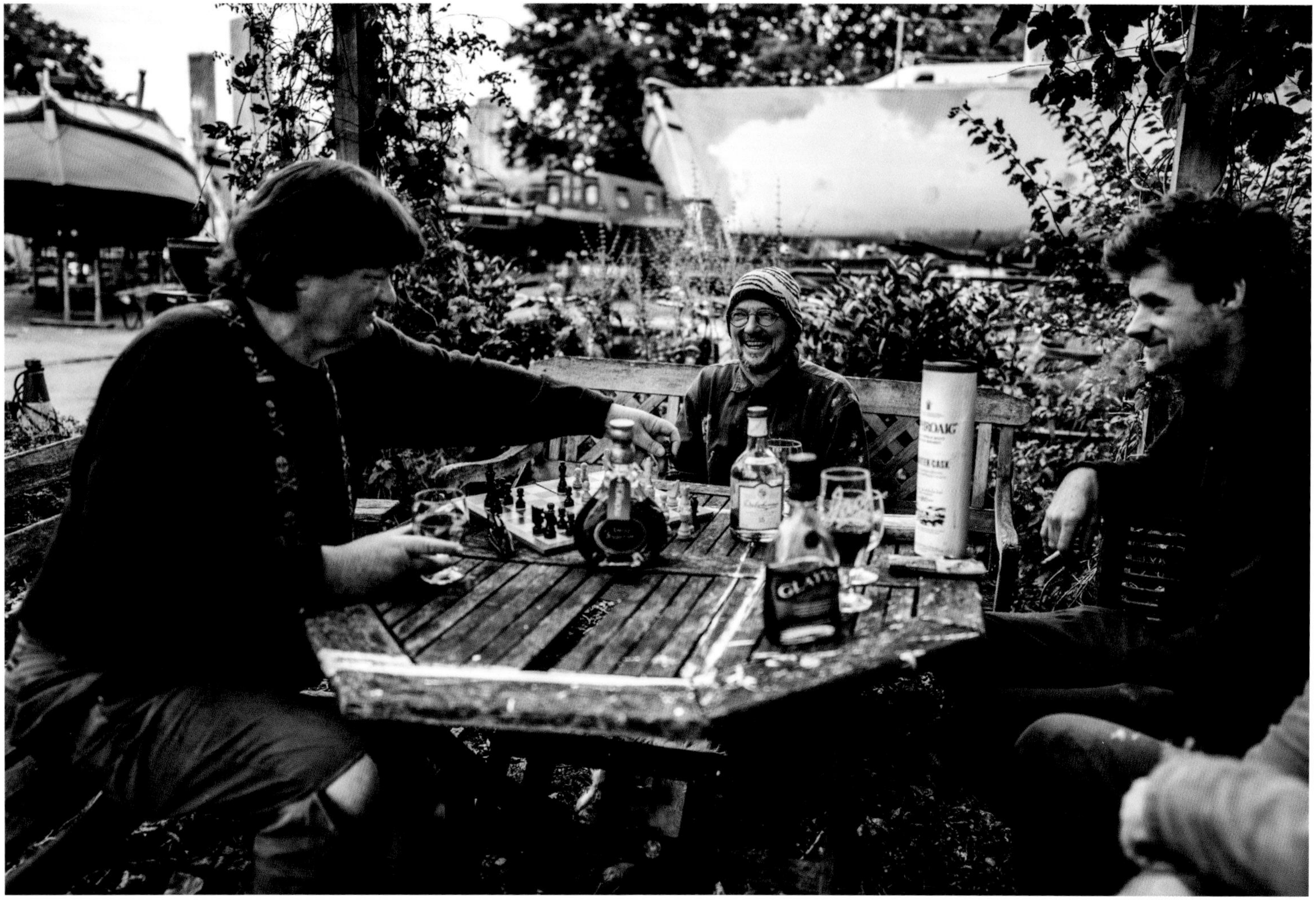

Community spirit

The barbecue at South Dock Marina boatyard is its social hub. At the end of the working day, the chess board comes out and people start to gather around to chat, eat, drink whisky and play. The exchange of practical boat tips, technical information and general gossip is the lifeblood of people who work and live in the marina. If anyone has a problem, there is usually someone available to provide an answer.

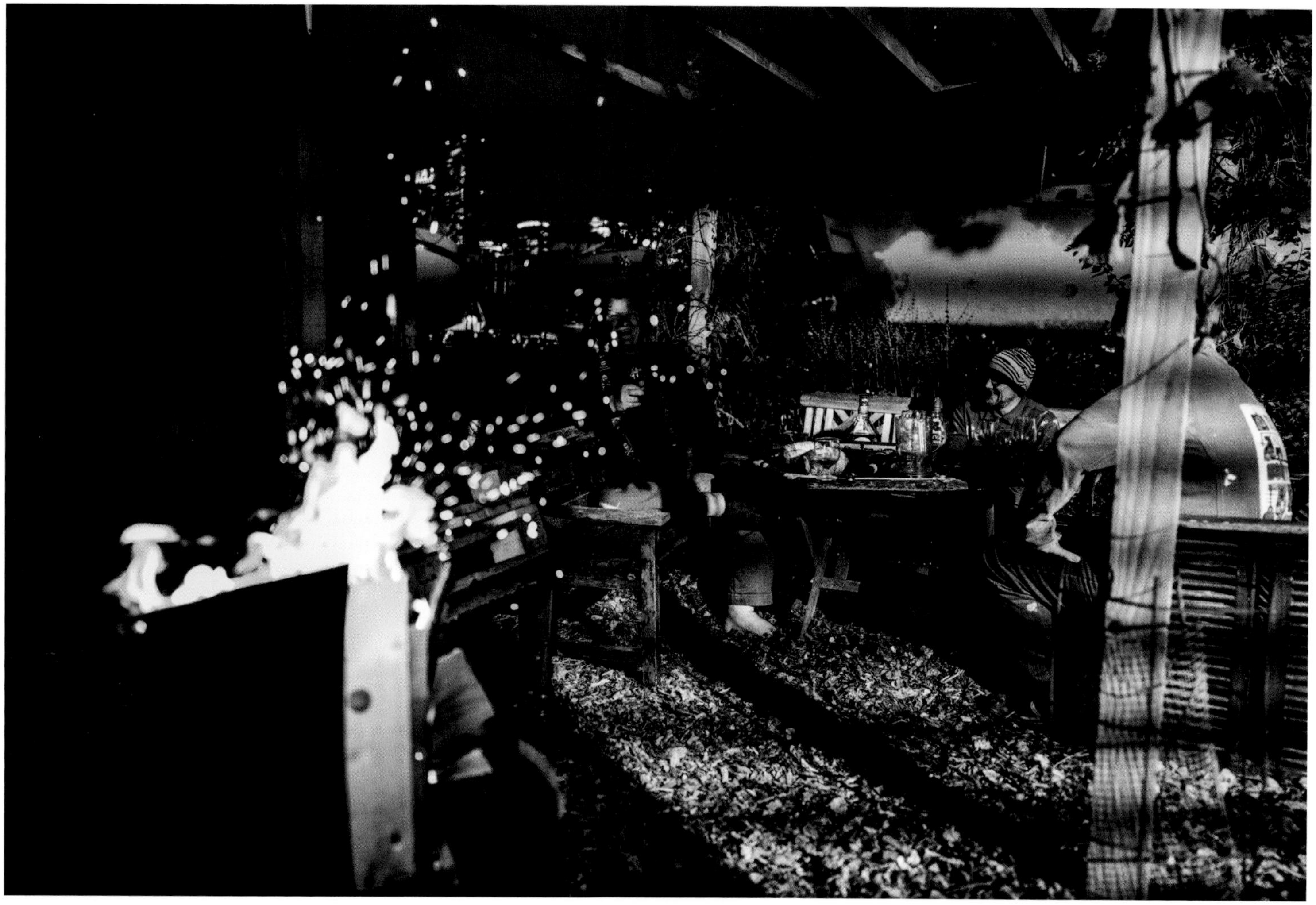

Social time

As the evening progresses, the fire is used for a barbecue and the party atmosphere grows. Boat hulls can still just be seen in the background but repairs and all things work-related can wait for another day.

Skill sets

Any boat owner knows the continual battle against the decaying effects of water but it's doubly so for those with liveaboards who have to deploy a wide range of expertise.

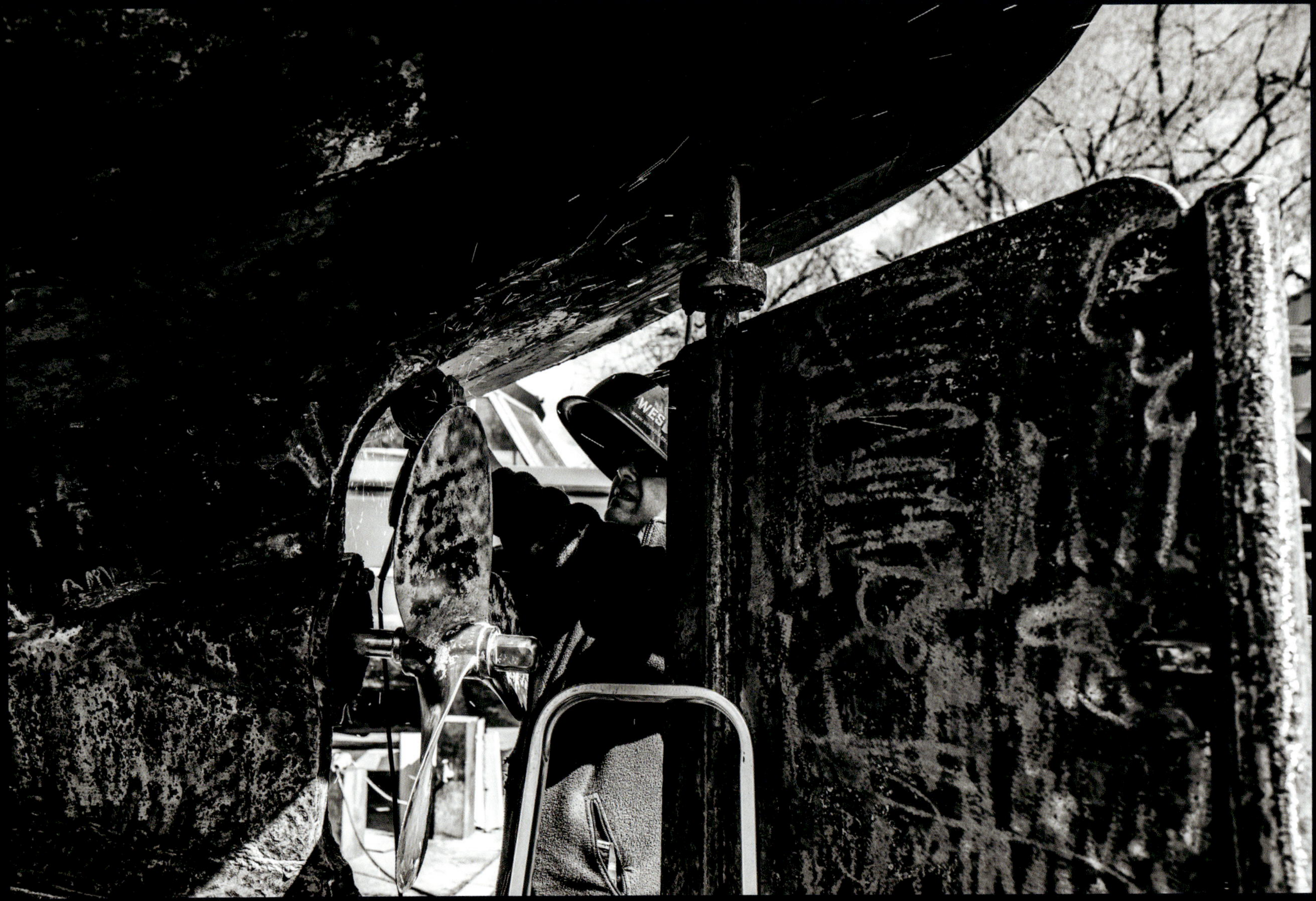

Sub-aqua engineering

Mike is used to having to don his diving gear and extend his engineering skills below the waterline. Here he is securing bolts for *Arcadia*'s new extension bracket on to her underwater concrete base. Protection rules for such work are strictly observed, with another safety diver in the water, just out of shot, in case of any problems.

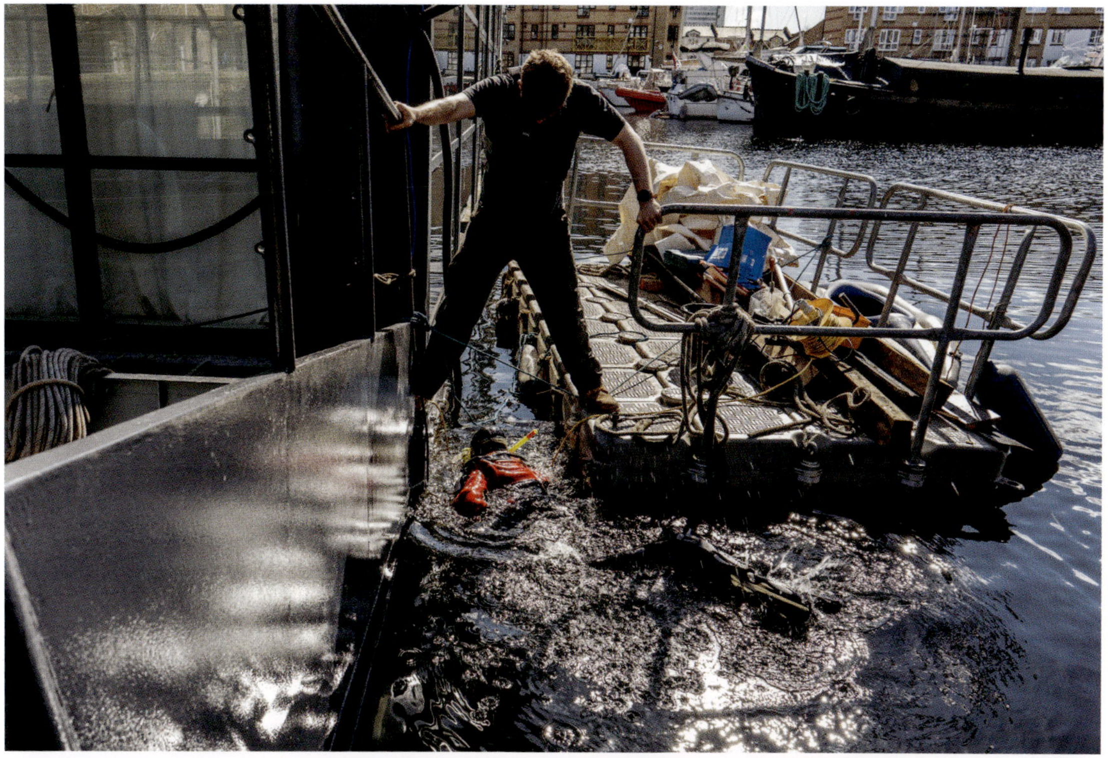

Tight corners

Fine-tuning boat engines often requires contortionist skills within challengingly limited space. Brenden's slim, youthful frame, as well as his skills as a mechanic, give him a definite advantage. He's been working on the Thames in some capacity since his early teens and there is little that he doesn't know about boats and the ways of the river.
www.osheasmarineservices.com

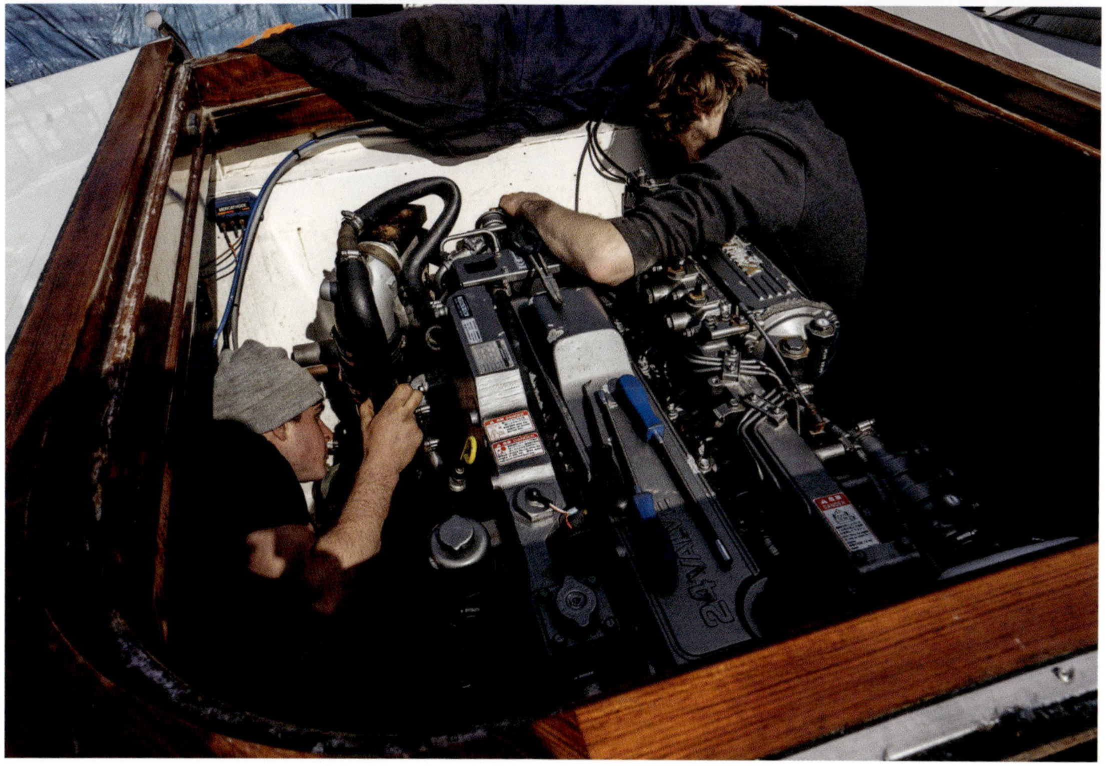

Boats galore

‹ A steady stream of boats needing repair comes through South Dock Marina boatyard every year, including those with emergency leaks requiring immediate attention. Mike's metalwork skills are much in demand. In this case, he's having to sort out problems caused by layers of previous repairs around the propellor shaft of an old Dutch barge. Water has got inside and is now mixing with his welding material to create an unhelpful pumice layer. As ever, Mike finds a solution.

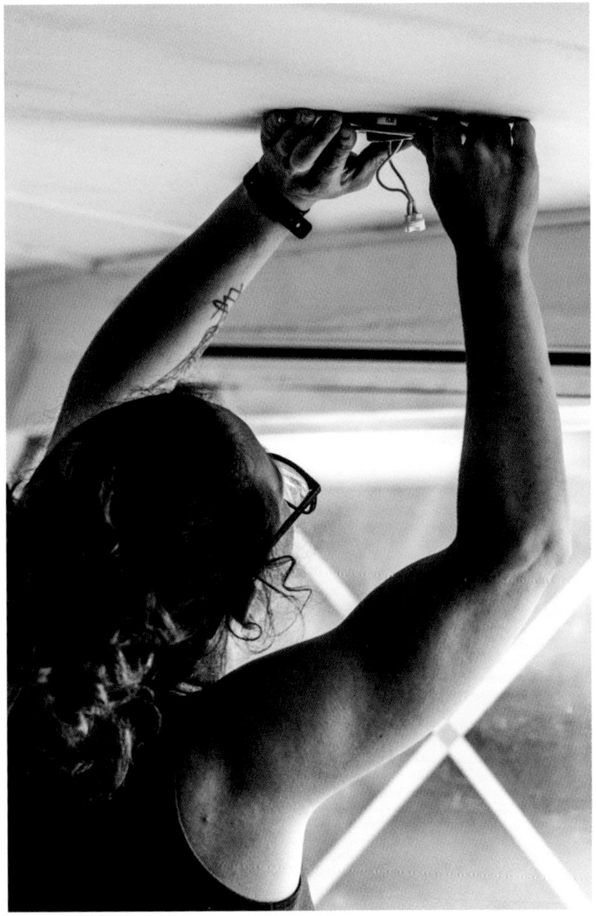

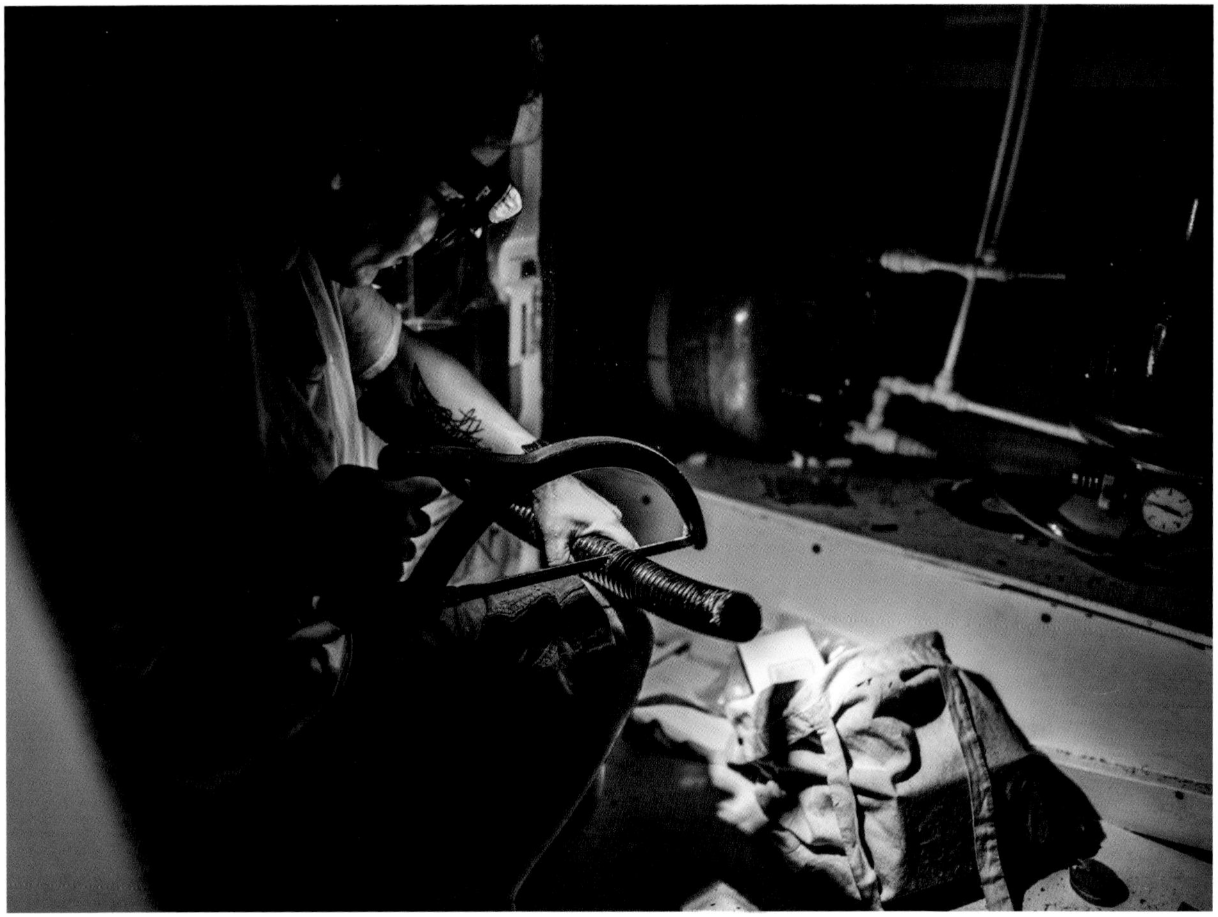

Bilge work

Specialising in both marine electrics and plumbing, Jay has a workshop in South Dock Marina boatyard and is called upon to work all over London's dock and canal network. She's equally expert at wiring up or installing pipework to meet the particular needs of boat dwellers, having discovered this niche several years ago while living on a friend's boat and realising the high demand for providing neat solutions to fit tight onboard spaces.

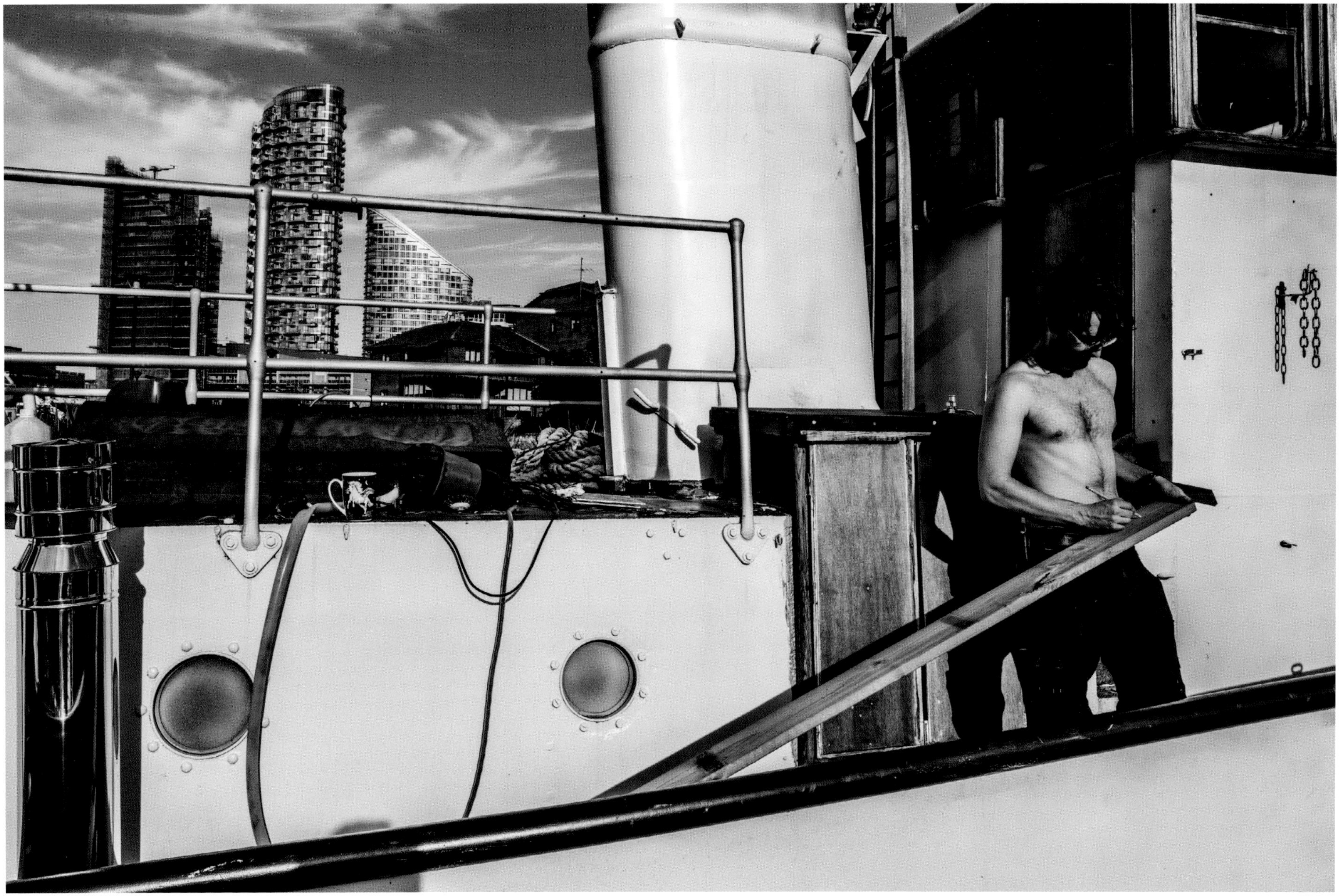

Stripping back

In Blackwall Basin on the Isle of Dogs, Inigo is completely renovating *Adie*, an early 20th-century tug, readying her for resale as a liveaboard. This has already involved stripping back her hull and deck to the metal, spending 1,000 hours grinding it all clean and then painting. Now Inigo is installing new bespoke decks, with expertise built up since he was a philosophy student at Oxford and had to create a cheap place to live on a wrecked boat. He became hooked on this practical contrast to academia and loves the holistic necessity of mastering all the skills needed to rebuild boats.

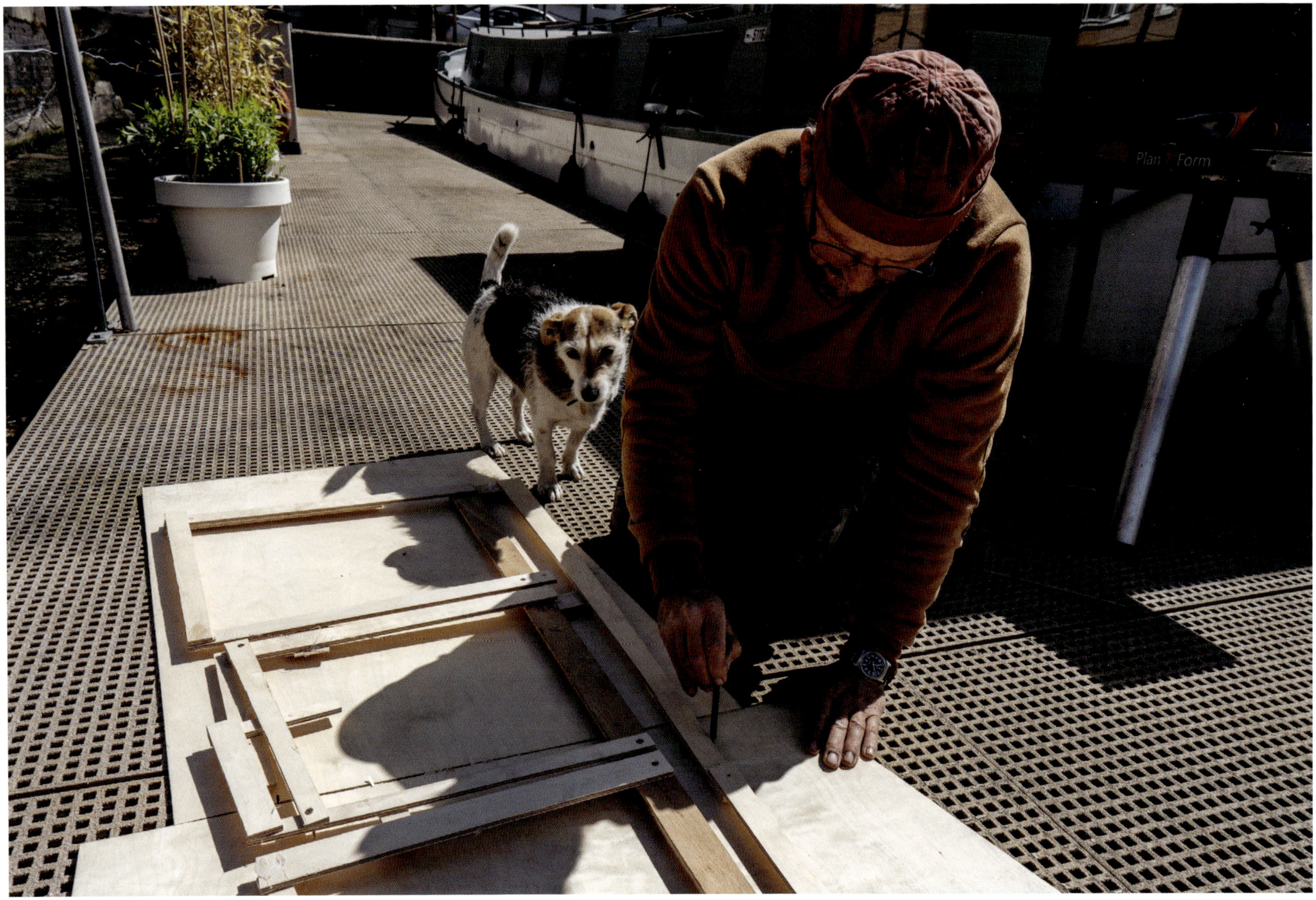

A watchful eye

As a marine carpenter, Nick has found a constant demand for his specialist work from boat owners in South Dock Marina since 1989. Here he is using templates that he's created to cut tailored pieces of birchwood to line a Dutch barge's small utility space with tricky curves. As usual, Tilly is on hand to monitor her master's work.

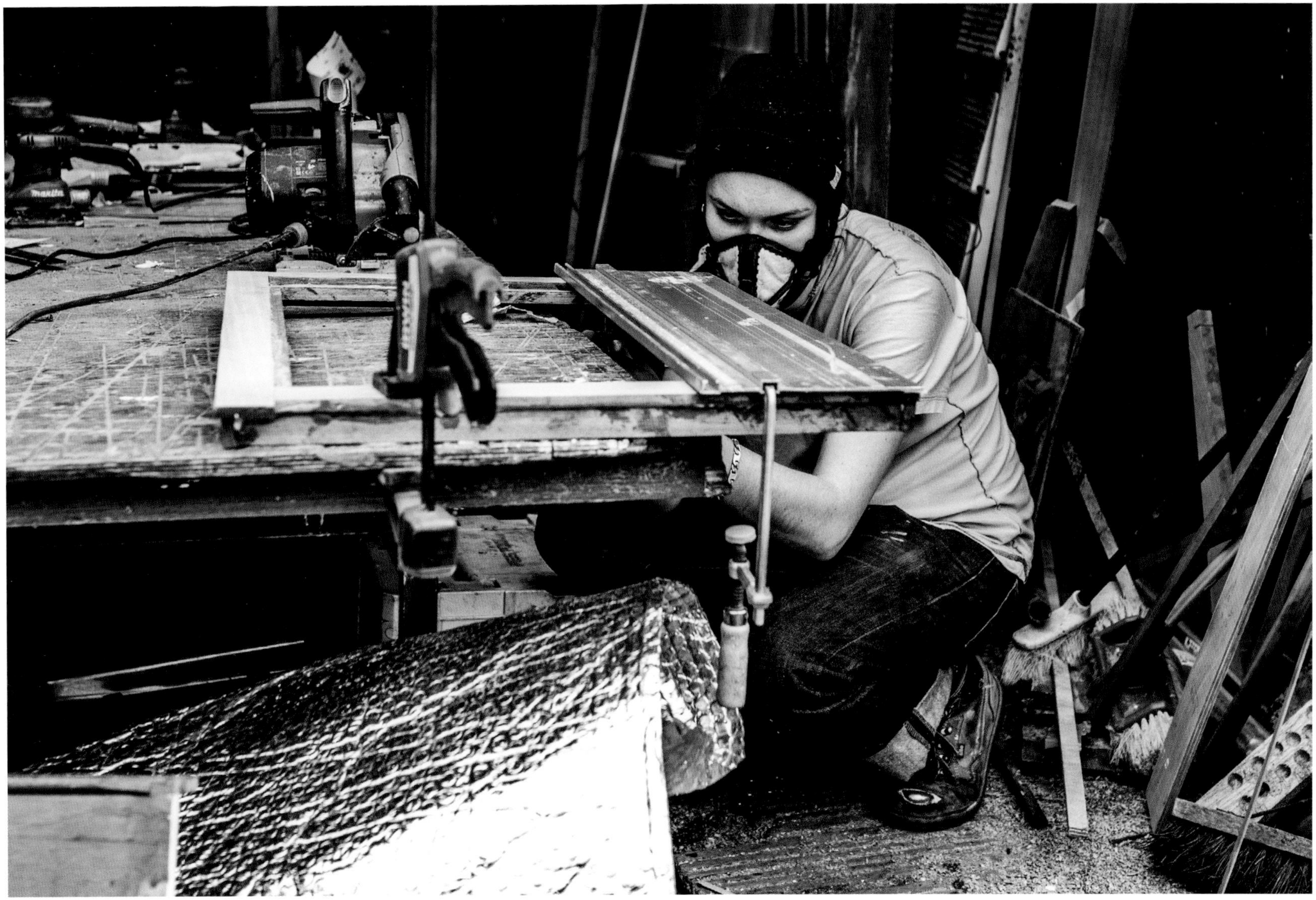

Transferable skills

Frances is working as an apprentice for Nick at his converted shipping container workshop in South Dock Marina boatyard. Still in her early 20s, she has already qualified in general woodworking but is now keen to learn the complicated specifics of marine carpentry, where there are very few straight lines and using a spirit level to fit items like this window frame on a bobbing boat would be a waste of time.

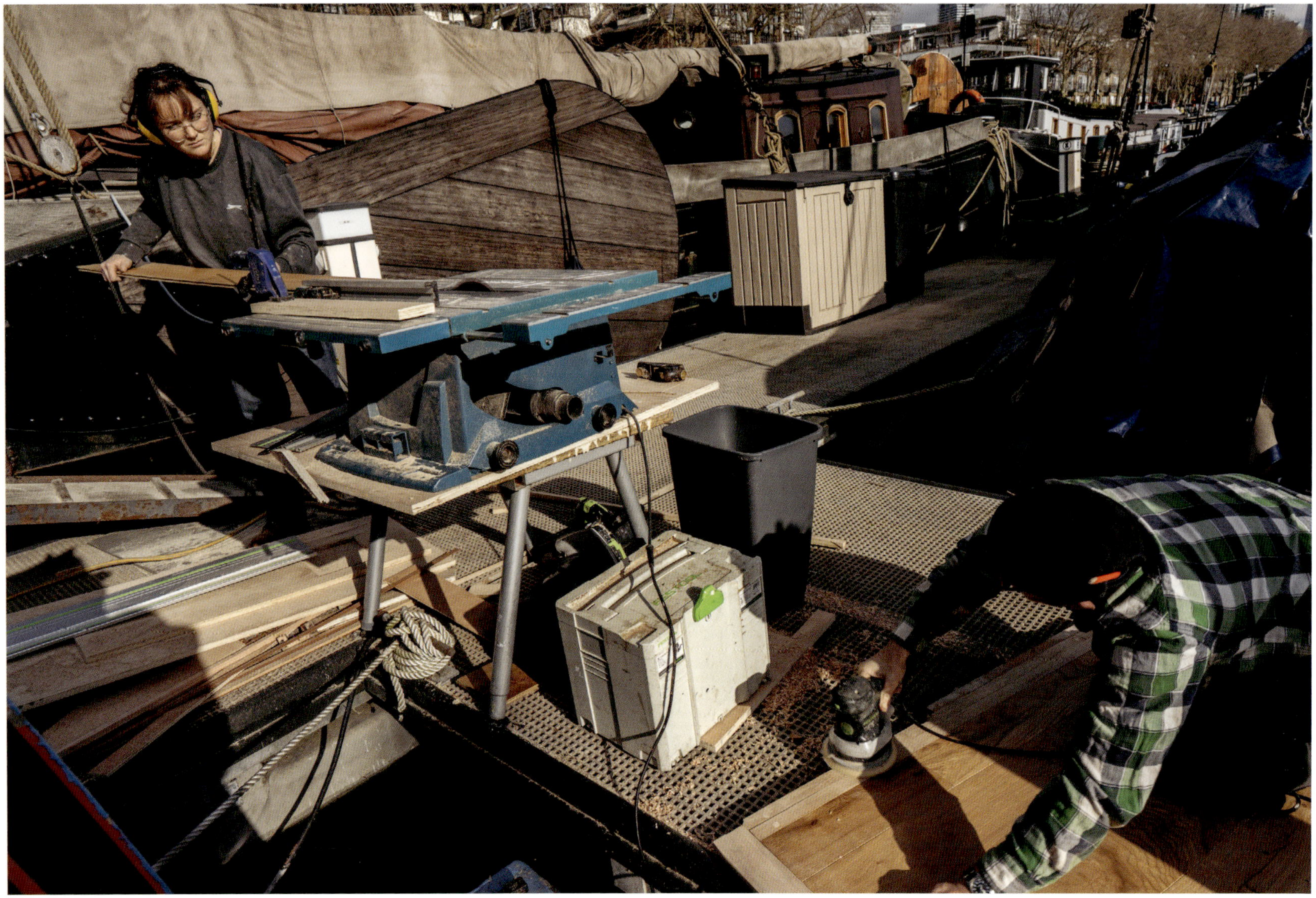

Boat-shaped jigsaw puzzle

Out in the marina, Frances and Nick prepare to lay a new wood floor inside a 'closed'-type ship's lifeboat. Now a liveaboard, just large enough for one person, this is by no means straightforward, as the boat's fibreglass construction was originally designed to be curved for maximum buoyancy, so every piece of wood must be cut to fit exactly. Bespoke hatches also have to be incorporated to allow access to the bilges underneath that house the engine, plumbing and electrics.

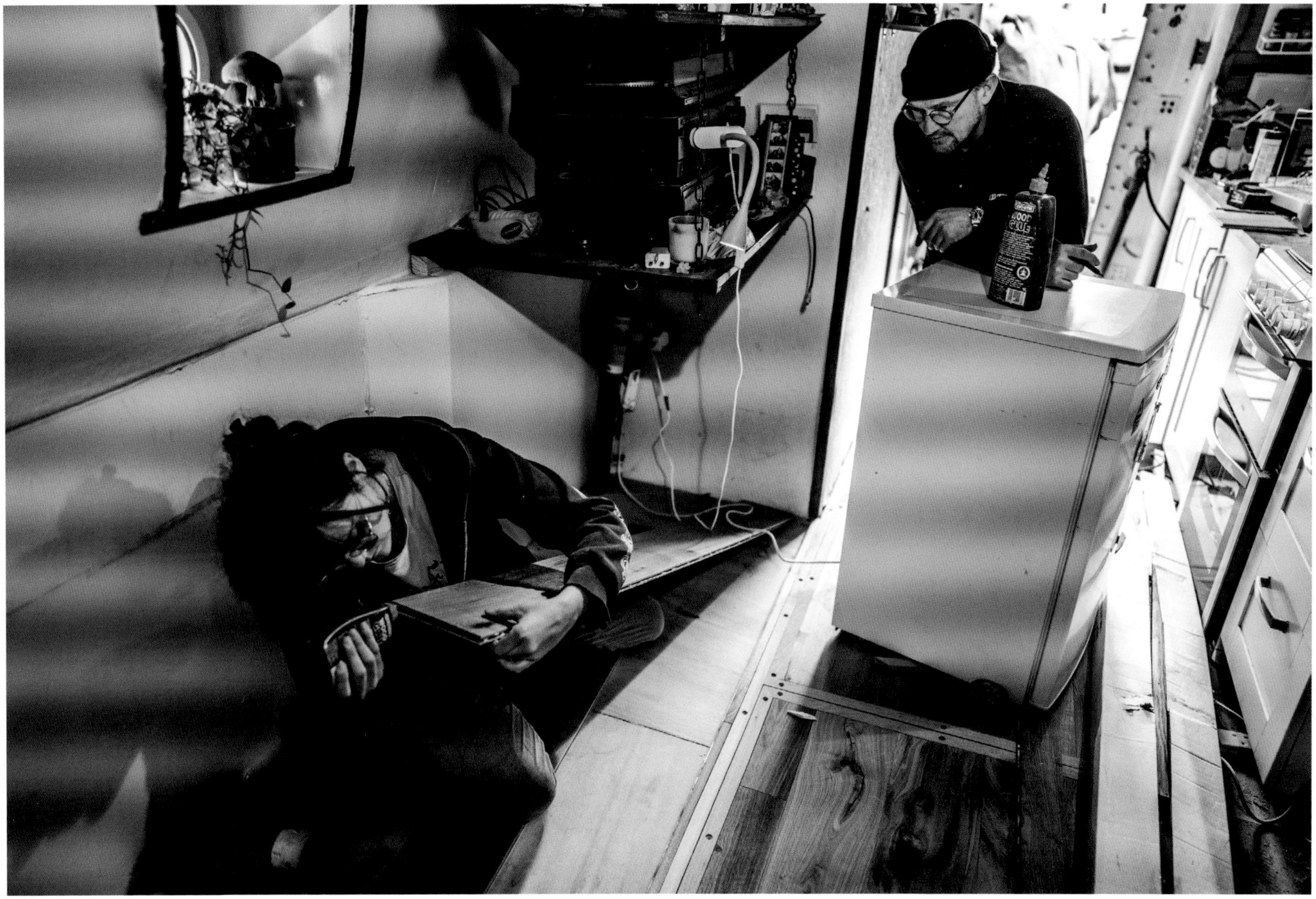

Learning curve

Inside the lifeboat's unusually shaped interior, Nick guides Frances in fitting each plank into its allotted place. By the time they've finished, the owner will have a beautiful hardwood floor, robust enough to stand the test of time. It's a real lesson in careful planning and craftsmanship.

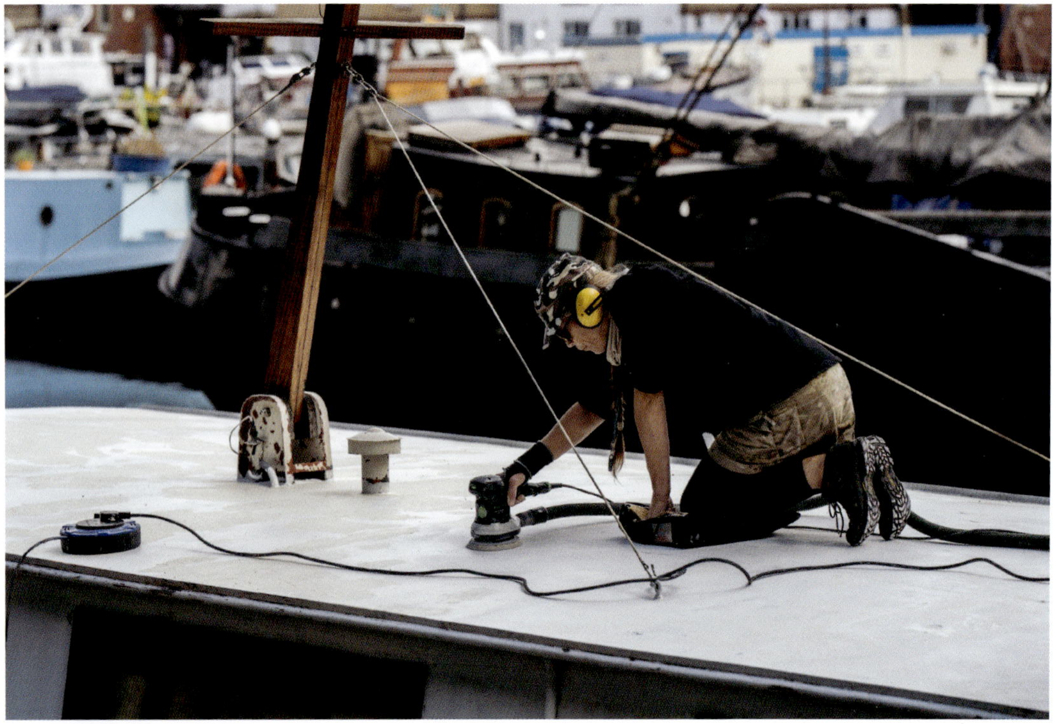

Smooth operator

Good paintwork is a boat's first line of defence against the ill effects of wind and water, and an electric sander is the essential tool for getting rid of old paint and then achieving the best results with a light sanding in between coats. Nina is a dab hand with the sander and as a long-time assistant to marine carpenter, Nick, can often be seen creating fine finishes in South Dock Marina, wearing her trademark khaki and headphones.

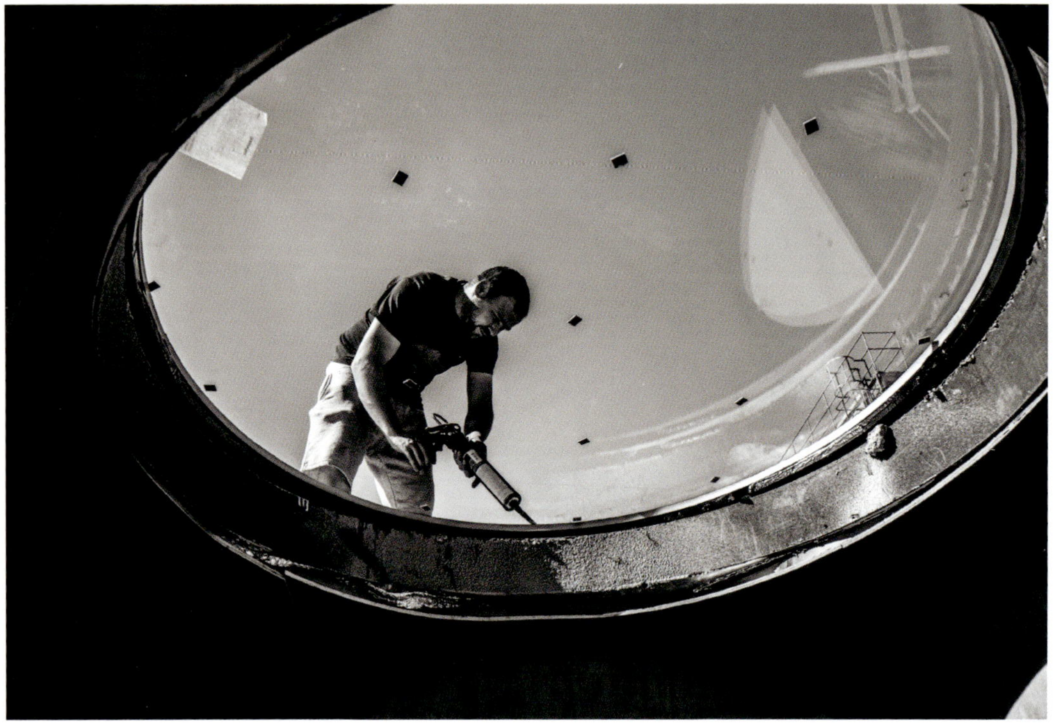

Watertight

Surrounded by water and open to the elements all year round, boats in the marinas need to have every possible nook and cranny thoroughly sealed. After the installation of a large skylight like this, a particularly careful application of an ultra-waterproof marine sealant is needed to make sure that the connection between window frame and steel roof won't leak.

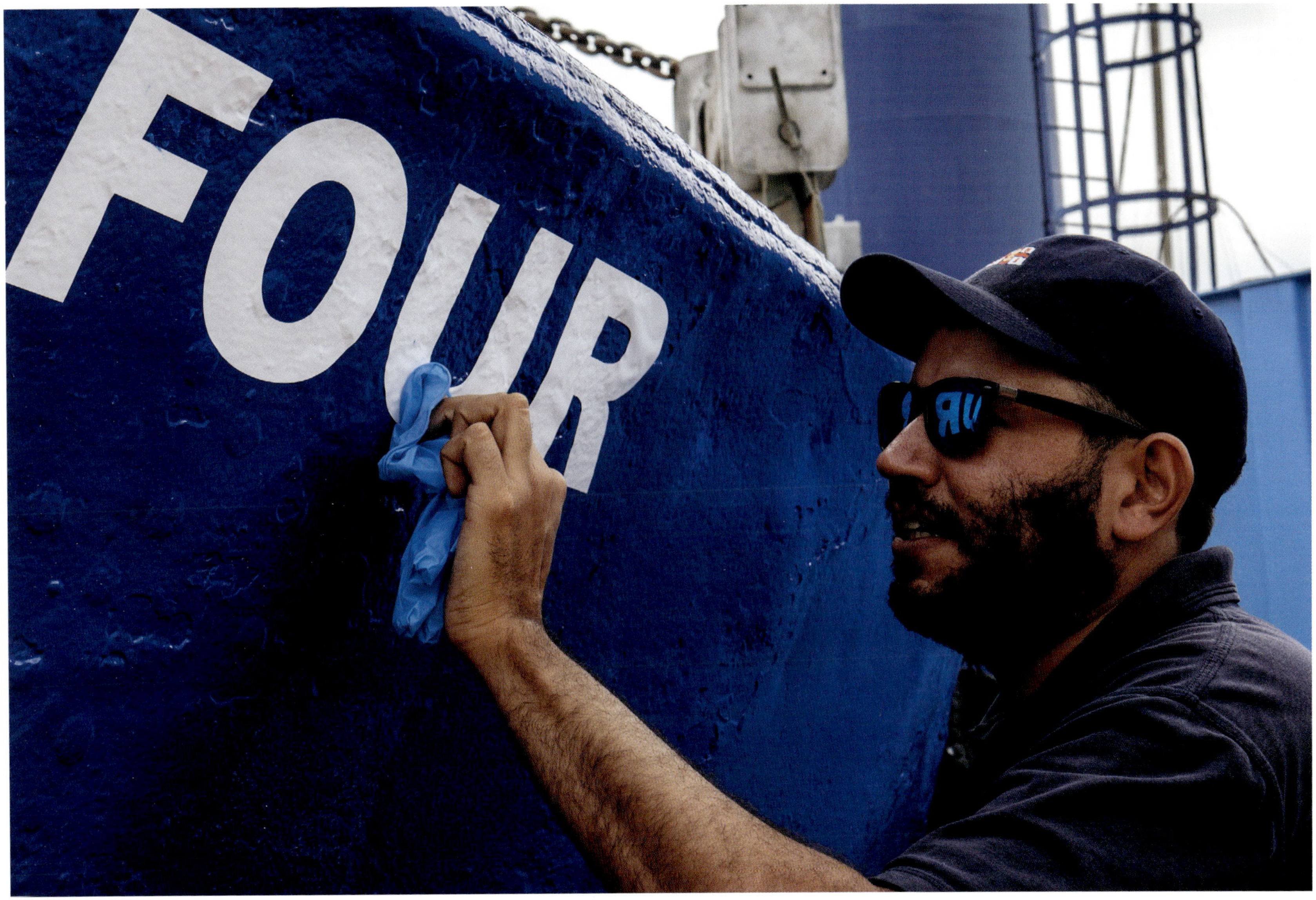

Signing up

Physically naming a boat is an important finishing touch and Simon's custom-made vinyl decals are a popular option. Robust and offering an almost infinite choice of lettering style, his wording handiwork can be seen throughout South Dock Marina and beyond. The wearing of cool sunglasses is always part of the deal.

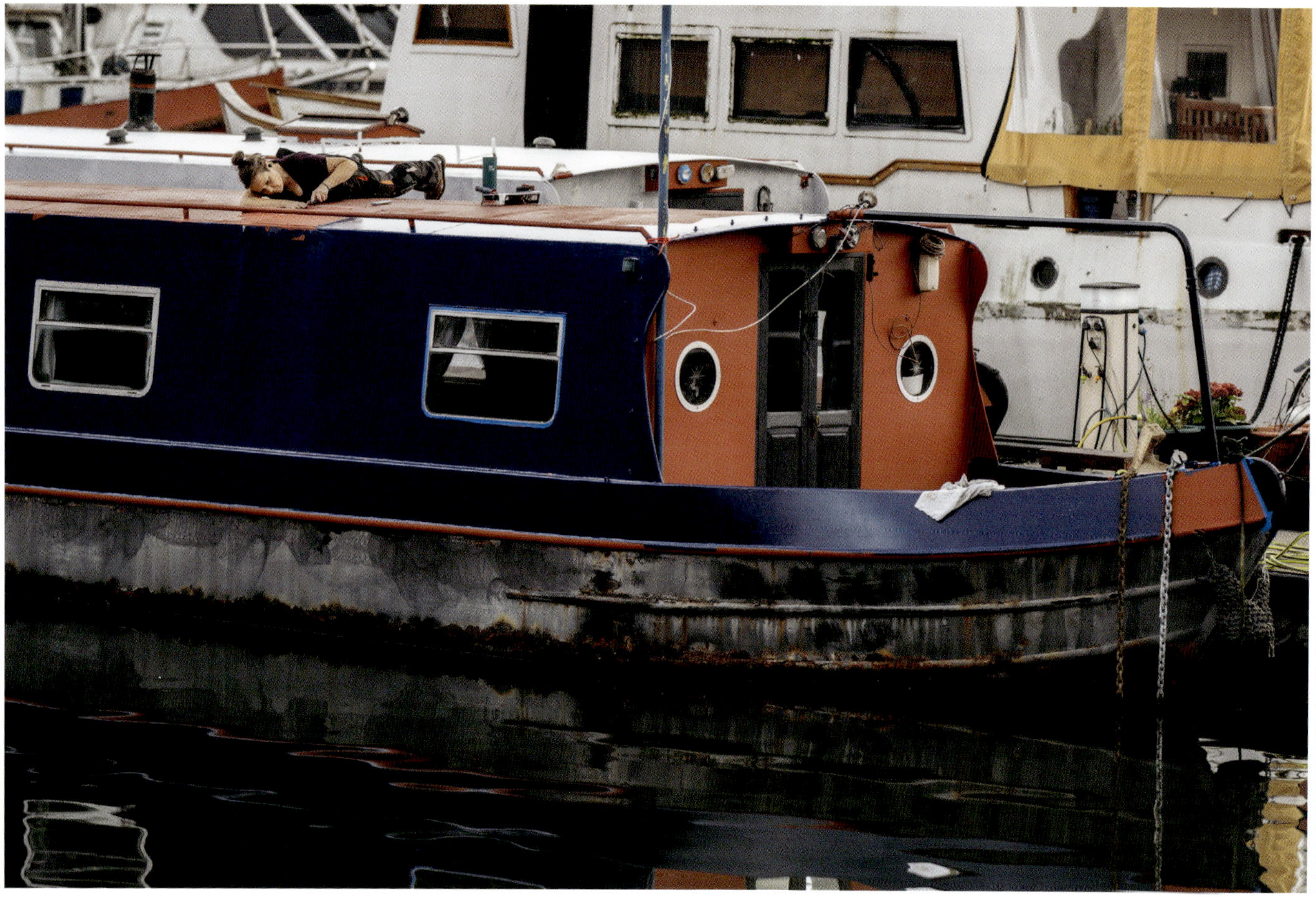

Colourful transformation

James' narrowboat isn't scheduled to come out of the water for its five-year survey but he's keen to smarten her up above the waterline and has hired Fizz to do a facelift at his mooring in the middle of South Dock Marina. Eagle-eyed and very methodical, she has soon located and is repairing any and every rust hole with special body filler. Then, with characteristic agility, she completes a thorough paint job.

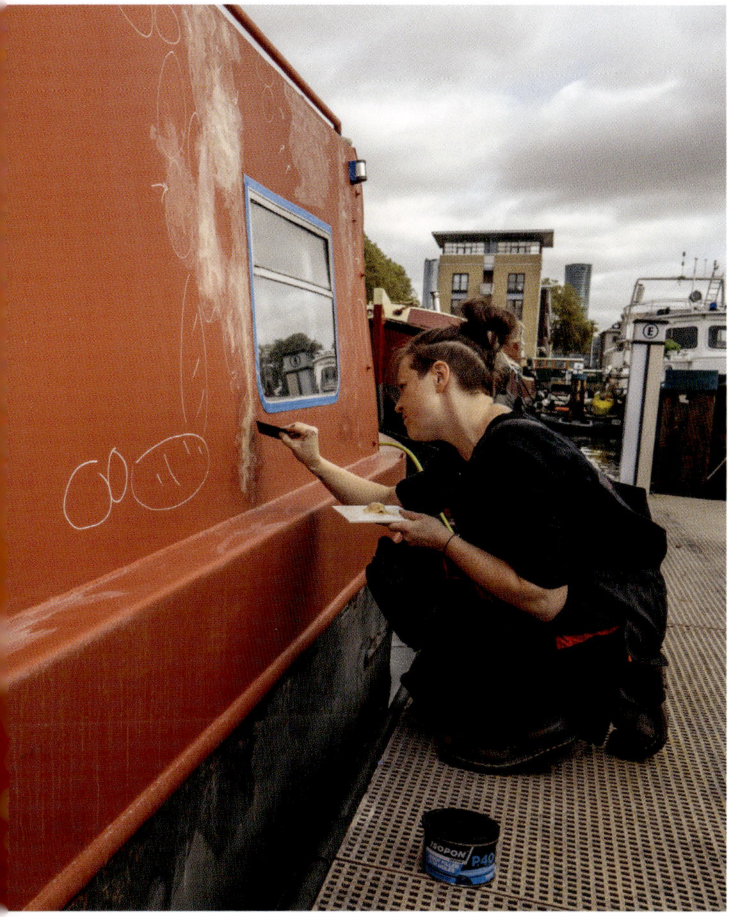

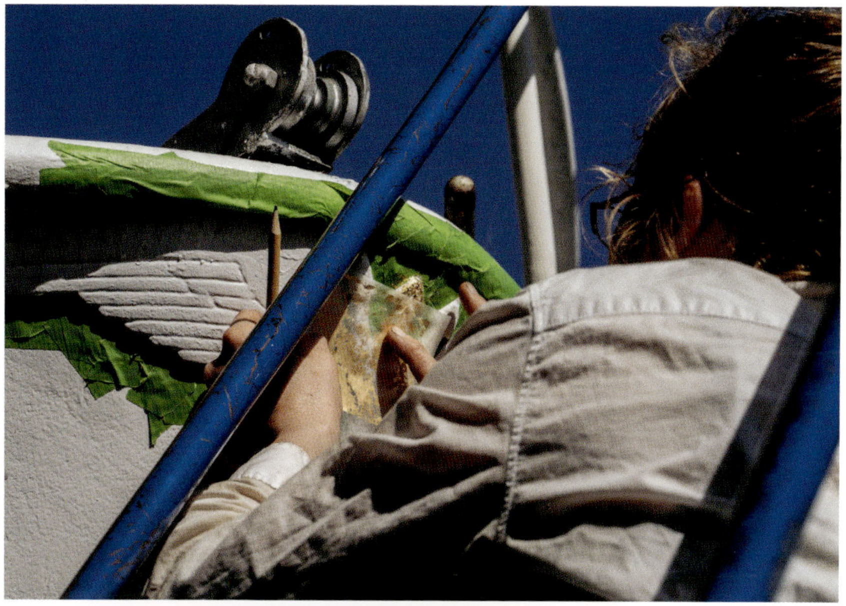

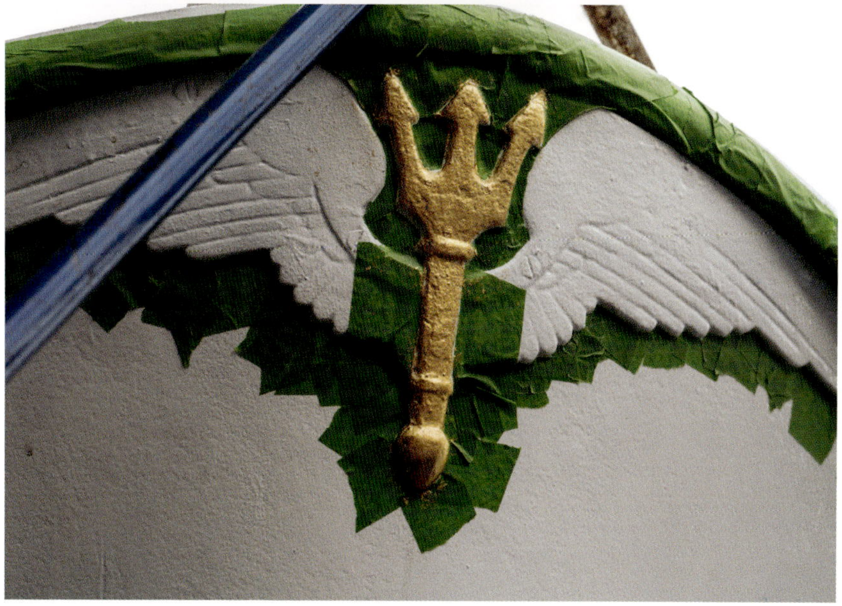

Golden touch

Before she completes the refurbishment of her boat *Ramesses II* in the boatyard, artist Charlie has decided how to highlight the trident feature on the bow. Her skill in applying five coats of gold leaf pays off. Now she can remove the masking tape and paint the hull a rich blue colour to set it off beautifully.

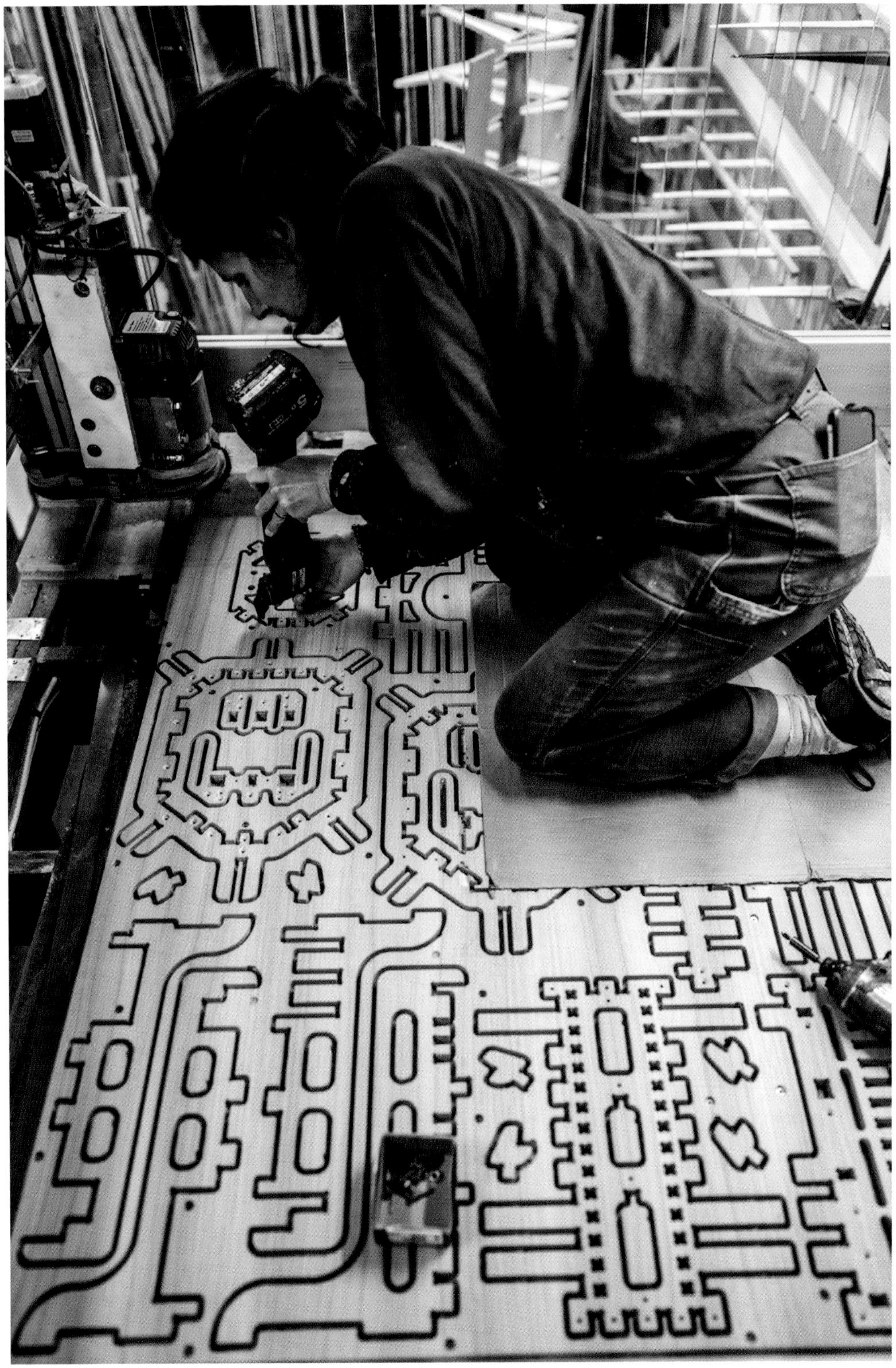

Creating a pattern

Every inch in the close confines of a boat's interior counts, so furniture has to be carefully thought through. Even better if it can be specially designed. Commissioned to create a multipurpose table, Rebecca has programmed the CNC machine in her Studio Shillito boatyard workshop to cut out over 50 separate pieces of birch plywood to a blueprint created by her architectural designer husband, Simon.

Signature style

This may be highly sophisticated digital fabrication but traditional techniques kick in when it comes to putting it all together. Rebecca favours mechanical joining to glues, as this means there aren't any toxic fumes to worry about and the product is not only robust but can easily be disassembled for transportation or repair. It's a unique blend of computer-savvy and eco-friendly practicality.

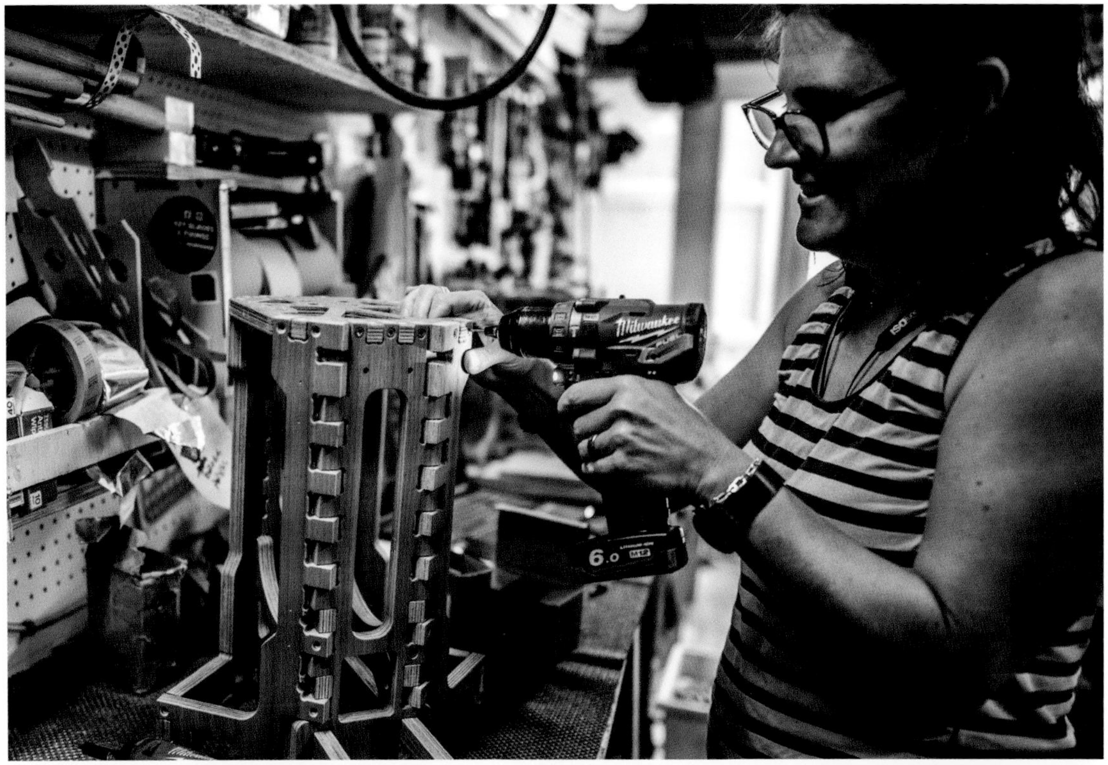

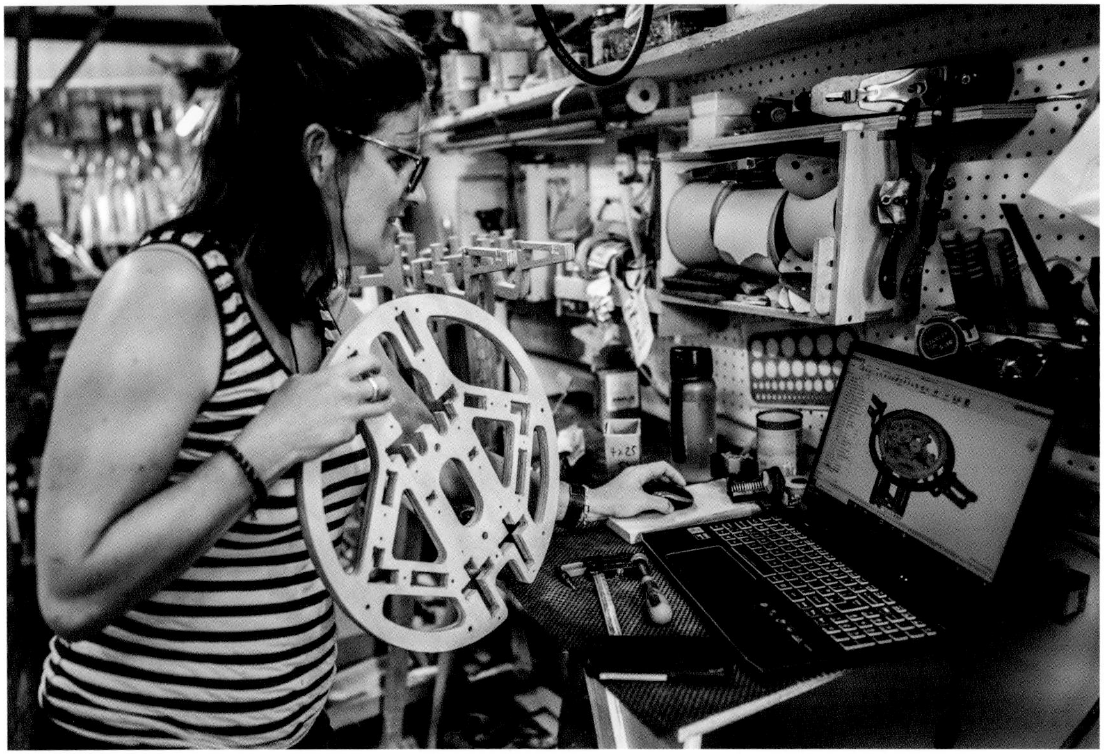

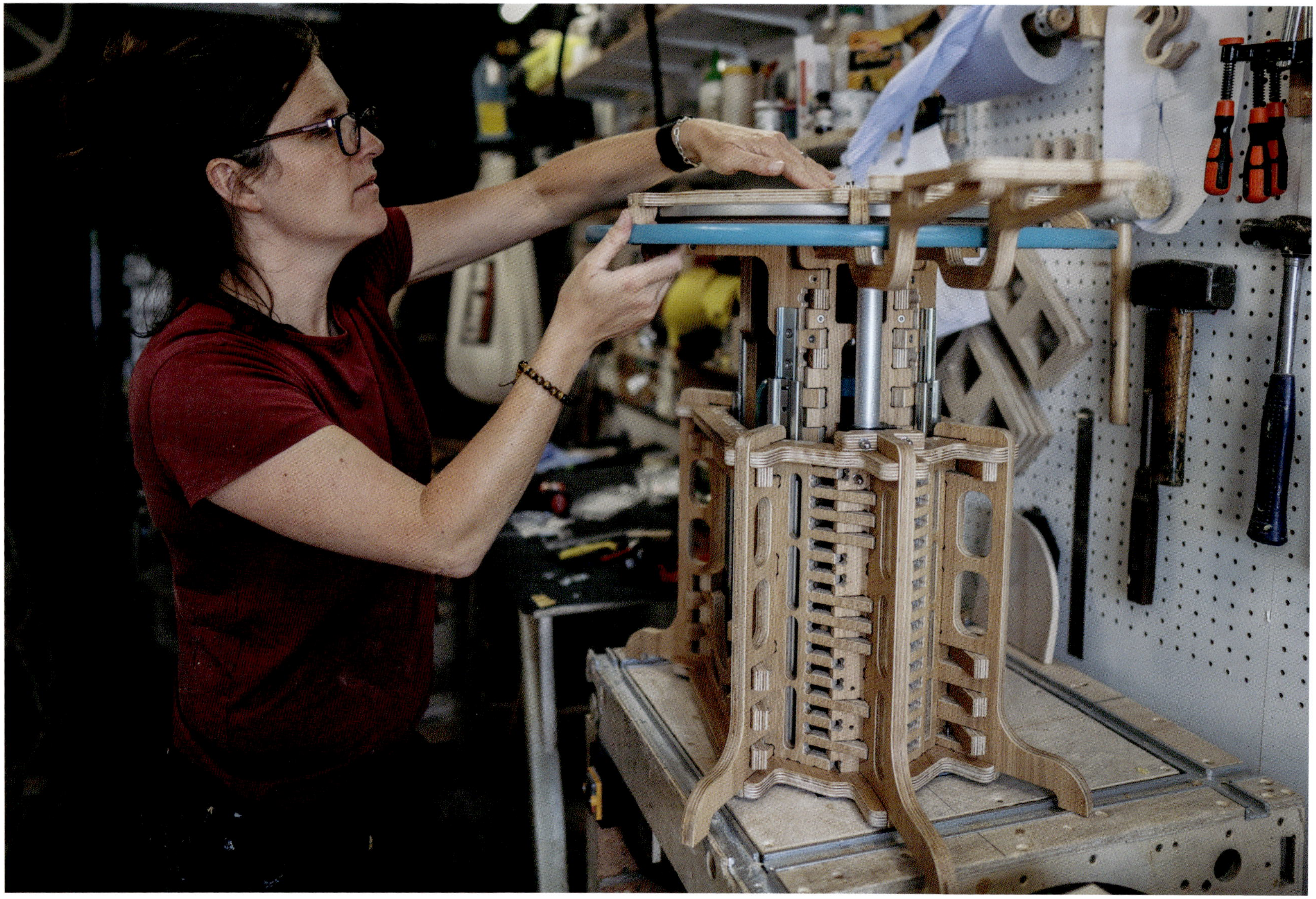

Fun, form and function

The table's practical use is to provide an adjustable surface: it is designed to achieve this through an ingenious series of different-sized interlocking wooden cogs that alter its height. But Rebecca and Simon also like to give their bespoke products a distinctive sense of playful beauty, often adding a 'pop' of colour, hand-finishing with good old-fashioned liquid-applied paint.

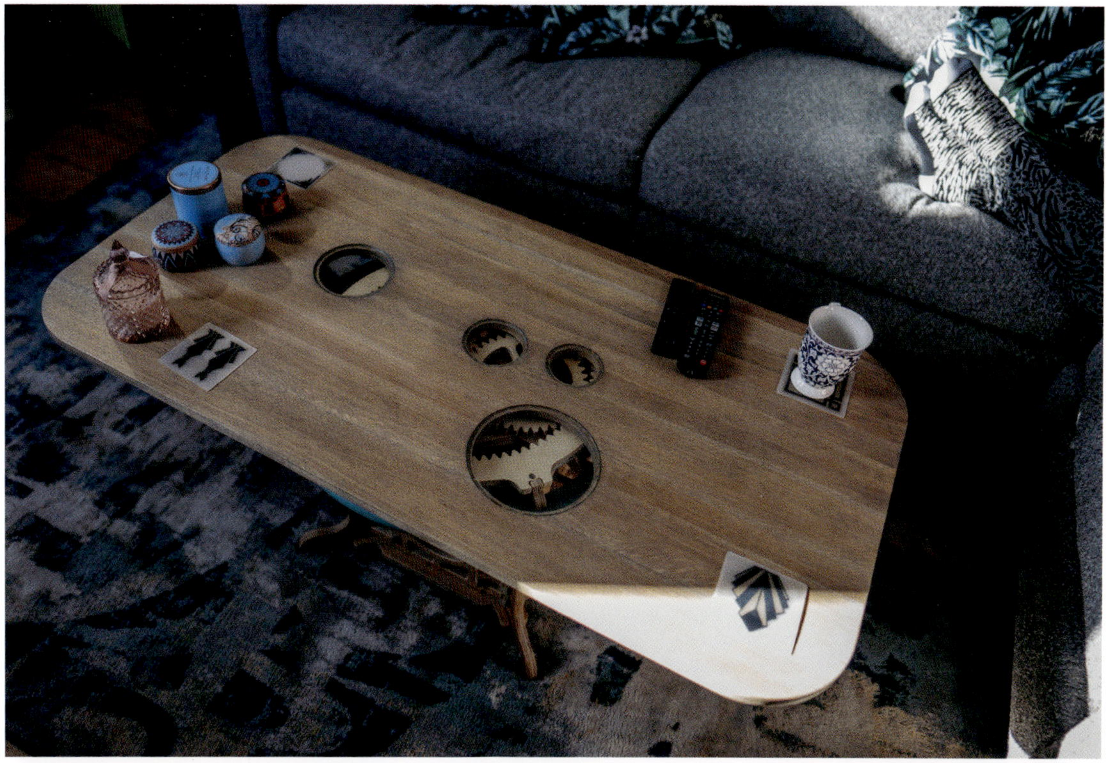

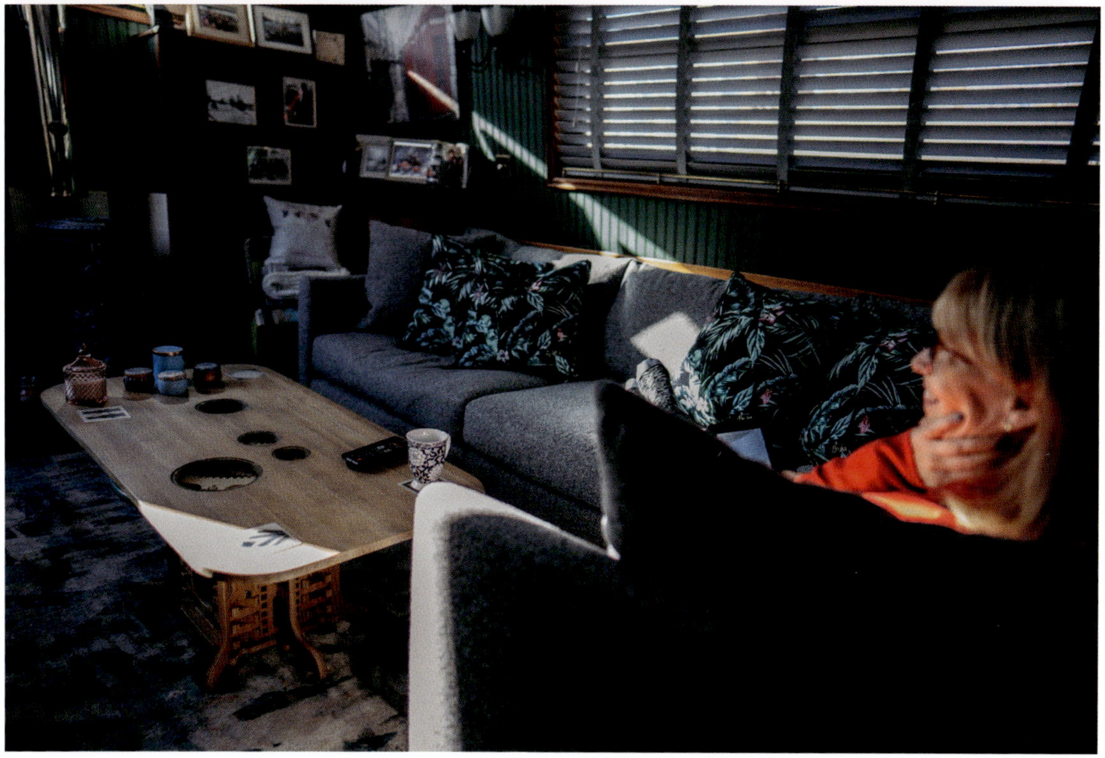

One satisfied boat owner

Finally in situ, the table now graces Julie's beautiful Dutch barge in Greenland Dock. She is thrilled, as, with limited space, it can easily be adjusted to different heights and is also a beautiful, unique piece of design. When Julie has guests for dinner and needs to raise it from being a sofa table to a higher dining surface, all she has to do is turn one wheel.

Restoring past glories

Fine craftsmanship transforms
two beautiful but neglected classics.

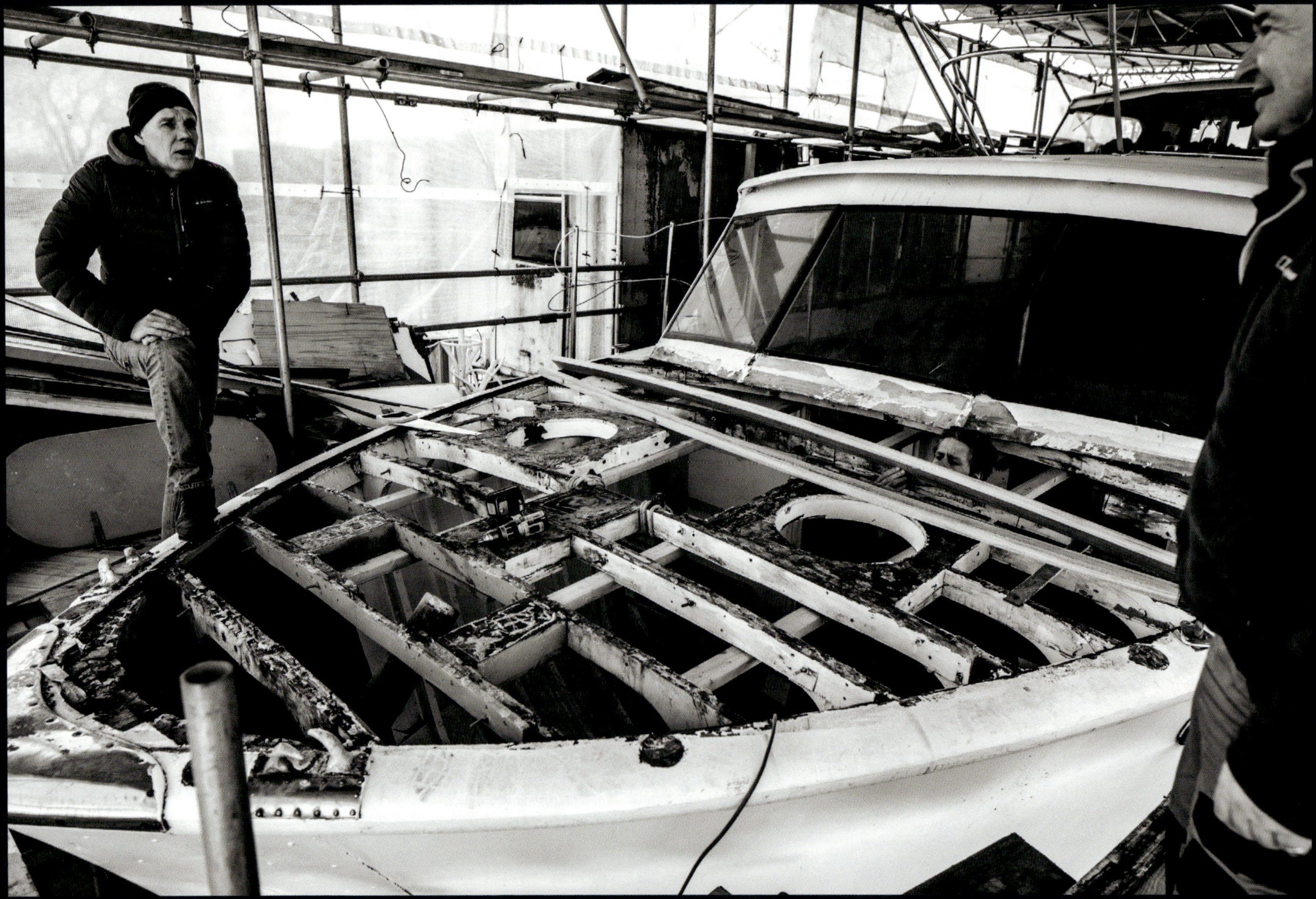

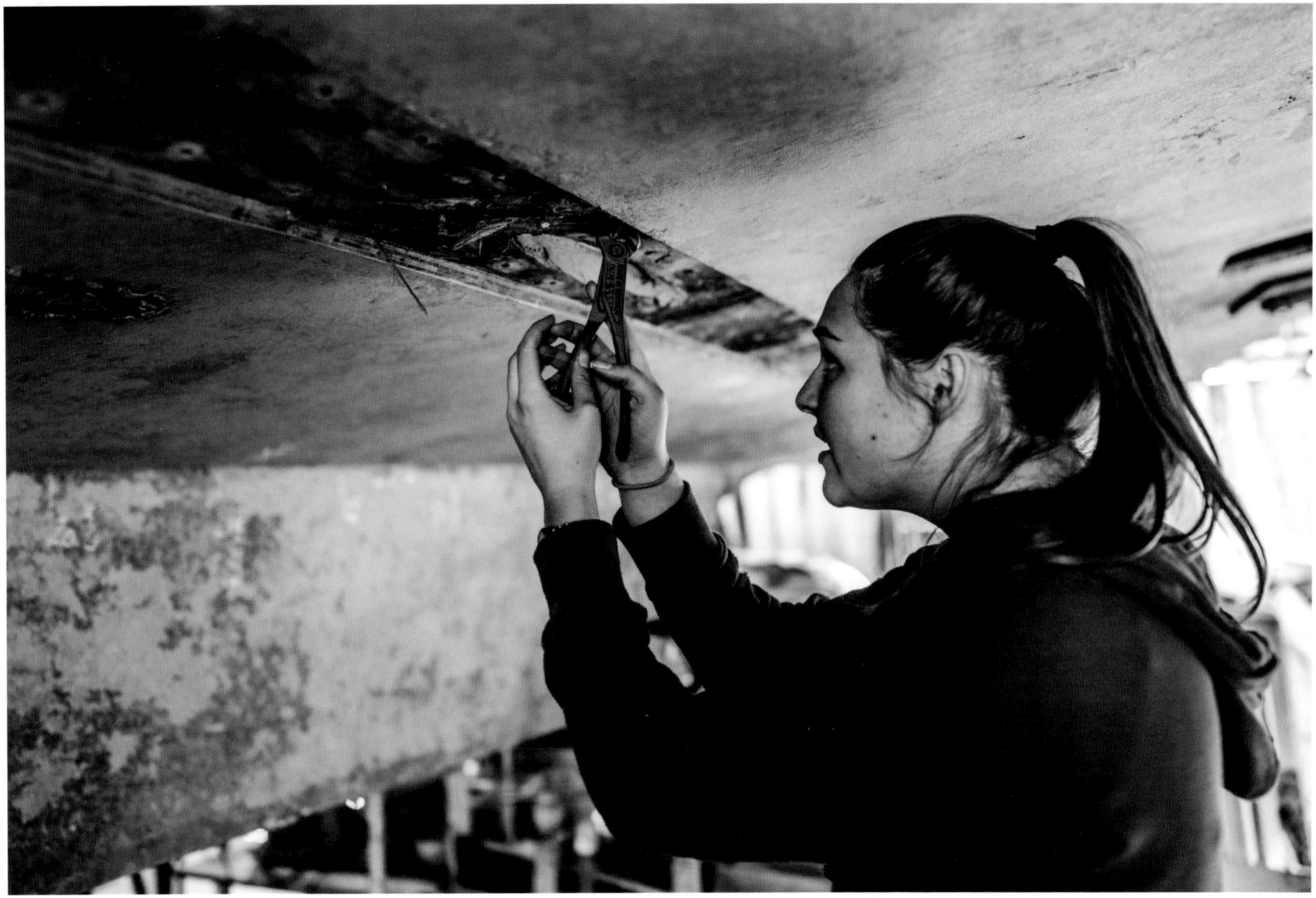

A chequered history

‹ Looking at her now, it's hard to imagine that *Maserati* was the superyacht of her time. Built in 1964 by top British shipyard Morgan Giles, she was built for speed (as her name suggests) and for luxury use in the Mediterranean. Only six were ever made in this large, almost 16-metre 'Monaco class' and she was beautifully hand-built, using the finest marine woods and finishes. Many years and several appallingly shoddy repairs later, she has arrived in South Dock Marina boatyard for a complete strip-back and rebuild to professional standards. Once she is fully restored as a piece of glamorous 1960s history, she will be moored as a liveaboard in the fittingly upmarket surroundings of St Katharine Docks.

Starting at the bottom

Octavia painstakingly prepares the ravaged hull for resealing. Rot is everywhere in this neglected wooden boat but it's obviously a priority to identify and remove any in her main body to make her watertight once more.

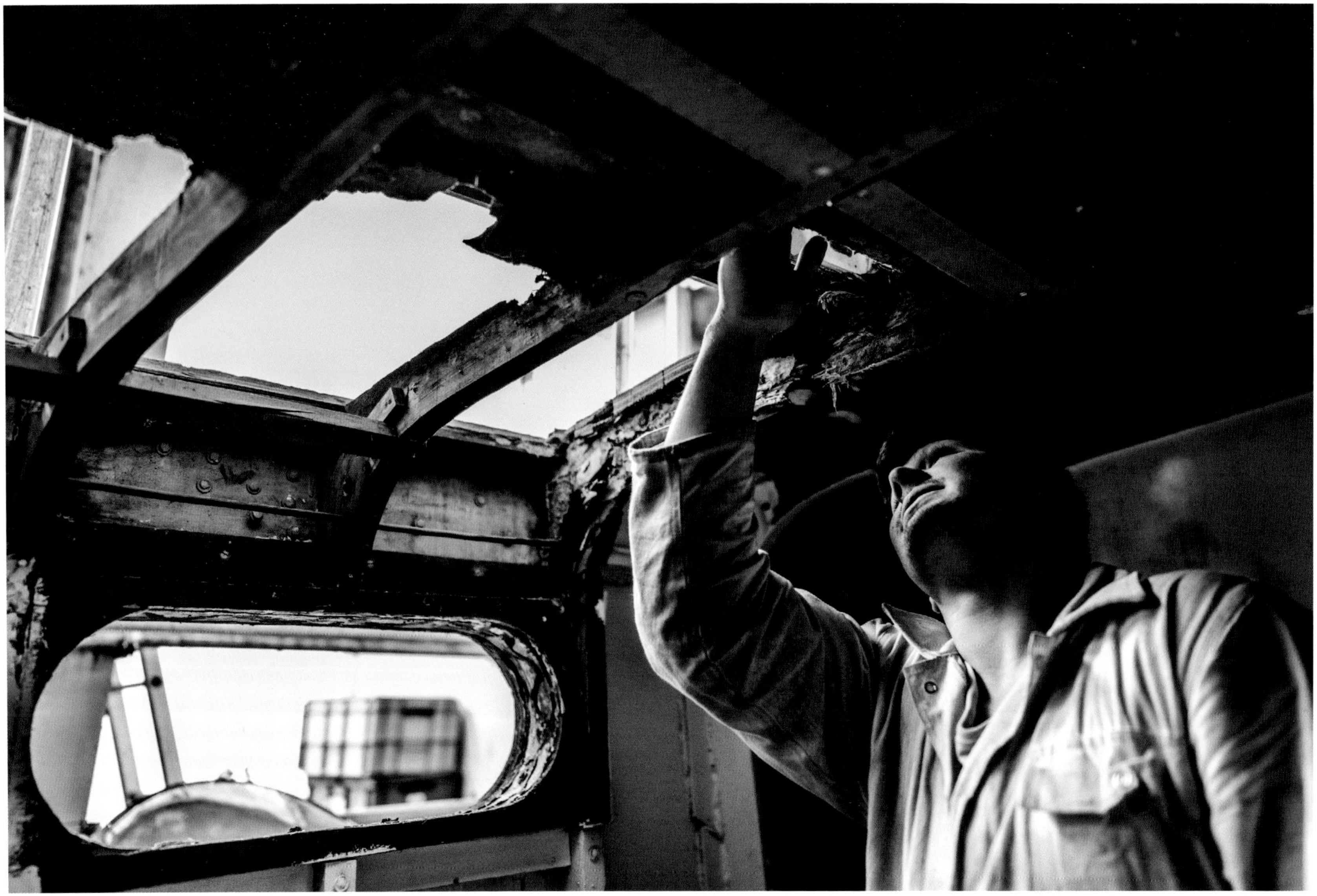

Open to the skies

The rot is so bad in one of cabins that Alex can pull whole sections away with his bare hands. This will need careful stripping back and the deck above will have to be completely rebuilt, including the supporting framework.

Drilling in unison

In the recently stripped-out part of the boat that will become the kitchen and living area, Justin and Octavia are now on to the next stage of installing a new floor structure. They are following *Maserati*'s original blueprints as closely as possible.

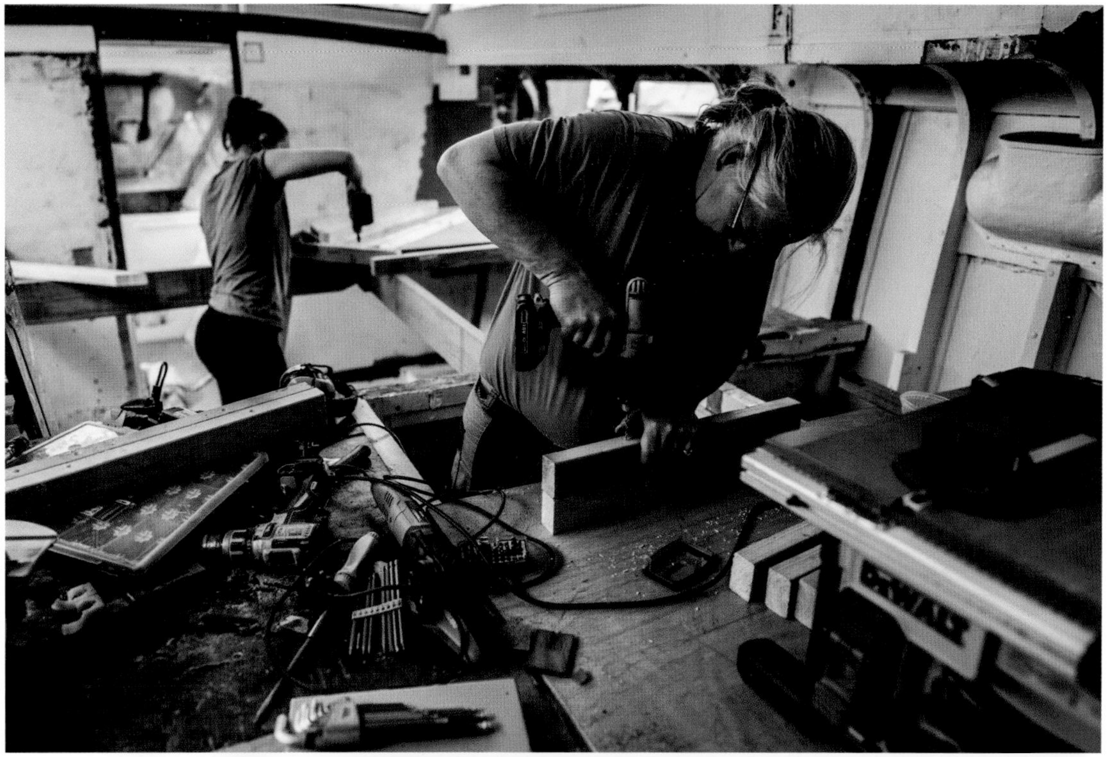

Creating the curve

As an experienced marine carpenter, Wayne is using the strenuous but effective method of a block pivot with foot-pressure and rope-pulling to fit new planks of top-quality marine oak into a new part of the main hull. To maintain the overall shape of the boat, the team can't clear and replace rotten wood all at once but have to work section by section, making it very time-consuming.

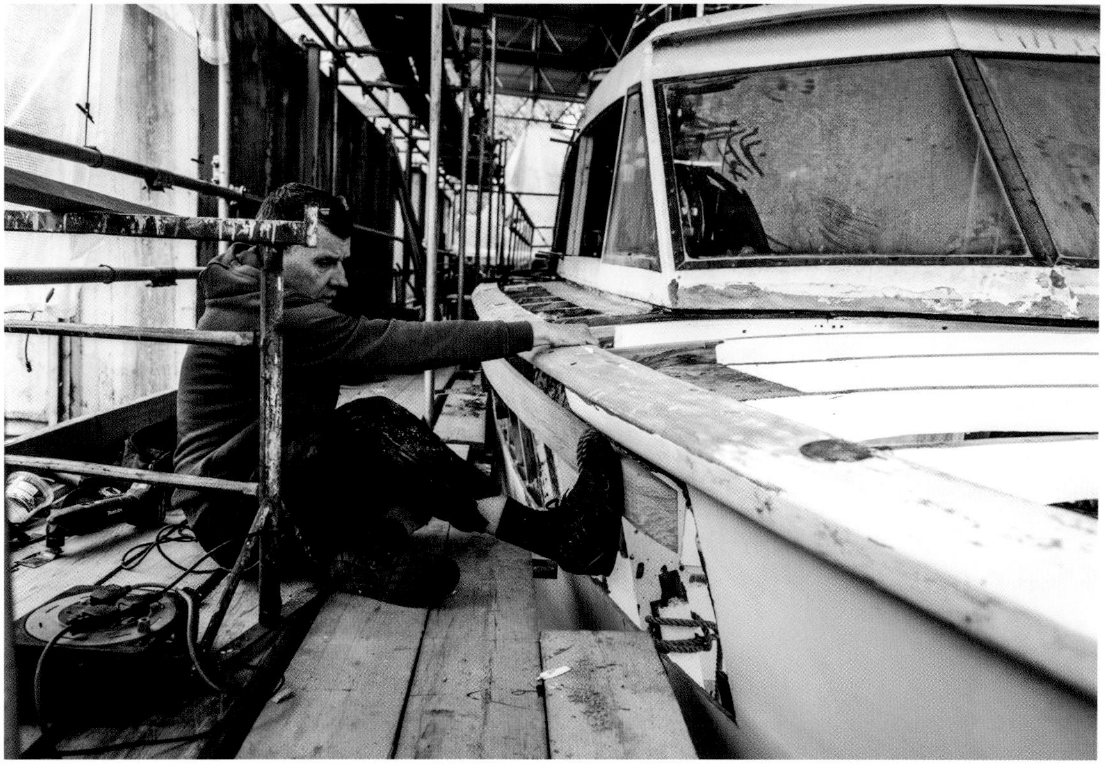

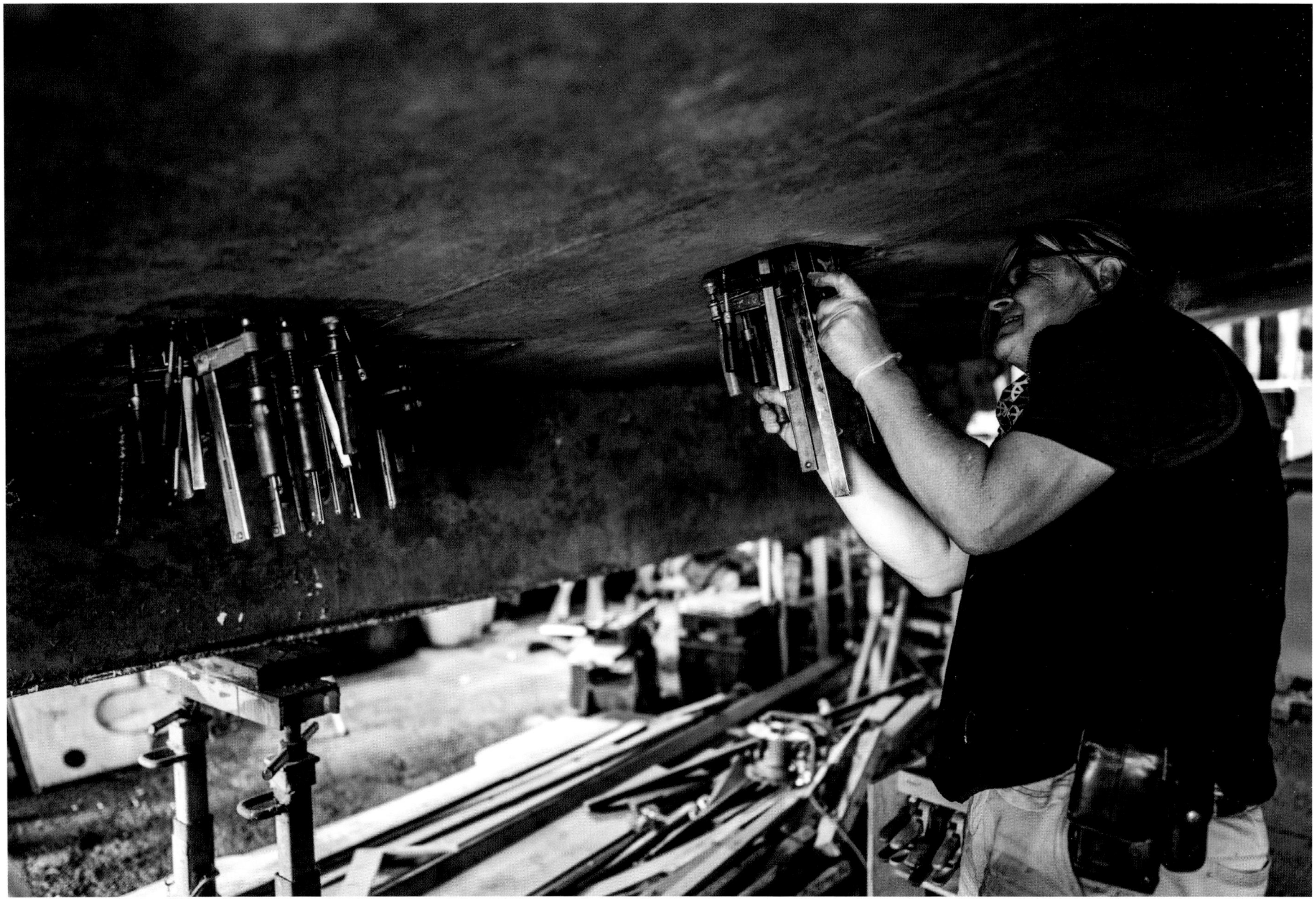

Holding it together

A forest of clamps grows out of *Maserati*'s hull as the many holes made by rotten wood have now been plugged both internally and externally with a double layer of wood riveted into place. These multiple braces pressurise the added layer of industrial-strength epoxy to help glue everything together for a watertight seal.

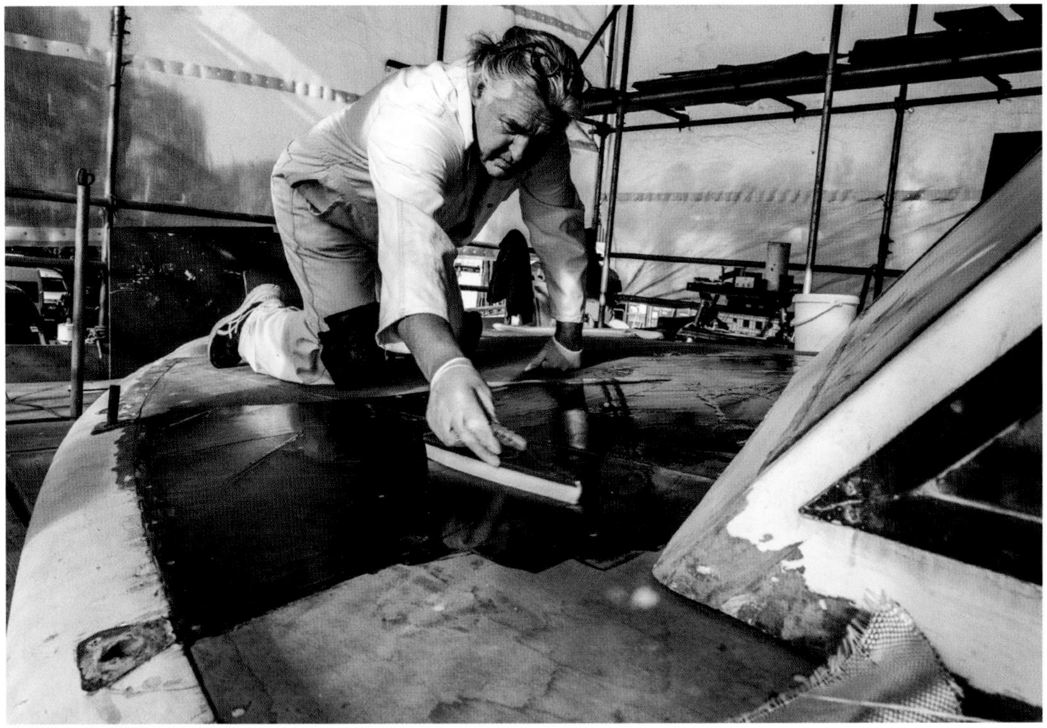

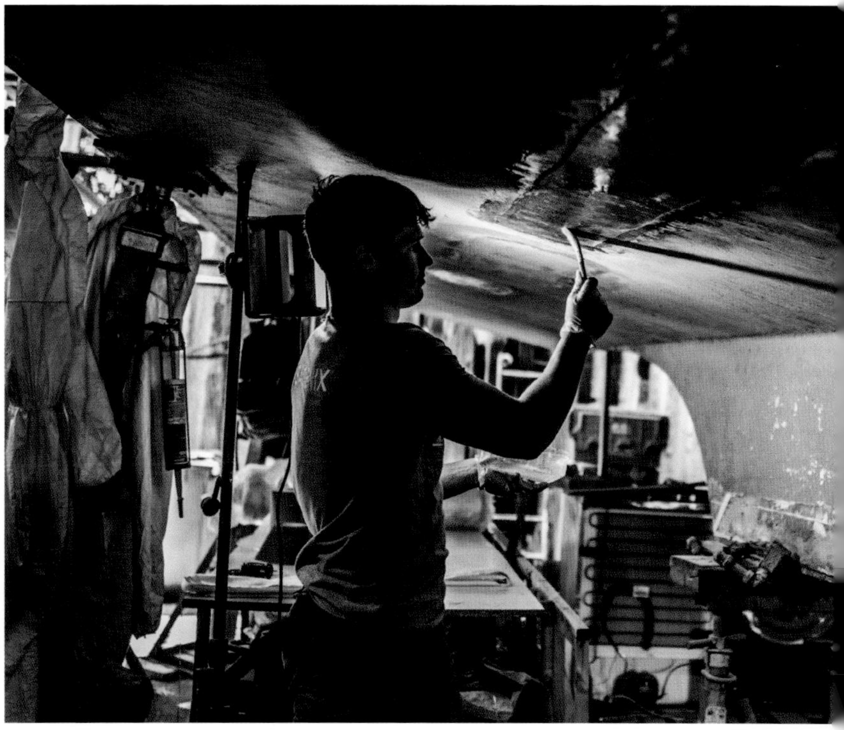

No expense spared

With all the replacement decking in marine plywood complete, it's time to create a waterproof layer of protection. Previous refits have used cheap fibreglass, which soon peels off. Justin is now laying down top-quality woven sheets and is spreading long-lasting epoxy resin to bind it all to the deck. Its high performance comes with a matching price tag but anything else would be a false economy. Two more layers will go on, the last being a fine fibreglass 'tissue' to create the best smooth finish for painting.

Bottoming out

Although the many rot repairs have taken well, the whole hull also gets a good coating of long-lasting epoxy resin. Once sanded, this will make the best surface for the anti-fouling paint layers to come.

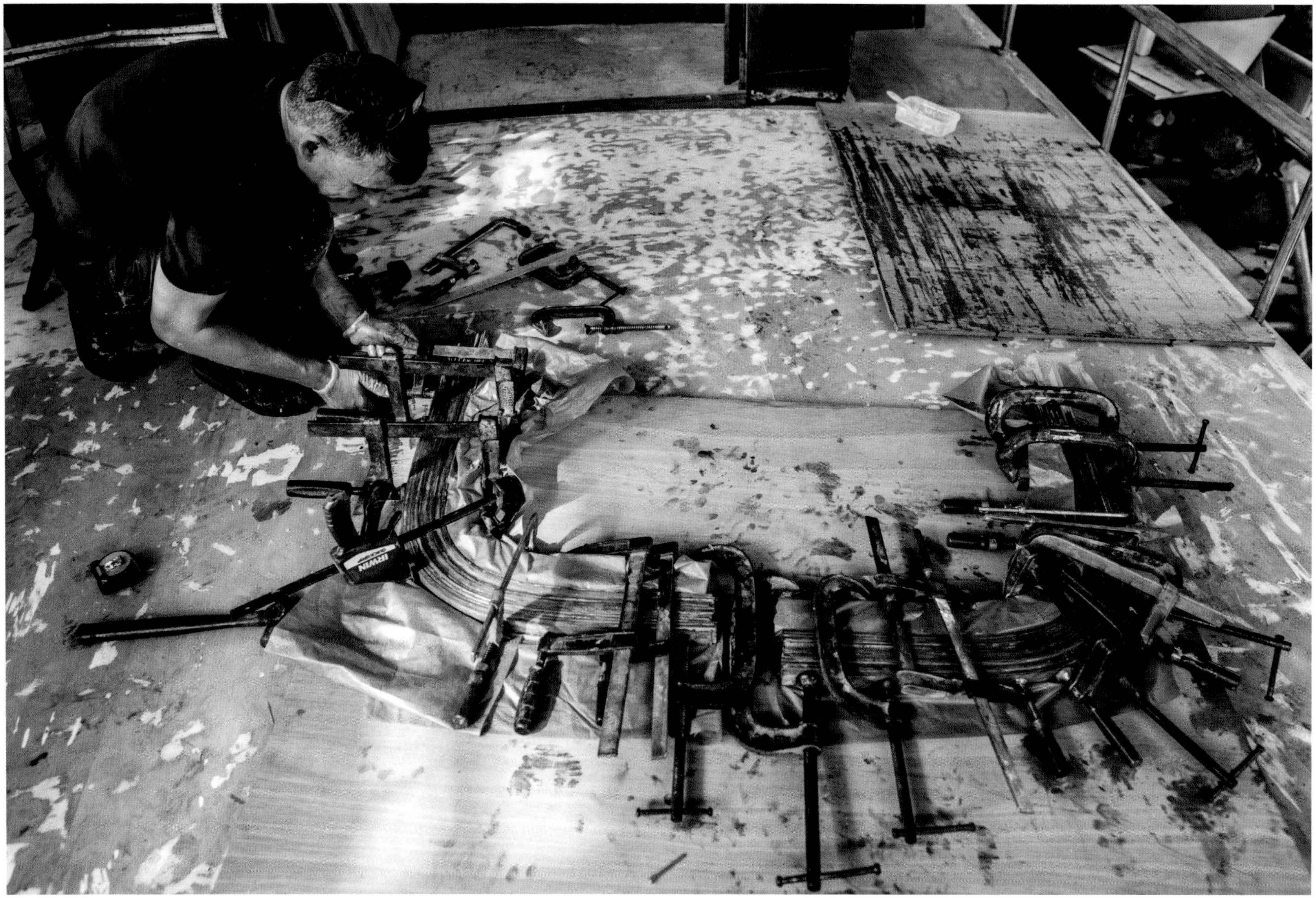

Wood wizardry

All *Maserati*'s distinctively shaped wooden window frames have completely rotted and need to be recreated. Wayne's answer is to combine seven layers of marine plywood with glue and then cleverly bend them all into the correct shape with an impressive array of clamps.

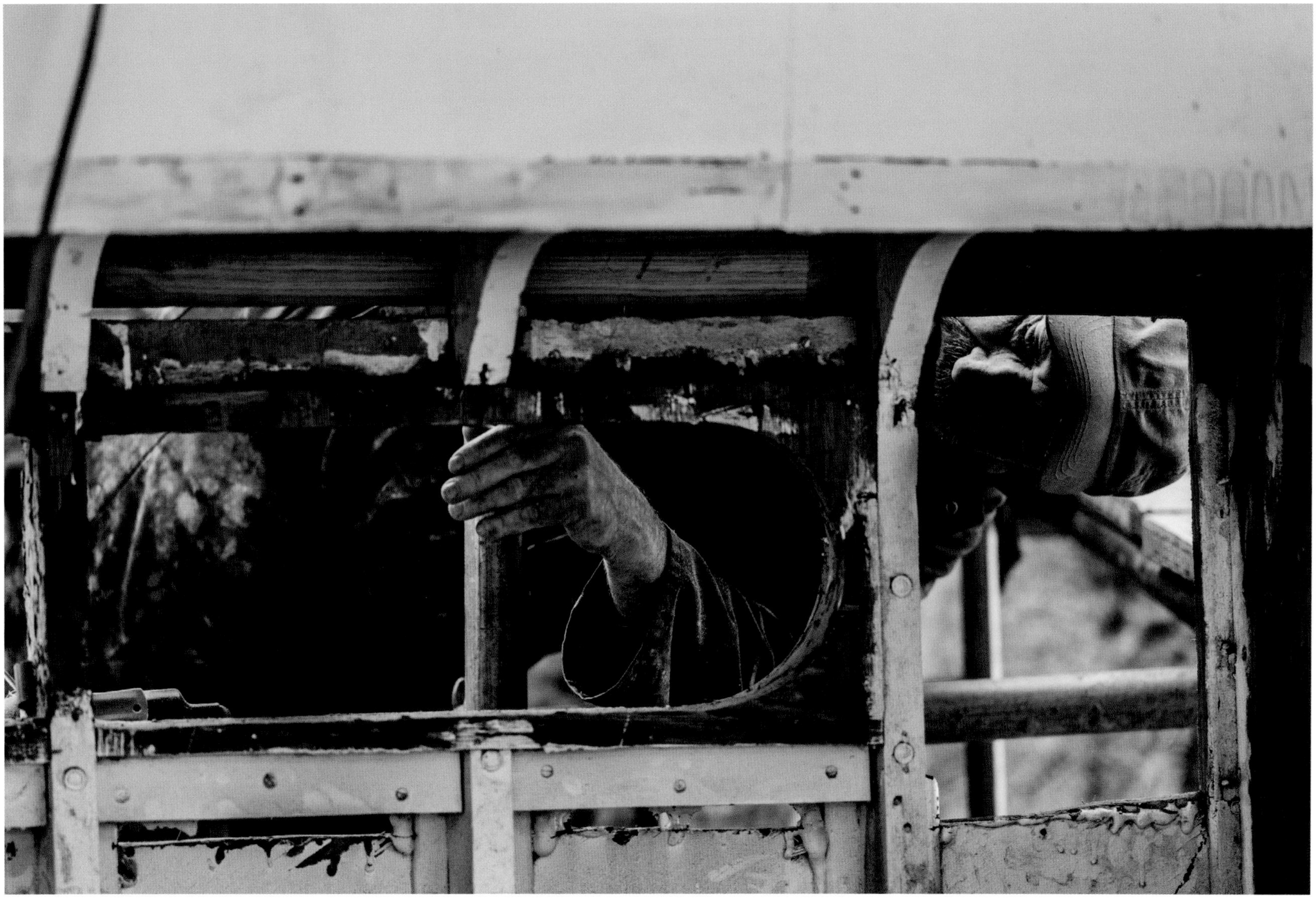

Side view

Fellow marine carpenter, Chris, fits a new supporting strut for one of the exterior windows. Having *Maserati* in dry dock, surrounded by scaffolding and platforms at the right level, is the only way to do such complicated rebuilding.

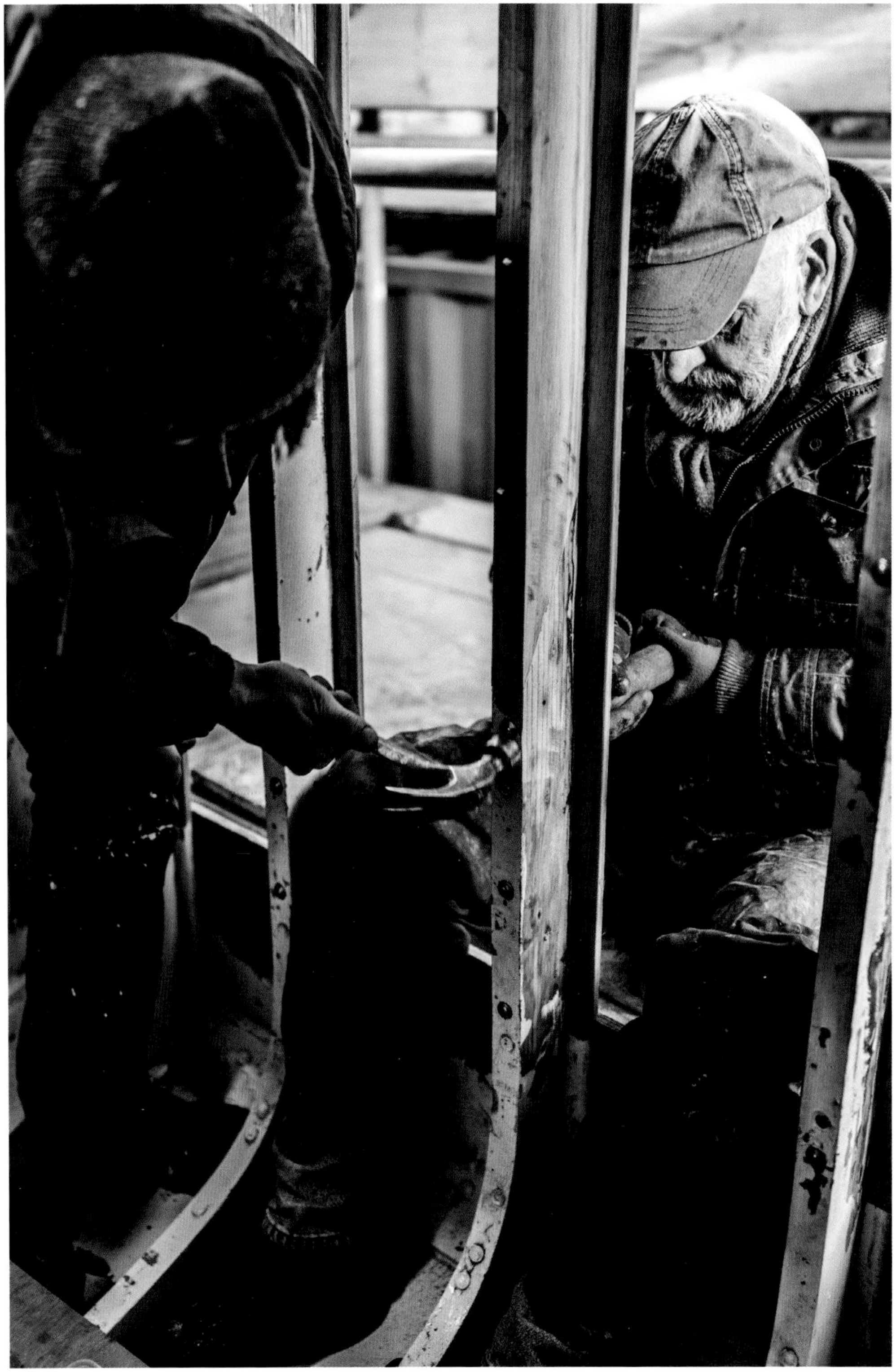

Riveting stuff

Practised teamwork is needed to fit the large new struts recreating the sides of the rear cabin. Experts at the centuries-old boat-building practice of riveting, Chris and Wayne are hammering in copper 'rivet' nails secured with dish-shaped 'rove' caps. One holds a special 'dolly' tool against the end of the nail to hold it firm while the other quickly hammers the rove flat and clips off the excess.

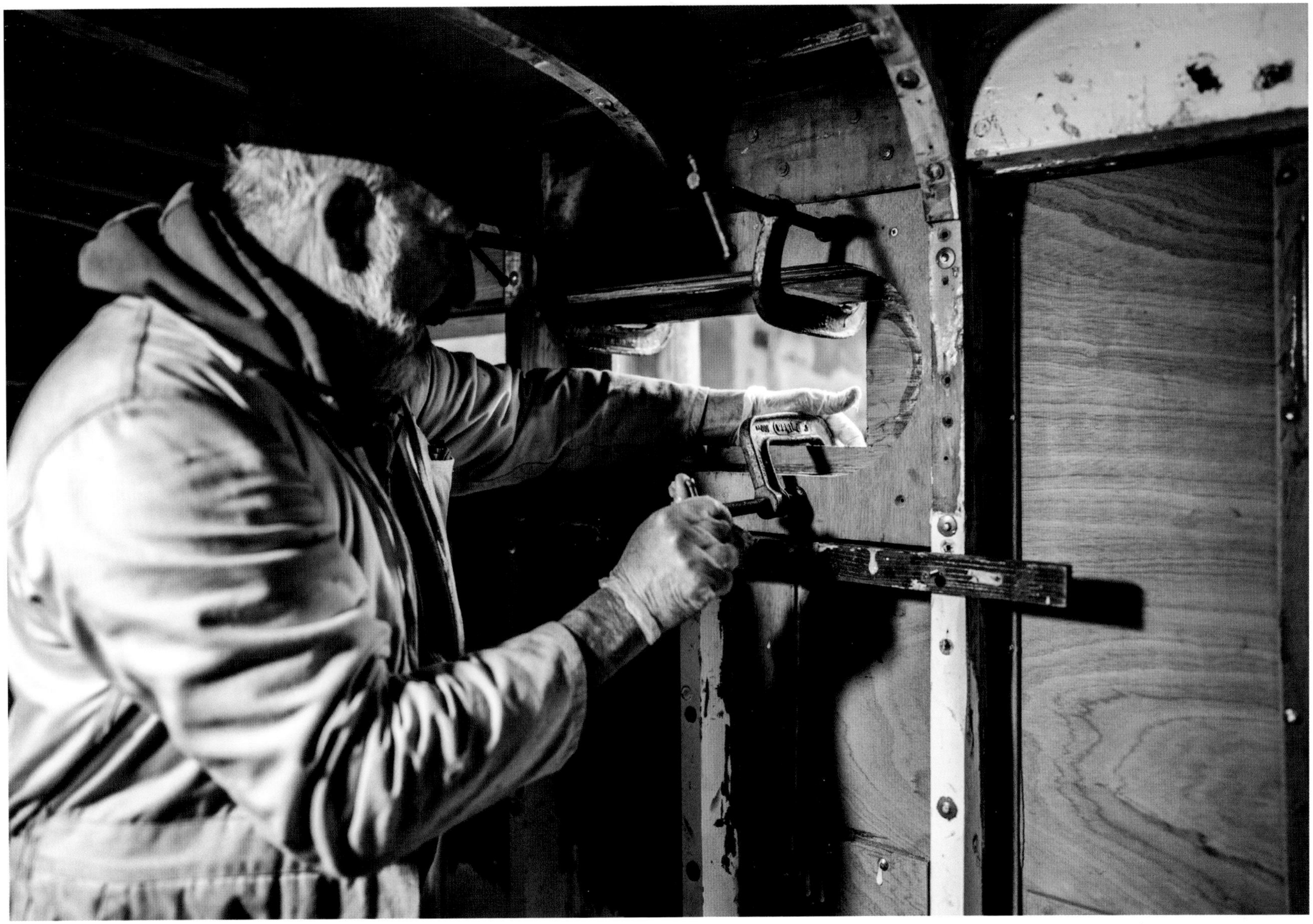

Saving time

Modern technology now helps move things on. Rebecca's pre-prepared interior window frames arrive, precision-cut by Studio Shillito's computer-controlled CNC machine. A perfect fit, Chris clamps them into place. With a clever merging of old and new techniques, *Maserati*'s cabins are taking shape.

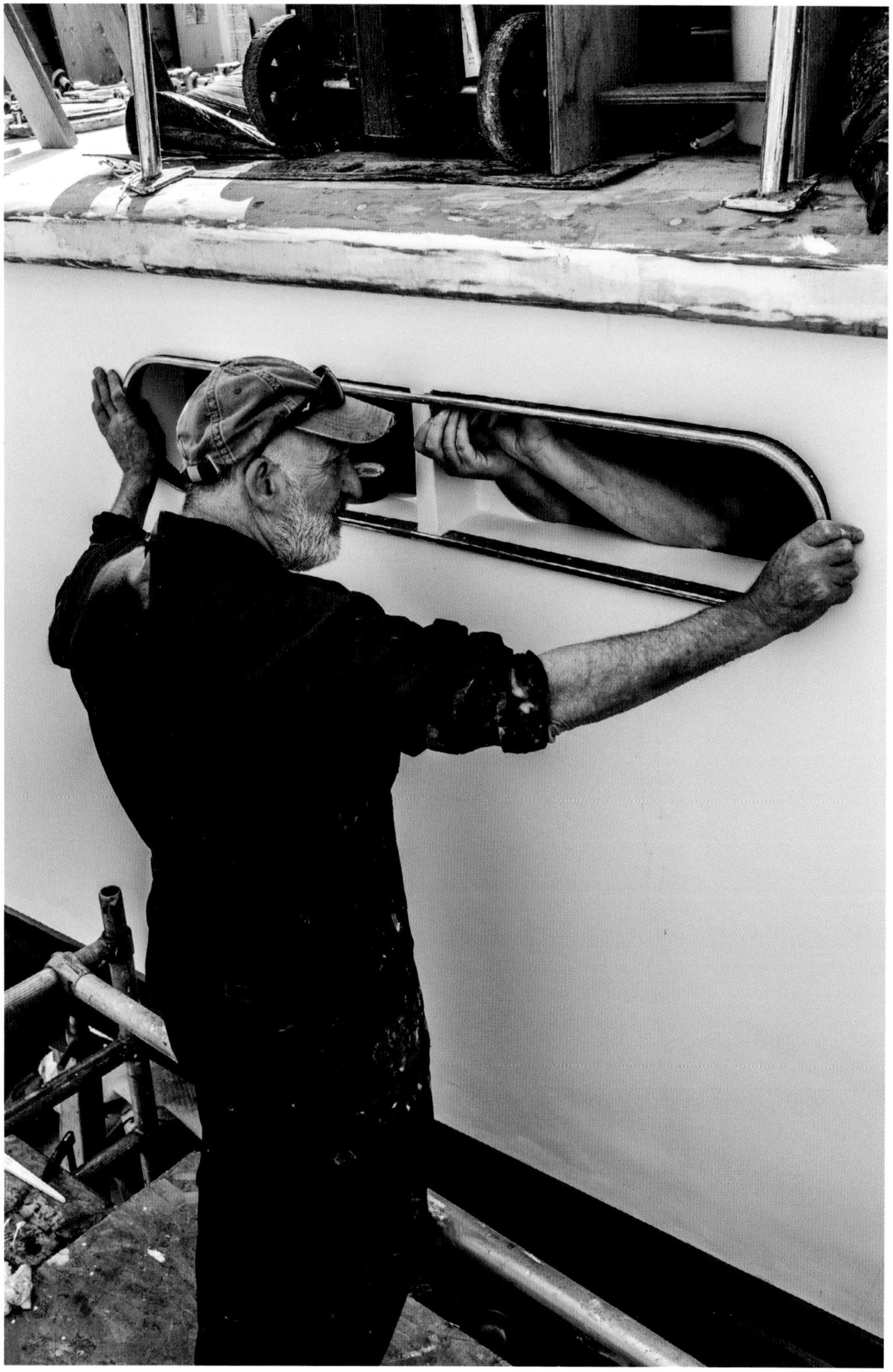

Trimming up

Chrome was very much part of *Maserati*'s original elegant design. Standing high up on the boatyard's scaffolding, Chris holds a carefully preserved rim against one of the reconstructed windows while Justin screws it back into place.

All hands on deck

Launch time is fast approaching and the pressure is on to finish the final exterior painting. There is a considerable expanse of hull to cover and three coats to apply, with sanding between each coat needed for a smooth finish.

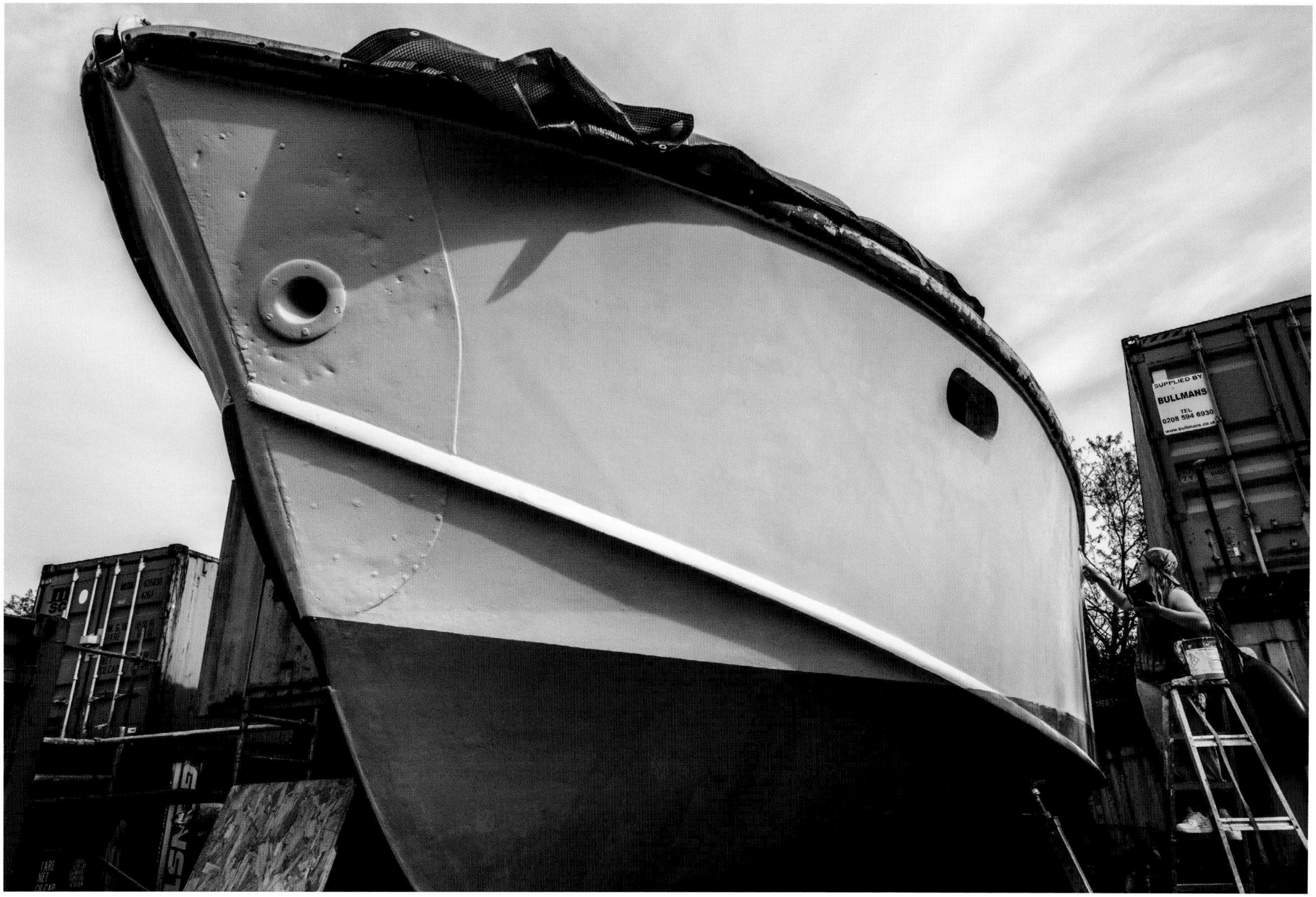

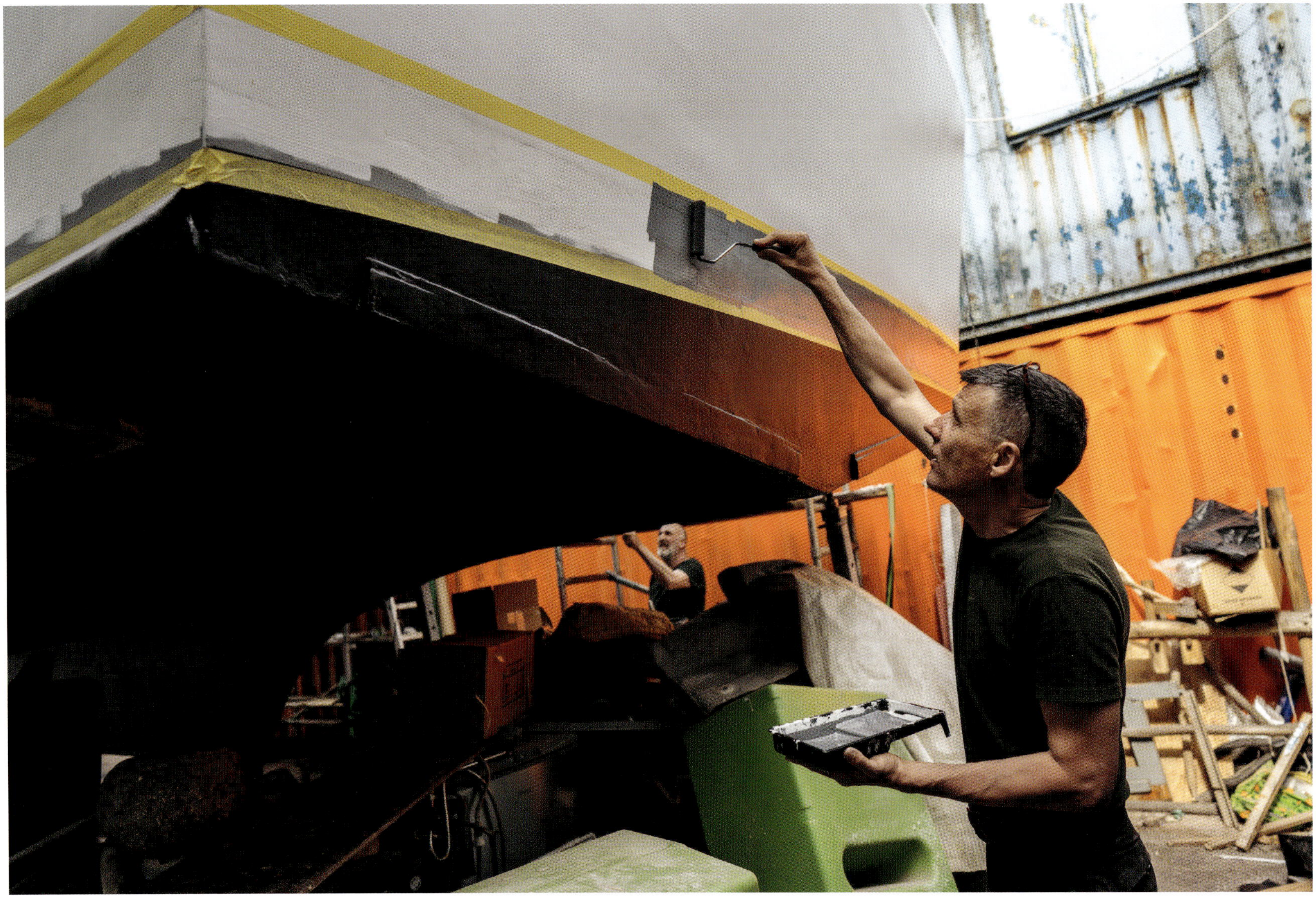

Sitting pretty

Wayne and Chris are priming a 15-centimetre-wide band ready for the red paint that will mark out and give added protection to the hull at the expected waterline. The level at which a boat sits in the water governs where this 'boot top' is painted. It's a tricky calculation that involves estimating the weight of liveaboard items such as beds, fridges and even people once the boat is fully loaded.

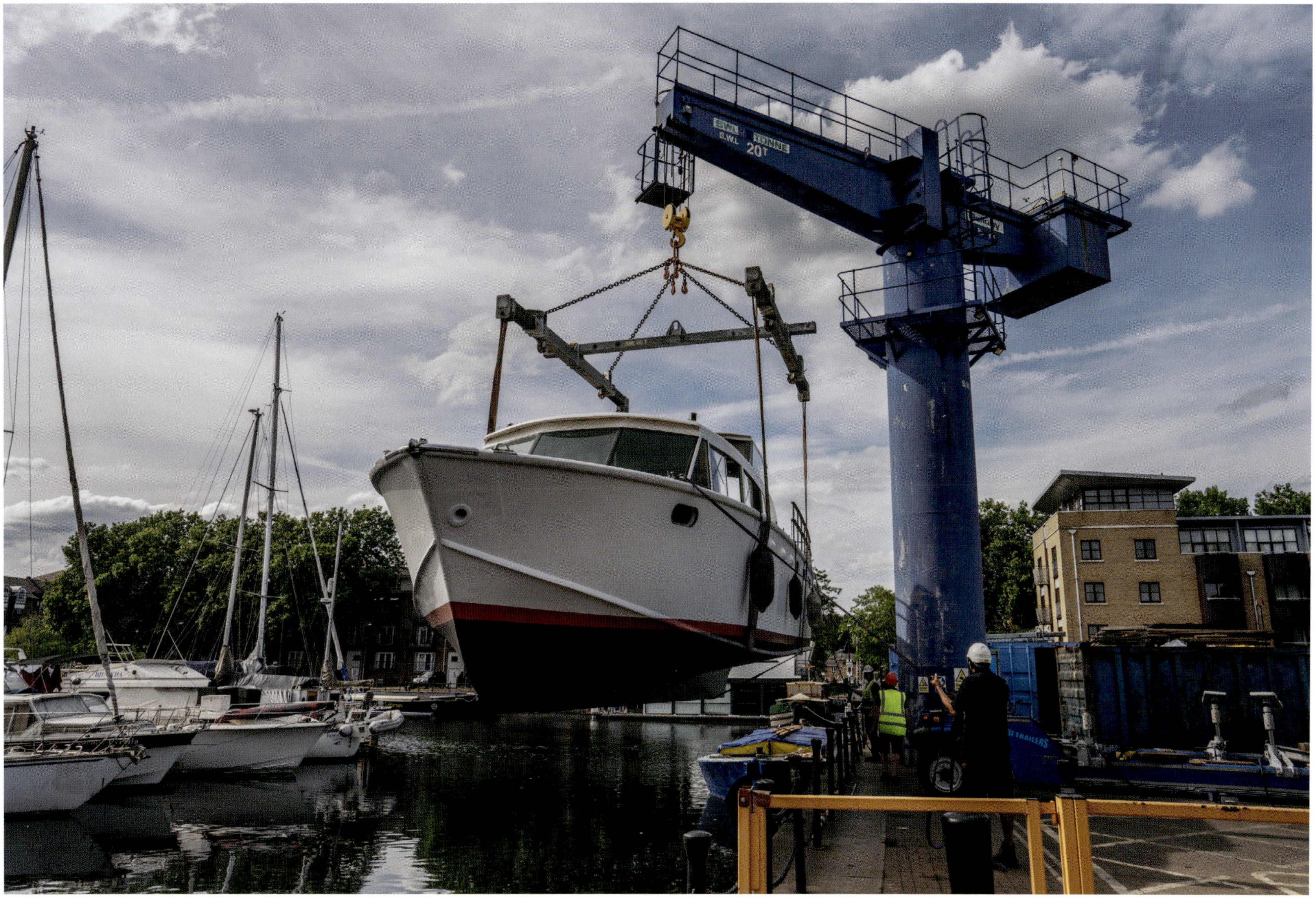

The big day

After over a year in South Dock Marina's boatyard, *Maserati* is finally returned to the water. Once lowered, she is left sitting in the crane slings overnight as a safety measure but after thousands of hours of expert woodwork and a great deal of fibreglassing and epoxy, she proves fully watertight, as expected.

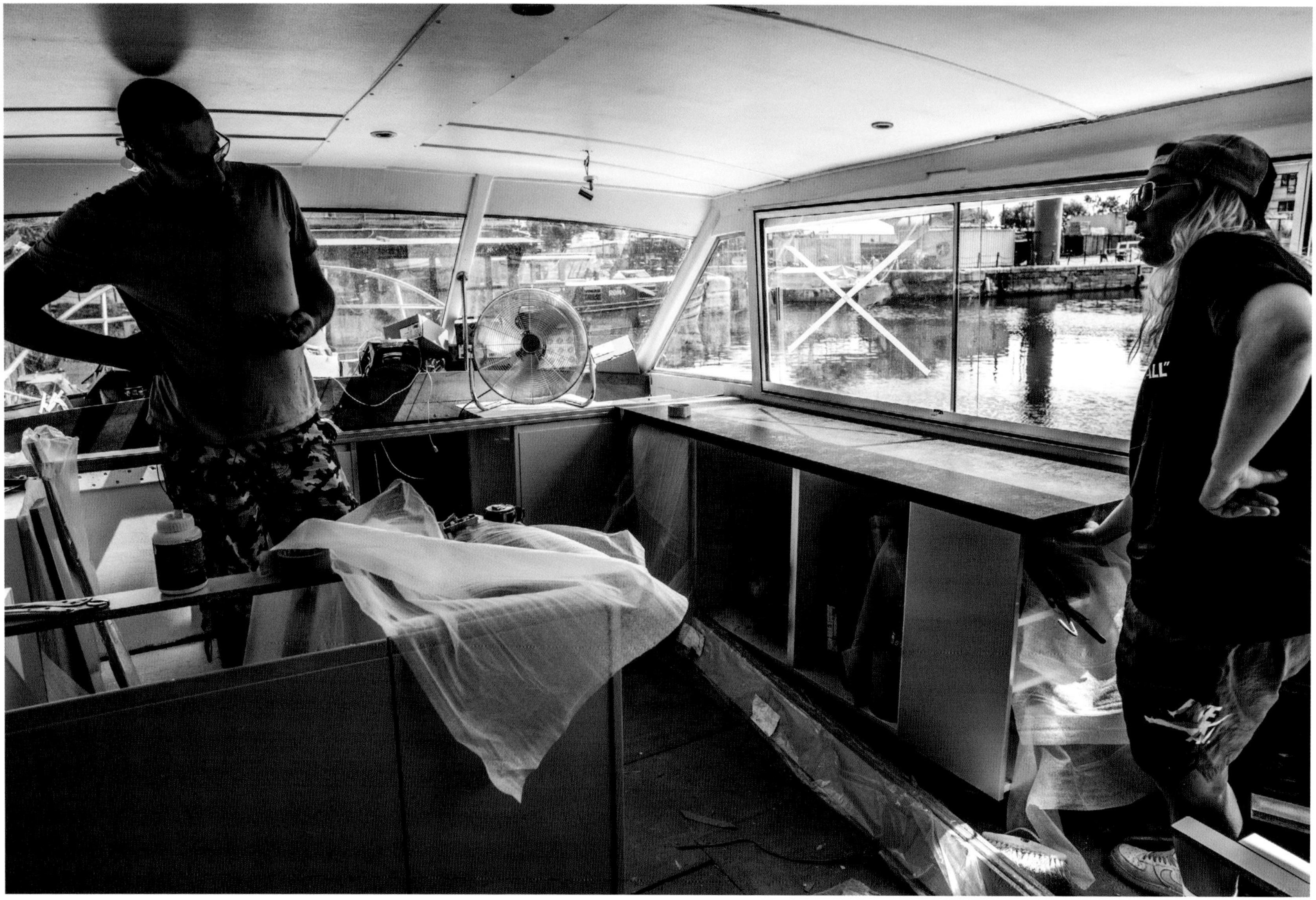

Domestic design

Now the process of creating a living space begins and the non-nautical work takes over. Carpenter Josh is working out how best to fit a kitchen into *Maserati*'s transformed interior.

Specialised marine carpentry may no longer be required but for this floating home, considerable skill is needed to fit square units within the curved sides of a boat.

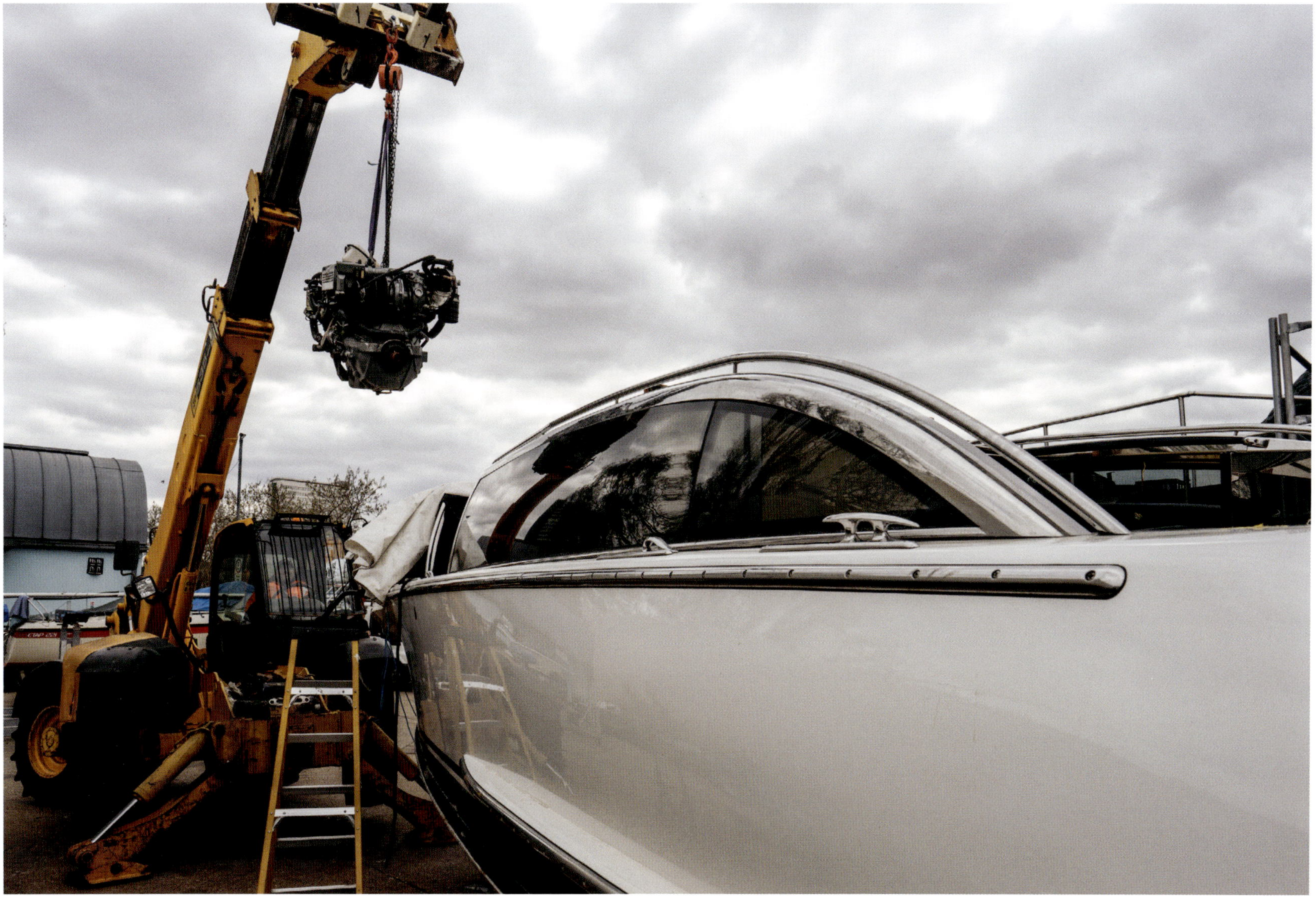

Return to luxury

Work starts on a classic Venetian-crafted water limousine in South Dock Marina boatyard. Philip and Mariana run Thames Limo, specialising in VIP trips on the river, and this will be the latest addition to their elegant, high-speed fleet. Originally handmade in the famous Marina Serenella shipyard in Murano, the boat was knocked about and uncared for as a modern superyacht's runabout tender. Now Philip plans a complete refit of her mahogany and leather interior, with a full technological update, but first her powerful engine needs attention. www.thameslimo.co.uk

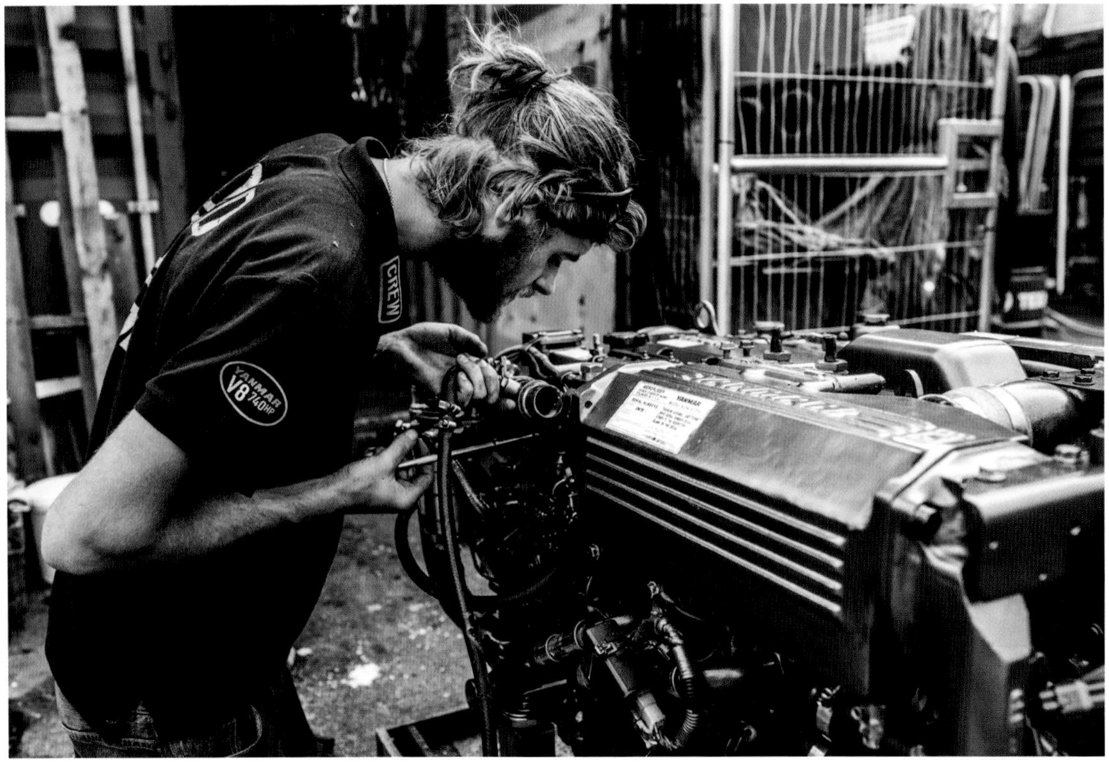

Fine tuning

Years of neglect have resulted in a serious reduction in this impressive machine's performance. Brenden has to use all his mechanical skills to clean and replace various essential parts.
www.osheasmarineservices.com

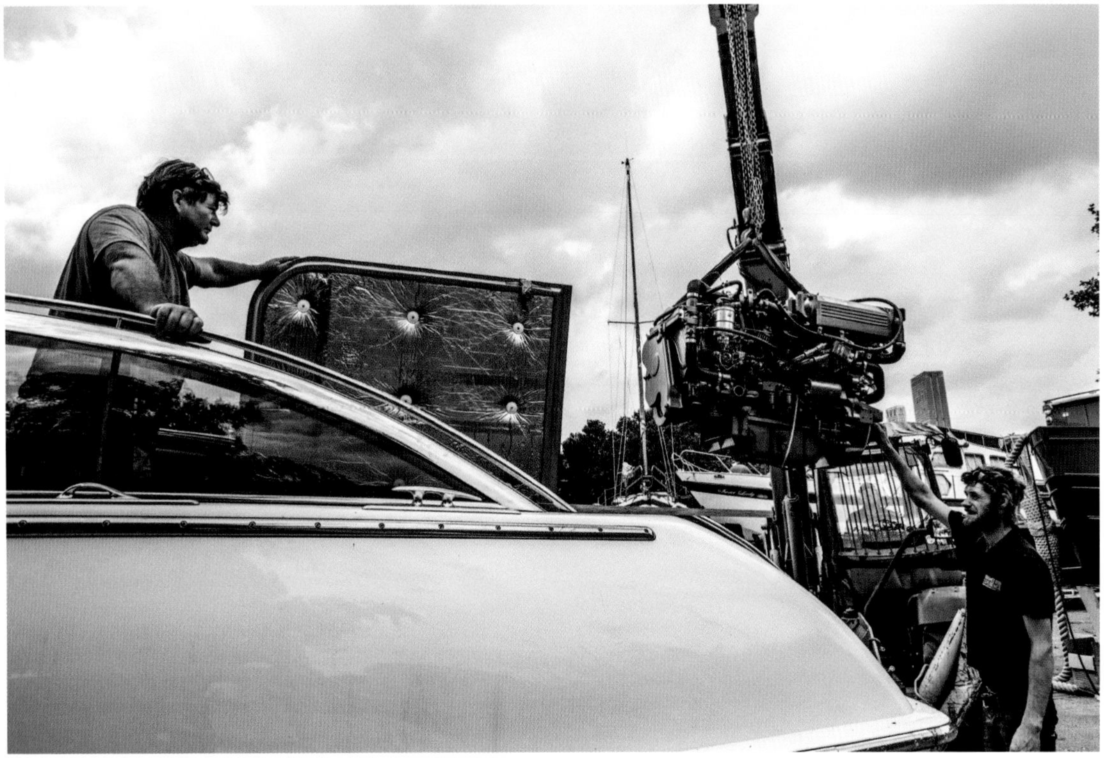

Power restored

Looking as shiny as new and with a relined hatch to match, *Grazia*'s refurbished engine is carefully lifted back into place under the watchful eye of owner Philip. He will be expecting a speedy 35 knots from her.

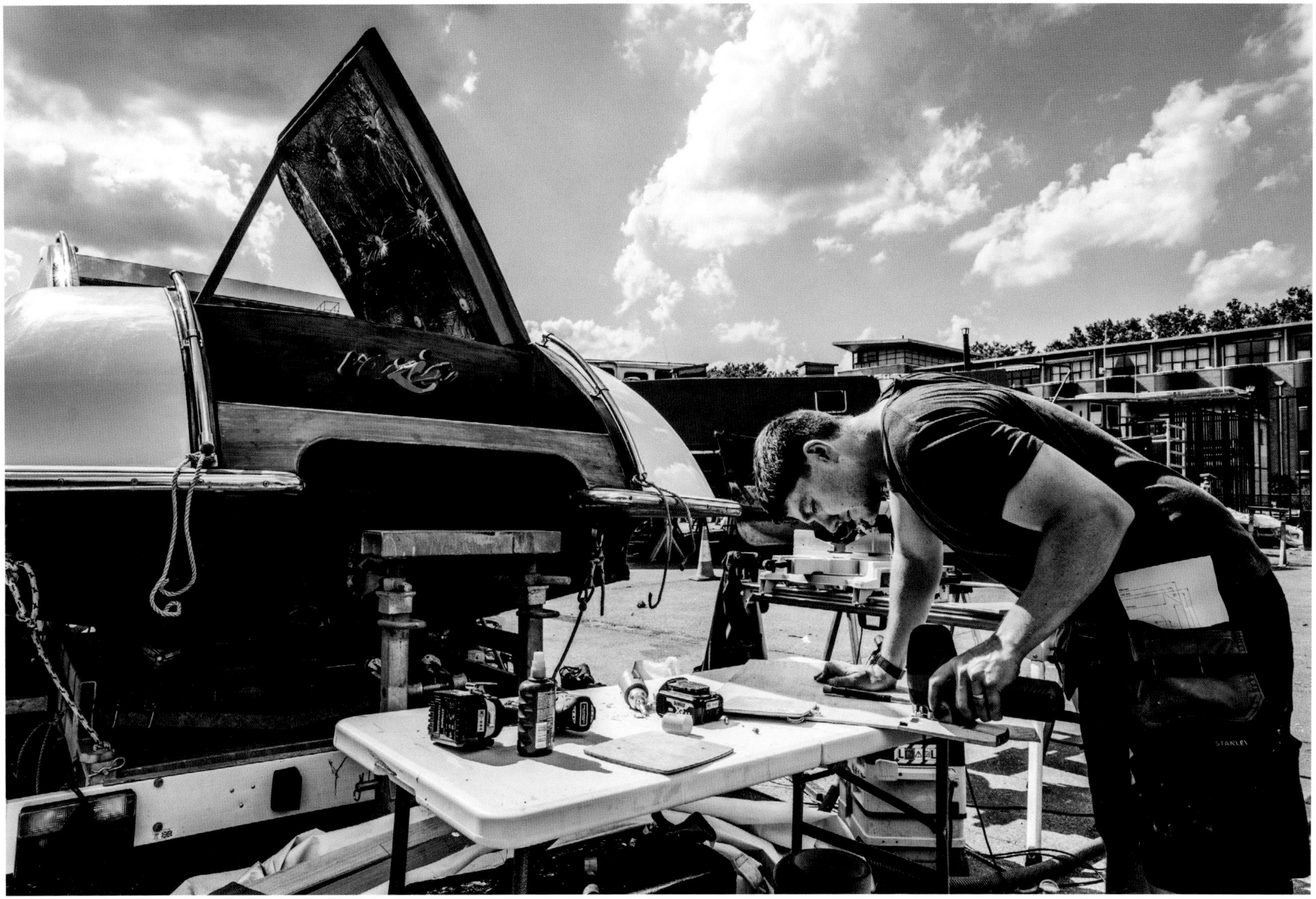

Craft with technology

Having worked on other Thames Limo restorations, Jamie is used to Philip's high standards. This time, he is enjoying having to match the mastery of Venetian craftsmanship. All the original mahogany interior has been restored and he's now creating a new wood dashboard to encompass newly required technology like satellite navigation.

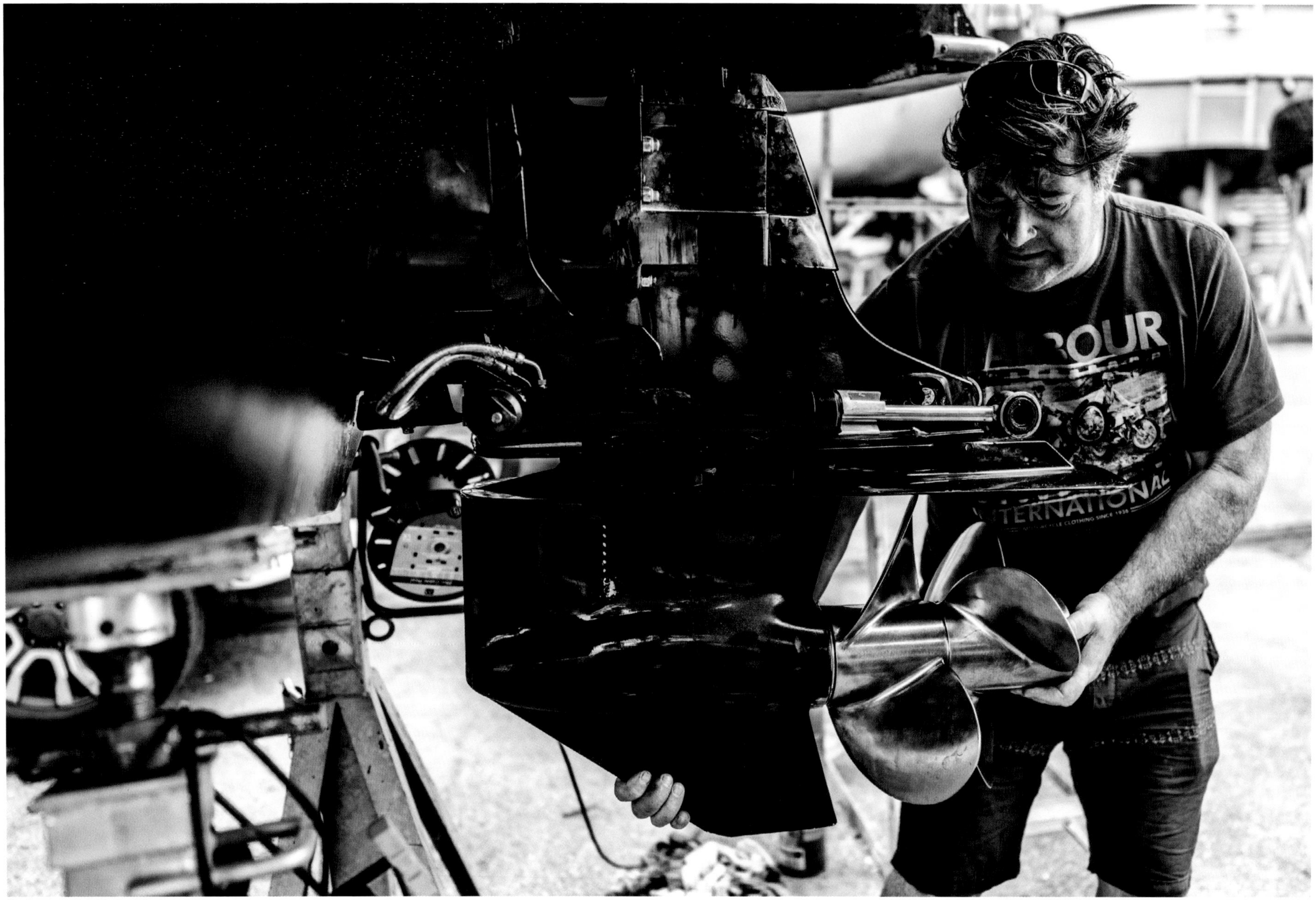

Final checks

Meticulous in his methods, Philip inspects the alignment of the engine 'drive leg'. It has been a lengthy and complicated refit but he now thinks *Grazia* is ready.

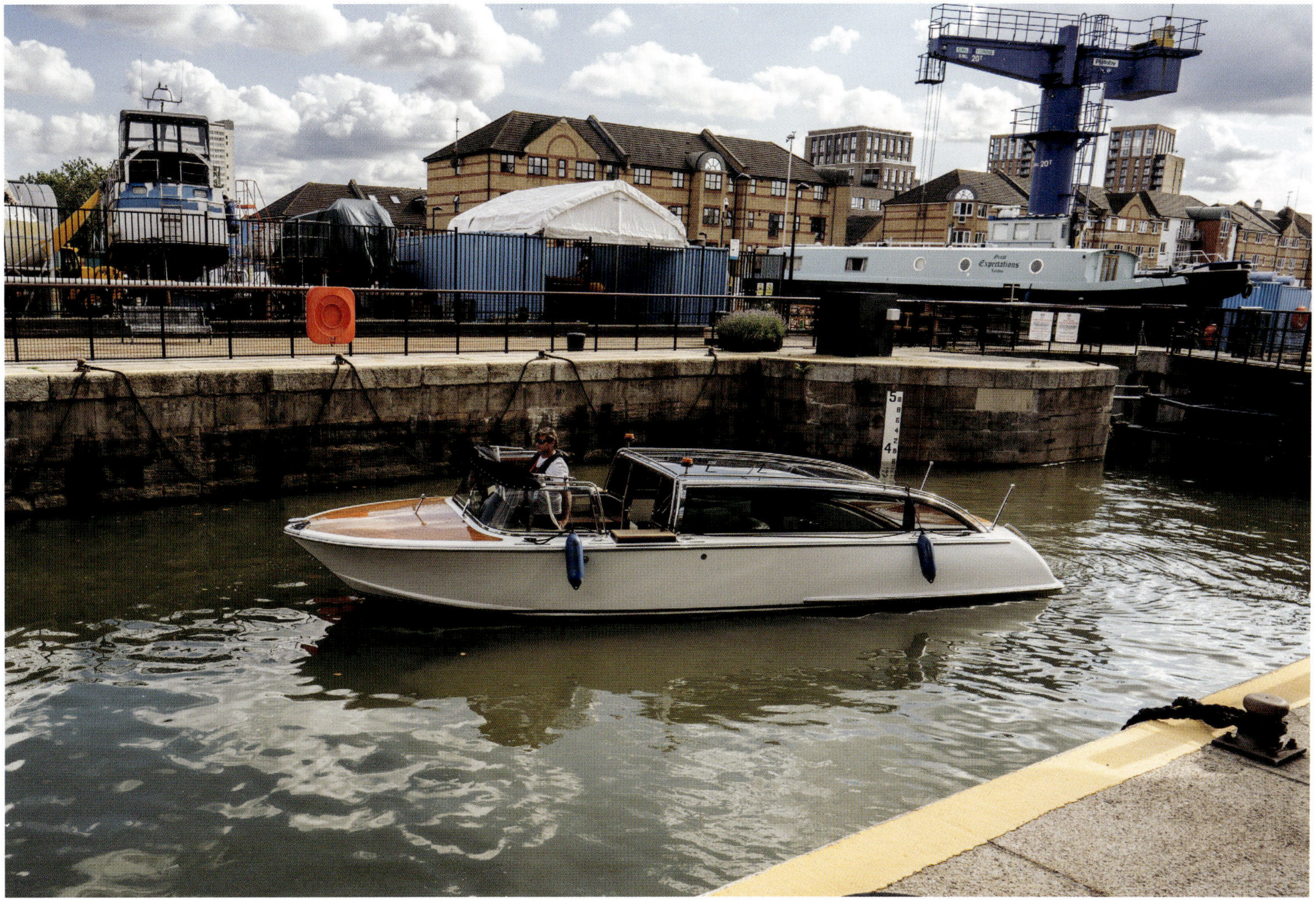

Successful relaunch

It's an exciting moment of anticipation as Philip waits for the South Dock Marina lock gates to open. He will then finally open up the throttle and head up-river to take *Grazia* back to Thames Limo's base at Imperial Wharf, Chelsea.

Nautical heritage

Enthusiasts celebrating Britain's seafaring past
and international connections find a home in these docks.

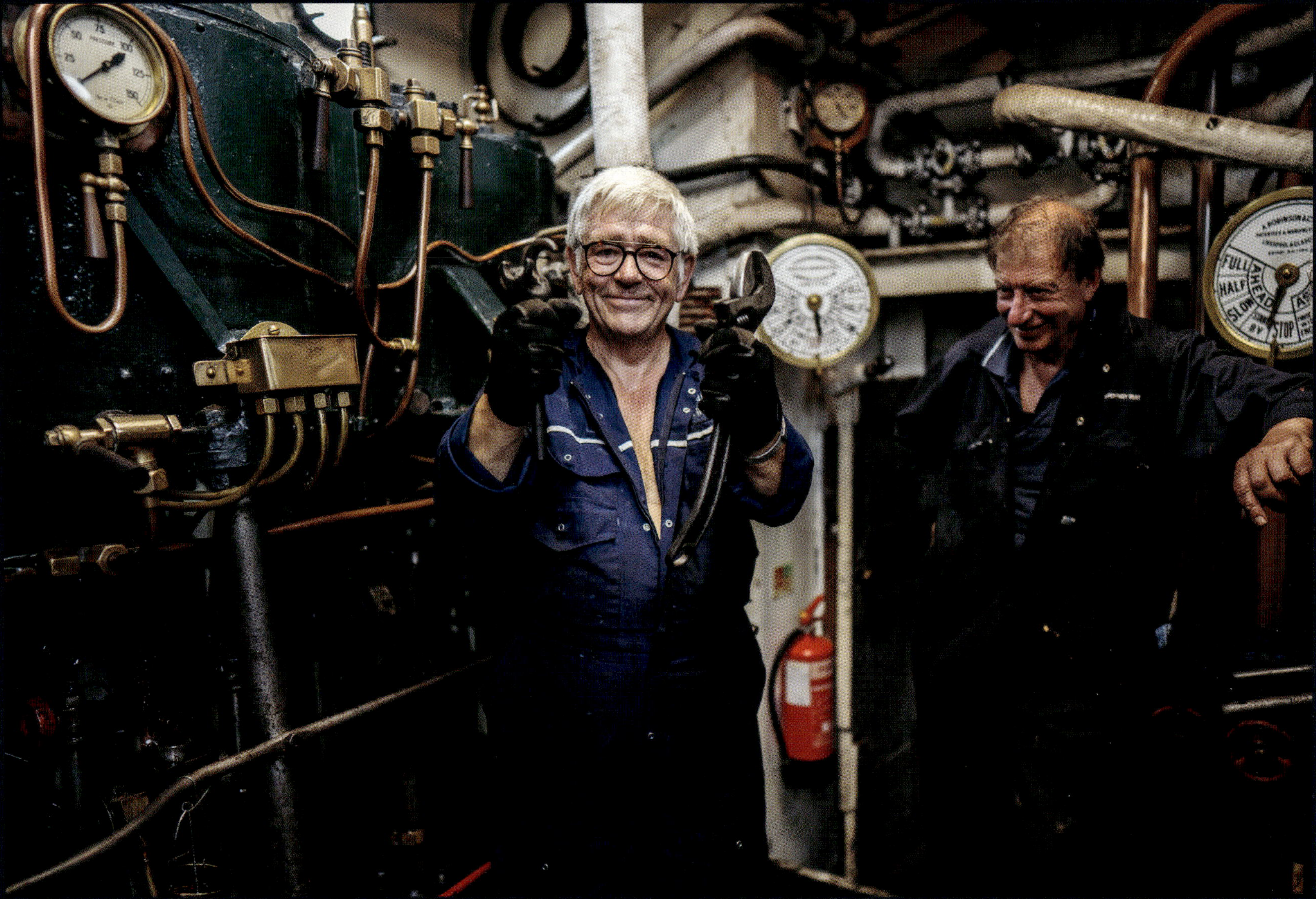

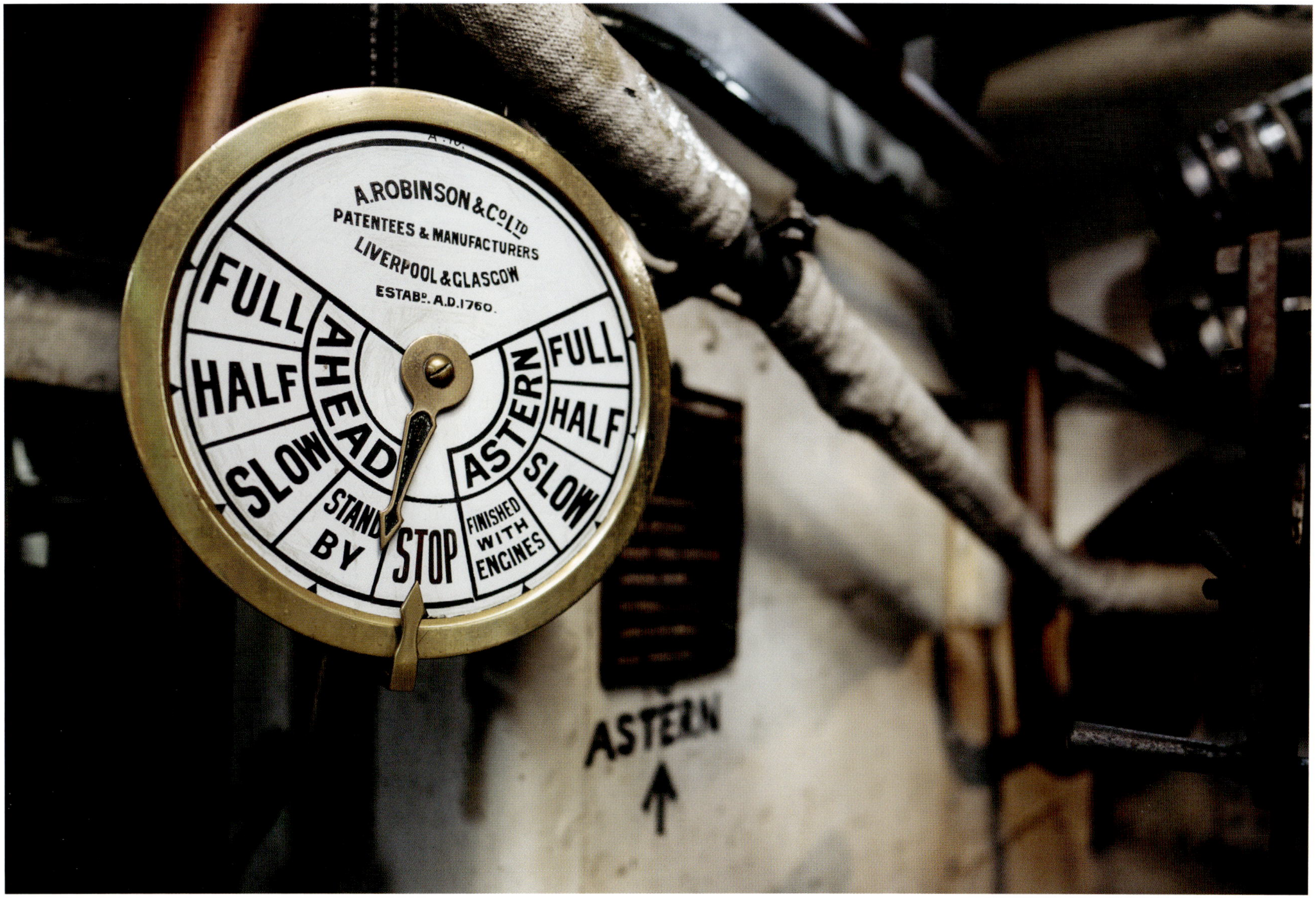

Ready for action

Spanners to the fore, a band of enthusiastic volunteers keeps *Portwey* going as one of the last steam-powered, twin-engined working tugs in the UK. Built in 1927 and now moored in the Isle of Dogs West India Docks, she had a busy working life on the Dorset and Devon coasts before being usurped by diesel-engined tugs in the 1960s. Saved from the scrapyard by Dartmouth's assistant harbour master, the Steam Tug Portwey Trust took over her running in 2000 and now does Steam Experience Days in dock as well as Thames excursions. She's much loved but new recruits for her upkeep are always needed.
www.stportwey.co.uk

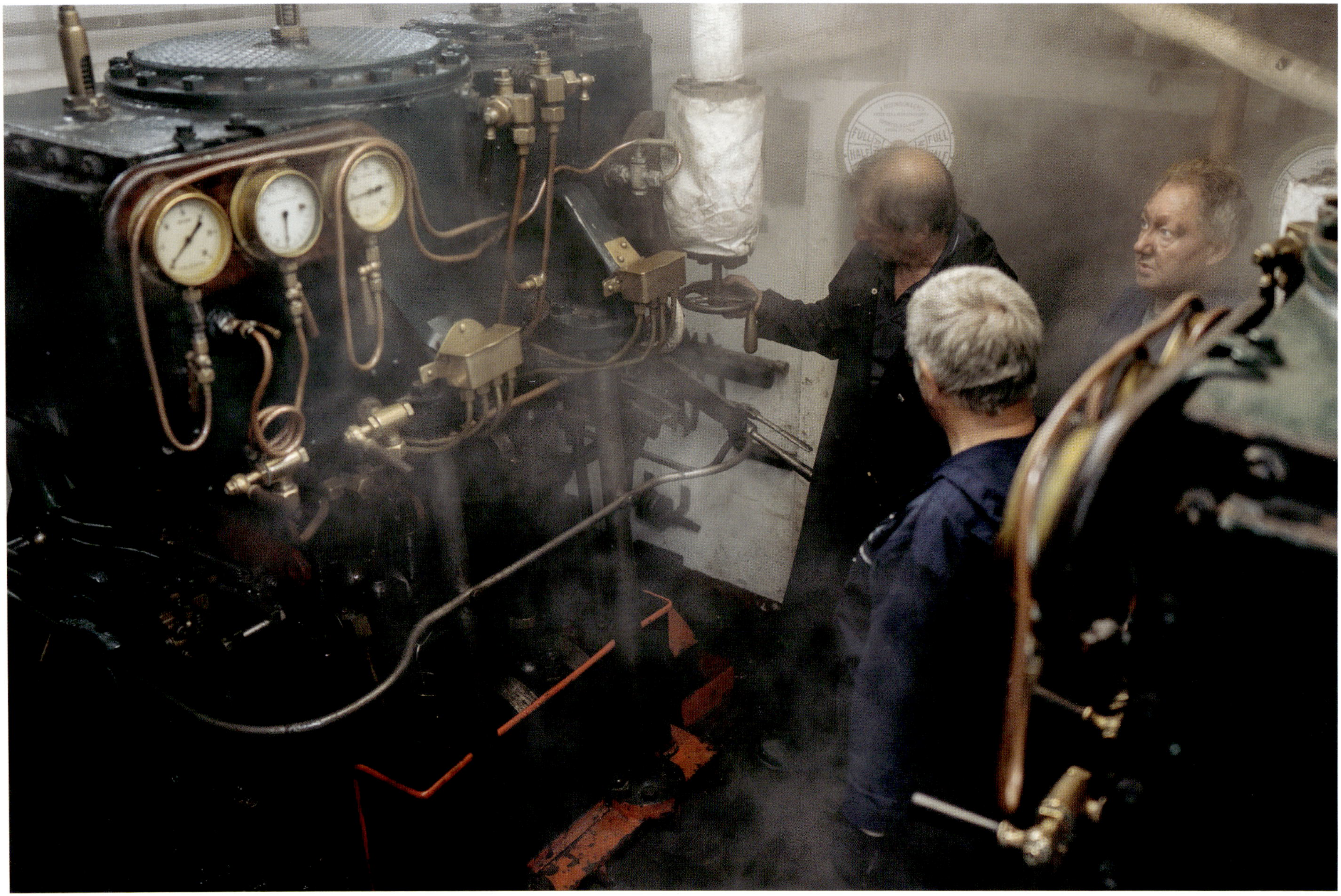

All steamed up

Every 14 months, a marine engineer surveyor arrives to inspect *Portwey*'s entire system, requiring a lot of coal shovelling and a full testing of her two huge engines. Such elements as the safety-pressure valves and water-level gauges have to be checked and as part of the process, the team is now warming the engines through, producing an impressive amount of interior steam.

Letting off steam

Conjuring up romantic memories of a long-gone era, *Portwey* creates a dramatic contrast to the 21st-century towers surrounding her on the Isle of Dogs.

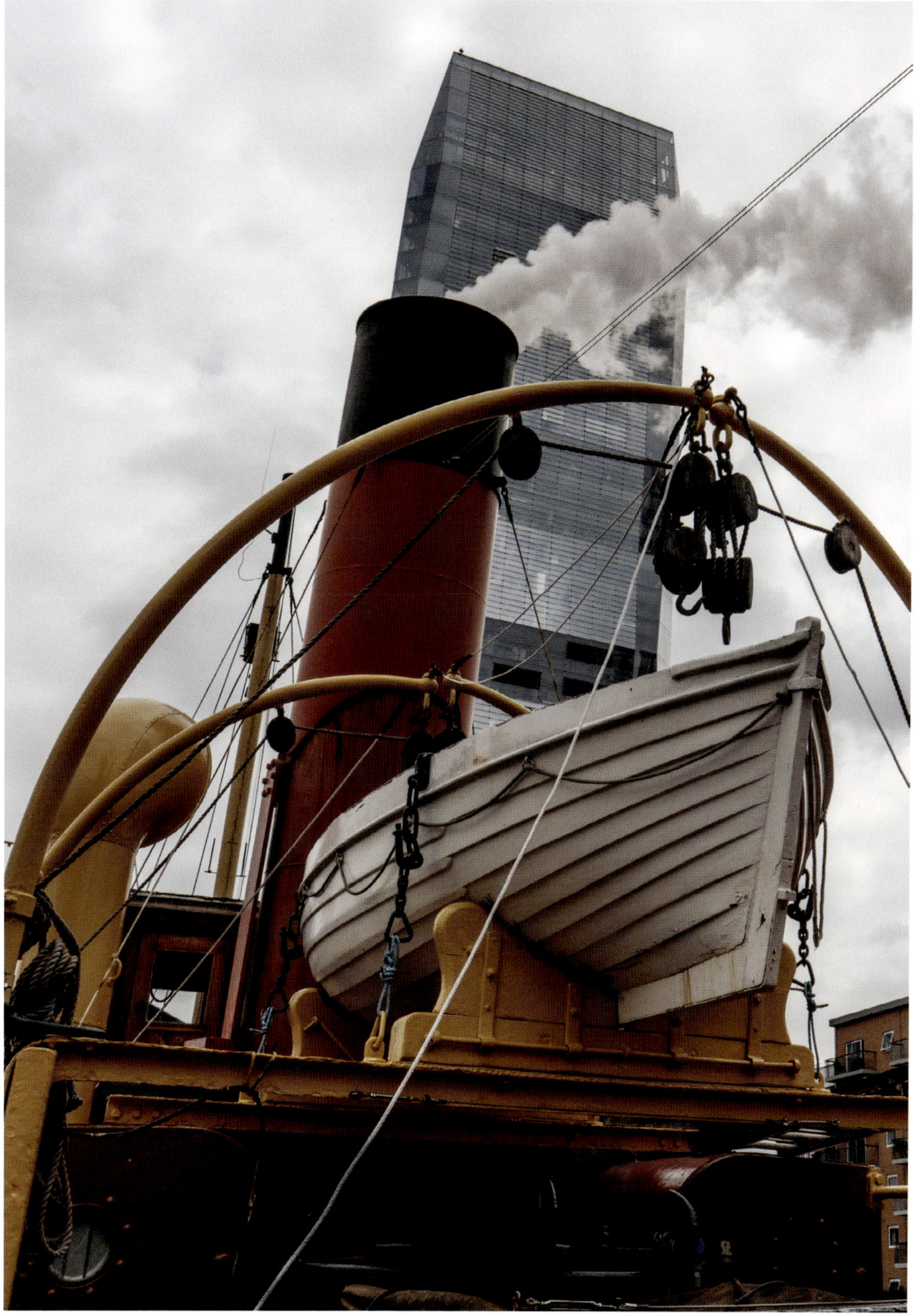

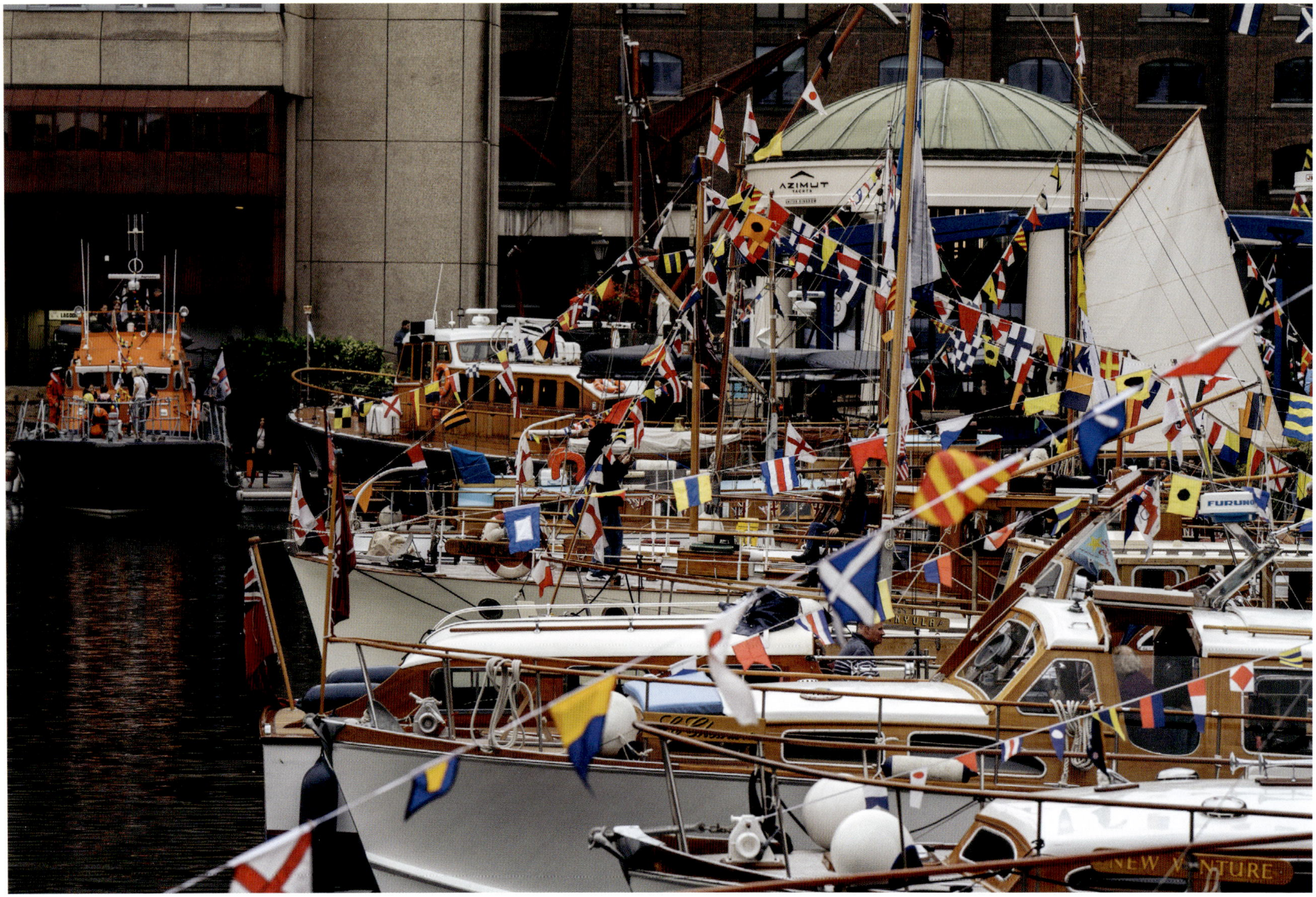

Classic celebration

For one weekend every September, St Katharine Docks' central basin is filled with 40 or so beautifully preserved vintage vessels for the increasingly popular Classic Boat Festival.

A highlight is seeing the line-up of Dunkirk Little Ships, an inspiring reminder of their vital role in crossing the Channel to rescue trapped Allied soldiers in 1940.

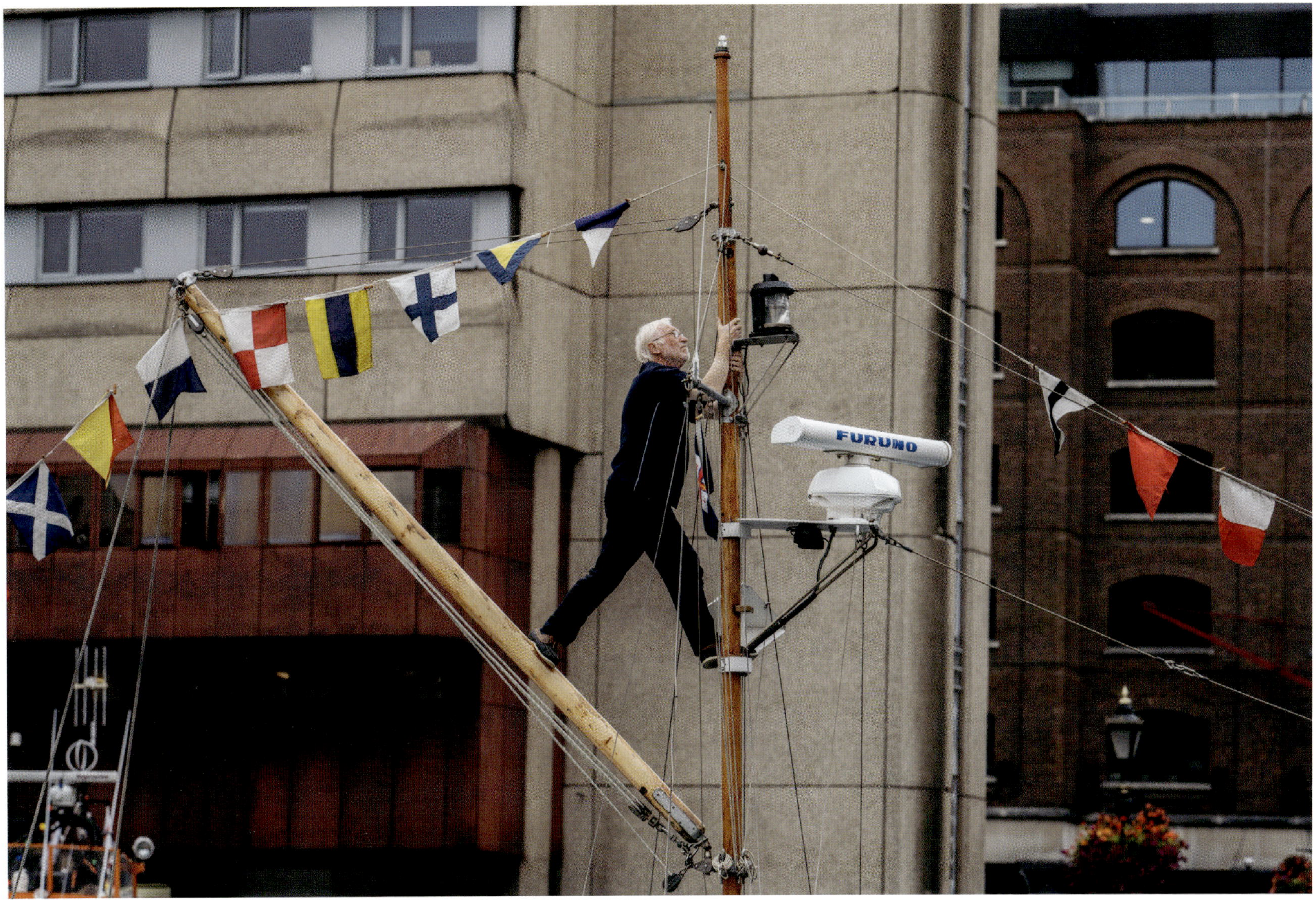

Flagging up

When the bunting on your historic Little Ship needs adjusting, there's only one way to do it.

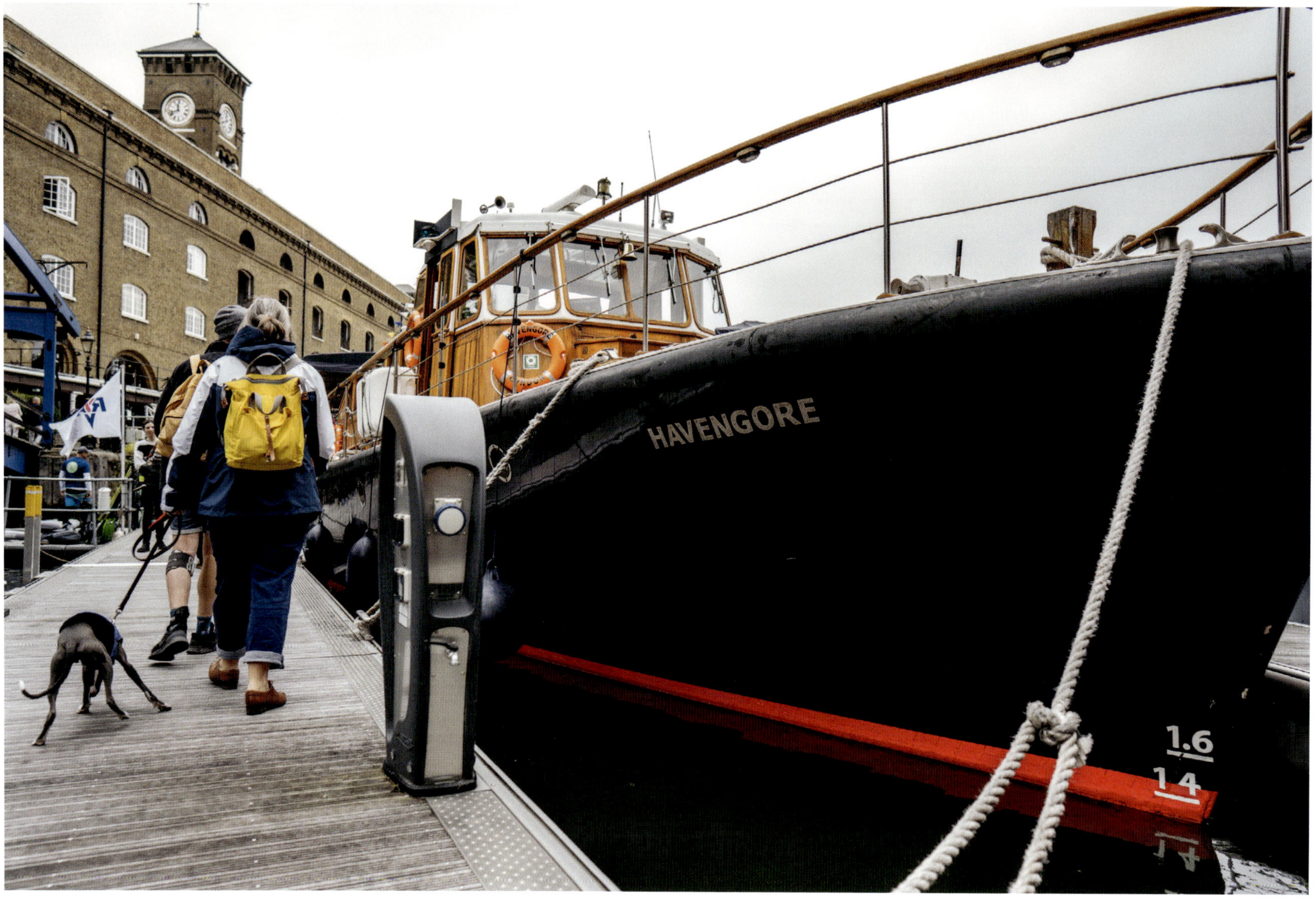

Steeped in history

Another big draw at the Classic Boat Festival is MV *Havengore*, most famous for acting as the funeral cortege barge to carry Sir Winston Churchill's coffin along the Thames in 1965. Since then, she has continued to be central to national events, memorably carrying nine members of the royal family during the Thames pageant for the Queen's Diamond Jubilee in 2012, and in 2016 leading the flotilla for the Queen's 90th Birthday River Parade.
www.havengore.com

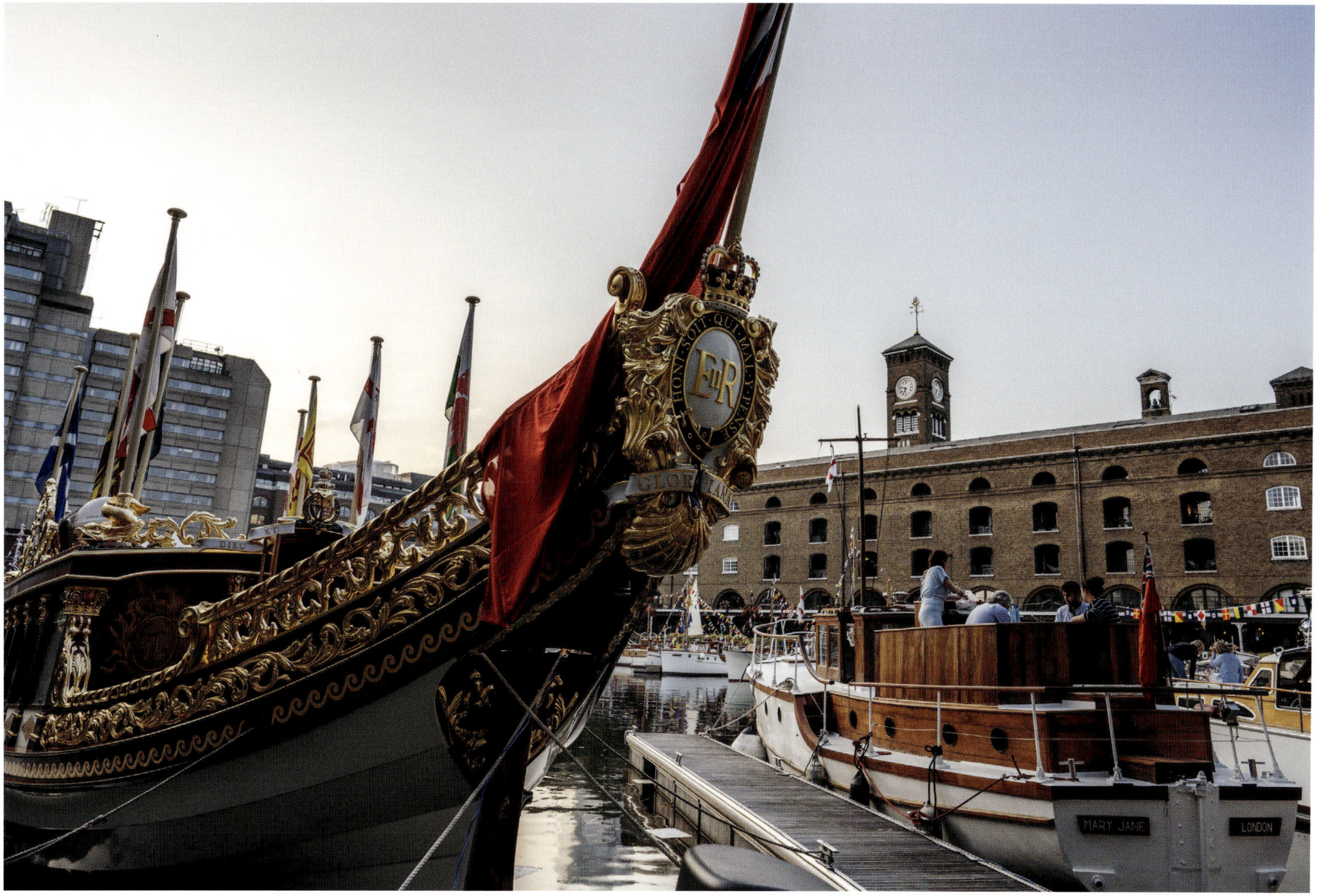

Golden centrepiece

Perhaps the biggest attraction at the festival is the chance to see the Queen's rowbarge *Gloriana* close-up. Commissioned privately to celebrate the Queen's 2012 Diamond Jubilee, she was the first royal barge to be built in over 250 years, inspired by traditional designs from the 18th century. By leading the Thames Diamond Jubilee pageant, she opened up a whole new chapter in the ceremonial use of the river that had died out in the mid-19th century. At almost 27-metres long, fully gilded in gold leaf and with room for 18 oarsman, she is a spectacular sight and continues to be part of celebrations and pageants on the Thames.

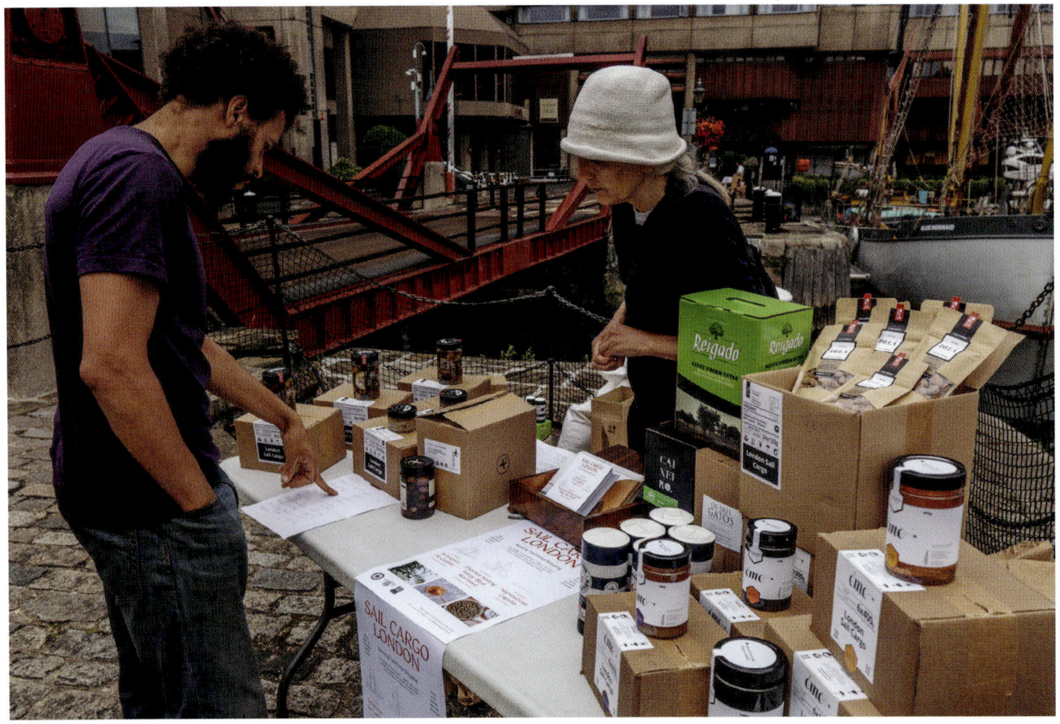

Fair trade

Setting up their stall in St Katharine Docks, Sail Cargo London is part of a network of people selling goods around the world under sail only. This cargo of high-quality, fair-trade foodstuffs has just been unloaded from the sailing barge *Blue Mermaid* in the background. Pre-orders from their website can now be picked up. As they say: 'Farmer – sailor – trader – you'. It has the added advantage of a short supply chain and this low-carbon, traditional way of trading is growing fast.
www.raybelcharters.com/sail-cargo-goods

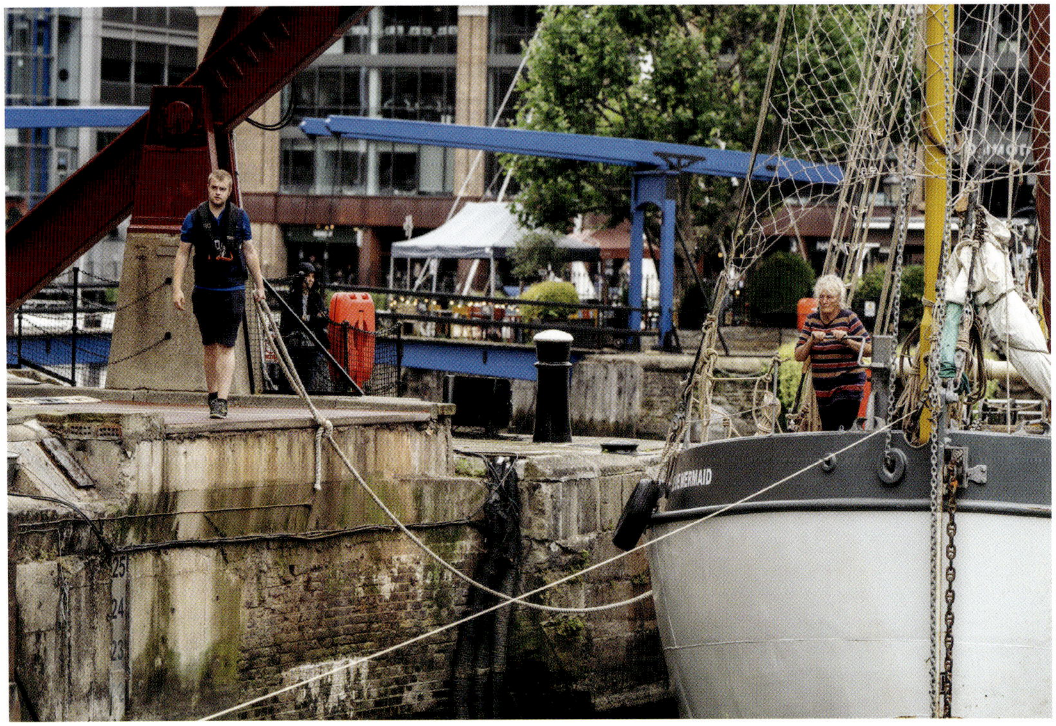

Lock manoeuvres

Having delivered her cargo, *Blue Mermaid* now leaves St Katharine Docks the way she came in, using the traditional 'warping' method for vessels without engines. This involves the expert use of ropes and a winch to ease her into the lock, ready for exiting into the Thames; efficient, peaceful and most importantly, emission-free.

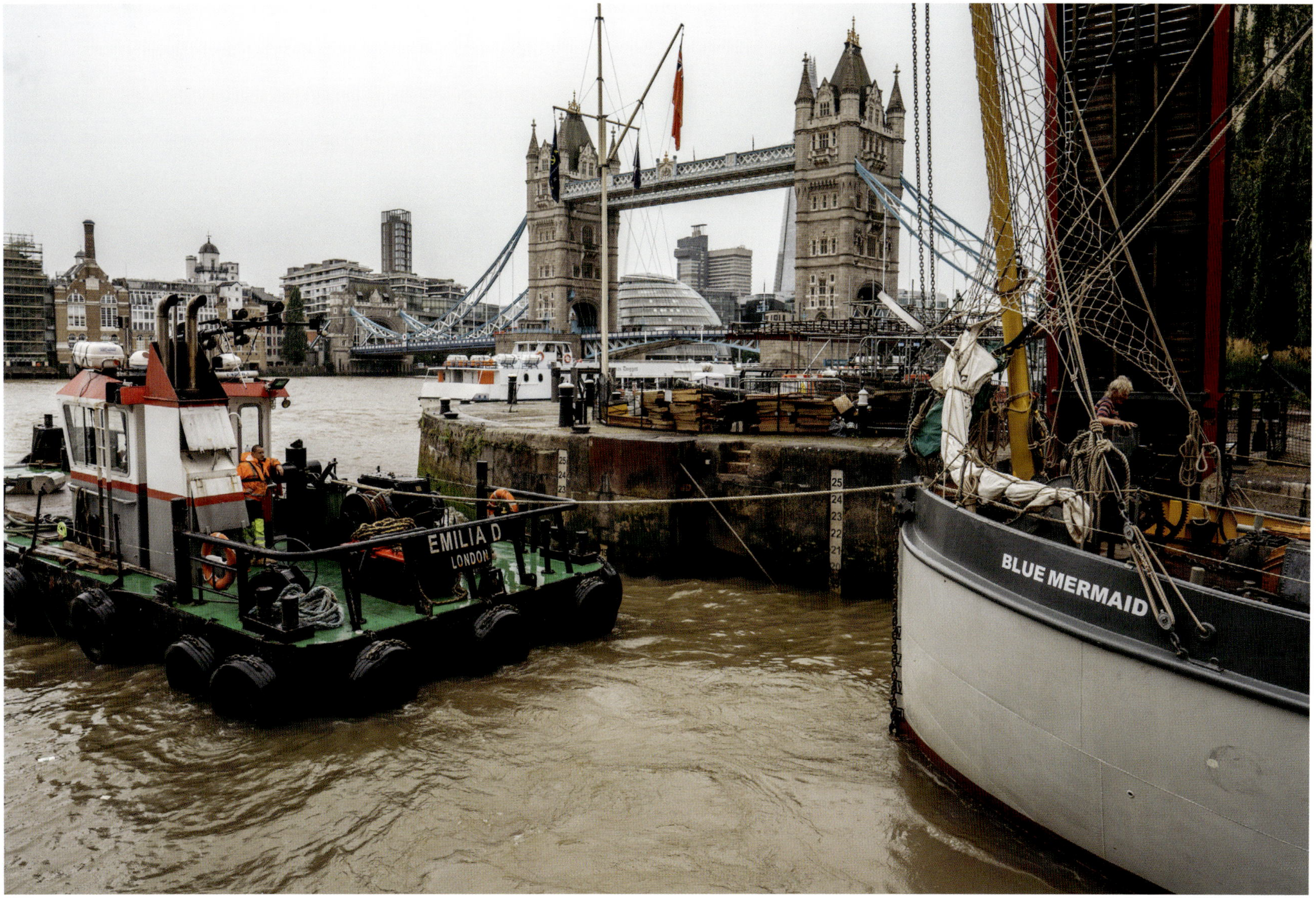

Tugged out

As a faithful replica of the original Thames sailing barge that was lost during the Second World War, *Blue Mermaid* is very capable of sailing down-river but it is helpful to get a start from a tug provided by Thamescraft, subsidised by Sea-Change Sailing Trust supporter Chris Livett. Once past Woolwich, *Blue Mermaid* will set sail for Maldon in Essex where she provides young people and vulnerable adults with the chance to learn life skills by living and working aboard a traditional sailing vessel.
www.seachangesailingtrust.org.uk

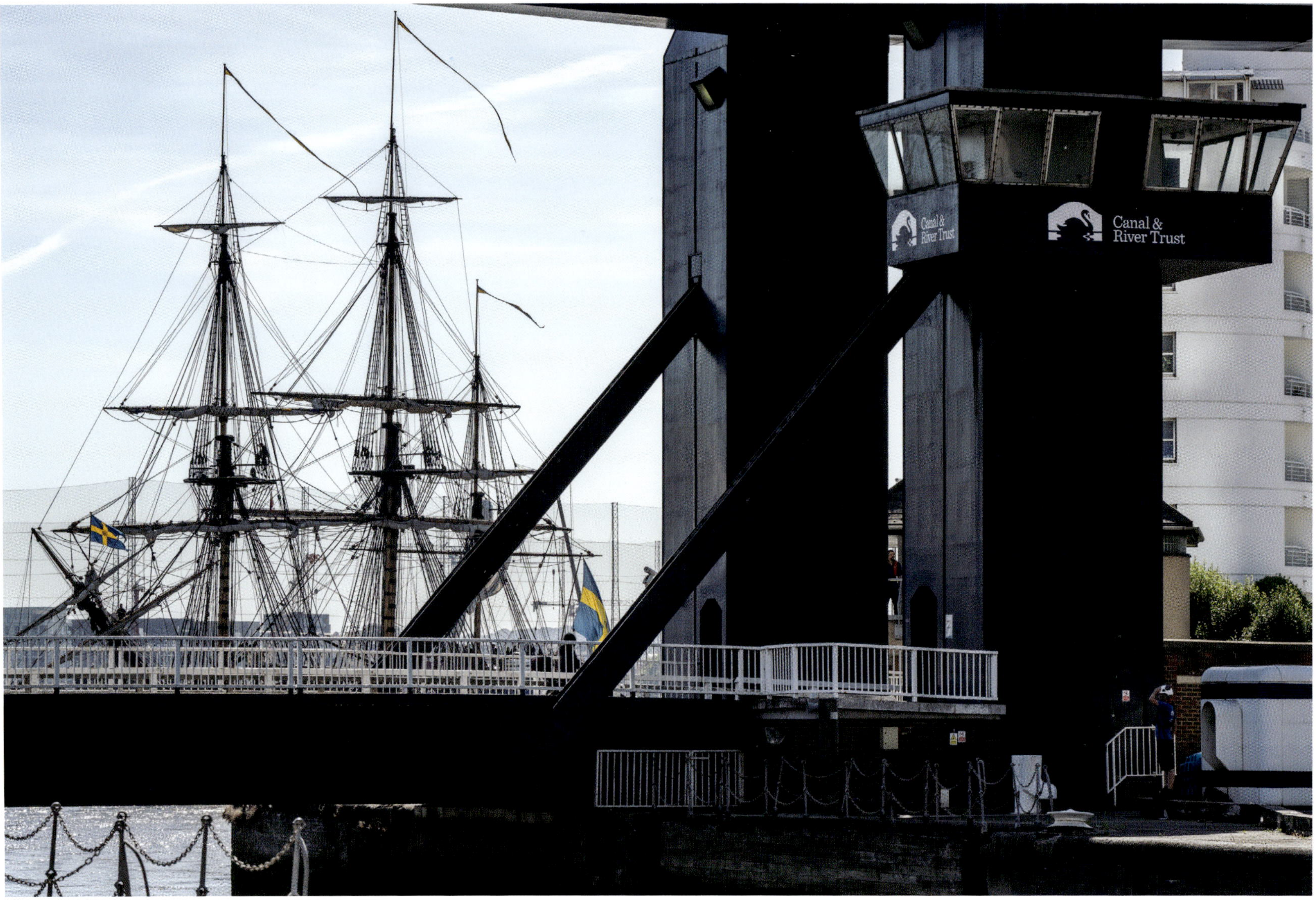

Reincarnation

Like a magnificent ghost from the past, *Götheborg* arrives outside West India Docks awaiting entry into the Isle of Dogs. The Canal & River Trust team are preparing to lift the road bridge for this extraordinary replica of a Swedish East Indiaman. As the world's largest ocean-going wooden sailing ship, she has just created a sensation going up- and down-river through Tower Bridge.

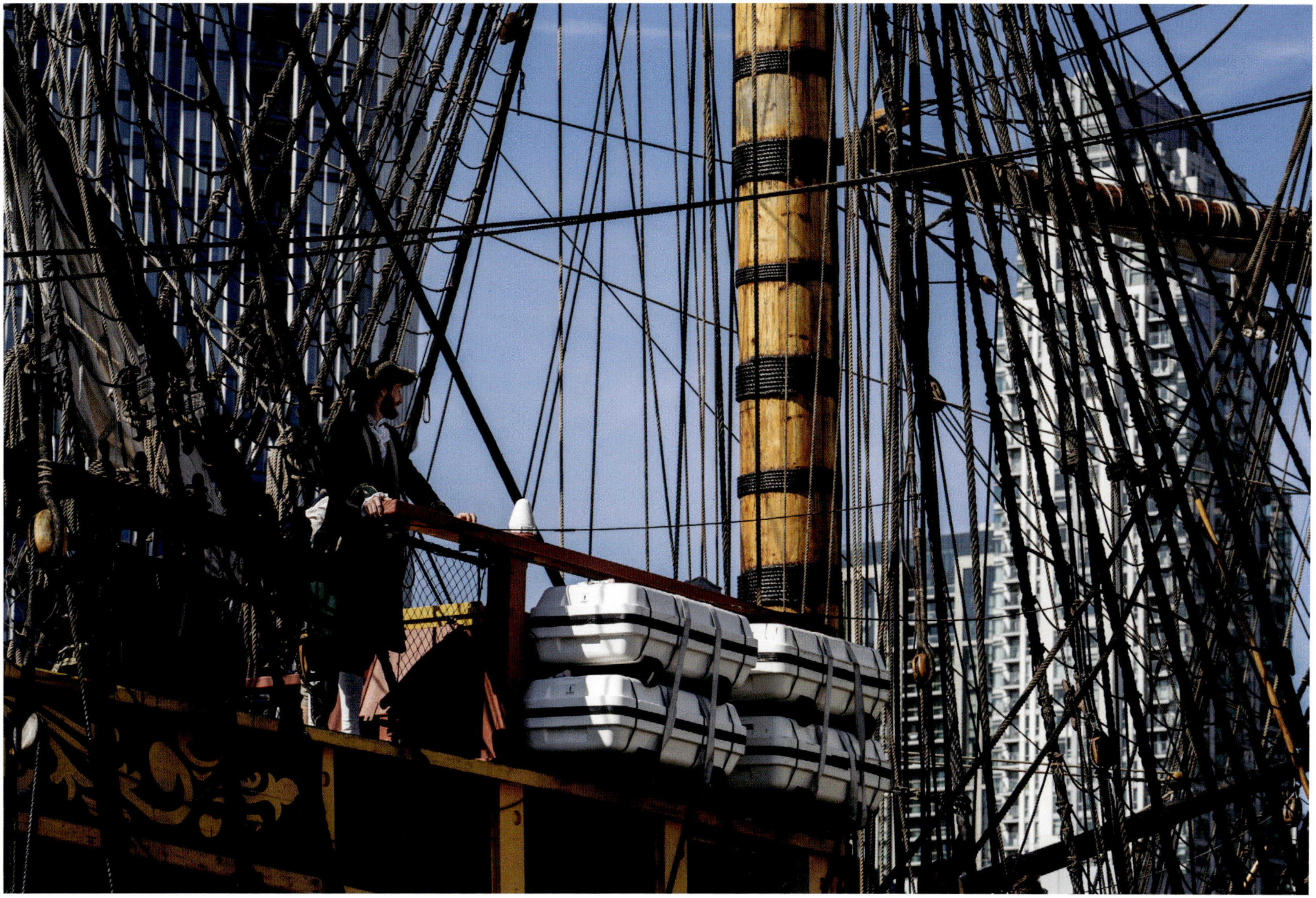

Two ships in one

Götheborg is a recreation of the original (which sank in 1745) and was built between 1996 and 2005 using purely traditional 18th-century methods and materials, including 20 tons of handmade hemp rigging. She voyages around the world as a unique working museum, attracting both paying deckhands keen to enjoy the full sailing experience and enthusiastic visitors in ports. But there are also modern comforts and safety additions, such as air-conditioning and fire extinguishers, well hidden inside. One of the few exterior hints of this dual timescale are the necessary lifeboats on deck.

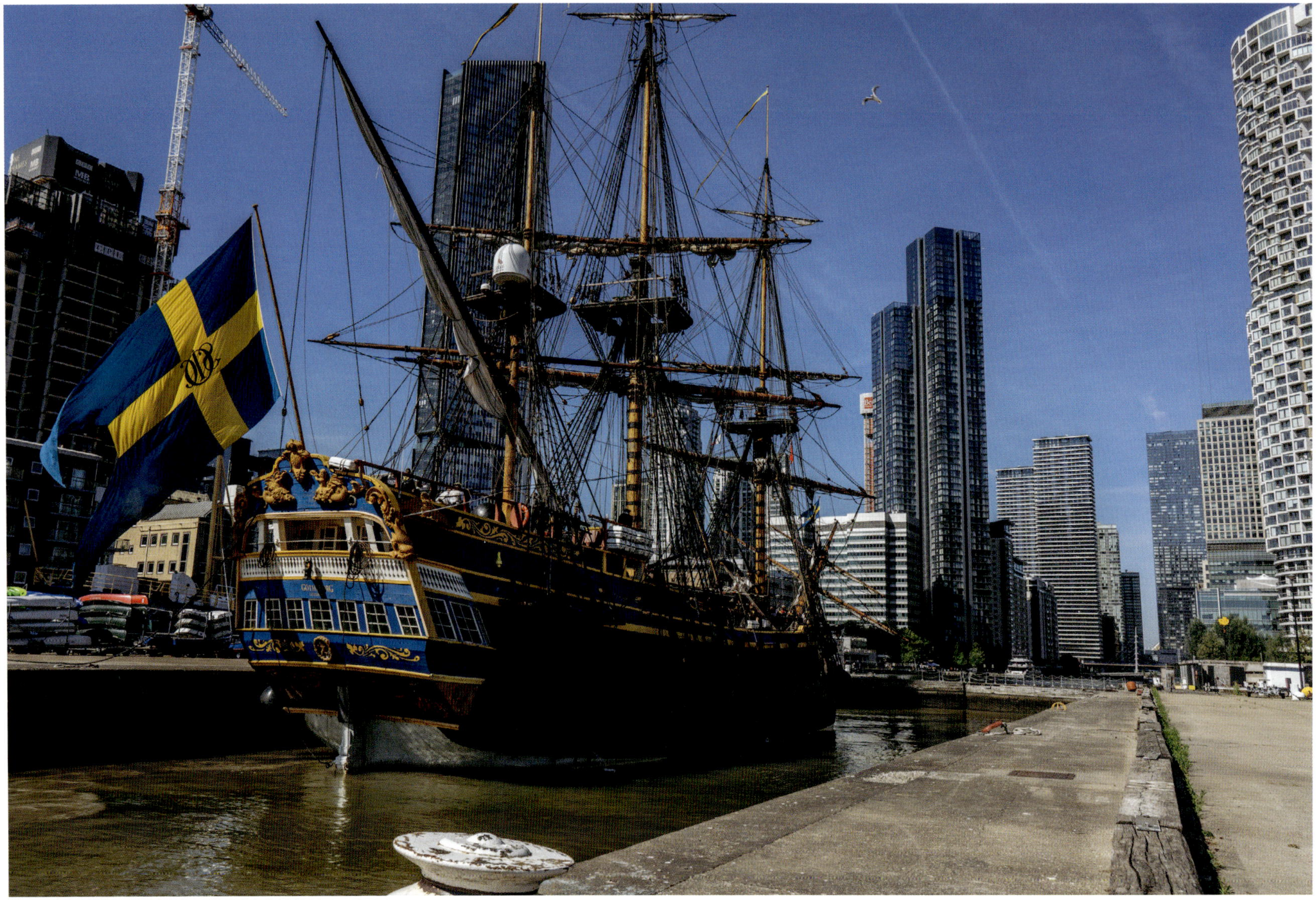

Voyaging attraction

Flying the unique Swedish East India Company's 'swallowtail' flag, the 788-ton *Götheborg* moves smoothly on towards her West India Docks mooring. Her arrival has been eagerly awaited and all the 20 professional crew, as well as the 50 volunteers and paying deckhands, are primed to greet the many expected visitors. After a few days, she will head off to her next port of call to continue her latest expedition. www.gotheborg.se

Multiple timelines

Built in Goa in 1997, the traditional barque design of the Indian Navy's INS *Tarangini* brings echoes of 18th-century sailing history. As she arrives at the Isle of Dogs, she highlights more layers from West India Docks' past in the 19th-century lock and in the 20th-century engineering feats of the quayside cranes and huge road bridge. The 21st century also gets a look-in with the O2's yellow spires visible on the other side of the river.

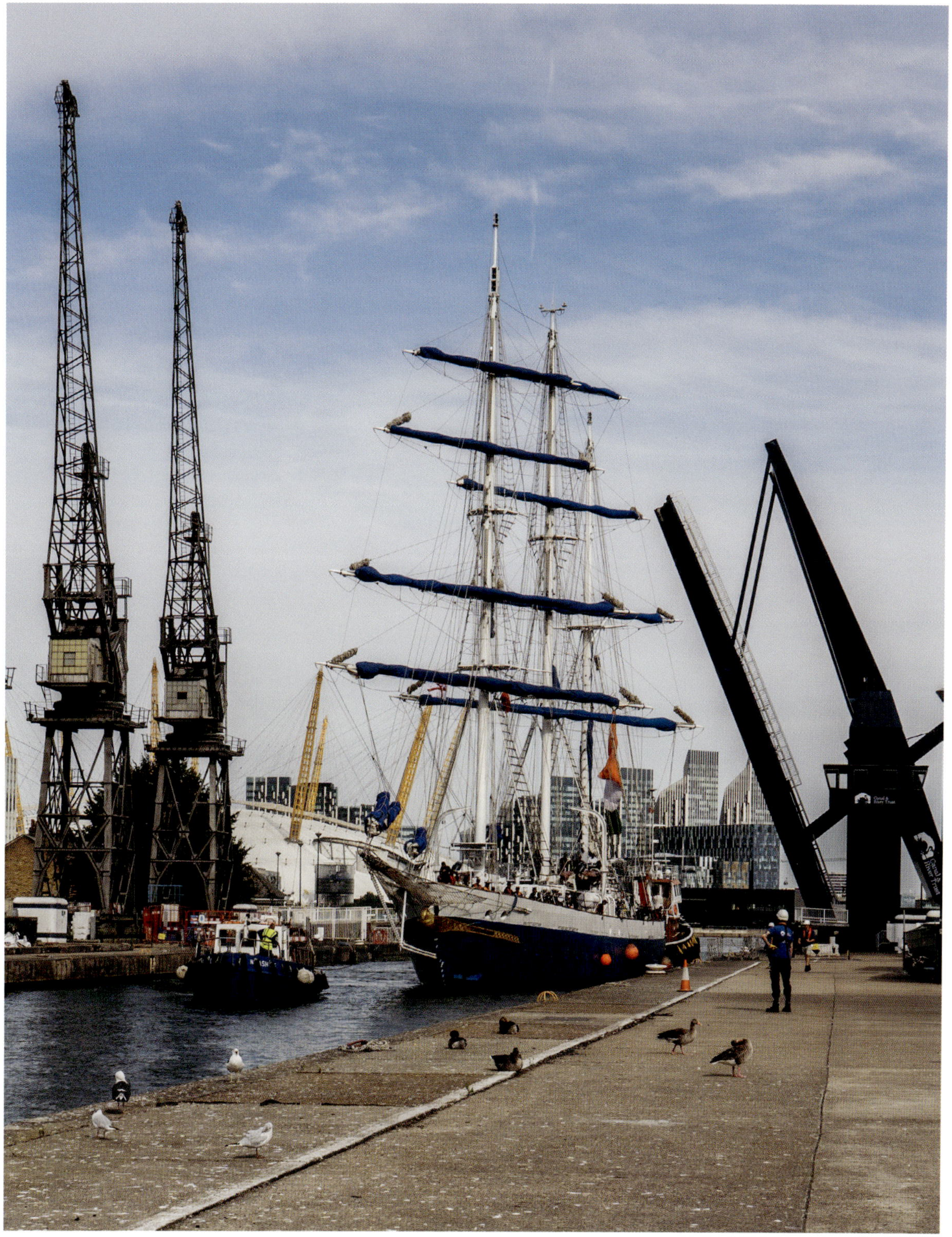

Watery pastimes

Where commerce and trade once dominated,
Londoners pursue recreation and fun.

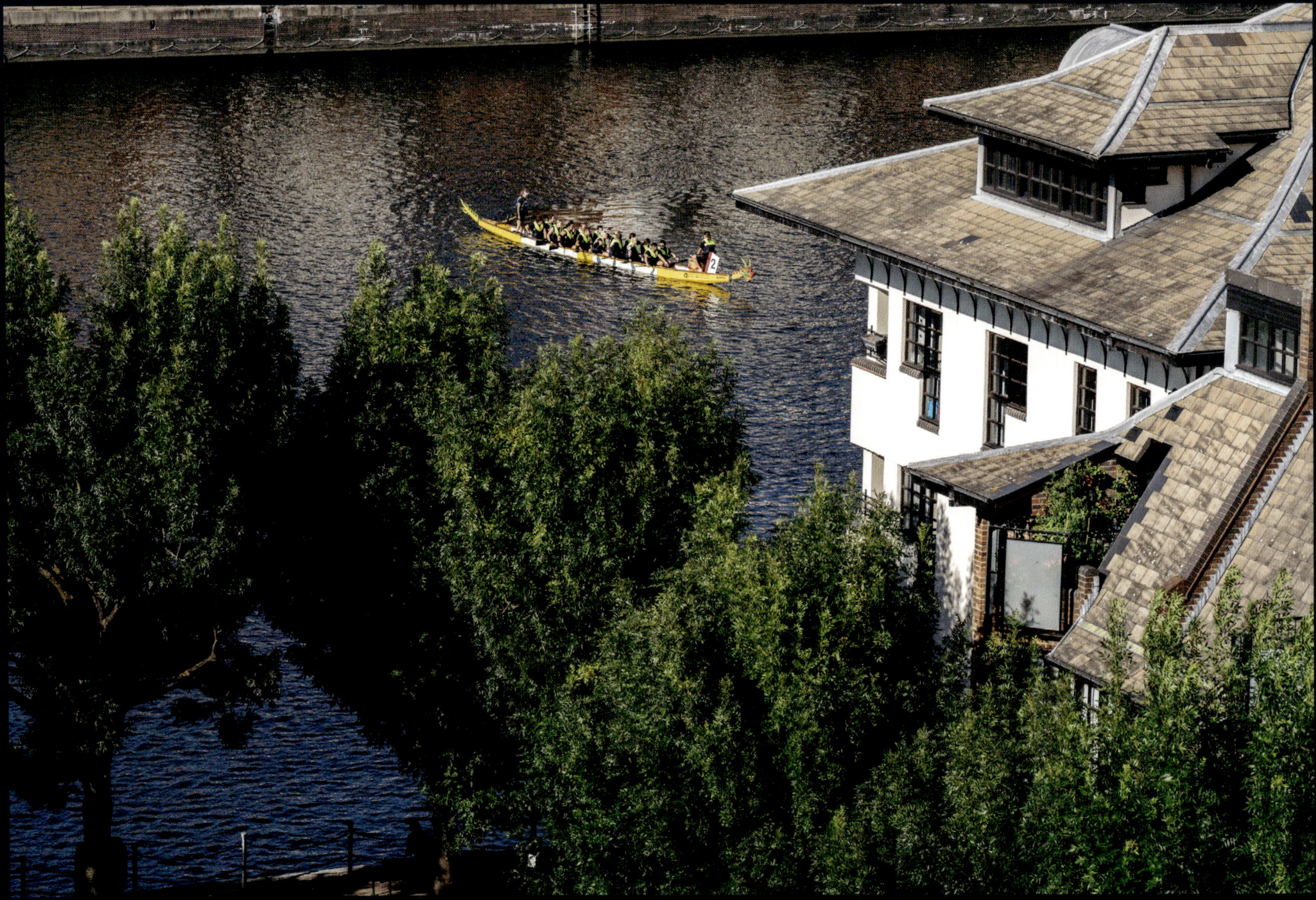

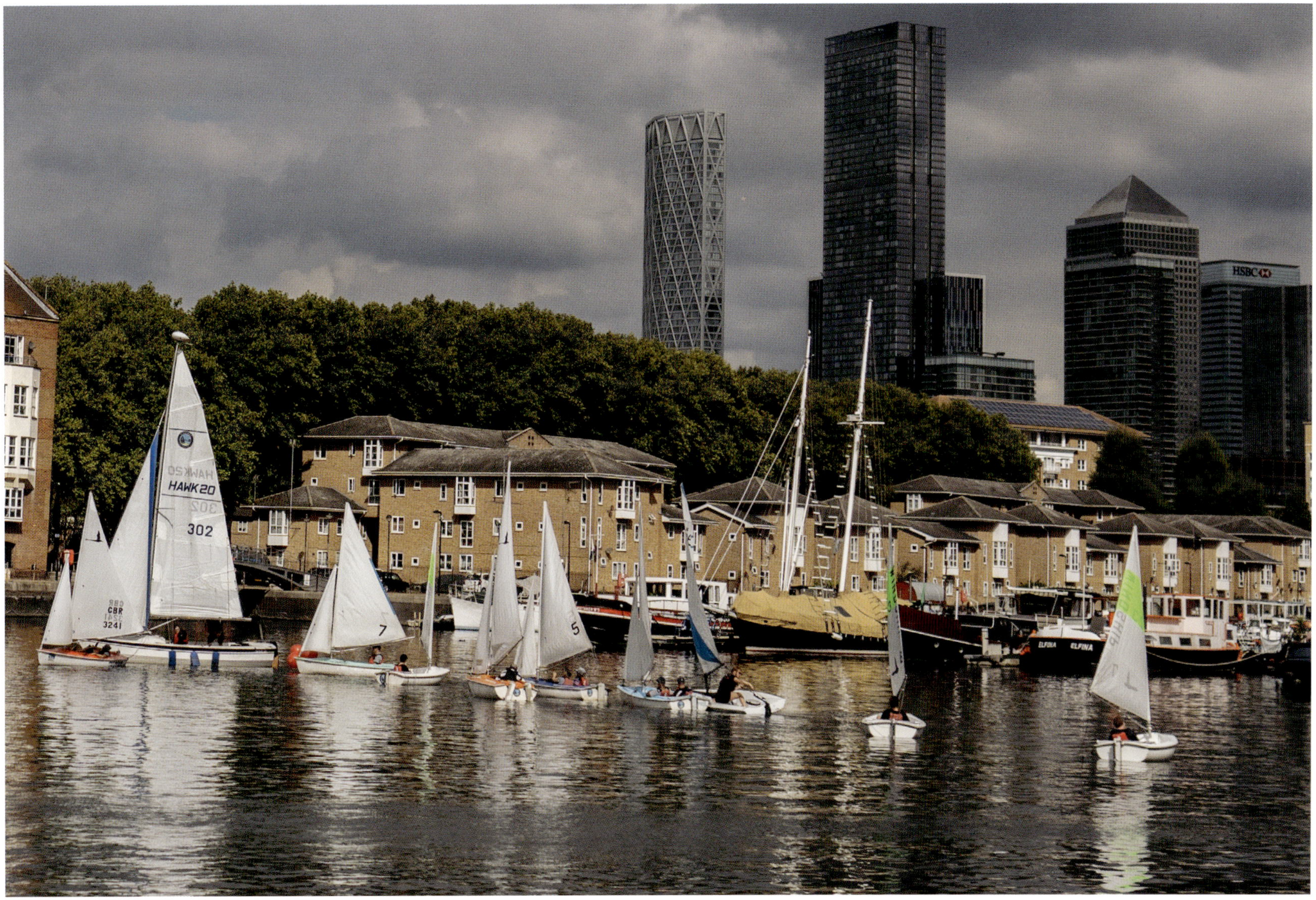

From whales to dragons and hawks

Greenland Dock in Surrey Quays was named after the 18th-century Greenland whalers who used its quayside to boil blubber and produce oil. At 690 metres in length, this vast expanse of water no longer accommodates whales but often hosts dragon boat racing and sailing boats going by such names as *Hawk 20*. The Surrey Docks Fitness & Watersports Centre is its busy focal point, offering a tempting range of waterborne activities, including kayaking, canoeing, windsurfing and paddleboarding. When everyone is out on a sunny afternoon, it's an amazing sight for central London.

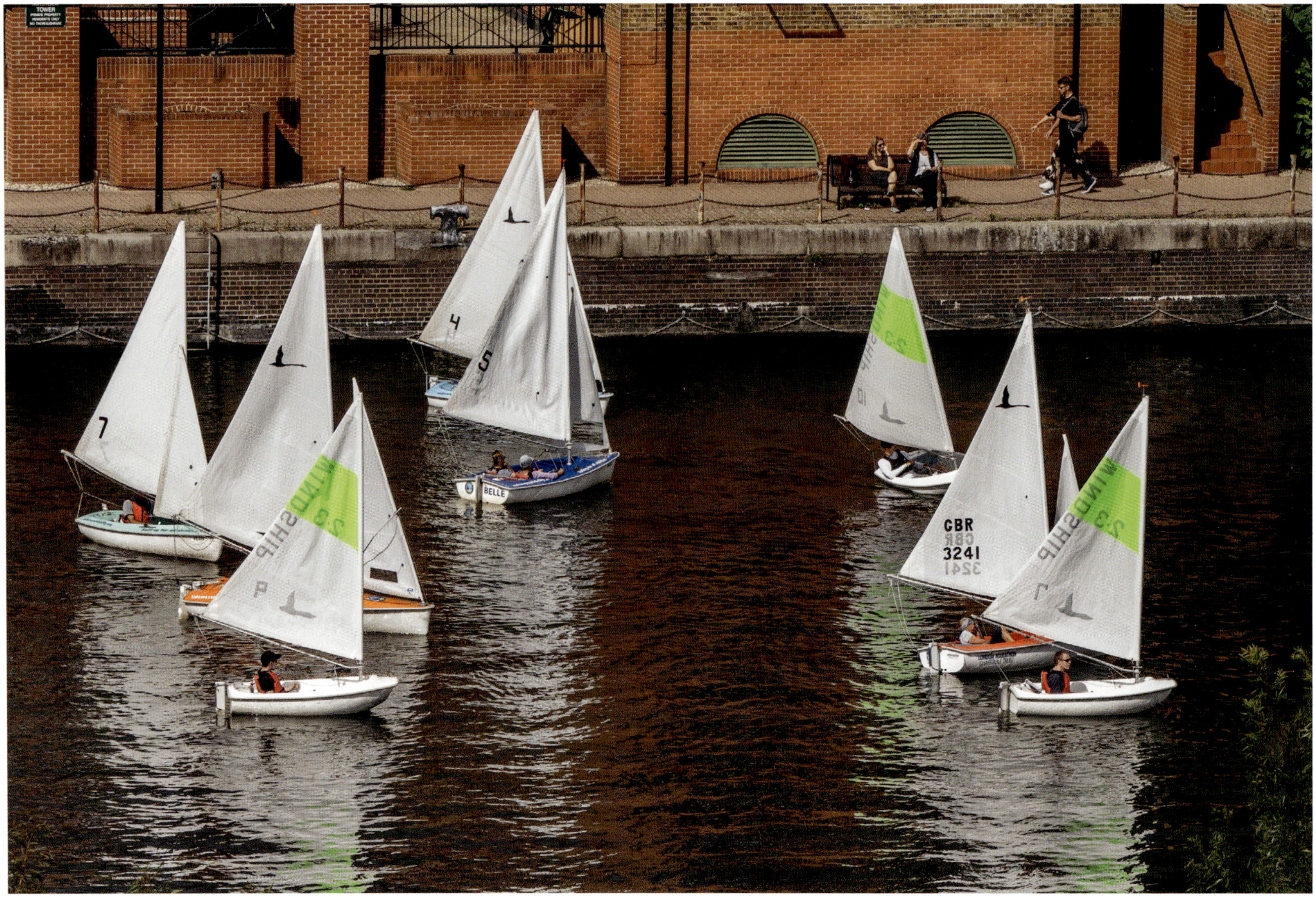

‘Bart’s Bash’

This annual global event run by the Andrew ‘Bart’ Simpson Foundation fits right in with Tideway Sailability’s own ethos. As many members as possible are out on Greenland Dock every September to take part in ‘Bart’s Bash’, designed to raise funds and promote the founders’ belief that everyone should have a chance to enjoy sailing. Tideway Sailability’s specially adapted boats for stability and ease-of-use allow anyone, with or without a disability, to have a go.

All aboard

Experienced volunteers Dave and Mark use Tideway Sailability's dockside hoist to gently swing Hanni into one of their specialist dinghies to join her sister and carer, Nalan. With a weighted keel and a joystick to steer with, this boat can't capsize and can be easily controlled.

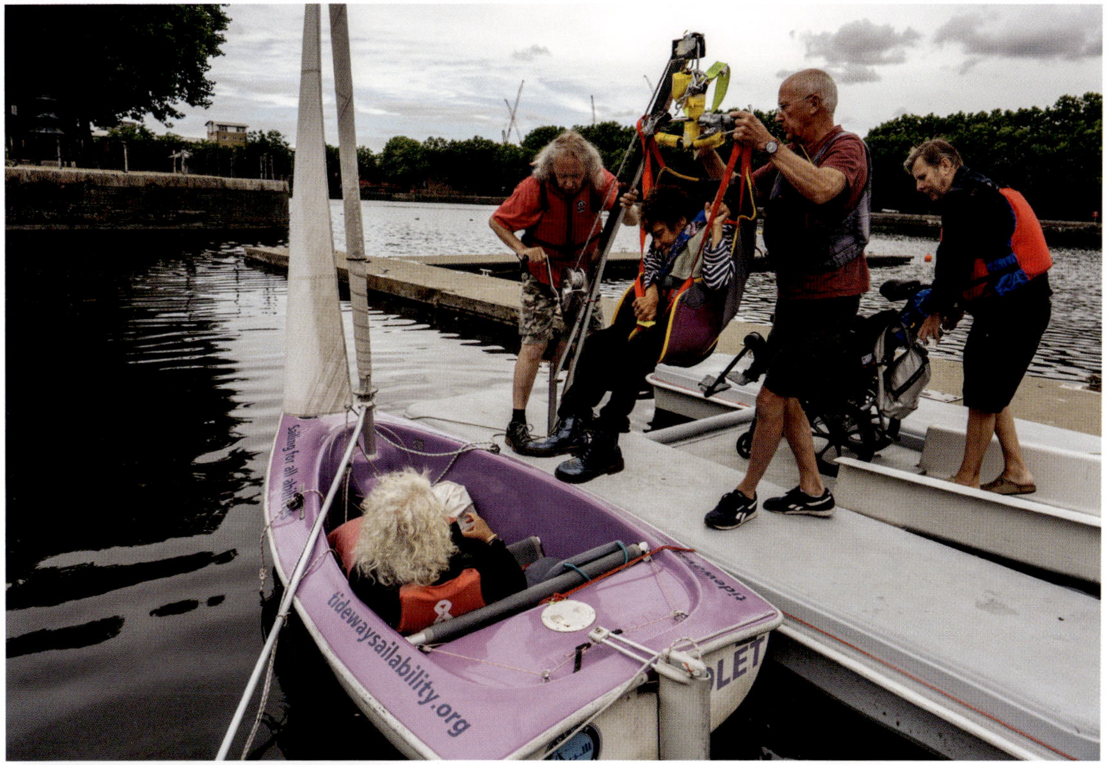

Freedom on the water

Nalan often brings her sister three times a week to sail around Greenland Dock. She loves the whole experience, particularly because she can see how Hanni finds it so liberating and fulfilling. Now they are coming in to dock, ready to be received by Paul, one of Tideway Saleability's long-serving volunteers.
www.tidewaysailability.org.uk

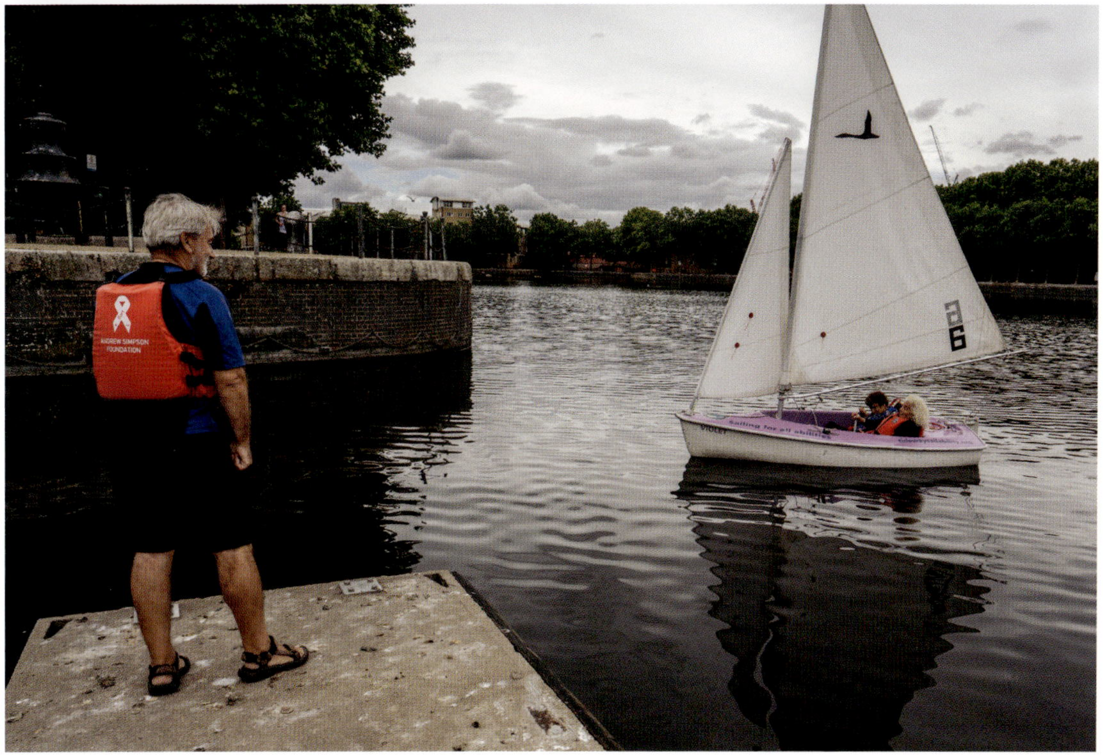

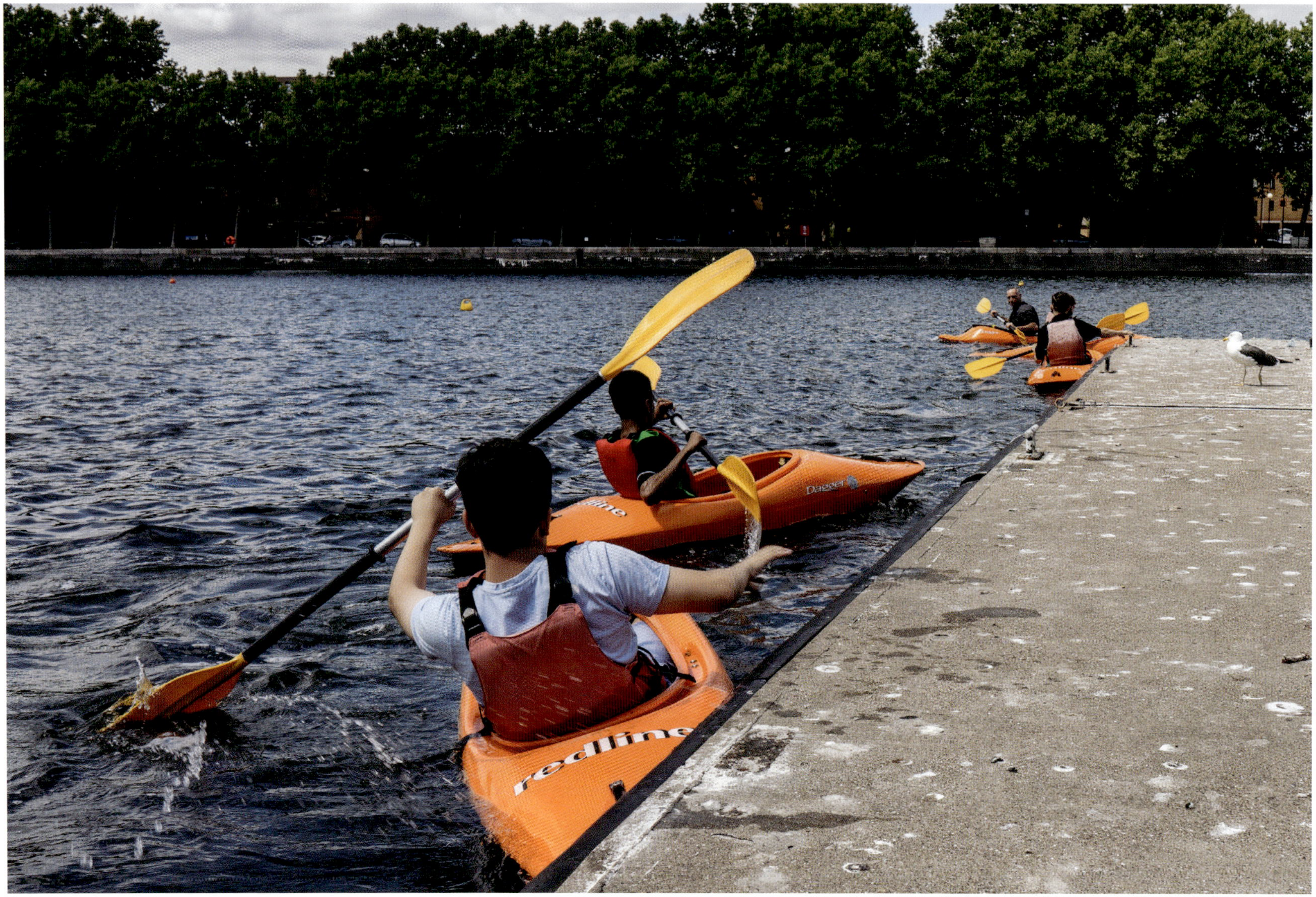

Watersport challenge

A group of 16-year-olds from a local school are being coached in how to handle a kayak. Several have never been in a boat before but after a first session learning the basics within the enclosed safety of the pontoons, they have gained confidence and are now heading out into Greenland Dock's open water under the watchful eye of instructor, Ben. The Surrey Docks Fitness & Watersports Centre works hard with schools to make sure that any child can benefit from this amazing water asset on their doorstep.

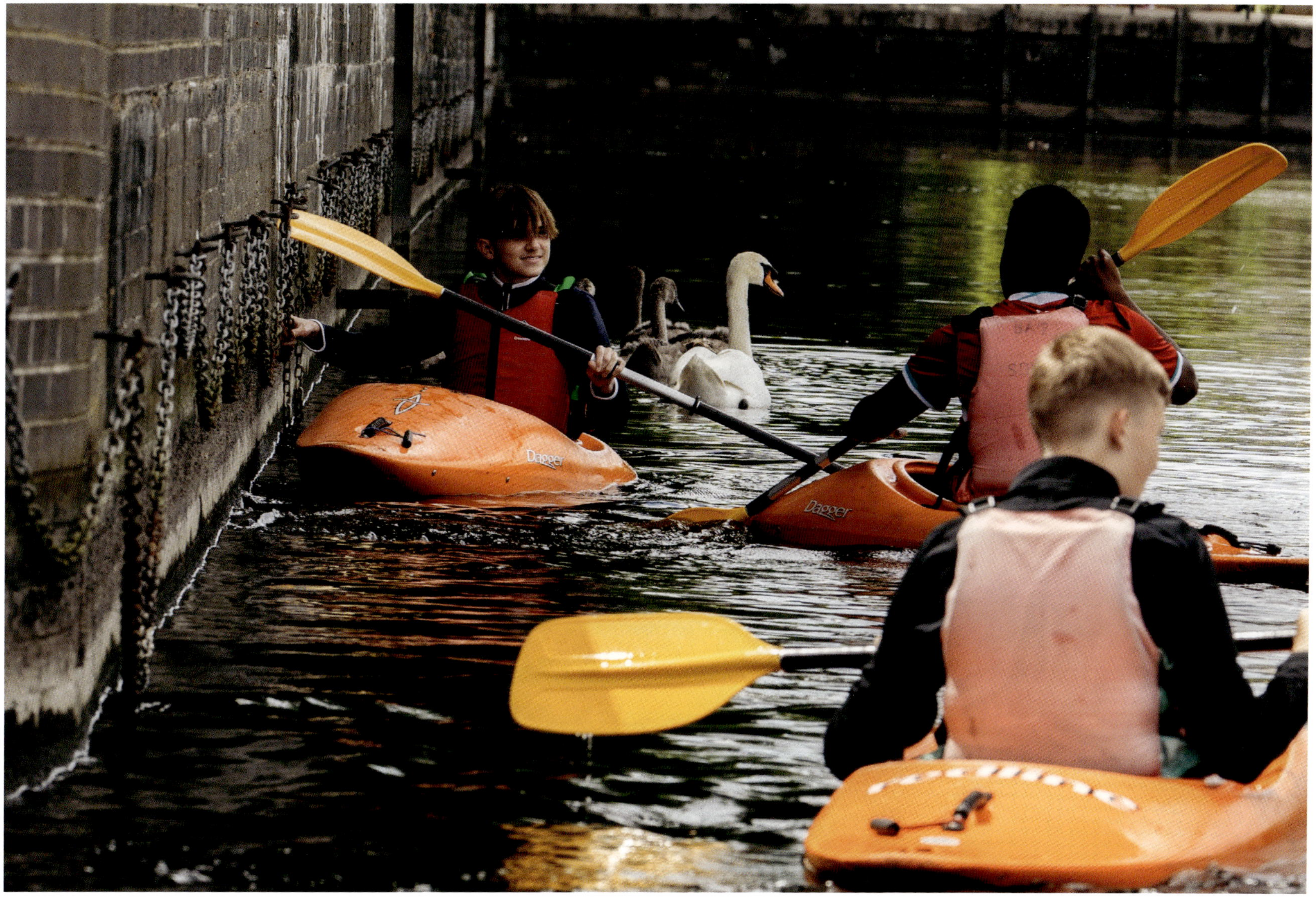

Raising the bar

James and his classmates have made it all the way around Greenland Dock and the sense of achievement is obvious. Now they will be tested further to reach the next level of kayaking skill. The Surrey Docks Fitness & Watersports Centre teaches to accredited standards and they like to set challenges. www.everyoneactive.com/centre/surrey-docks-water-sports-centre

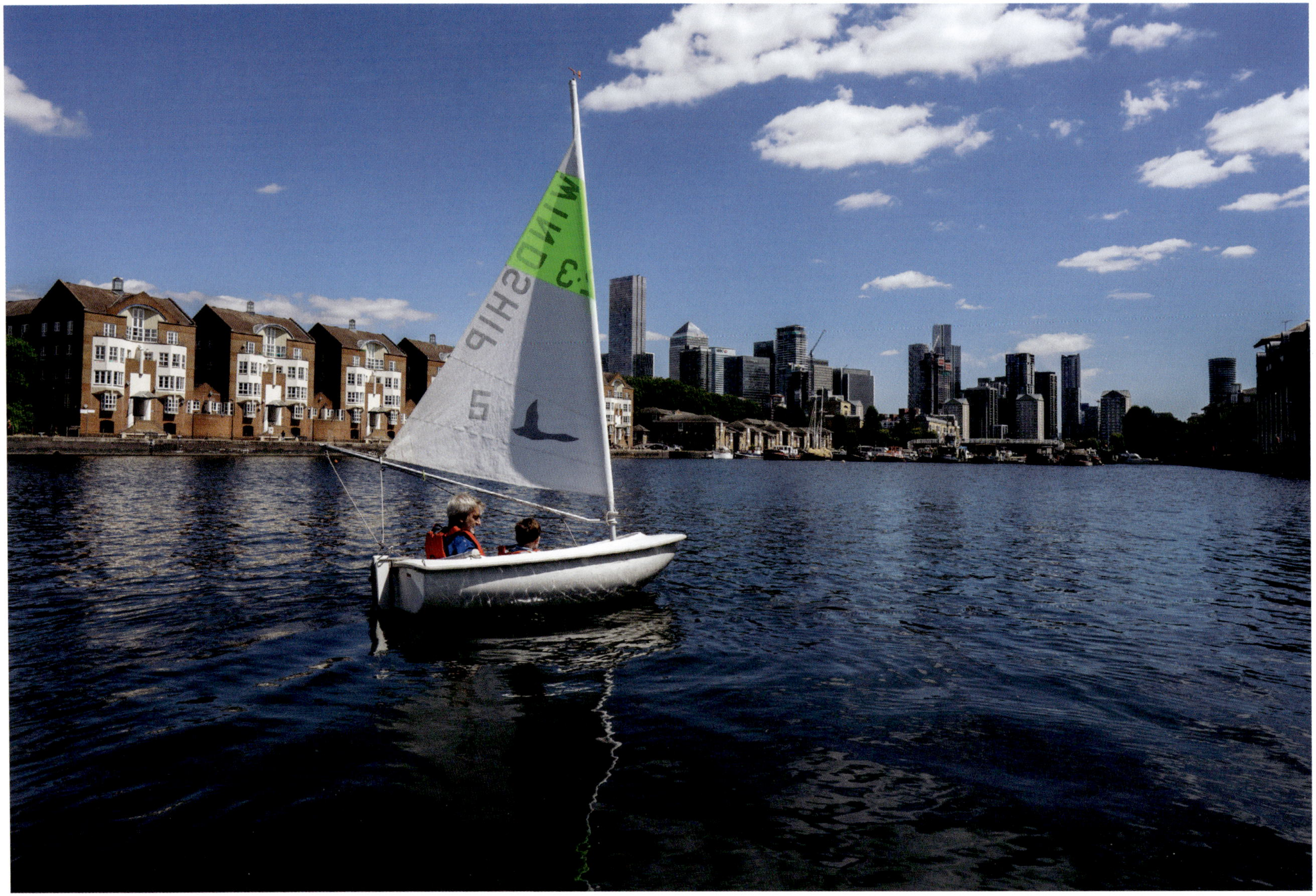

Expanding horizons

For a four-day Festival of Sailing organised by the PE & School Sports Network, children from the ages of five to eleven with Special Educational Needs and Disabilities (SEND) are invited to come sailing, often for the first time, at Greenland Dock. Given their own boat and personal teacher, the effect on these children is wonderful to see, as they soon learn how to use the joystick to steer and begin to get the feel of the boat moving with the wind. The PE & School Sports Network works with over 100 schools in South East London to develop all sports.
www.lpessn.org.uk

Scouting on water

A Water Activity Open Day at the Dockland Scout Project on the Isle of Dogs involves over 80 scouts and cubs having a great deal of fun learning how to stay afloat and move boats about in different ways. Centred on the HQTS *Lord Amory* moored in West India Docks, trained volunteers give expert instruction on kayaking, canoeing, rowing and sailing and take full advantage of the huge stretches of open water surrounding them. It's a remarkably colourful and exuberant transformation of these old docks.

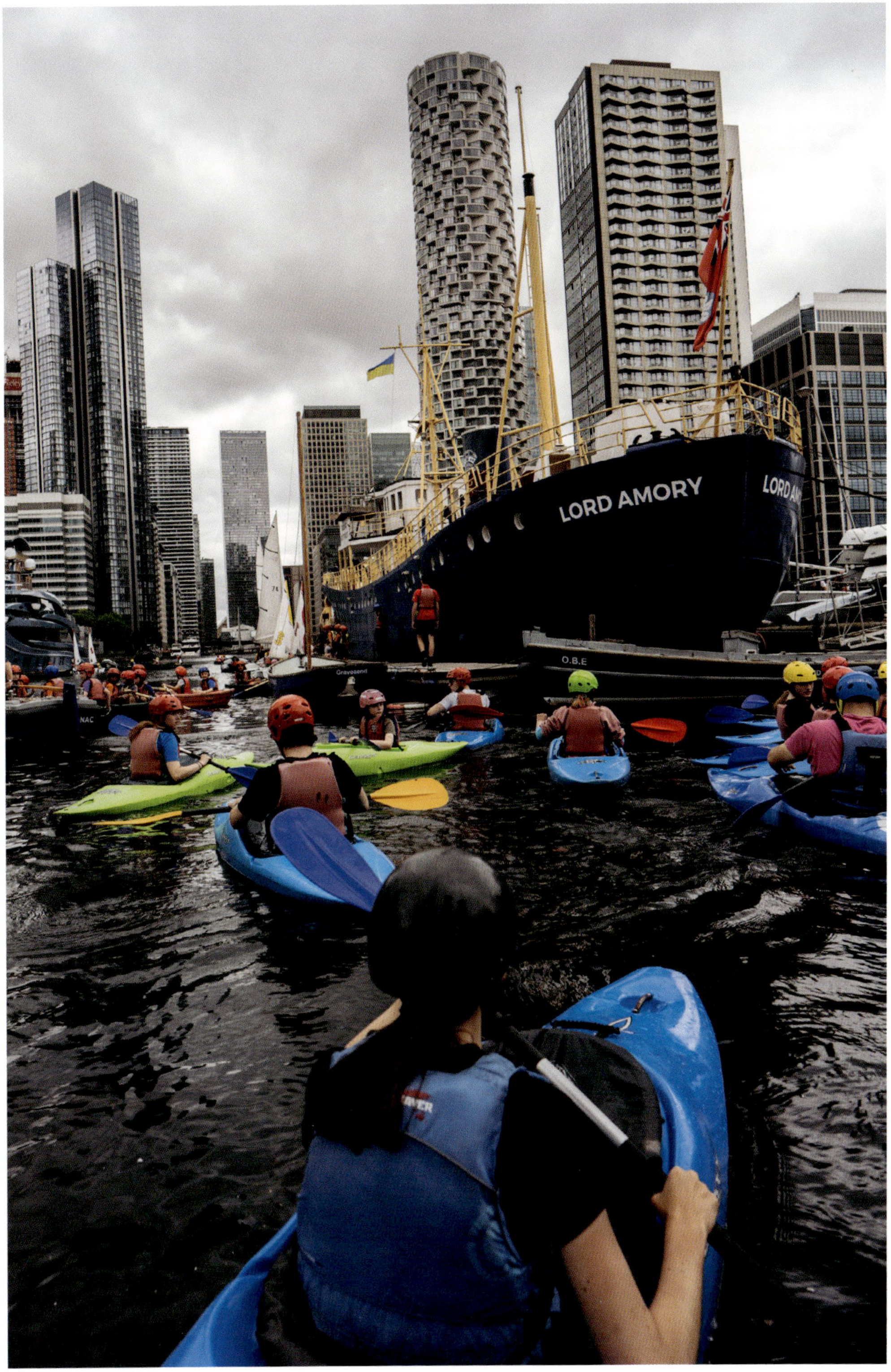

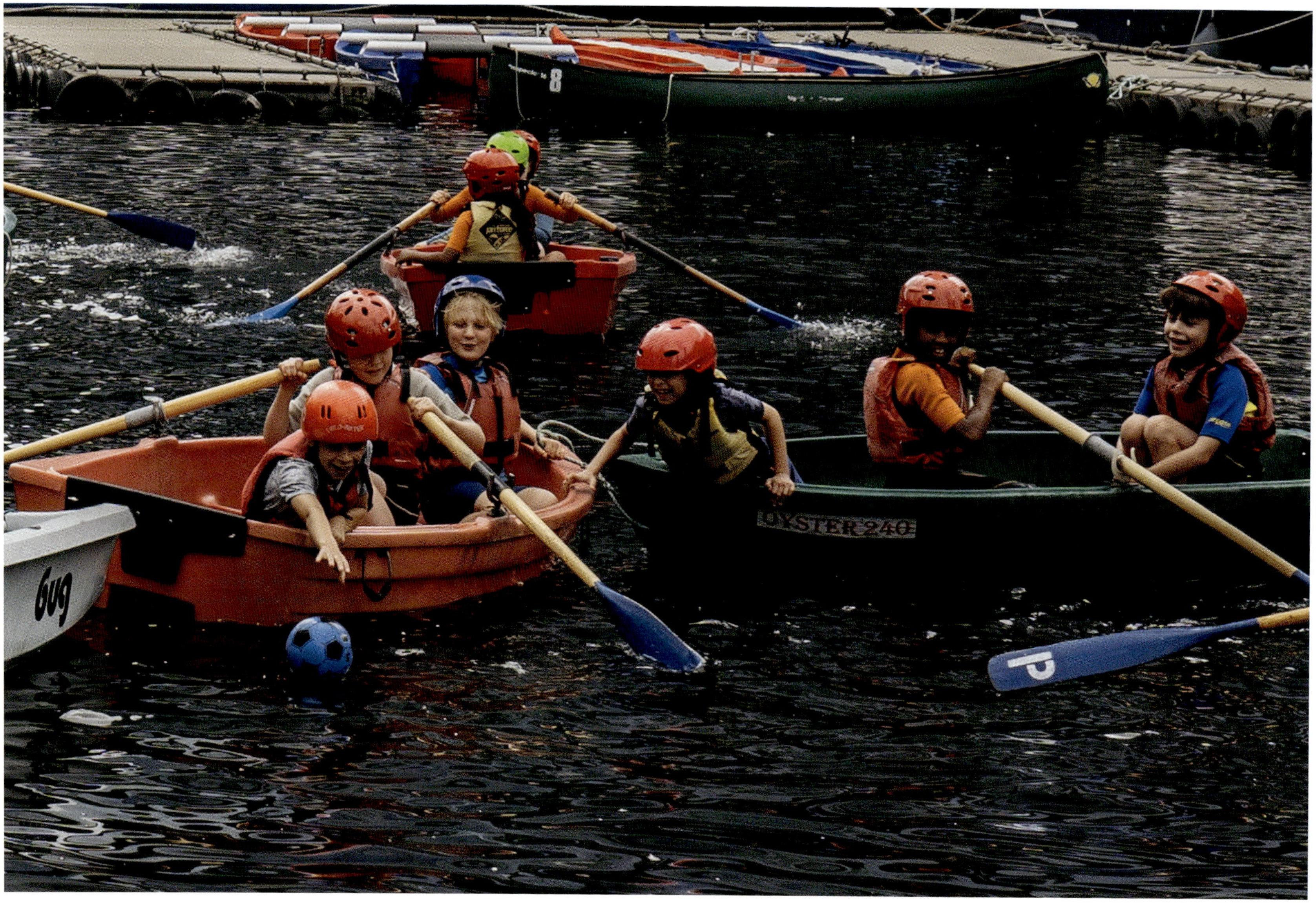

Floating target

One activity for Cubs is to learn how best to manoeuvre a rowboat in order to capture a floating ball. It's a real test of rowing control as well as being huge fun.

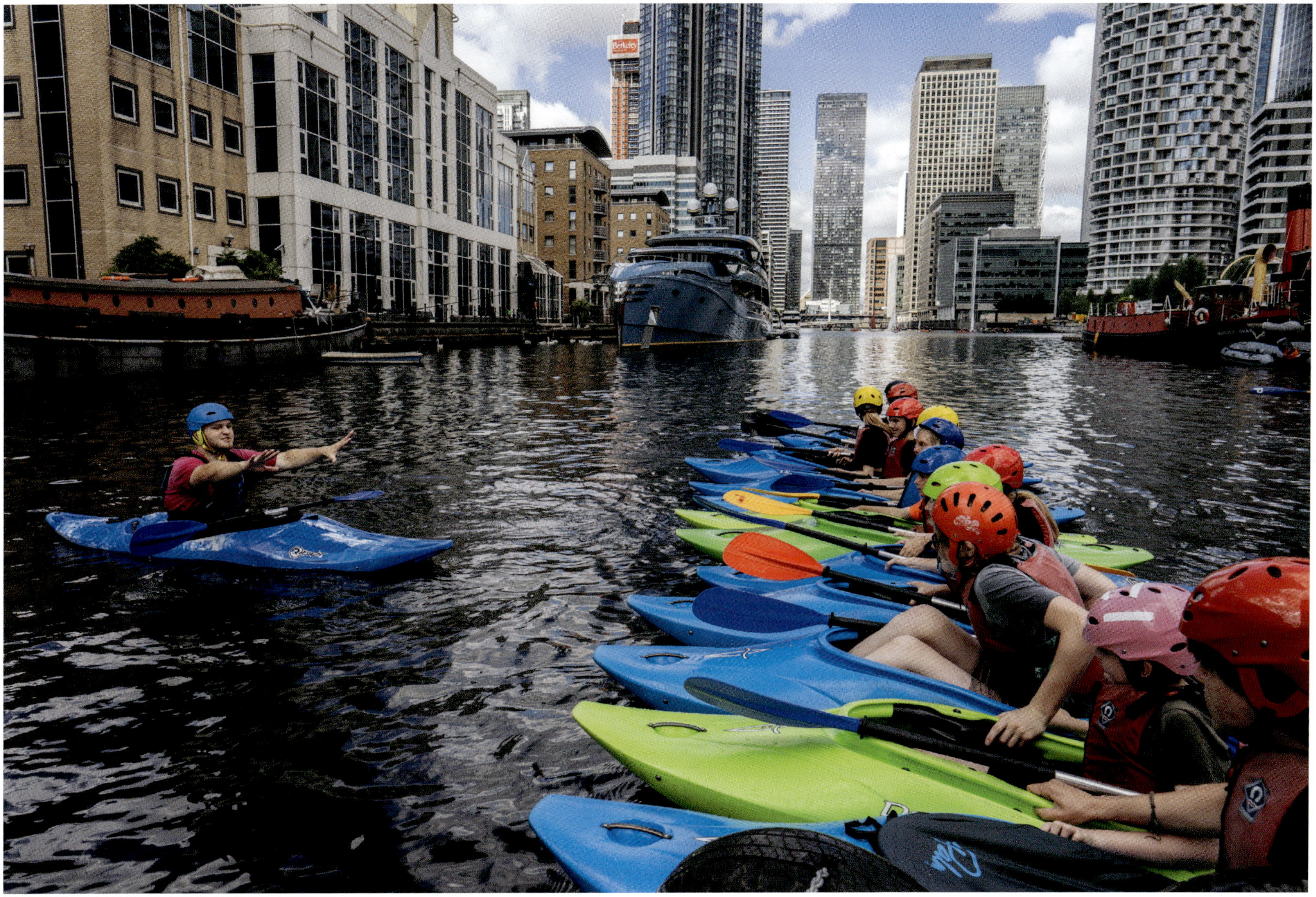

Straight down the dock

This older group of Scouts has just mastered enough kayaking skills to follow its instructor up West India Docks and back, carefully avoiding the unusual obstacle of a superyacht. Now it's on to the next challenge in this carefully structured day of learning activity.
www.lordamory.org

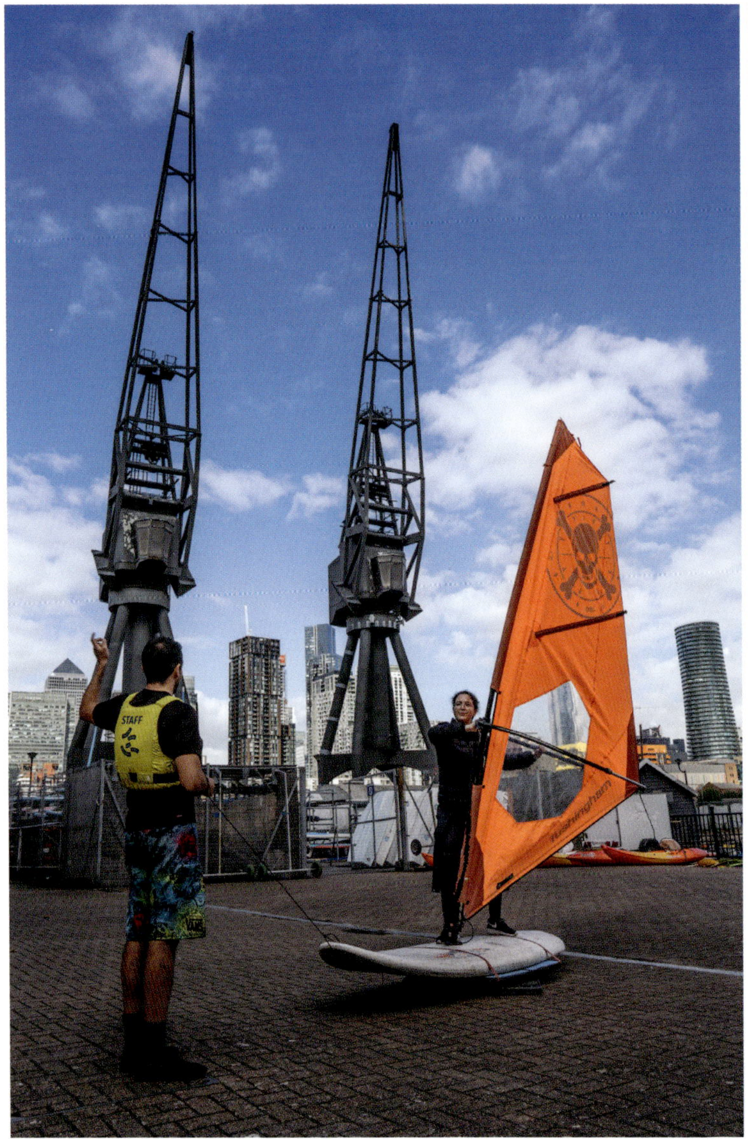

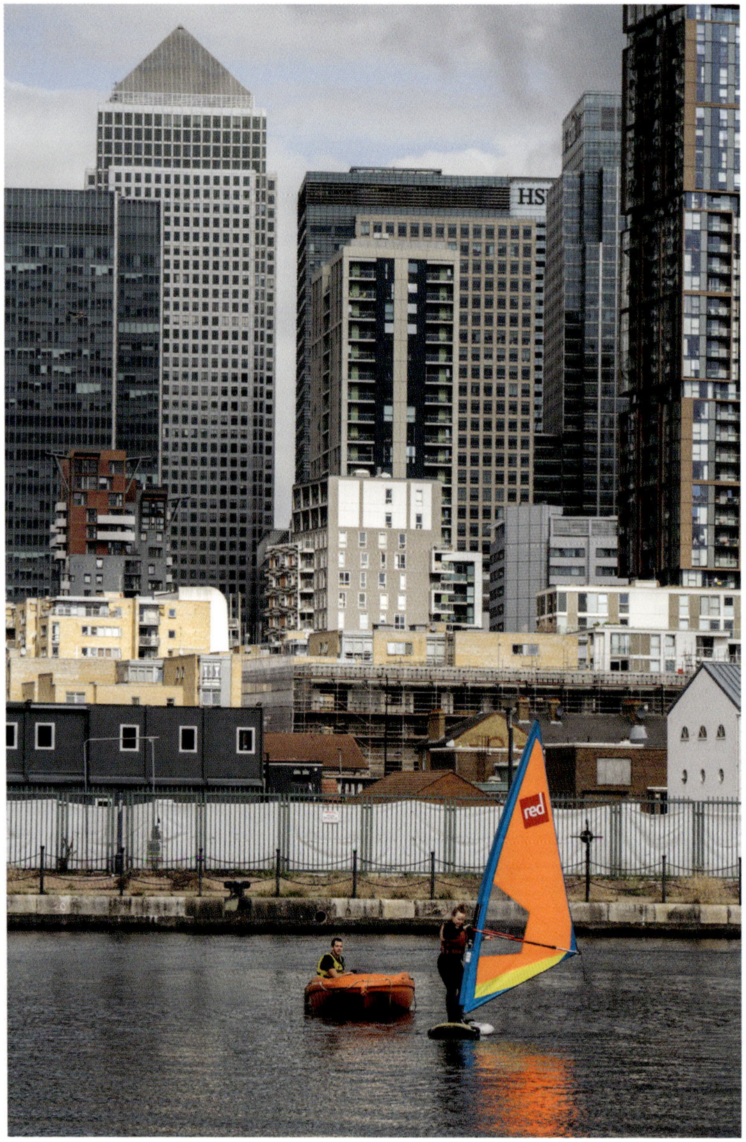

Mastering the basics

Under towering reminders of the Isle of Dogs' previous life, Albert starts a windsurfing beginners' course by teaching the rudiments on dry land. As part of the accredited watersports tuition schemes at the Docklands Sailing and Watersports Centre, this will be two full days of learning how to balance and turn with confidence and then harness the wind to take you where you want to go.

Putting it into practice

The moment of truth out on the waters of Millwall Dock itself, against the still-expanding backdrop of Canary Wharf's commercial and residential towers.

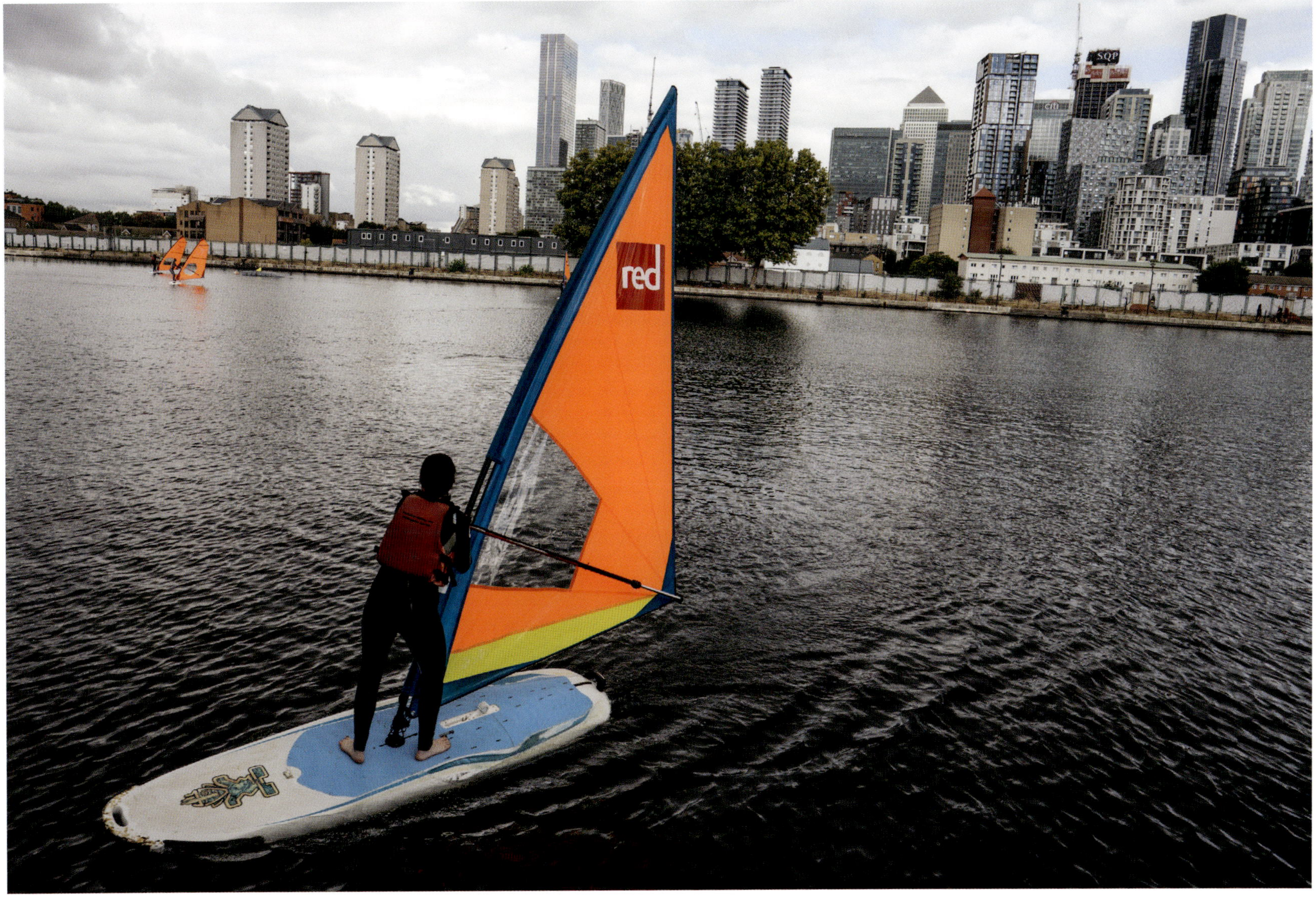

Sporting opportunity

Now spread out across the vast expanse of this old dock, Albert's pupils can safely hone their turning techniques. Thanks to the inspired decision by the London Docklands Development Corporation to set up the watersports centre in the late 1980s, Millwall Dock has offered several generations the chance to experience watersports affordably and become a highly popular part of recreational life on the Isle of Dogs.
www.dswc.org

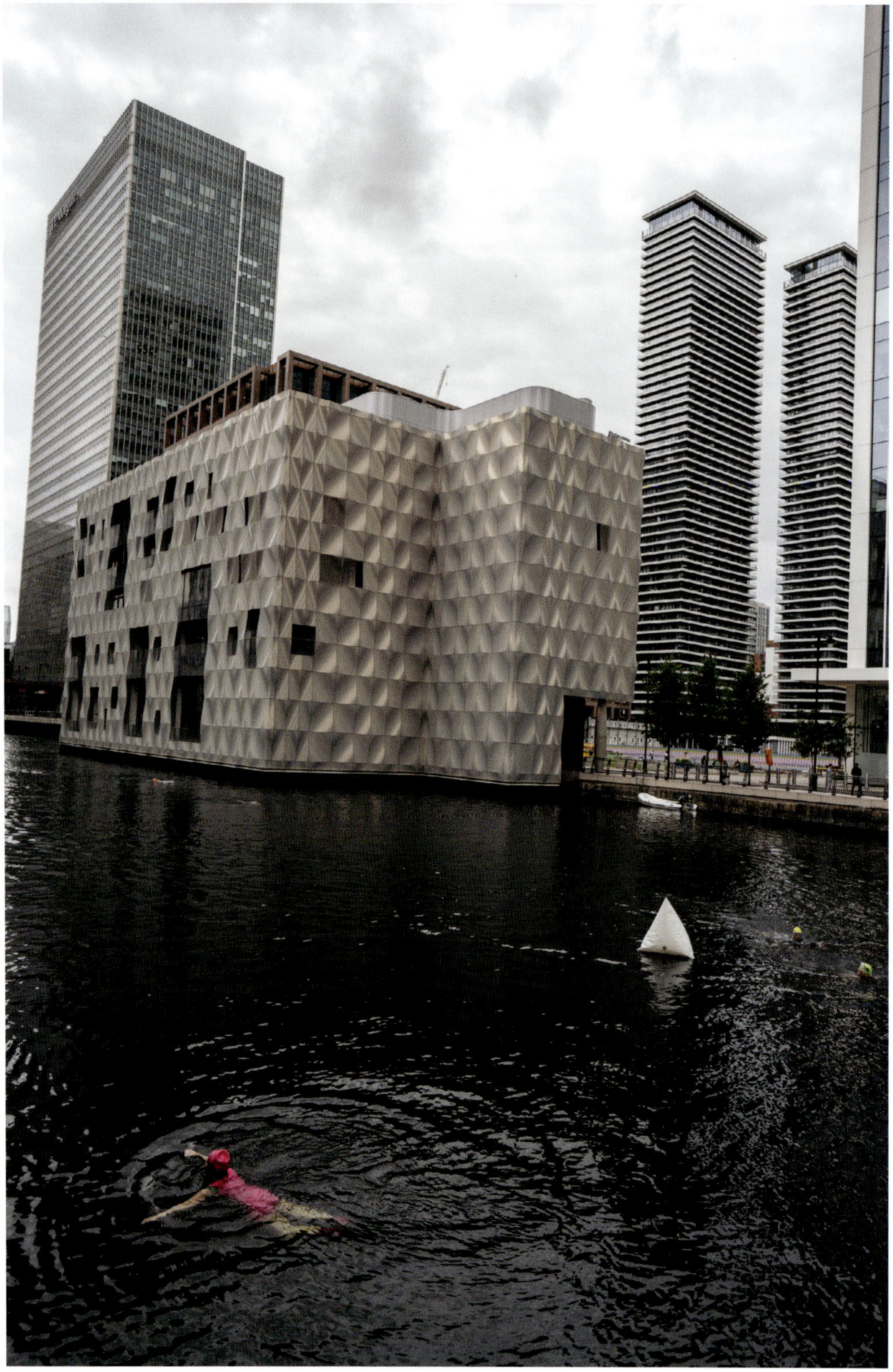

A dip in the dock

Unsupervised swimming is forbidden in the deep waters of the Isle of Dogs but Love Open Water now runs morning, lunchtime and evening sessions for those keen to take the plunge safely. Local office workers and others can access gently via a floating deck and then swim off around Middle Dock, admiring Canary Wharf's towers as they go. Trained lifeguards in kayaks patrol the area and brightly coloured headgear is required for good visibility. Regular attendee Tina sports a full pink ensemble for good measure.

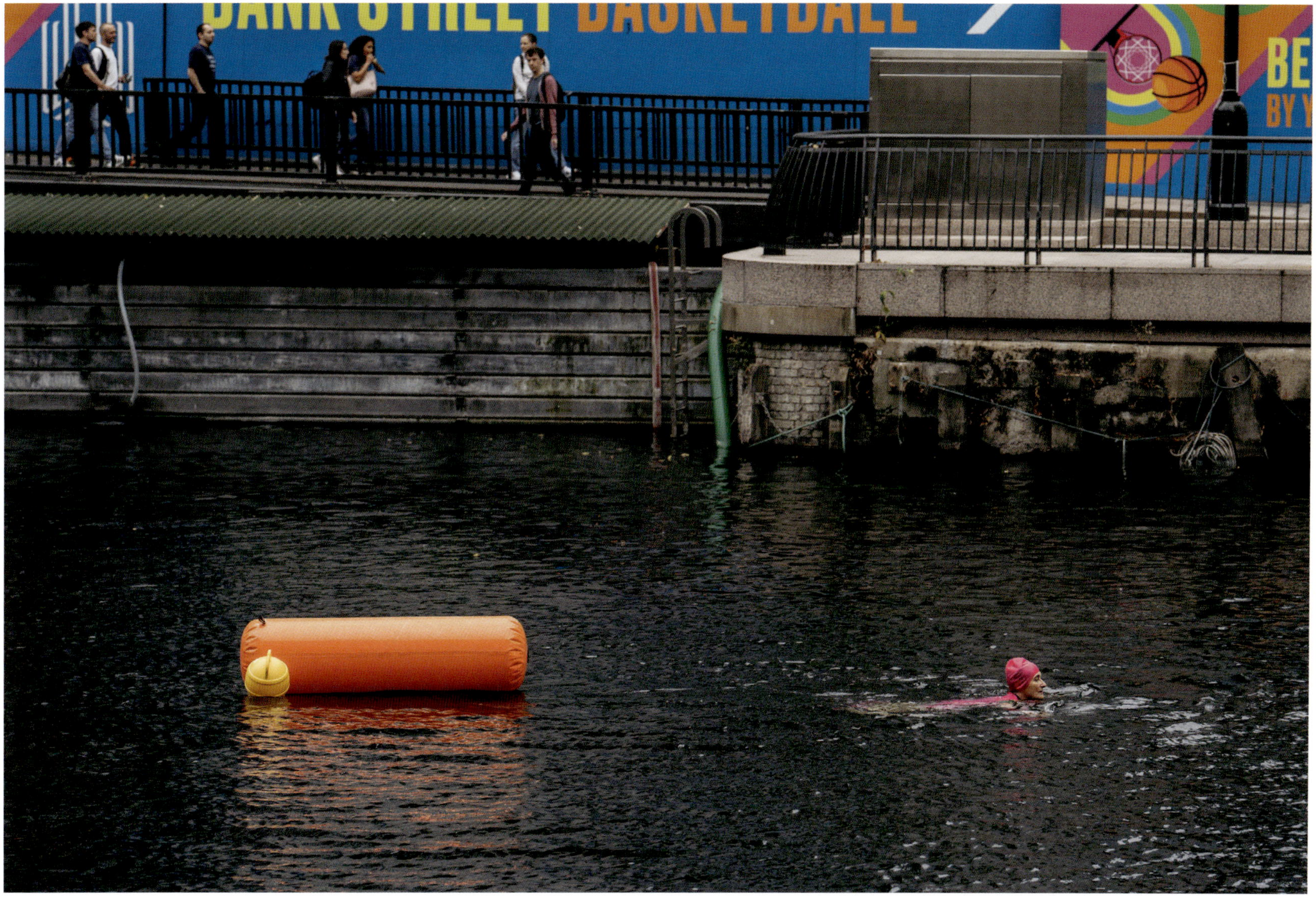

Quality control

These colourful swimmers serenely completing circuits of Middle Dock create an eye-catching temptation for those busily walking above them on the quayside. Numbers are growing, with new recruits quickly reassured that regular testing of the water's cleanliness rate it as 'excellent'.
www.loveopenwater.co.uk/canary-wharf

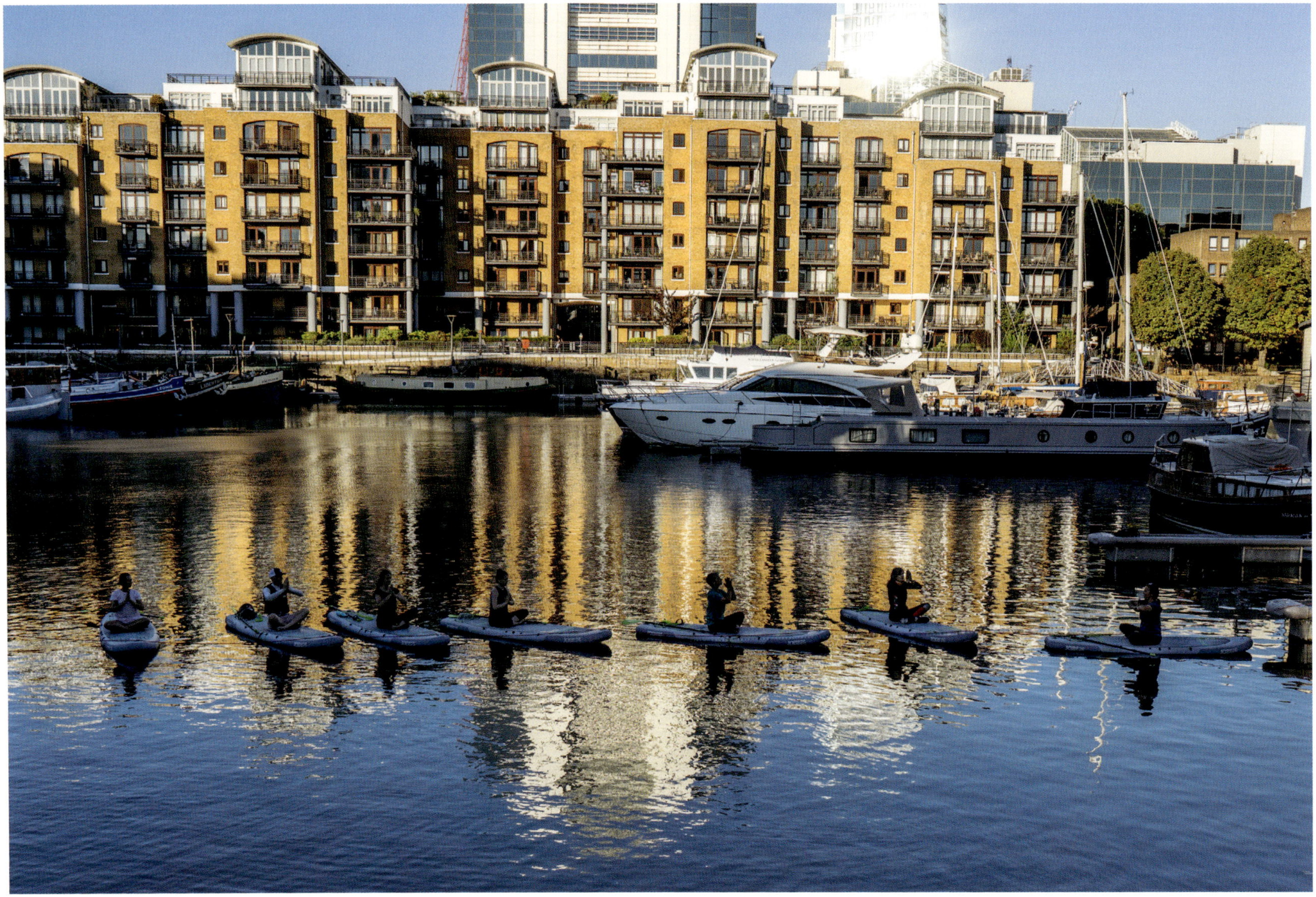

Adventure yoga

On a summer's evening in St Katharine Docks, Jennifer Cordero leads one of her regular SUP (Stand Up Paddleboarding) yoga groups through their moves. Despite the unstable nature of their platforms, these paddleboarders are managing to find great calm on the enclosed waters. Instability is all part of the experience as they learn to adapt to the motion of the board and improve focus. Paddleboarding London runs normal SUP classes in several locations along London's canals but St Kats is where it enjoys offering yoga devotees something to fit the tranquillity of the location.

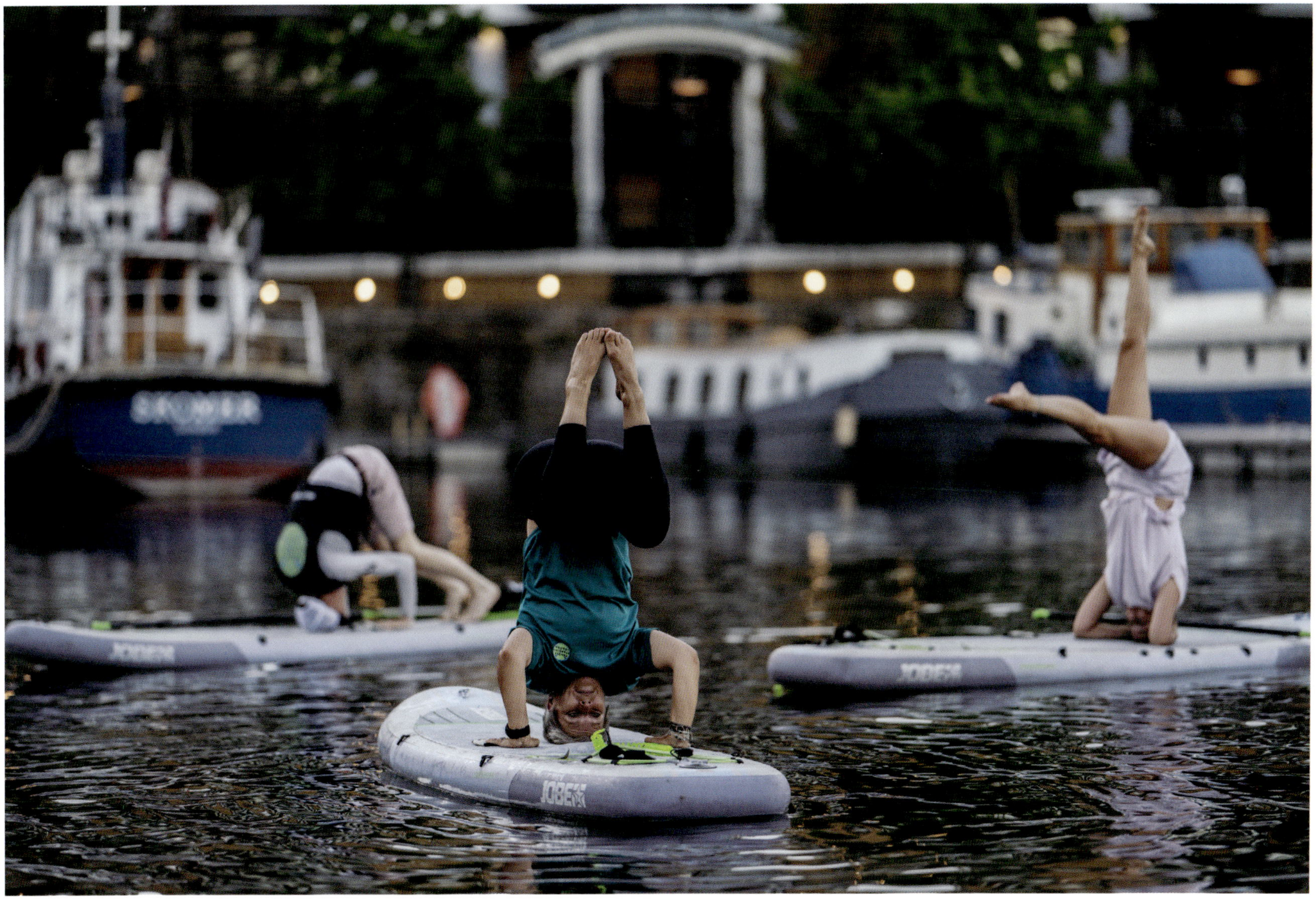

Challenging finale

After a final relaxing meditation using the gentle rocking motion of the water, the session ends with an unexpected headstand competition. With everyone feeling very relaxed by now, this was remarkably successful. www.paddleboardinglondon.co.uk

Culture on the water

Taking advantage of their central and picturesque locations, new initiatives are bringing the arts into the docks.

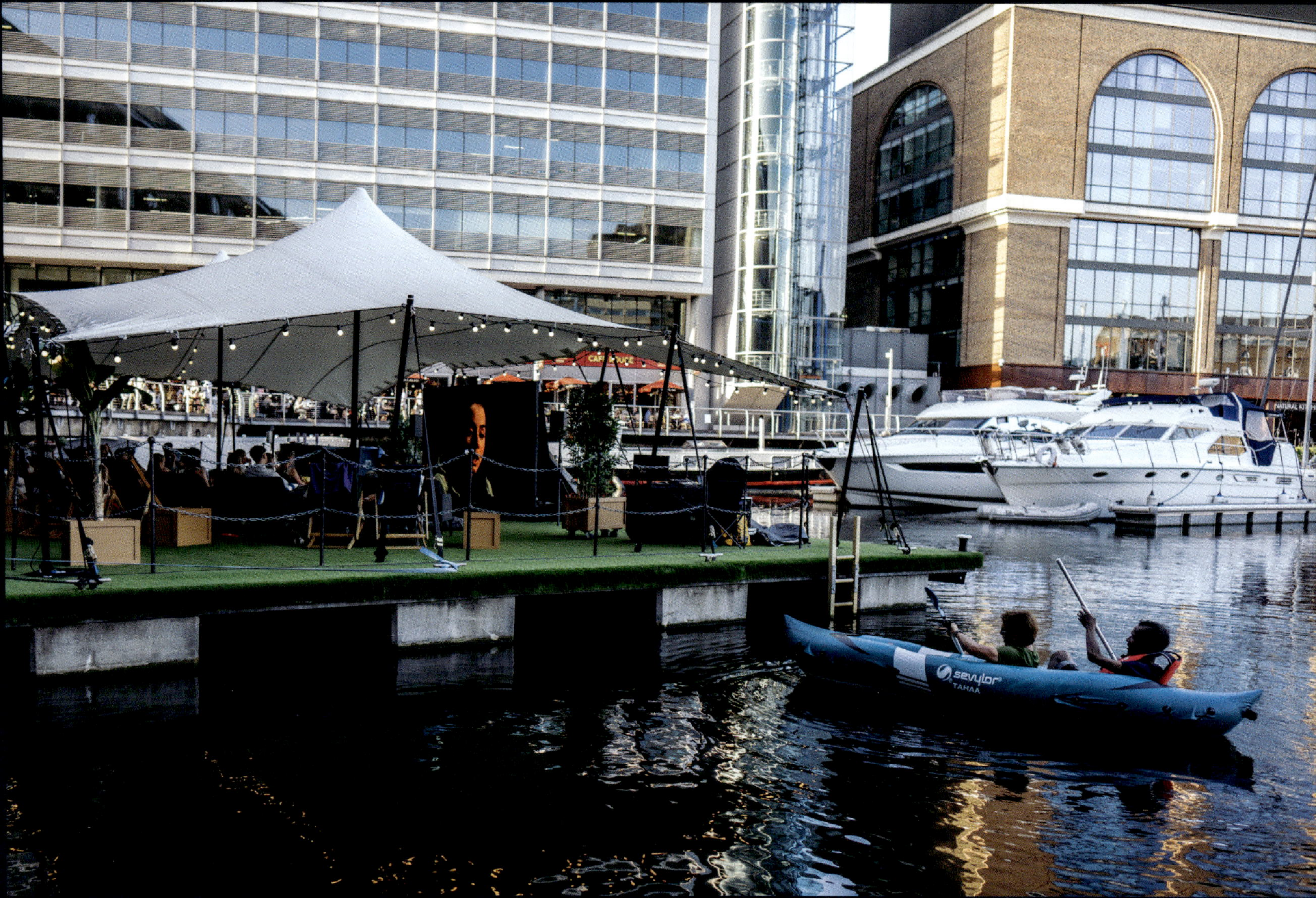

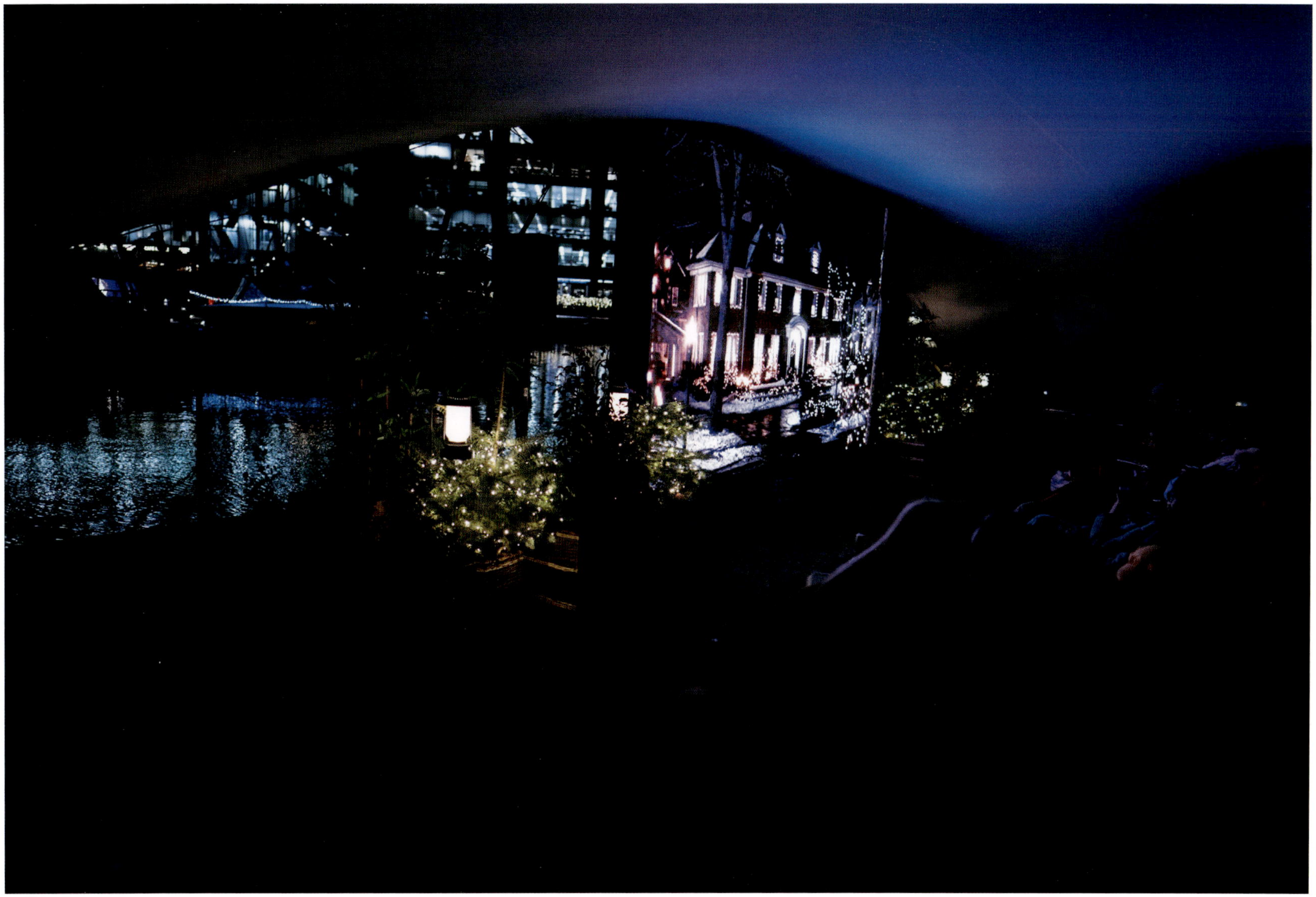

Floating film

Recreational life at St Katharine Docks centres on a large, buoyant platform, best known for metamorphosing into a floating cinema in both summer and winter. Film fans at these popular festivals lie back on sofas and deckchairs and enjoy the entertainment whilst bobbing among the marina's boats, with the occasional appearance of waterborne gatecrashers. In winter, they can cosy up in blankets with mulled wine, hot chocolate and festive lights.

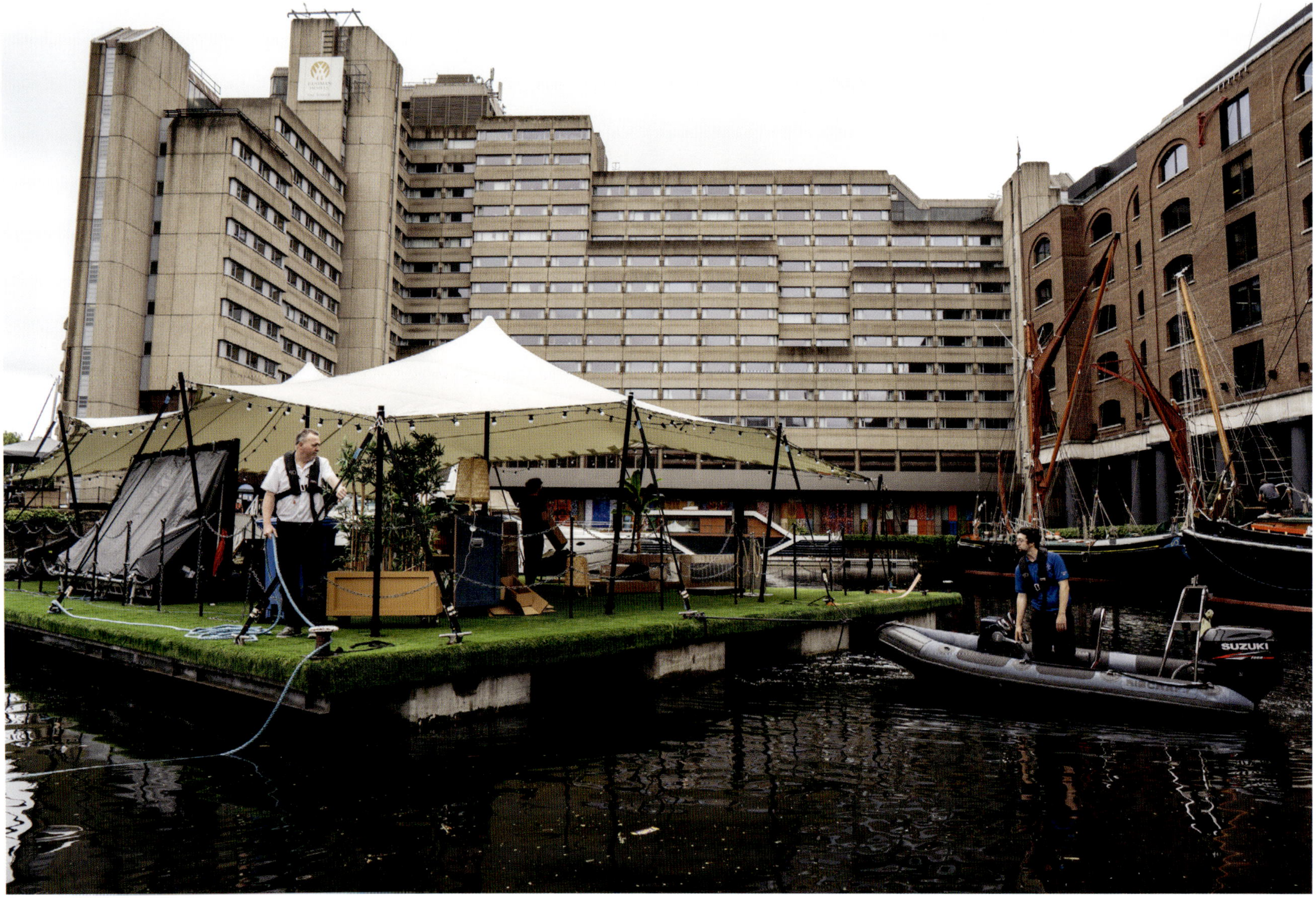

On the move

This entertainment platform has no fixed mooring in St Katharine Docks, so the marina team has become expert at shifting its location. To move this large, engine-less and unwieldy structure demands a combination of rope and dinghy work to manoeuvre past the historic Thames barges moored close by.

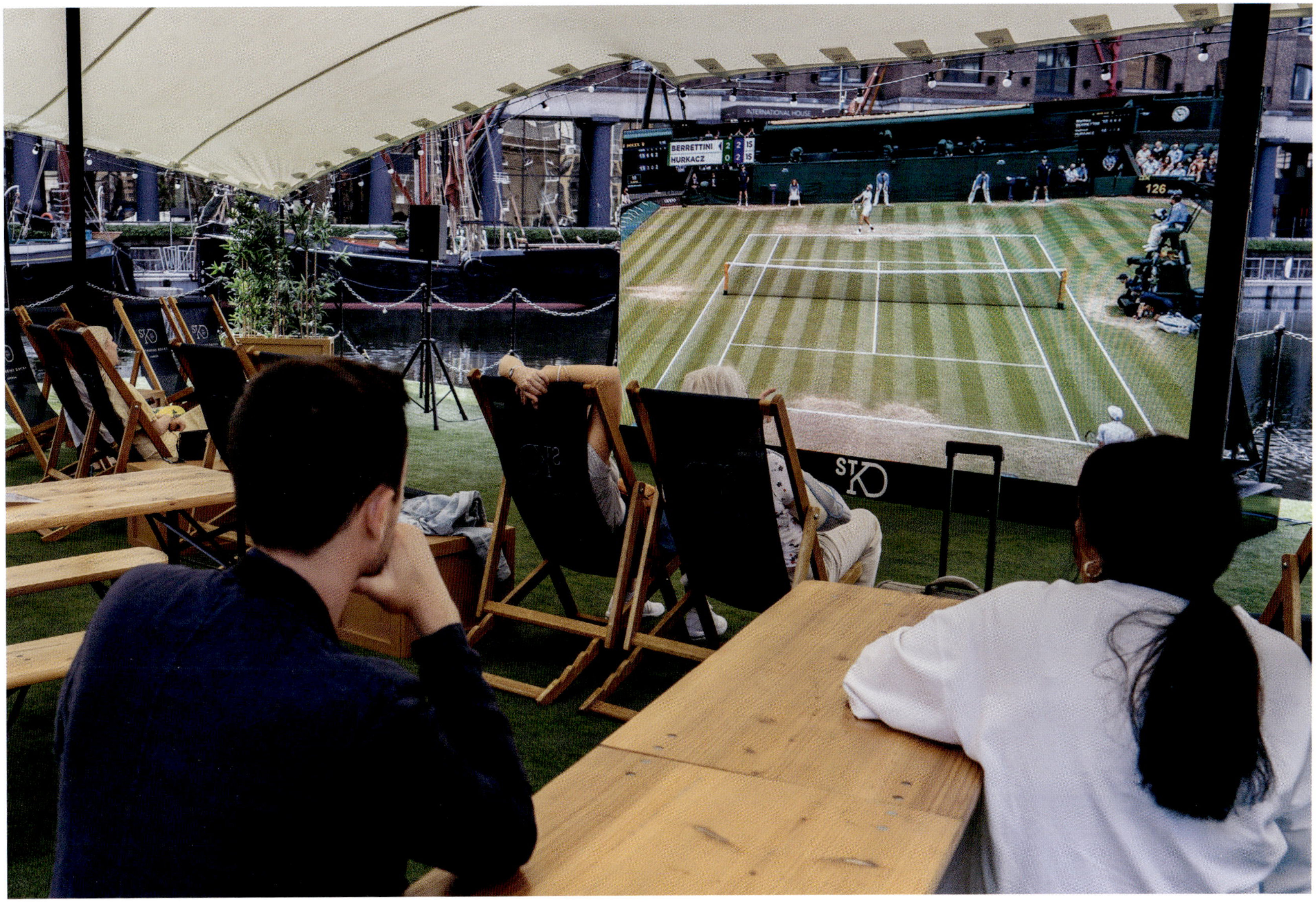

Sporting viewpoint

July finds the St Katharine Docks' platform in much demand for watching Wimbledon. Sitting under its sun-shading canopy, surrounded by water and boats while sipping champagne and eating strawberries, is certainly a very pleasant way to enjoy the tournament.
www.skdocks.co.uk

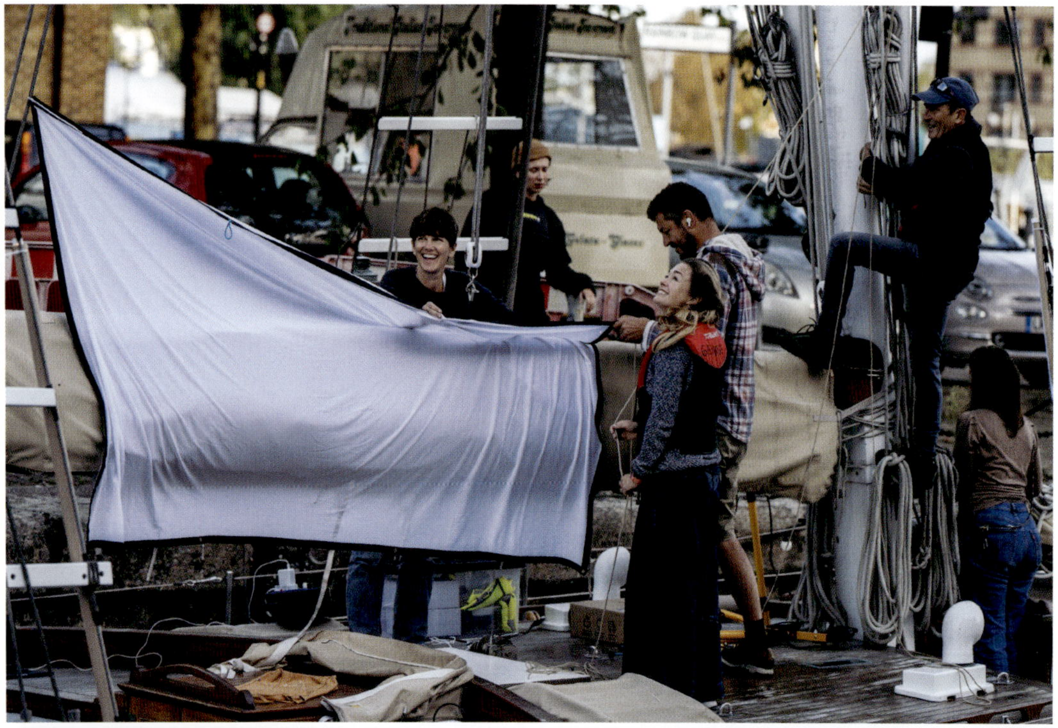

Community set-up

Fellow boat dwellers have turned out in force to help Sammy and Nicole of Shadowboxer Theatre prepare for an outside screening of their latest film. It's all part of the network of support that flourishes in Surrey Quays' South Dock Marina. Amongst a great deal of chat and laughter, it isn't long before they've worked out the best way of setting up a screen between two masts.

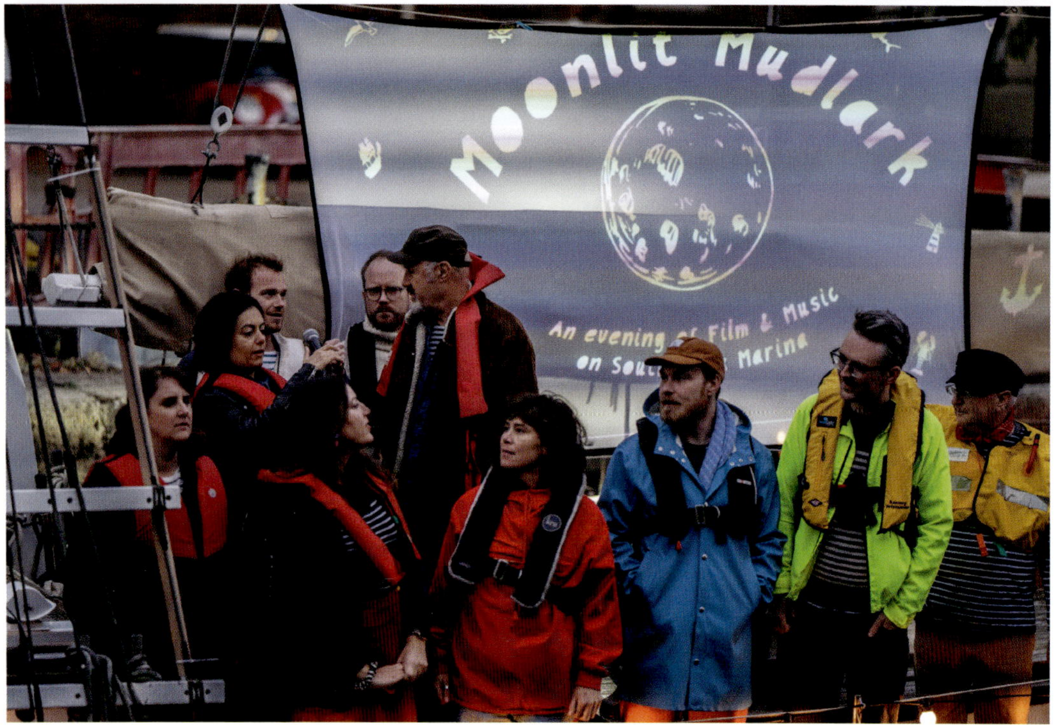

Nautical night

Using animated shadow puppetry, 'Moonlit Mudlark' tells the story of a girl living on a boat in Greenland Dock, so Sammy and Nicole are particularly pleased to have been able to create this local screening as part of the annual Totally Thames Festival. Now the sea shanty singers arrive to provide the evening's musical element and having donned lifejackets, start rehearsing.

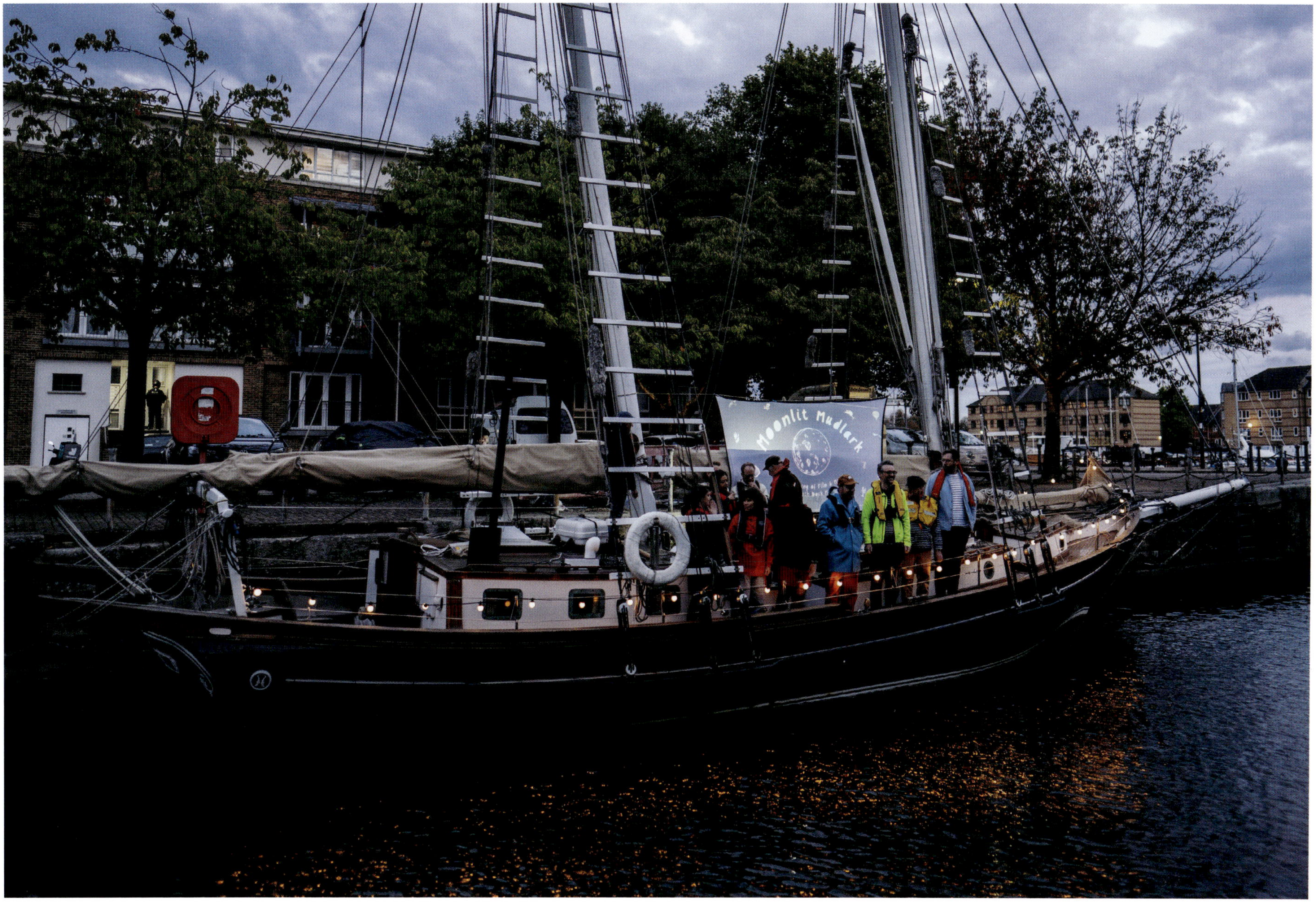

Magical setting

The beautiful schooner *Nathanael* has been specially moved across from its usual mooring in Greenland Dock to be used as both a cinema and a stage. Preparations are almost complete and the audience is beginning to gather on the quayside. Once darkness falls, the show begins to an enthusiastic response.
www.shadowboxertheatre.com

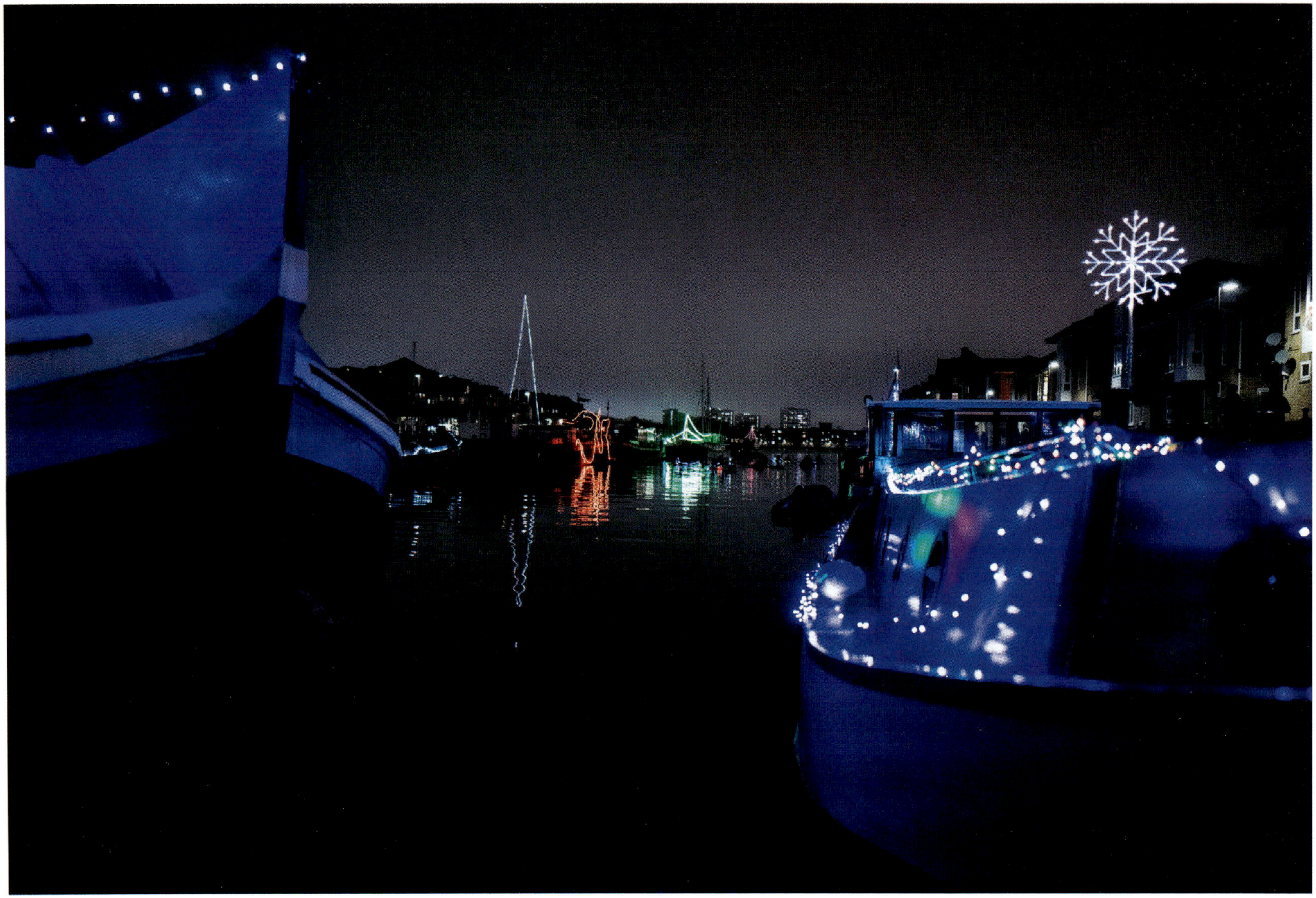

Festival of lights

Now into its fifth year, the Greenland Dock Festival galvanises boat owners and land-based residents all around Surrey Quays' South Dock Marina to vie with each other for the best light display. Organised by local business Marine Canvas Hut, the ambition and artistry increases every year, lifting the gloom of December nights and bringing together the whole community for events and celebrations.

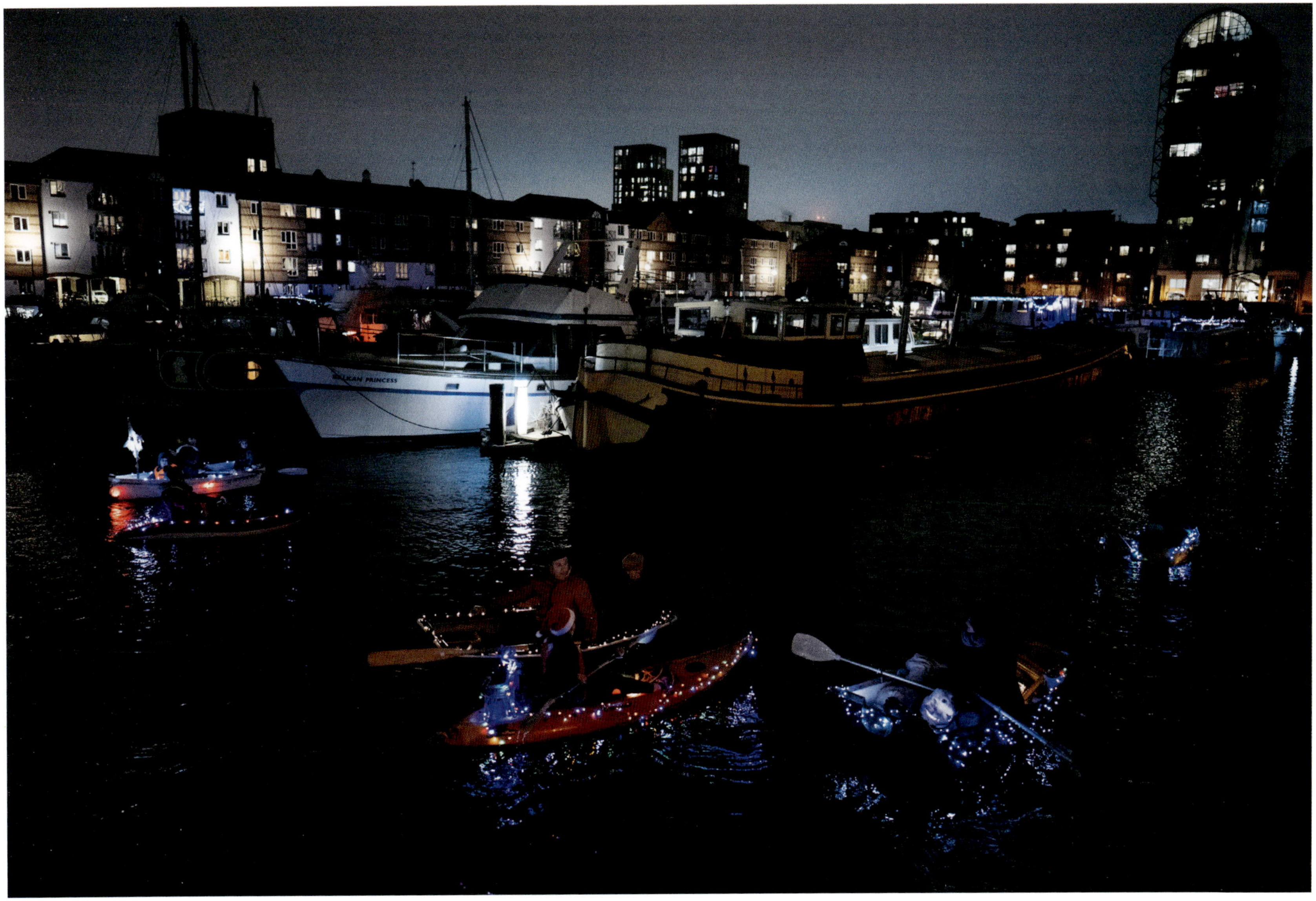

Illuminated kayak parade

Local boat owners gather for a highlight of the Greenland Dock Festival. In costumes and decorated dinghies, rowing boats and kayaks, they set off on a circuit around Surrey Quays' South Dock Marina singing sea shanties and attracting a crowd of local families to follow them along the quayside and join in this community, non-profit event. www.greenlanddockfestival.co.uk

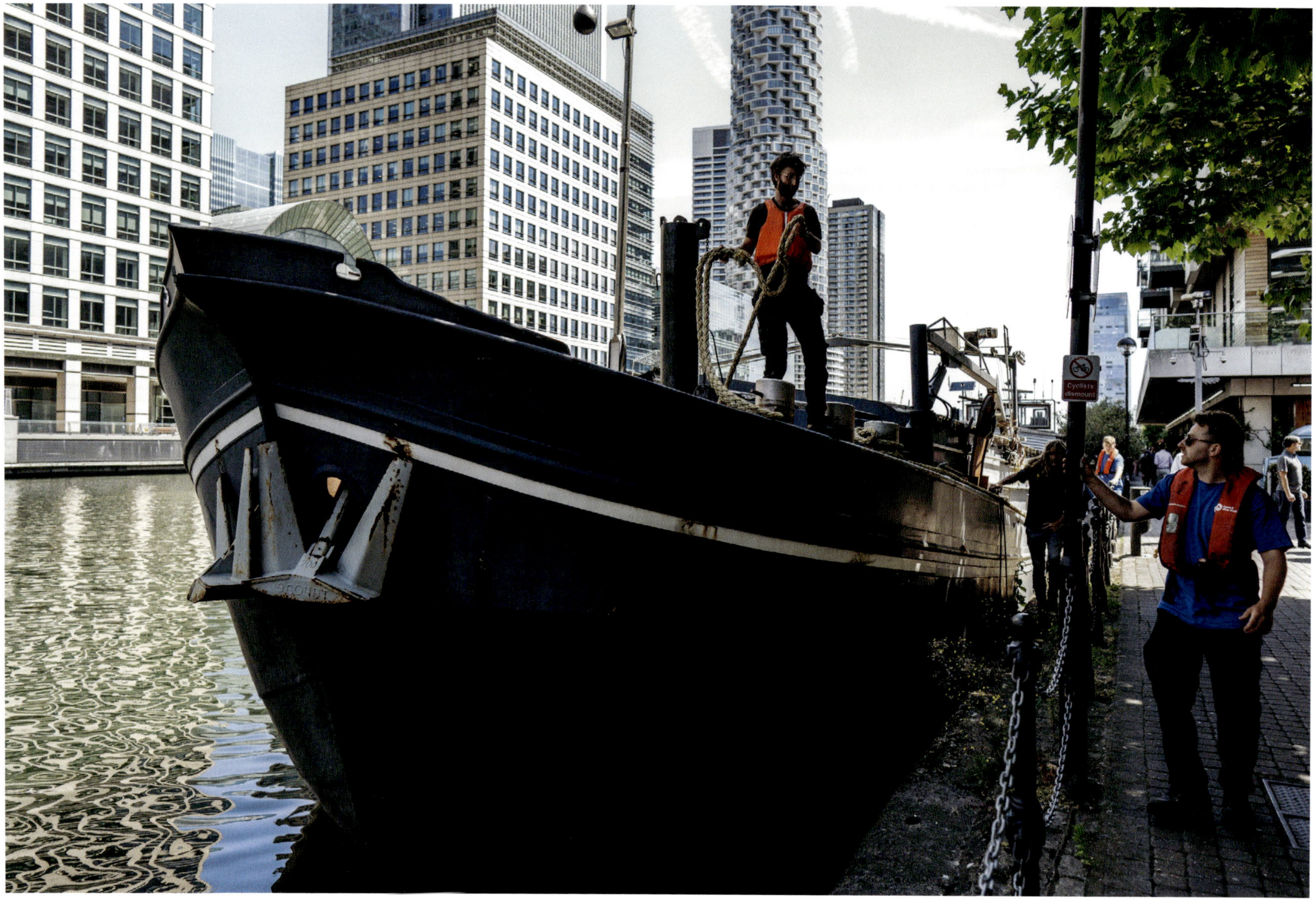

'Theatreship' arrival

After a 30-hour journey across the North Sea from Holland, *Fiat* finally moors up in West India Docks. As a 305-ton bulk dry-cargo carrier built in 1913, Inigo has chosen her as the perfect vessel to transform into a new theatre and community space for the Isle of Dogs. Considerable renovation is needed but once ready she will celebrate a wide range of art forms and host both global as well as local artists.

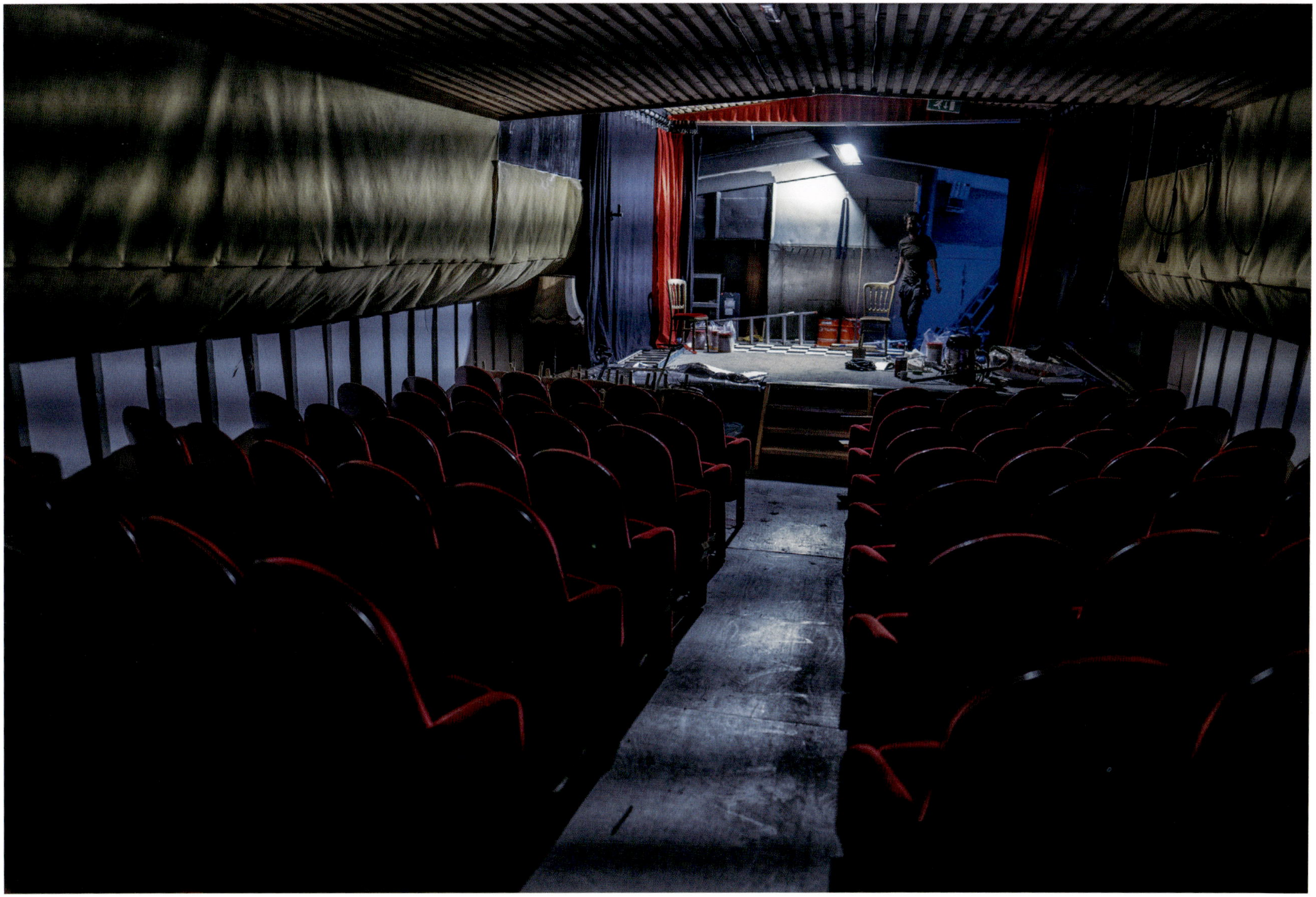

Enterprising plans

It helps that a previous owner has already installed a stage and some plush, tiered seating in *Fiat*'s old cargo hold but these will have to be temporarily removed in order to make good the ship's structure and install proper ventilation and lighting. Next door to this 100-seat theatre, the original wood floor and fittings will be kept for a community bar, and a canopied café will be created on the spacious top deck.

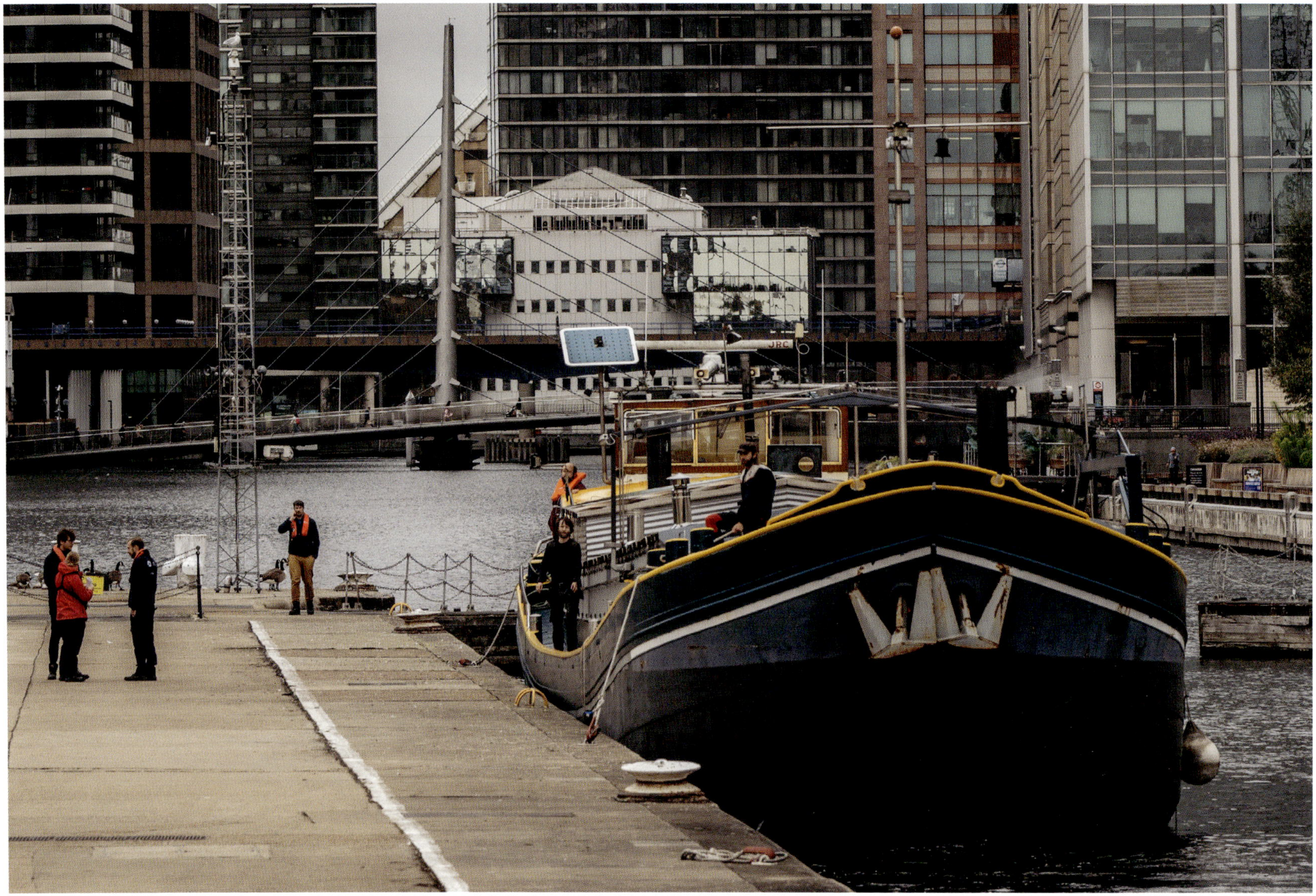

Bridging vision

After a few weeks restoring her exterior paintwork, including a new yellow and blue colour scheme to highlight her elegant prow, *Fiat* heads out for an important survey down-river before returning for more renovation. Once ready, the Canal & River Trust plan to moor her on a new Arts and Heritage Berth. This will host other boats of interest, such as steam tug *Portwey*, and will aim to encourage more interaction between modern Canary Wharf and the historical Isle of Dogs.
www.theatreship.co.uk

All pulling together

Most of the boatyard turns out to help manoeuvre a new 'culture boat' called *Exposure* into her berth in Surrey Quays' South Dock Marina. The brainchild of photographer and filmmaker George Gottlieb, this unique vessel has been designed in Portsmouth and built up in layers on top of an old 'lighter' barge. Much work still needs to be done internally but the plan is to develop her as a studio and events space for a wide range of arts.

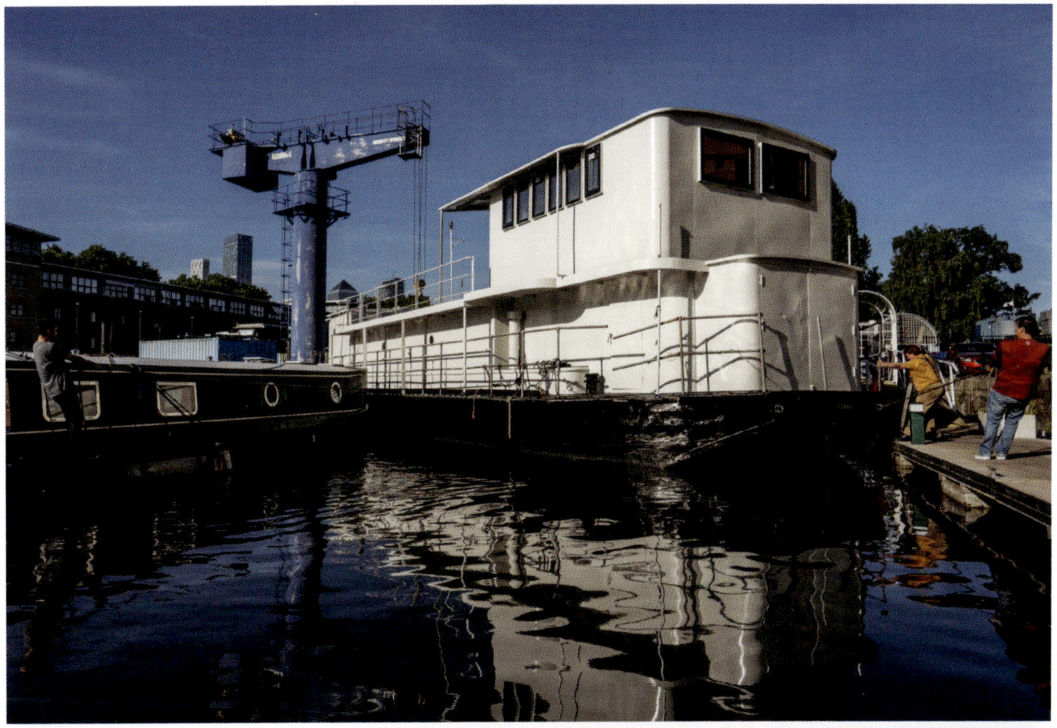

Creative space

The immense proportions of the boat's interior will be a big attraction, allowing flexible use for all sorts of artistic endeavours. Full insulation is already in place and carpentry work has now started, using recycled wood as much as possible, including old scaffolding planks for side storage benches and salvaged flooring from a demolished school in Manchester.

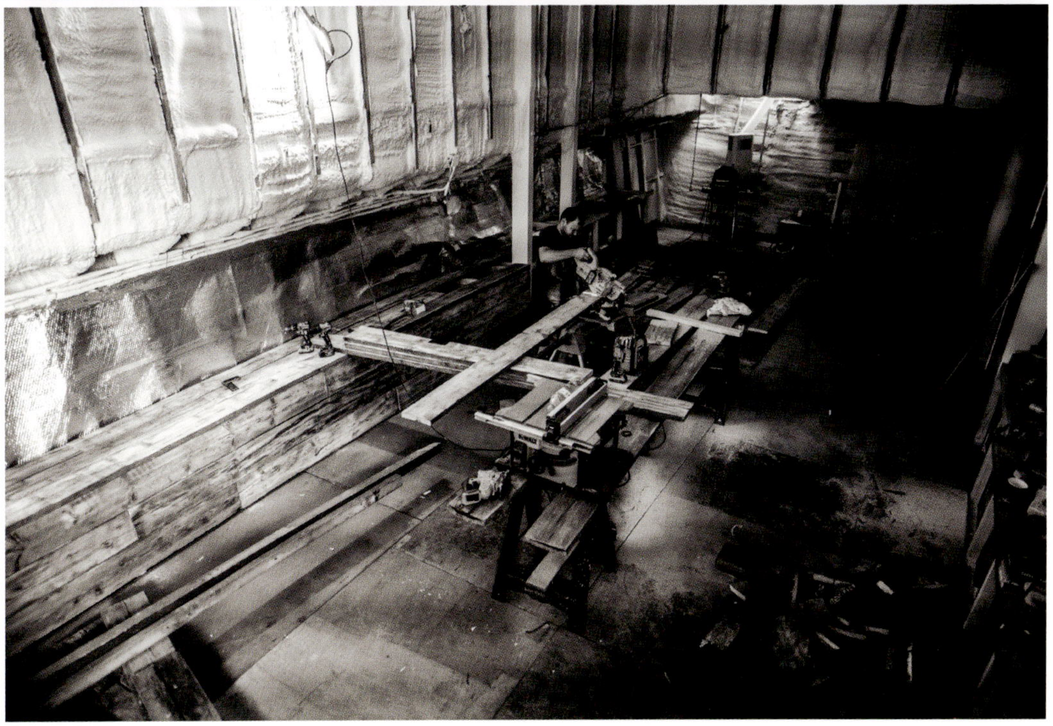

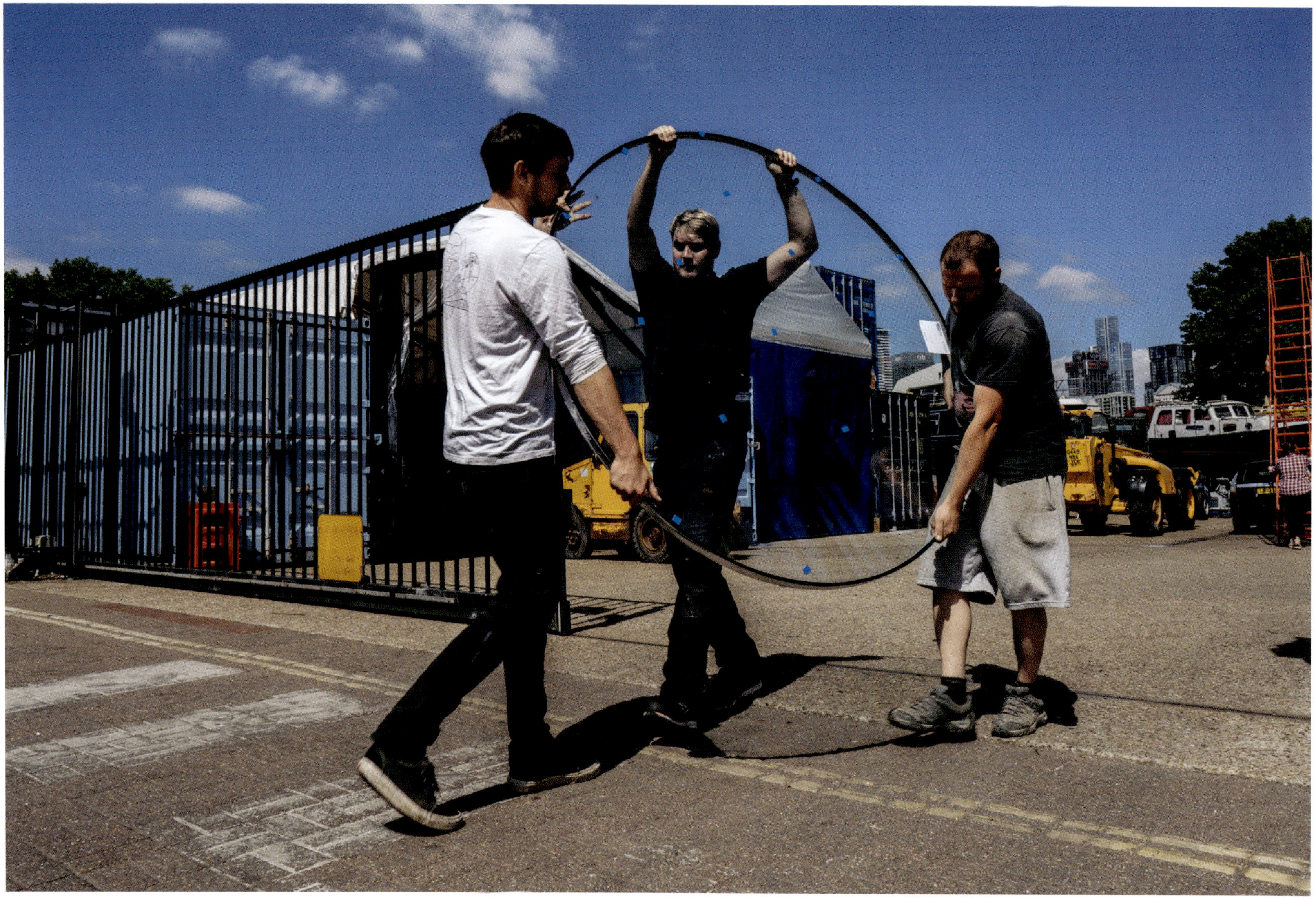

Glass protection

George gets some help bringing over a weighty, specially designed skylight from the boatyard for immediate installation on *Exposure*. Making her watertight is a priority before any rain arrives.

Rooftop teamwork

After some careful and strenuous hoisting in the midday sun, the skylight is finally in place and fits perfectly.

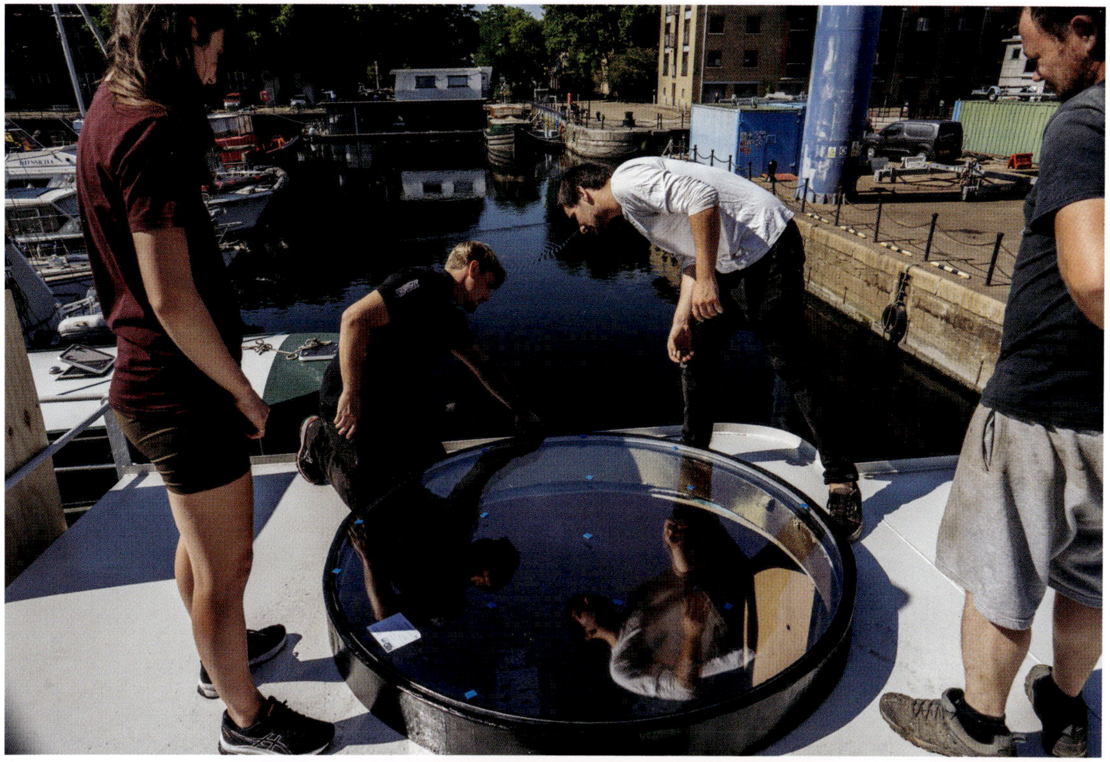

Making it happen

The circular skylight is the last of three to be installed, joining a square and a rectangle to not only allow in natural light but also add elegance and fun to what will be *Exposure*'s important entrance area. George and his partner, Isabel, now discuss the next step in fitting out and completing this exciting new arts venue for Surrey Quays.
www.boatstudios.co.uk

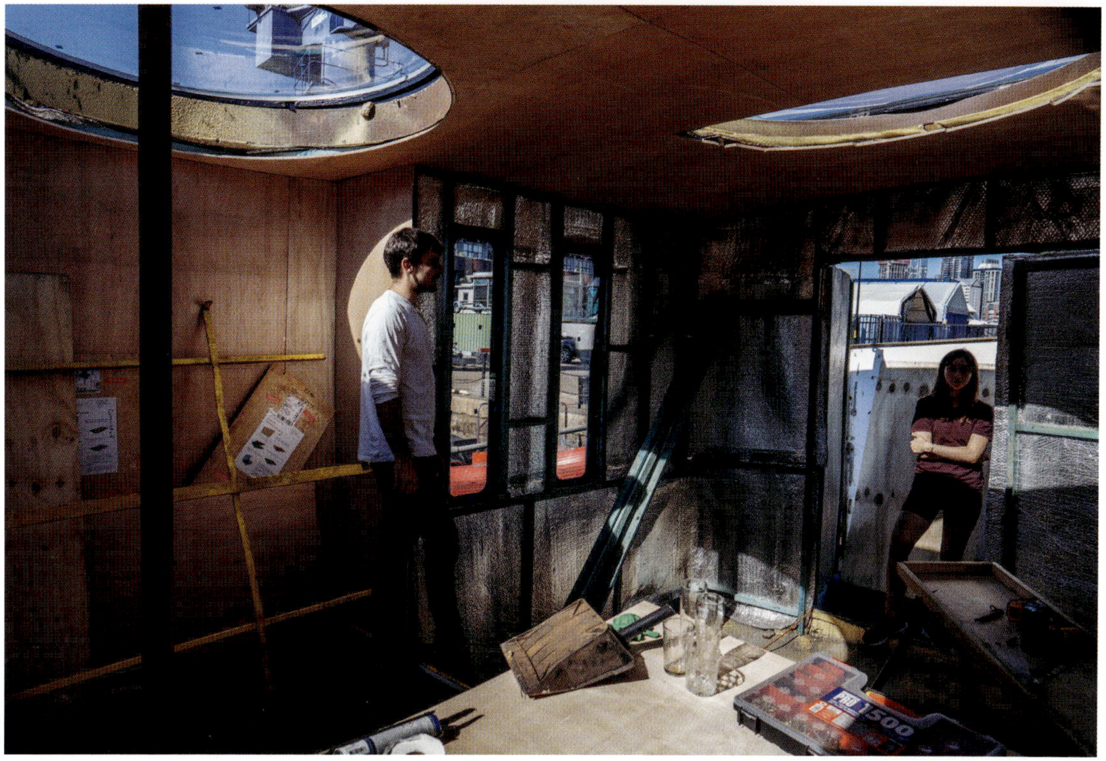

Acknowledgements

I am very grateful to everyone in the boating communities of St Katharine Docks, the Isle of Dogs and Surrey Quays' South Dock Marina for allowing me to take photographs over the last 18 months. Thank you for being so welcoming and for your patience with my continually popping up to ask questions and snap away while you worked or went about your daily life. I will try and name as many of you as I can but please forgive me if I leave anyone out – you are no less thanked.

Paul Atkins, Nalan Bedding, British Marine, Patricia and Miryam Brizuela, Canal & River Trust Central & Docklands team, James Capper, Eva Chesswas, Lou and Tim Clark, Wayne Clark, Justin, Octavia and Alex Crowe, 'D.J.' Wayne, DiveCo Marine Ltd., Dockland Scout Project, Docklands Sailing and Watersports Centre, Fizz Forsey, Julie Gaudion, *Götheborg* team, George Gottlieb, Francois Greeff, Frances Harding, Richard Henderson, Ian Hugo, Island Global Yachting Marinas, Patrick Keating, Derek Kendall, Nick Kenny, Inigo Lapwood, Chris Lees, Love Open Water, Josh Metter, Charlie Murphy, Simon Mustafa, Chris Nursey and the *Portwey* team, Brenden O'Shea, Chris Olley, Philip and Mariana Otto, Paddleboarding London, PE & School Sports Network, Mike Pearce, Raybel Charters, Dan Re'em, Rev. Marcus Nodder, John, Anna and Artu Rhodes, Bill Robinson and Phil, Sea-Change Sailing Trust, Shadowboxer Theatre, Rebecca, Simon, Eli and Penny Shillito, Skuna Boats, Claire Slater, Dean Smith, SOCOTEC, South Dock Marina team, St Katharine Docks Marina team, Alex Stele, Surrey Docks Fitness & Watersports Centre, Paul Tetlow, Thames Marine Services, Simon Thomas, Tideway Sailability volunteers, Nina Tranter, Felix Trench, Jay White, Mark and Sarah Wilson, Max Wilson.

From the non-boating contingent, particular thanks for support should definitely go to Tina Baxter for managing to decipher my handwriting, collate my notes and provide social media savvy; to the font of all knowledge about London, Matt Brown, for penning the Introduction; to Jana Gough for her forensic eye on the text and not least, to Lord Heseltine for very kindly writing the Foreword.

The whole team at Unicorn Publishing have again been outstanding with advice, expertise and support – thank you to Ian, David, Lucy, Ramona and Felicity.

Especial thanks, of course, to Peter, Ria and Remi for being here to hold my hand and feed me chocolate throughout.

Published in 2023 by Unicorn
an imprint of Unicorn Publishing Group
Charleston Studio, Meadow Business Centre, Lewes BN8 5RW
www.unicornpublishing.org

ISBN 978-1-911397-31-1

10 9 8 7 6 5 4 3 2 1

Designed by Felicity Price-Smith
Printed by FineTone Ltd

Front cover: Urban transformation

In the tranquil residential waterway that is now Blackwall Basin on the Isle of Dogs, Inigo installs new roof-decking on a liveaboard boat against the contrasting backdrop of Canary Wharf's towers. Forty years ago, this same view would have only contained derelict warehouses and redundant shipping cranes.